Intermediate
Mathematical
Statistics

Intermediate Mathematical Statistics

G.P. BEAUMONT

*Senior Lecturer, Department of Statistics and Computer Science,
Royal Holloway College, London*

CHAPMAN AND HALL
LONDON AND NEW YORK

First published 1980
by Chapman and Hall Ltd
11 New Fetter Lane, London EC4P 4EE

© *G. P. Beaumont 1980*

Printed in Great Britain by
J. W. Arrowsmith Ltd., Bristol

ISBN 0 412 15480 3

Published in the USA
by Chapman and Hall
in association with Methuen, Inc.
733 Third Avenue, New York, NY 10017

British Library Cataloguing in Publication Data

Beaumont, G P
   Intermediate mathematical statistics.
   1. Mathematical statistics
   I. Title
   519.5   QA276   79-4061

   ISBN 0 412 15480 3

Contents

Preface

This book covers those basic topics which usually form the core of intermediate courses in statistical theory; it is largely about estimation and hypothesis testing. It is intended for undergraduates following courses in statistics but is also suitable preparatory reading for some postgraduate courses.

It is assumed that the reader has completed an introductory course which covered probability, random variables, moments and the sampling distributions. The level of mathematics required does not go beyond first year calculus. In case the reader has not acquired much facility in handling matrices, the results in least squares estimation are first obtained directly and then given an (optional) matrix formulation. If techniques for changing from one set of variables to another have not been met, then the appendix on these topics should be studied first. The same appendix contains essential discussion of the order statistics which are frequently used for illustrative purposes.

Introductory courses usually include the elements of hypothesis testing and of point and interval estimation though the treatment must perforce become rather thin since at that stage it is difficult to provide adequate justifications for some procedures—plausible though they may seem. This text discusses these important topics in considerable detail, starting from scratch. The level is nowhere advanced and proofs of asymptotic results are omitted. Methods deriving from the Bayesian point of view are gradually introduced and alternate with the more usual techniques.

Many illustrative examples have been included since the average student typically grasps the import of a theorem by seeing how it is applied. Each chapter contains exercises which either give practice in techniques or take a previous example a little further. At the end of the book will be found a selection of typical questions for which brief solutions are provided.

London, June 1979   G. P. B.

Acknowledgements

I am indebted to the following sources for permission to publish:
The Senate of the University of London, and the Universities of Birmingham, Edinburgh, Exeter, Leicester, Leeds, Manchester, Reading and Wales, for questions from past examination papers.

The publishers, C. Griffin and Company Limited for two exercises from *Exercises in Probability and Statistics* by N. A. Rahman.

The publishers, Oliver and Boyd, Edinburgh, and the R. A. Fisher Royalty Fund, University of Adelaide, for two brief quotations from *Statistical Methods and Scientific Inference* by Sir Ronald Fisher.

I wish to thank Mr C. P. Chalmers, Professor D. R. Cox, Professor P. R. Freeman, Professor H. J. Godwin, Dr H. W. Peers and Professor A. Stuart for reading and commenting on parts of this book. They are not responsible for any errors—or any inability on my part to profit from their advice!

I also wish to thank Miss E. Atherton for typing the manuscript.

Notation

Random variables are denoted by capital letters, such as X, and the obtained value of such a random variable by the corresponding lower case letter x. $t(X_1, X_2, \ldots, X_n)$ means a function of the random variables $X_1, X_2, \ldots, X_n$ and is also referred to as the statistic T. The corresponding numerical value, for observed x_1, $x_2, \ldots, x_n$, is written $t(x_1, x_2, \ldots, x_n)$. The variance of X is written $V(X)$, the covariance of X and Y as $\text{Cov}(X, Y)$ and the conditional distribution of X given $Y = y$ is often shortened to the distribution of X given y. In Appendix 1, the rth order statistic is written $X_{(r)}$, but in illustrative examples elsewhere may be denoted as Y_r.

Unknown parameters are usually denoted by the Greek letters $\theta, \phi, \ldots$, numerical *estimates* of such parameters by $\hat{\theta}, \hat{\phi}, \ldots$, and the corresponding random variables, or *estimators* by $\hat{\Theta}, \hat{\Phi}, \ldots$.

Matrices, which are used rather sparingly, are also written as capitals but in bold type. The matrix of constants, A, with a_{ij} as the element in its ith row and jth column is also written (a_{ij}), with determinant $\det(a_{ij})$. Column and row vectors of *random variables* are denoted by $\mathbf{X}, \mathbf{X}'$ and the corresponding vectors with numerical components by $\mathbf{x}, \mathbf{x}'$. Similarly $\hat{\boldsymbol{\Theta}}$ for the estimator of θ.

We shall say a random variable has a probability density function (p.d.f.) whether it is continuous or discrete. Where the context is merely referential, the functional notation $f(.), d(.), \ldots$ has been contracted to $f, d, \ldots$ Logarithms are always natural and the base e is therefore not displayed. $\sum_{i=1}^{n} X_i$ is frequently shortened to $\sum_{1}^{n} X_i$ and even $\sum X_i$ where ambiguity is scarcely possible.

Some departures from the notational rules occur where strict adherence would be clumsy.

Those methods of statistical analysis which rely on the sample data as the main source of relevant information and for which the long-run frequency interpretation of probability is paramount are often called 'classical'. This usage is rooted in the long history and predominant role of such techniques. Methods which combine prior information with the sample data and express conclusions in terms of posterior probabilities are qualified as Bayesian, in virtue of the role played by Bayes' theorem to effect the combination. It is to be hoped that the presentation leaves no doubt as to whether any particular technique is classical or Bayesian. In the chapter on interval estimation, the term confidence interval is reserved for the classical construction and Bayesian confidence interval for the construction based on a posterior distribution.

Standard distributions

Univariate

(1) *Bernoulli*, with parameter θ $(0 < \theta < 1)$.
A discrete random variable X with p.d.f.

$$f(x|\theta) = \theta^x(1 - \theta)^{1-x}, \quad x = 0, 1.$$

$E(X) = \theta$, $V(X) = \theta(1 - \theta)$.

(2) *Geometric*, with parameter θ $(0 < \theta < 1)$.
A discrete random variable X with p.d.f.

$$f(x|\theta) = \theta(1 - \theta)^{x-1}, \quad x = 1, 2, \dots.$$

$E(X) = 1/\theta$, $V(X) = (1 - \theta)/\theta^2$.

(3) *Binomial*, with parameters n and θ $(n = 1, 2, \dots; 0 < \theta < 1)$.
A discrete random variable X with p.d.f.

$$f(x|n, \theta) = \binom{n}{x}\theta^x(1 - \theta)^{n-x}, \quad x = 0, 1, \dots, n.$$

$E(X) = n\theta$, $V(X) = n\theta(1 - \theta)$.
It will be assumed that n is a known positive integer.

(4) *Poisson*, with parameter θ $(\theta > 0)$.
A discrete random variable X with p.d.f.

$$f(x|\theta) = \theta^x \exp(-\theta)/x!, \, x = 0, 1, \dots.$$

$E(X) = \theta$, $V(X) = \theta$.

(5) *Negative binomial*, with parameters r and θ $(r > 0; 0 < \theta < 1)$.
A discrete random variable X with p.d.f.

$$f(x|r, \theta) = \binom{x-1}{r-1}\theta^r(1 - \theta)^{x-r}, \quad x = r, r+1, \dots.$$

$E(X) = r/\theta$, $V(X) = r(1 - \theta)/\theta^2$.

(6) *Uniform*, with parameter θ $(\theta > 0)$.
A continuous random variable X with p.d.f.

$$f(x|\theta) = 1/\theta, \quad 0 < x < \theta.$$

$E(X) = \theta/2, V(X) = \theta^2/12$.
Also known as the rectangular distribution.
(7) *Exponential*, with parameter $\lambda (\lambda > 0)$.
A continuous random variable X with p.d.f.

$$f(x|\lambda) = \lambda \exp(-\lambda x), \quad x > 0.$$

$E(X) = 1/\lambda, V(X) = 1/\lambda^2$.
It is sometimes convenient to regard the mean as the parameter,
in which case the density is written $(1/\lambda)\exp(-x/\lambda)$.
(8) *Gamma*, with parameters $\alpha, \lambda(\alpha > 0, \lambda > 0)$.
A continuous random variable X with p.d.f.

$$f(x|\alpha, \lambda) = \lambda(\lambda x)^{\alpha-1} \exp(-\lambda x)/\Gamma(\alpha), \quad x > 0.$$

$E(X) = \alpha/\lambda, V(X) = \alpha/\lambda^2$.
Also referred to as the $\Gamma(\alpha, \lambda)$ distribution.
(9) *Beta*, with parameters $\alpha, \beta(\alpha > 0, \beta > 0)$.
A continuous random variable X with p.d.f.

$$f(x|\alpha, \beta) = \frac{\Gamma(\alpha + \beta)}{\Gamma(\alpha)\Gamma(\beta)}x^{\alpha-1}(1-x)^{\beta-1}, \quad 0 < x < 1.$$

$E(X) = \alpha/(\alpha + \beta), V(X) = \alpha\beta/(\alpha + \beta)^2(\alpha + \beta + 1)$.
Also referred to as the Beta (α, β) distribution.
(10) *Normal*, with parameters $\mu, \sigma(-\infty < \mu < +\infty, \sigma > 0)$.
A continuous random variable X with p.d.f.

$$f(x|\mu, \sigma) = \frac{1}{\sqrt{(2\pi)}\sigma}\exp\left[-\tfrac{1}{2}(x - \mu)^2/\sigma^2\right], \quad -\infty < x < +\infty.$$

$E(X) = \mu, V(X) = \sigma^2$.
Also referred to as the $N(\mu, \sigma^2)$ distribution.
(11) *Pareto*, with parameters θ_0, α $(\theta_0 > 0, \alpha > 0)$.
A continuous random variable X with p.d.f.

$$f(x|\theta_0, \alpha) = \alpha\theta_0^\alpha/x^{\alpha+1}, \quad x > \theta_0.$$

$E(X) = \alpha\theta_0/(\alpha - 1), V(X) = \alpha\theta_0^2/(\alpha - 1)^2(\alpha - 2), \alpha > 2$.
(12) *Chi-square*, with parameter $n(n = 1, 2, \ldots)$.

A continuous random variable X with p.d.f.

$$f(x|n) = (\tfrac{1}{2})\left(\frac{x}{2}\right)^{(n/2)-1} \exp(-x/2)/\Gamma(n/2), x > 0.$$

$E(X) = n$, $V(X) = 2n$.

Also referred to as the χ_n^2 distribution, with n degrees of freedom. Evidently a χ_n^2 distribution is also a $\Gamma(\frac{n}{2}, \frac{1}{2})$ distribution.

(13) *Student's t*, with parameter n $(n = 1, 2, \dots)$.

A continuous random variable X with p.d.f.

$$f(x|n) = \frac{1}{\sqrt{(n\pi)}} \frac{\Gamma[(n+1)/2]}{\Gamma(n/2)} \frac{1}{[1+(x^2/n)]^{(n+1)/2}}, \quad -\infty < x < +\infty$$

$E(X) = 0$ $(n > 1)$, $V(X) = n/(n-2)$ $(n > 2)$.

Also referred to as the t_n distribution, with n degrees of freedom.

(14) F, with parameters, m, n $(m, n = 1, 2, \dots)$.

A continuous random variable X with p.d.f.

$$f(x|m,n) = \frac{\Gamma[(m+n)/2]}{\Gamma(m/2)\Gamma(n/2)} \left(\frac{m}{n}\right)^{m/2} \frac{x^{(m/2)-1}}{[1+(mx/n)]^{(m+n)/2}}, \quad x > 0.$$

$E(X) = n/(n-2)$, $(n > 2)$, $V(X) = 2n^2(m+n-2)/m(n-2)^2(n-4)$, $n > 4$.

Also referred to as the $F_{m,n}$ distribution with m,n degrees of freedom. The order of the integers m,n is material.

Bivariate

(1) *Trinomial*, with positive parameters n, θ_1, θ_2 $(0 < \theta_1 + \theta_2 < 1, n = 1, 2, \dots)$

The discrete random variables X_1, X_2 have joint p.d.f.

$$f(x_1, x_2|n, \theta_1, \theta_2) = \frac{n!}{x_1! x_2! (n - x_1 - x_2)!} \theta_1^{x_1} \theta_2^{x_2} (1 - \theta_1 - \theta_2)^{n - x_1 - x_2}$$

x_1, x_2 non-negative integers such that $x_1 + x_2 \leqslant n$. The marginal distribution of X_i is binomial with parameters n, θ_i $(i = 1, 2)$. Covariance $(X_1, X_2) = -n\theta_1\theta_2$.

(2) *Bivariate normal*, with parameters $\mu_1, \mu_2, \sigma_1, \sigma_2, \rho$ $(-\infty < \mu_i < +\infty, \sigma_i > 0, |\rho| < 1)$.

The continuous random variables X_1, X_2 have joint p.d.f.

$$f(x_1, x_2 | \mu_1, \mu_2, \sigma_1, \sigma_2, \rho) =$$

$$\frac{1}{2\pi\sigma_1\sigma_2\sqrt{(1-\rho^2)}} \exp\left\{ -\frac{1}{2(1-\rho^2)}\left[\left(\frac{x_1 - \mu_1}{\sigma_1}\right)^2 \right.\right.$$

$$\left.\left. - 2\rho\left(\frac{x_1 - \mu_1}{\sigma_1}\right)\left(\frac{x_2 - \mu_2}{\sigma_2}\right) + \left(\frac{x_2 - \mu_2}{\sigma_2}\right)^2 \right]\right\},$$

$$-\infty < x_1 < +\infty, \quad -\infty < x_2 < +\infty.$$

The marginal distribution of X_i is $N(\mu_i, \sigma_i^2)$ $(i = 1, 2)$. Covariance $(X_1, X_2) = \rho\sigma_1\sigma_2$.

The use of particular letters for the parameters of standard distribution is not invariable. For instance, for some purposes it is convenient to refer to the normal distribution as $N(\theta_1, \theta_2)$ or even $N(\theta, \sigma_0^2)$. Other variations agree with customary usage, i.e. binomial (n, p).

The marginal distribution of X is ... Covariance ...

Introduction

We begin by previewing some of the topics which will be subsequently discussed in greater detail.

Before carrying out a formal analysis, the statistician will have a tentative mathematical model for the process which generated the data. Since the data generally show haphazard variation, the model will include statements of the type of population which may have been sampled.

Example 1. A simple model for a queueing process specifies:
(1) There is a single queue in which first come is first served.
(2) There is a single server. The durations of service times for customers have independent exponential distributions with a common mean.
(3) Regardless of the number in the queue, the inter-arrival times between incoming customers have independent exponential distributions with a common mean.

The model is partly organizational and partly statistical and has the following implications arising solely by virtue of the properties of exponential distributions:
(a) However long the server has spent on the current customer, the residual time to finish his service is again exponential.
(b) The waiting time for the nth customer to arrive has a gamma distribution.
(c) The number of customers arriving in a fixed time has a Poisson distribution.
[Exercise 2 contains calculations to support these claims.]

The appropriateness of any model will itself have to be assessed. This may be done by examining past records of such a process and seeing whether the 'fit is good'. In a famous experiment, dogs were exposed to electric shocks which could be avoided by jumping away. The centre of interest was on the number of trials taken to learn that a warning signal heralded a shock. The data for each dog consisted of a series of successes and failures in avoidance. A great many models have been proposed to explain the 'learning process', each of which had implications in terms of mean number of trials to learning, number of trials to first avoidance, and so on. These implications were compared with the experimental evidence. Notice that in this kind of analysis, almost all the work will have to be statistical since it is not possible to observe directly the learning process in a dog's brain.

Although the theory of checking the overall suitability of a model is important, it is not the subject of this text. We are concerned rather in using the data to draw conclusions about the parameters of the distributions which may have been sampled. This activity is the core of *statistical inference*. Since the data are subject to random variation, any inferences we draw will be uncertain. The only useful procedures will be those for which the degree of uncertainty is measurable in terms of probabilities. Our next examples outline, briefly, different techniques attempting to answer certain kinds of inference problem. We proceed intuitively and at this stage questions about 'best' procedures must be postponed.

Suppose we compute from the data a single function of the observations to serve as an estimate of an unknown parameter. Such a statistic, viewed as a random variable, is called a *point estimator*. The numerical value of an estimator for a particular sample is the estimate.

Example 2.   We have a random sample of values for an exponential distribution with unknown mean θ. It seems natural to estimate θ by the sample mean $\bar{x}$. Now the expected value of the mean of a random sample is the distribution mean when this exists. That is, $E(\bar{X}) = \theta$ and we say $\bar{X}$ is an *unbiased estimator* of θ. We can grasp this property by noting that repeated use of the sample average from independent random samples will not lead to a systematic over- or underestimate of θ. In general, if T is taken to be the estimator of θ, then $E(T) - \theta$ is known as the *bias*.

An estimator may lose some of its charms as soon as we become aware of competitors. For instance, the mean of a uniform distribution over $(0, \theta)$ is $\theta/2$. The mean of a random sample still estimates

$\theta/2$ without bias. But, from considerations of symmetry, so does the sample median. Which estimator shall we choose? A well-established criterion for resolving this quandary is to prefer the estimator with the smaller variance. But this then prompts the question: 'is there an unbiased estimator of θ with minimum variance?'

If unbiasedness is thought to be of prime importance, then we must be on the alert for certain difficulties.

(a) Just because some function of the observations, $t(X_1, X_2, \ldots X_n)$, is an unbiased estimator of θ, we do not automatically have an unbiased estimator of $\phi(\theta)$. That is to say

$$E[\phi\{t(X_1, X_2, \ldots, X_n)\}] \not\equiv \phi[E\{t(X_1, X_2, \ldots, X_n)\}]$$

For example, $E(1/\bar{X}) \neq 1/E(\bar{X})$

(b) A change in the conditions under which the sample is drawn may introduce bias. Thus in Example 2, suppose because of un-avoidable external limitations, each value can only be determined if it is less than x_0; otherwise it is lost. If we average the $m(\leqslant n)$ observed values less than x_0, then we tend to underestimate the distribution mean. [See Exercise 3.]

Point estimators appear to focus unduly on one possible value of the parameter. This overemphasis can be countered by computing instead an *interval estimator*. That is to say, a set of values, determined from the data, in which θ is thought to lie. When θ is regarded as a fixed constant we cannot speak of the probability of it being in an interval as if it had a distribution. On the other hand, one or both of the end-points of such an interval will be functions of the observations and it is proper to speak of the probability that the lower end lies below the parameter and simultaneously the upper end lies above the parameter. Naturally, only intervals of a type for which this probability does not depend on θ are of any use.

Example 3. We have a random sample of n observations from an exponential distribution with unknown mean θ, and we are particularly interested in finding a value which is very likely to be below θ. The smallest observation in the sample is a possible candidate. Now it may be shown that the minimum of the sample from this distribution has *another* exponential distribution but with mean θ/n. Hence the probability that it lies below θ is

$$\int_0^\theta (n/\theta)\exp(-ny/\theta)\mathrm{d}y = 1 - \exp(-n)$$

Hence the interval of positive numbers exceeding the minimum sample observation contains θ with probability $1 - \exp(-n)$. This probability does not depend on θ and rapidly approaches 1 as the sample size increases.

Estimation techniques are attempts to locate a parameter. A closely related problem is posed by the question: 'Is the parameter here–or there?' Typical examples for one parameter are:

(a) is $\theta = \theta_1$ or $\theta = \theta_2$?
(b) is $\theta < \theta_0$ or $\theta \geqslant \theta_0$?
(c) is θ inside or outside the interval (θ_1, θ_2)?

Each of (a), (b), (c) consists of a pair of conjectures or *hypotheses* about θ. One possibility is to say that any sample must be declared to be in favour of one conjecture or the other. To this end innumerable rules, known as *hypothesis tests*, can be devised. In the case of (a), one such test suggests that $\theta = \theta_1$ be preferred to $\theta = \theta_2$ if and only if the joint probability density of the sample values, when $\theta = \theta_1$, exceeds the joint probability density of the sample values, when $\theta = \theta_2$.

Example 4.   Suppose we have a single value from an exponential distribution with mean θ. Then for the rule just proposed, θ_1 will be preferred to θ_2 if and only if

$$\theta_1^{-1} \exp(-x/\theta_1) > \theta_2^{-1} \exp(-x/\theta_2)$$

If $\theta_1 > \theta_2$, this implies $x > [(\theta_1 \theta_2)/(\theta_1 - \theta_2)] \log(\theta_1/\theta_2) = c$.
We can draw a false conclusion in two different ways. For we may obtain a sample value $x > c$ when in fact $\theta = \theta_2$ or we may have $x < c$ when $\theta = \theta_1$. However, the probabilities of each of these events can be calculated.

Exercise 1.   For Example 4, calculate $\Pr[X > c | \theta = \theta_2]$ and $\Pr[X < c | \theta = \theta_1]$.

The ideas just presented will be developed and extended. We here content ourselves with one slight modification.

In some applications, the interest is not so much in the probabilities as in the economic consequences of reaching wrong decisions. A simple scheme for the costs in deciding between $\theta = \theta_1$ or $\theta = \theta_2$ would be: a correct decision costs nothing; to decide that $\theta = \theta_2$ when in fact $\theta = \theta_1$ costs a units; to decide that $\theta = \theta_1$ when in fact $\theta = \theta_2$ costs b units. The average costs of this scheme for Example 4 are $a[1 - \exp(-c/\theta_1)]$ and $b \exp(-c/\theta_2)$ respectively.

So, even with a pair of simple conjectures, two different measures of performance are available for any particular rule. Thus if we are concerned with probabilities only, we may be mistaken in one of two distinct ways:

(a) We decide $\theta = \theta_1$, when in fact $\theta = \theta_2$; let $\Pr[\text{Decide } \theta = \theta_1 | \theta = \theta_2 \text{ is the case}] = \alpha$.

(b) We decide $\theta = \theta_2$ when in fact $\theta = \theta_1$; let $\Pr[\text{Decide } \theta = \theta_2 | \theta = \theta_1 \text{ is the case}] = \beta$.

Should it happen that for two different rules, I, II, based on the same data, $\alpha_I < \alpha_{II}$ *and* $\beta_I < \beta_{II}$, then rule I is superior to rule II, But since we may have $\alpha_I < \alpha_{II}$ and $\beta_I > \beta_{II}$, no direct ordering of the rules is feasible. One way out of the dilemma is to fix one of the probabilities, say α, and search for the rule which has smallest β. This has been an important principle in traditional or classical hypothesis testing. The difficulty is not avoided by taking costs into account since there are again two expected costs, according as $\theta = \theta_1$ or $\theta = \theta_2$.

The matter would be resolved if we had a justifiable method for combining the separate probabilities (or costs) and thus of imposing an order. A linear combination of the probabilities can be made if a further assumption about the experimental situation is warranted. We have regarded the unknown parameter as fixed, but with nothing said about how it was fixed. Suppose we assume that, before the data were collected, θ was itself freshly drawn from a known distribution. In the case when θ is either θ_1 or θ_2 this amounts assigning a known probability p that θ_1 was drawn and thus of $1 - p$, that it was θ_2. If such be the case, then we have

$$\Pr[\text{Wrong decision}] = \Pr[\text{Deciding } \theta = \theta_2 | \theta = \theta_1] \Pr[\Theta = \theta_1] + \Pr[\text{Deciding } \theta = \theta_1 | \theta = \theta_2] \Pr[\Theta = \theta_2]$$
$$= \beta p + \alpha(1 - p)$$

The application we have just made, seriously under-rates the extra scope conferred by the use of such a *prior distribution* for a parameter. For instance we can calculate the probability that $\Theta = \theta_1$, conditional on the obtained data. More generally, if Θ has a continuous distribution we can attach explicit probabilities to such events as

$\Theta \leqslant \theta_0$, both before and after obtaining the data. The latter would be obtained by applying Bayes' formula. Techniques of estimation or hypothesis testing based on the assumption of a prior distribution are known as *Bayesian* methods.

But, it may be demanded, in what circumstances would we expect a prior distribution to be available? One type of situation is non-controversial. This is when there is a solid mass of previous data in which a parameter was well determined and we have what amounts to a picture of its variability.

This is the case for some long-running manufacturing processes. Thus, suppose the output consists of containers of fluid and part of the quality control is to determine whether a chemical constituent has reached a certain level. Any particular container can be checked by readings on small test amounts, though these observations are subject to error. It seems reasonable that prior information about the levels achieved should be combined with the new data to make inferences about the current batch. Not surprisingly, it is usual to employ distributions which agree comfortably with the information available and yet contrive to enjoy mathematical tractability. For instance, it might be assumed that the test readings are distributed $N(\theta, \sigma_1^2)$ where σ_1^2 is known, and that the mean Θ has a prior distribution $N(\theta_0, \sigma_0^2)$ where both θ_0, σ_0^2 are known.

More controversially, it has been argued that any individual has prior convictions about the true state of affairs before collecting the data. These beliefs are rooted partly in experience in related fields and partly in a kind of inside information which is difficult to express in the form of a probability distribution, though it may be put in broad terms. It is claimed that such features can be made explicit by forcing the holder of such views to consider the odds that he would accept in a bet concerning some readily grasped property of the distribution of a parameter. A suitable prior distribution is then selected to agree with the subjective beliefs so elicited. Suppose, for example, that a sample of individuals are asked for their voting intentions on a particular issue with a view to estimating the proportion of a large population which can be expected to support a proposal on the issue. Then, subject to some assurances about how the sample was drawn, the obvious estimator is the proportion of the sample indicating support. However, an expert in social science studying the issue expresses the conviction that with probability three-quarters the true proportion is greater than 0.5, and with probability one-half the true proportion is greater than 0.6. One way of taking his views into account is to select that member of a suitable family of prior distributions which matches his claims. 'Suitable' here means that members of the family are readily compounded with the distribution of the sample number in favour. (If this sampling distribution is taken to be binomial then we shall later see that the family of beta distributions is suitable.)

Of course, it is entirely possible that we have no prior information, yet we may be loath to part with some of the advantages accruing from the use of prior distributions. In that case we would be obliged to nominate a prior distribution which reflects our ignorance. If Θ is discrete and takes a finite number of values, then this might be done by giving each such value equal probability. When Θ is continuous and lies in a bounded interval, then much the same idea is conveyed by choosing a uniform prior distribution over that same interval. Already a doubt creeps in – for apparently the same degree of ignorance does not extend to Θ^2, which does not then have a uniform distribution over the interval. Further, it would appear that we cannot allow a uniform distribution over the whole real line, for the integral of such a density is infinite. Fortunately, if we do use such an *improper density* we shall find that the conditional distribution of the parameter given the data has a proper density.

Exercise 2. (Intended to confirm the results of Example 1(*a*), (*b*), (*c*).)
(*a*) If X has the probability density function (p.d.f.) $f(x|\theta) = \theta^{-1} \exp(-x/\theta), x > 0$, show that $\Pr[X \geqslant x] = \exp(-x/\theta)$. Show further that $\Pr[X \geqslant x_0 + x | X \geqslant x_0]$ also equals $\exp(-x/\theta)$.
(*b*) If X has p.d.f. $f(x|\theta) = \theta^{-1} \exp(-x/\theta)$, check that the moment generating function (m.g.f.) of X, $E(\exp Xt)$, is $1/(1-\theta t)$. Hence the m.g.f. of the sum of n independent random variables having this distribution is $1/(1-\theta t)^n$. Verify that the random variable with density $\theta^{-1}(x/\theta)^{n-1}\exp(-x/\theta)/(n-1)!$ also has m.g.f. $1/(1-\theta t)^n$.
(*c*) The time intervals between successive events are independent random variables with a common exponential distribution with mean θ. Suppose N_t is the number of events in the fixed interval $(0,t)$ and T_n is the time to the nth event. Since $N_t \geqslant n$ if and only if $T_n \leqslant t$, show that

$$\Pr[N_t = n] = \Pr[T_n \leqslant t] - \Pr[T_{n+1} \leqslant t]$$

Deduce that $\Pr[N_t = n] = (t/\theta)^n \exp(-t/\theta)/n!$ which corresponds to a Poisson distribution with parameter t/θ.

Exercise 3. If X has p.d.f. $f(x|\theta) = \theta^{-1}\exp(-x/\theta)$, then the p.d.f. of X, given $X \leqslant x_0$, is

$$\theta^{-1}\exp(-x/\theta)/[1-\exp(-x_0/\theta)], \qquad 0 \leqslant x \leqslant x_0$$

Hence show that the mean of this conditional distribution is

$$\theta - [\{x_0\exp(-x_0/\theta)\}/\{1-\exp(-x_0/\theta)\}]$$

CHAPTER ONE

Sufficiency

1.1 Introduction

In any statistical analysis we attempt to use all the data. The reader will already be accustomed to the idea of condensing the raw data into one or more summary statistics without perhaps dwelling overlong on the possibility that valuable information may thereby have been cast away. Suppose, for instance, that a coin is tossed independently n times and that the data are the sequence of heads and tails obtained. If it is desired to estimate the probability, θ, of a head on an individual toss and if r is the total number of heads, then it is known that R/n is an unbiased estimator of θ. There is, however, a more pervasive and general property enjoyed by the statistic R. In a sense it contains all the information about θ that the sample affords. More precisely, the conditional probability of any feature that may be displayed by the sample, given that it contains just r heads, does not depend on θ at all. For example, the conditional probability that the first toss was a head is

$$\theta \binom{n-1}{r-1} \theta^{r-1} (1-\theta)^{n-r} \Big/ \binom{n}{r} \theta^r (1-\theta)^{n-r} = r/n$$

regardless of θ. This merely reflects the circumstance that any one of the r available heads may with equal probability $1/n$ have been the first result. In like manner, the conditional probability of any sequence, compatible with the given r, does not depend on θ. In a wide sense, the conditional distribution of any statistic given r cannot be used to make any inference about θ because its conditional distribution does not depend on θ. It is 'sufficient' to know r and this very word is employed in a technical sense.

Definition. Let the random variables $X_1, X_2, \ldots, X_n$ have joint

9

probability density function $f(x_1, x_2, \ldots, x_n | \theta)$. The statistic $t(X_1, X_2, \ldots, X_n)$ is said to be a single *sufficient* statistic for θ if the conditional distribution of $X_1, X_2, \ldots, X_n$ given t does not depend on θ.

Example 1. $X_1, X_2, \ldots, X_n$ is a random sample from the Poisson distribution with parameter λ. Show that $T = \sum_1^n X_i$ is sufficient for λ. The joint probability density function of the sample values is

$$f(x_1, x_2, \ldots, x_n | \lambda) = \prod_1^n f_i(x_i | \lambda)$$
$$= \prod_1^n (\lambda^{x_i} e^{-\lambda} / x_i !)$$
$$= \lambda^{\Sigma x_i} e^{-n\lambda} \Big/ \prod_1^n x_i !$$

In this case it is known that $\sum_1^n X_i$ has another Poisson distribution but with parameter $n\lambda$. Hence the probability density function of T is

$$h(t | \lambda) = (n\lambda)^t e^{-n\lambda} / t !, \qquad t = 0, 1, \ldots$$

so that the conditional probability density function of $X_1, X_2, \ldots, X_n$ given $T = t$ is

$$g(x_1, x_2, \ldots, x_n | t, \lambda) = \frac{f(x_1, x_2, \ldots, x_n | \lambda)}{h(t | \lambda)}, \quad \text{provided} \sum_1^n x_i = t$$
$$= \frac{\lambda^{\Sigma x_i} e^{-n\lambda} / \prod x_i !}{(n\lambda)^t e^{-n\lambda} / t !}, \quad \text{provided} \sum_1^n x_i = t$$
$$= \frac{t !}{\prod x_i !} \left(\frac{1}{n}\right)^t, \quad \text{provided} \sum_1^n x_i = t$$

As this does not depend on the unknown parameter, T is sufficient for λ. In this instance we recognize the conditional distribution as multinomial with parameters $t, \theta_i = 1/n, i = 1, 2, \ldots, n$. The restriction $\sum_1^n x_i = t$ should be noted. The conditional distribution has, so to speak, one dimension less than the original sample space.

Exercise 1. $X_1, X_2, \ldots, X_n$ is a random sample from the binomial distribution with known parameter m and unknown parameter θ.

Show that the statistic $T = \sum_{1}^{n} X_i$ is sufficient for θ. Identify the conditional distribution of X_1 given $T = t$.

$$\left[\text{Ans.} \quad \binom{m}{x_1}\binom{nm-m}{t-x_1} \Big/ \binom{nm}{t} \right]$$

Exercise 2. $X_1, X_2, \ldots X_n$ is a random sample from the distribution with p.d.f. $f(x|\theta) = \theta(1-\theta)^{x-1}, x = 1, 2, \ldots$. Show that $T = \sum_{1}^{n} X_i$ is sufficient for θ.

Example 2. $X_1, X_2, \ldots, X_n$ is a random sample from the normal distribution $N(\mu, \sigma^2)$ where σ_0 is known. Show that $T = \sum_{1}^{n} X_i$ is sufficient for μ.

The joint probability density function of the sample values is

$$f(x_1, x_2, \ldots, n_n | \mu, \sigma_0) = \prod_{1}^{n} f_i(x_i | \mu, \sigma_0)$$

$$= \prod_{1}^{n} \frac{1}{\sqrt{(2\pi)}\sigma_0} \exp\left[-\tfrac{1}{2}(x_i - \mu)^2 / \sigma_0^2 \right]$$

$$= \frac{1}{\{\sqrt{(2\pi)}\}^n \sigma_0^n} \exp\left[-\tfrac{1}{2}\sum(x_i - \mu)^2 / \sigma_0^2 \right]$$

The distribution of $T = \sum_{1}^{n} X_i$ is normal $N(n\mu, n\sigma_0^2)$ with probability density function

$$h(t | \mu, \sigma_0) = \frac{1}{\sqrt{(2\pi n)}\sigma_0} \exp\left[-\tfrac{1}{2}(t - n\mu)^2 / n\sigma_0^2 \right]$$

Hence the conditional probability density function of $X_1, X_2, \ldots, X_n$ given $T = t$ is, provided $\sum x_i = t$,

$$g(x_1, x_2, \ldots, x_n | t, \mu, \sigma_0) = \frac{\sqrt{(2\pi n)}\sigma_0}{\{\sqrt{(2\pi)}\sigma_0\}^n} \exp\left[-\tfrac{1}{2}\{n\sum(x_i - \mu)^2 \right.$$
$$\left. - (t - n\mu)^2\}/n\sigma_0^2 \right]$$

$$= \frac{\sqrt{n}}{\{\sqrt{(2\pi)}\sigma_0\}^{n-1}} \exp\left[-\tfrac{1}{2}(n\sum x_i^2 - t^2)/n\sigma_0^2 \right],$$

Since g does not depend on μ, $\sum_{1}^{n} X_i$ is sufficient for μ.

Such conditional distributions are troublesome to manipulate and difficult to identify. We take a closer look at the present case when $n = 2, \sigma_0 = 1$.

$g(x_1, x_2 | t, \mu)$

$$= \frac{1}{\sqrt{\pi}} \exp\left[-\tfrac{1}{2}(2x_1^2 + 2x_2^2 - t^2)/2 \right], \qquad x_1 + x_2 = t$$

$$= \frac{1}{\sqrt{\pi}} \exp\left[-\tfrac{1}{2}(2x_1^2 + 2(t - x_1)^2 - t^2)/2 \right]$$

$$= \frac{\sqrt{2}}{\sqrt{(2\pi)}} \exp\left[-\tfrac{1}{2}(x_1 - t/2)^2/(1/\sqrt{2})^2 \right]$$

This is the probability density function of a normal distribution with mean $t/2$ and variance $1/2$. The joint distribution of X_1, X_2, given $X_1 + X_2$, is effectively one-dimensional and all the probability lies on the line $x_1 + x_2 = t$. Such a distribution is said to be *singular bivariate normal*. We still correctly deduce that $E(X_1 | X_1 + X_2 = t) = t/2$.

Exercise 3. $X_1, X_2, \ldots, X_n$ is a random sample from the normal distribution $N(\mu_0, \sigma^2)$ where μ_0 is a known constant. Show that $T = \sum_1^n (X_i - \mu_0)^2$ is sufficient for σ.

Exercise 4. $X_1, X_2, \ldots, X_n$ is a random sample from the gamma distribution $\Gamma(\alpha_0, \lambda)$, where α_0 is a known constant. Show that $T = \sum_1^n X_i$ is sufficient for λ.

Exercise 5. X_1, X_2 is a random sample of two from the distribution with probability density function $f(x | \theta) = \theta x^{\theta - 1}$, $0 < x < 1$, $\theta > 0$. Show that $X_1 X_2$ is sufficient for θ.

Example 3. $X_1, X_2, \ldots, X_n$ is a random sample from the rectangular distribution over $(0, \theta)$. Show that $T = \max(X_1, X_2, \ldots, X_n)$ is sufficient for θ.

The joint probability density function of the sample is

$$f(x_1, x_2, \ldots, x_n | \theta) = \prod_{1}^{n} f_i(x_i | \theta)$$
$$= \prod_{1}^{n} \frac{1}{\theta}, \qquad 0 < x_i < \theta$$
$$= \frac{1}{\theta^n}, \qquad 0 < x_i < \theta$$

The probability density function of T is

$$h(t) = n \left(\frac{t}{\theta} \right)^{n-1} \frac{1}{\theta}, \qquad 0 < t < \theta$$

Hence the conditional probability density function of the sample values given t is

$$g(x_1, x_2, \ldots, x_n | t, \theta) = \begin{cases} \dfrac{1/\theta^n}{nt^{n-1}/\theta^n}, & \max(x_1, x_2, \ldots, x_n) = t \\ 0 \text{ otherwise} \end{cases}$$

$$= \frac{1}{nt^{n-1}}, \qquad \max(x_1, x_2, \ldots, x_n) = t.$$

This does not depend on θ, *not even as regards the domain in which g is positive*.

The conditional distribution of X_i given $T = t$ is somewhat peculiar. For there is a discrete probability that X_i is actually equal to t and otherwise it is continuously distributed over the open interval $0 < x_i < t$.

Exercise 6. For Example 3, show that $f_i(x_i | t) = (n - 1)/nt$, $0 < x_i < t$. Calculate $E(X_i | T = t)$ and thence $2E\left(\sum_1^n X_i | T = t \right)$. [Ans. $(n + 1)t/2n$, $(n + 1)t$. Recall $\Pr[X_i = t | t] = 1/n$]

Exercise 7. $X_1, X_2, \ldots, X_n$ is a random sample from the distribution with probability density function $f(x | \theta) = \exp(\theta - x)$, $\theta < x < \infty$. Show that $T = \min(X_1, X_2, \ldots, X_n)$ is sufficient for θ.

1.2 Factorization criterion

The process of confirming the sufficiency of a statistic by first obtaining its distribution is apt to prove laborious. The definition states that T is sufficient for θ if and only if

$$f(x_1, x_2, \ldots, x_n | \theta) = h(t | \theta)g(x_1, x_2, \ldots, x_n | t, \theta) \qquad (1.1)$$

where h is the probability density function of T and g does not depend on θ. Equation (1.1), known as the Fisher–Neyman criterion, imposes a particular kind of factorization of f. Provided that the region of the sample space where f is positive does not depend on θ, it will be sufficient to show that we can write

$$f(x_1, x_2, \ldots, x_n | \theta) = H(t, \theta)G(x_1, x_2, \ldots, x_n, t) \qquad (1.2)$$

where H is *some* non-negative function of t and θ, while G is non-negative and does not contain θ. We prove the result for continuous random variables.

Proof. Effectively we change the variables from $X_1, X_2, \ldots, X_n$ to $T, T_1, T_2, \ldots, T_{n-1}$ and find in *principle* the marginal distribution of T. The auxiliary statistics $T_1, T_2, \ldots, T_{n-1}$ are of no interest in themselves, except in so far as they provide a one-to-one transformation and a well-behaved Jacobian,

$$J = \frac{\partial(t, t_1, \ldots, t_{n-1})}{\partial(x_1, x_2, \ldots, x_n)}$$

The joint probability density of the new set of variables is

$$h(t, t_1, t_2, \ldots, t_{n-1} | \theta) = \{ f(x_1, x_2, \ldots, x_n | \theta)/|J| \}_{t, t_1, \ldots, t_{n-1}} \qquad (1.3)$$

which by Equation (1.2) is $= \{ H(t, \theta)G(x_1, x_2, \ldots, x_n, t)/|J| \}_{t, t_1, \ldots, t_{n-1}}$

$$= H(t, \theta)\{ G(x_1, x_2, \ldots, x_n, t)/|J| \}_{t, t_1, \ldots, t_{n-1}}$$

$$(1.4)$$

whence

$$h_1(t | \theta) = \int\int \ldots \int h(t, t_1, \ldots, t_{n-1} | \theta)dt_1 \, dt_2, \ldots, dt_{n-1}$$
$$= H(t, \theta)\int\int \ldots \int \{ G(x_1, x_2, \ldots, x_n, t)/|J| \} dt_1 \, dt_2 \ldots dt_{n-1}$$

$$(1.5)$$

Now it is assumed that the points where $f > 0$ do not depend on θ, hence the same can be said of h since the functions T_i are statistics, and finally of h_1 because the limits of the integrals in Equation (1.5) do not involve θ. The only way θ is involved is through $H(t, \theta)$ and *this* term cancels in

$$\frac{f(x_1, x_2, \ldots, x_n | \theta)}{h_1(t | \theta)} \qquad (1.6)$$

As this expression does not depend on θ, T is sufficient for θ. That the condition in Equation (1.2) is necessary evidently follows since Equation (1.1) is but a particular form of Equation (1.2).

Example 4. We briefly apply the result to our previous worked examples.

(a) The Poisson distribution

$$f(x_1, x_2, \ldots, x_n | \lambda) = (\lambda^{\Sigma x_i} e^{-n\lambda}) \bigg/ \prod_1^n x_i!$$

Since we may take $H(\sum x_i, \lambda) = \lambda^{\Sigma x_i} e^{-n\lambda}$, $G(x_1, \ldots, x_n) = 1/\prod x_i!$ and the points where f is positive do not depend on λ, we have that $T = \sum_1^n X_i$ is sufficient for λ.

(b) The normal distribution $N(\mu, \sigma_0^2)$

$$f(x_1, x_2, \ldots, x_n | \mu, \sigma_0^2) = \frac{1}{\{\sqrt{(2\pi)}\}^n \sigma_0^n} \exp\left[-\frac{1}{2} \sum_1^n (x_i - \mu)^2 / \sigma_0^2 \right]$$

$$= \frac{1}{\{\sqrt{(2\pi)}\}^n \sigma_0^n} \exp\left[\left(\mu \sum_1^n x_i - n\mu^2/2 \right) / \sigma_0^2 \right]$$

$$\times \exp\left[-\frac{1}{2} \sum_1^n x_i^2 / \sigma_0^2 \right]$$

Again the first factor is a function of $\mu, \sum x_i$ only, while the second does not contain μ, and $\sum_1^n X_i$ is sufficient for μ.

(c) The uniform distribution over $(0, \theta)$

$$f(x_1, x_2, \ldots, x_n | \theta) = 1/\theta^n, \qquad 0 < x_i < \theta$$

The condition of $0 < x_i < \theta$ means that the points such that $f > 0$ do depend on θ, so that the result cannot be applied directly. The restricted version of the factorization theorem we are using will serve to protect us from certain errors. Thus if a random sample is drawn from the distribution with probability density function $f(x | \theta) = \exp(\theta - x), x > 0$, we have

$$f(x_1, x_2, \ldots, x_n | \theta) = \prod_1^n e^{\theta - x_i} = e^{n\theta - \Sigma x_i}, \qquad x_i > \theta$$

This 'suggests' that $\sum X_i$ is sufficient for θ, though in fact this is not the case.

Example 5. Many standard cases are covered by considering a random sample from a member of the *regular* exponential family, for which the set of x in which $f(x) > 0$ does not depend on θ, and

$f(x|\theta) = \exp[a(\theta)b(x) + c(\theta) + d(x)]$. So that

$$f(x_1, x_2, \ldots, x_n|\theta) = \prod \exp[a(\theta)b(x_i) + c(\theta) + d(x_i)]$$
$$= \exp[a(\theta)\sum b(x_i) + nc(\theta) + \sum d(x_i)]$$
$$= \exp[a(\theta)\sum b(x_i) + nc(\theta)]\exp[\sum d(x_i)]$$

By this factorization, $\sum_1^n b(X_i)$ is seen to be a sufficient statistic for θ.

1.3 Distribution of statistics conditional on a sufficient statistic

Suppose T is sufficient for θ, then with the same change of variables that yielded equation (1.3),

$$\frac{h(t, t_1, t_2, \ldots, t_{n-1}|\theta)}{h_1(t|\theta)} = \left\{ \frac{f(x_1, x_2, \ldots, x_n|\theta)/|J|}{h_1(t|\theta)} \right\}_{t, t_1, \ldots, t_{n-1}}. \quad (1.7)$$

But by the sufficiency of T, the right-hand side of Equation (1.7) does not involve θ. Hence interpreting the left-hand side we have that the conditional distribution of $T_1, T_2, \ldots, T_{n-1}$, given t, does not depend on θ. Thence, by integration, nor does any subset of $T_1, T_2, \ldots, T_{n-1}$ given t. This property is sometimes the starting-point for the discussion of sufficiency. In practice, the commonest use is to observe that if T is sufficient for θ, the conditional distribution of any other statistic, S, given t, does not depend on θ.

The reader may have noticed that nothing has been said about uniqueness in connection with a single sufficient statistic. This is because, if T is sufficient, so is any other one-to-one function of T. This is most easily seen by changing the variable in Equation (1.1), or where the factorization applies, replacing t by the inverse function in Equation (1.2). If for example, $\sum_1^n X_i$ is sufficient for θ, so are $\bar{X}$, $a\bar{X} + b$, and $\exp[\sum X_i]$.

1.4 Joint sufficiency

There does not always exist a *single* sufficient statistic for a parameter. If we are not restricted to one function of the observations, can we always find a set of sufficient statistics? The answer is 'yes'. The sample values $X_1, X_2, \ldots, X_n$ are themselves sufficient. For instance, in the discrete case, the conditional probability of any sample is 0, except for the given set, when it is $1 - $ whatever θ. Moreover, for a continuous distribution, it is readily seen that the order statistics are sufficient, for the sample values, given the order statistics, can only be a permutation of the obtained values of the order statistics. Such a set would scarcely be regarded as a reduction of the data. To cover intermediate cases and also to allow more than one parameter, it is now convenient to broaden our discussion.

Definition. Suppose $X_1, X_2, \ldots, X_n$ have a joint distribution depending on parameters $\theta_1, \theta_2, \ldots, \theta_k$. The statistics $T_1, T_2, \ldots, T_r$ are said to be *jointly sufficient* for $\theta_1, \theta_2, \ldots, \theta_k$ if and only if the conditional distribution of $X_1, X_2, \ldots, X_n$ given $t_1, t_2, \ldots, t_r$ does not depend on any or all the θ_i.

In terms of the corresponding probability density functions we require

$$f(x_1, x_2, \ldots, x_n | \theta_1, \theta_2, \ldots, \theta_k)$$
$$= h(t_1, t_2, \ldots, t_r | \theta_1, \theta_2, \ldots, \theta_k) g(x_1, x_2, \ldots, x_n | t_1, t_2 \ldots, t_r) \quad (1.8)$$

where h is the probability density function of the joint distribution of $T_1, T_2, \ldots, T_r$ and g does not depend on the parameters.

We state, without proof, the equivalent factorization result when the region where $f > 0$ does not depend on the parameters:

$$f(x_1, x_2, \ldots, x_n | \theta_1, \theta_2, \ldots, \theta_k)$$
$$= H(t_1, t_2, \ldots, t_r, \theta_1, \theta_2, \ldots, \theta_k) G(x_1, x_2, \ldots, x_n) \quad (1.9)$$

Example 6. $X_1, X_2, \ldots, X_n$ is a random sample from the distribution $N(\mu, \sigma^2)$. Show that $\sum_1^n X_i, \sum_1^n X_i^2$ are jointly sufficient for μ, σ.

$$f(x_1, x_2, \ldots, x_n | \mu, \sigma) = \prod_1^n f_i(x_i | \mu, \sigma)$$

$$= \frac{1}{\{\sqrt{(2\pi)}\sigma\}^n} \exp\left[-\frac{1}{2} \sum_1^n (x_i - \mu)^2 / \sigma^2 \right]$$

$$= \frac{1}{\{\sqrt{(2\pi)}\sigma\}^n} \exp\left[-\frac{1}{2} \left\{ \sum_1^n x_i^2 - 2\mu \sum_1^n x_i + n\mu^2 \right\} \middle/ \sigma^2 \right]$$

Since this is a function of $\sum_1^n x_i, \sum_1^n x_i^2, \mu, \sigma$, it follows that $T_1 = $

$\sum_1^n X_i, T_2 = \sum_1^n X_i^2$ are jointly sufficient for μ, σ. Although T_1 is single sufficient for μ when σ is known, T_2 is not in general sufficient for σ when μ is known. For if we factorize f into

$$\frac{1}{\{\sqrt{(2\pi)}\sigma\}^n} \exp\left[-\frac{1}{2}\sum x_i^2/\sigma^2 \right] \exp\left[-\frac{1}{2}(n\mu_0^2 - 2\mu_0 \sum x_i)/\sigma^2 \right]$$

we observe that the second factor still depends on σ, unless $\mu_0 = 0$.

It is customary, for this distribution, to employ $U_1 = T_1/n = \bar{X}, U_2 = T_2 - T_1^2/n = \sum_1^n (X_i - \bar{X})^2$, which are also sufficient for μ, σ since T_1, T_2 can be expressed uniquely in terms U_1, U_2.

Exercise 8. $(X_1, Y_1), (X_2, Y_2), \ldots (X_n, Y_n)$ is a random sample of n pairs of values from a trinomial distribution with parameters m, θ_1, θ_2. Show that $T_1 = \sum X_i, T_2 = \sum Y_i$ are jointly sufficient for θ_1, θ_2 but that T_1 is not sufficient for θ_1 when θ_2 is known.

Perhaps more surprisingly, if T_1 is sufficient for θ_1 when θ_2 is known and T_2 is sufficient for θ_2 when θ_1 is known, we may not conclude that T_1, T_2 are jointly sufficient for θ_1, θ_2.

Example 7. (Due to J. Kiefer)
If $f(x_1, x_2, \ldots, x_n | \theta_1, \theta_2) = c(\theta_1, \theta_2) \exp(-\theta_1 \sum x_i - \theta_2 \sum x_i^2$
$$- \theta_1 \theta_2 \sum x_i^3), \qquad x > 0$$
then by direct factorization:

if θ_1 is known, $\sum X_i^2 + \sum X_i^3$ is sufficient for θ_2;

if θ_2 is known, $\sum X_i + \sum X_i^3$ is sufficient for θ_1.

However, we need $\sum X_i, \sum X_i^2, \sum X_i^3$ to obtain joint sufficiency for θ_1, θ_2.

Example 8. A random sample of three is drawn from the distribution with probability density function $f(x|\theta) = 1/2, \theta - 1 < x < \theta + 1$. Show that $Y_1 = \min(X_1, X_2, X_3), Y_3 = \max(X_1, X_2, X_3)$ are jointly sufficient for θ.

$$h(y_1, y_2, y_3) = 3! f(y_1|\theta) f(y_2|\theta) f(y_3|\theta) = 6/8,$$

where y_1, y_2, y_3 are the order statistics, $\theta - 1 < y_1 < y_2 < y_3 < \theta + 1$

$$h_{1,3}(y_1, y_3) = \int_{y_1}^{y_3} (6/8) dy_2 = (3/4)(y_3 - y_1),$$

$$\theta - 1 < y_1 < y_3 < \theta + 1.$$

Hence the conditional probability density function of Y_2 given y_1, y_3 is

$$\frac{1}{y_3 - y_1}, \qquad y_1 < y_2 < y_3$$

which does not depend on θ, either through its functional form or the interval for which it is positive. Hence Y_1, Y_3 are jointly sufficient for θ. A little further work shows that neither Y_1 nor Y_3 is single sufficient for θ. [This does not appear to rule out some function of Y_1, Y_3 being single sufficient.]

Exercise 9. For Example 8, calculate $E(Y_1), E(Y_3)$ and hence show that there cannot be a unique unbiased estimator of θ.

Exercise 10. $X_1, X_2, \ldots, X_n$ is a random sample from the $\Gamma(\alpha, \lambda)$ distribution. Show that $\prod_1^n X_i, \sum_1^n X_i$ are jointly sufficient for α, λ.

Exercise 11. $X_1, X_2, \ldots, X_n$ is a random sample from the continuous distribution with probability density function $f(x \mid \theta_1, \theta_2) = \exp\left[(\theta_1 - x)/\theta_2\right]/\theta_2$ for $\theta_1 < x, \theta_2 > 0$. Show that $\sum_1^n X_i$, $\min(X_1, X_2, \ldots, X_n)$ are jointly sufficient for θ_1, θ_2. [Hint: if $S = \sum X_i, T = \min(X_1, X_2, \ldots, X_n)$, find the joint p.d.f. of S, T by *considering* the conditional distribution of S given t and the marginal distribution of T.]

1.5 Minimal sufficiency

We now address ourselves more closely to the question of effecting the maximum reduction of the data in terms of sufficient statistics. Evidently, if we have a set $S_1, S_2, \ldots, S_r$ which is jointly sufficient for $\theta_1, \theta_2, \ldots, \theta_k$ but we can find another set $T_1, T_2, \ldots, T_l$ with $l < r$ then we shall have removed some redundancy. The case $l = r$ is not so clear, since it may be that the sets are not one-to-one functions of each other. For example, if we have a single value X from the normal distribution $N(0, \sigma^2)$, then $\exp\left[-\frac{1}{2}(x^2/\sigma^2)\right]/\sqrt{(2\pi)}\sigma$ is a function of x and of x^2 so that both are sufficient statistics. However, although x^2 is a function of x, this latter is not a one-to-one function of x^2. This kind of consideration leads to the definition of *minimal sufficient statistic*. A set of statistics is said to be minimal sufficient if its components are functions of any other set of sufficient statistics. This definition has a geometrical aspect. We may think of the sample space as divided up into mutually exclusive regions in which a set of sufficient statistics takes constant values.

Example 9. $X_1, X_2, \ldots, X_n$ is a random sample from the Bernoulli distribution with probability density function $f(x|\theta) = \theta^x(1-\theta)^{1-x}$, $x = 0, 1$. Consider a sample space which consists of the 2^n points of positive probability. It is easily seen that $T = \sum_1^n X_i$ is sufficient for θ. Also $t(x_1, x_2, \ldots, x_n)$ takes the values $0, 1, \ldots, n$. There are just $\binom{n}{r}$ points for which $\sum_1^n x_i = r$. By inspection of $f(x_1, x_2, \ldots, x_n|\theta)$, the statistics $U_1 = \sum_1^m X_i, U_2 = \sum_{i=m+1}^n X_i$ are jointly sufficient for θ. The points for which $U_1 = u, U_2 = r - u$ are such that $T = r$ for $u = 0, 1, \ldots, \max(m, r - m)$. The partition based on constant values of U_1, U_2 are subsets of the partitions induced by constant values of T. In this sense, the minimal sufficient statistics will provide the coarsest partition of the sample space. It is this idea which is exploited in the next result.

Construction of minimal sufficient statistics

Suppose there exist minimal sufficient statistics $T_1, T_2, \ldots, T_r$ for the parameters $\theta_1, \theta_2, \ldots, \theta_k$. Then by definition

$$f(x_1, x_2, \ldots, x_n|\theta_1, \theta_2, \ldots, \theta_k)$$
$$= h(t_1, t_2, \ldots, t_r|\theta_1, \theta_2, \ldots, \theta_k)g(x_1, x_2, \ldots, x_n|t_1, t_2, \ldots, t_r)$$

We now divide up the points of the sample space into sets according to the values of the minimal sufficient statistics. That is, $(x_1, x_2, \ldots, x_n)$, $(y_1, y_2, \ldots, y_n)$ will be in the same set if and only if $t_i(x_1, x_2, \ldots, x_n) = t_i(y_1, y_2, \ldots, y_n)$, $i = 1, 2, \ldots, r$. But in that case, for any two such samples, we must have

$$\frac{f(y_1, y_2, \ldots, y_n|\theta_1, \theta_2, \ldots, \theta_k)}{f(x_1, x_2, \ldots, x_n|\theta_1, \theta_2, \ldots, \theta_k)} = \frac{g(y_1, y_2, \ldots, y_n|t_1, t_2, \ldots, t_r)}{g(x_1, x_2, \ldots, x_n|t_1, t_2, \ldots, t_r)} \quad (1.10)$$

and this ratio does not depend on any of the parameters. We construct another partition of the sample space. For any fixed sample $x_1, x_2, \ldots, x_n$, we shall say that $y_1, \ldots, y_n$ lies in the same partition set, $P(x_1, x_2, \ldots, x_n)$ indexed by the fixed sample, if and only if

$$\frac{f(y_1, y_2, \ldots, y_n | \theta_1, \theta_2, \ldots, \theta_k)}{f(x_1, x_2, \ldots, x_n | \theta_1, \theta_2, \ldots, \theta_k)} = l(y_1, y_2, \ldots, y_n, x_1, x_2, \ldots, x_n) \quad (1.11)$$

where l does not depend on any of the parameters. If two samples satisfy Equation (1.10), then they satisfy Equation (1.11). That is, the partitions afforded by constant values of the minimal sufficient statistic are subsets of the partition generated by Equation (1.11) – which we will now show are themselves sufficient. For the conditional probability density function of $Y_1, Y_2, \ldots, Y_n$ given $P(x_1, x_2, \ldots, x_n)$ is

$$f(y_1, y_2, \ldots, y_n | \theta_1, \theta_2, \ldots, \theta_k) / \Pr[(Y_1, Y_2, \ldots, Y_n) \in P(x_1, x_2, \ldots, x_n)]$$

$$= \frac{f(x_1, x_2, \ldots, x_n | \theta_1, \theta_2, \ldots, \theta_k) l(y_1, y_2, \ldots, y_n, x_1, x_2, \ldots, x_n)}{\int f(x_1, x_2, \ldots, x_n | \theta_1, \theta_2, \ldots, \theta_k) l(y_1, y_2, \ldots, y_n) dy_1 dy_2 \ldots dy_n}$$

where the integral is over $P(x_1, x_2, \ldots, x_n)$, and as f cancels, does not depend on the parameters. Hence the partition sets in Equation (1.11) are themselves sufficient. Hence they are also minimal sufficient.

Example 10. $X_1, X_2, \ldots, X_n$ is a random sample from the distribution $N(\mu, \sigma^2)$.

$$\frac{f(y_1, y_2, \ldots, y_n | \mu, \sigma)}{f(x_1, x_2, \ldots, x_n | \mu, \sigma)} = \frac{\prod \{\exp[-\frac{1}{2}(y_i - \mu)^2 / \sigma^2] / \sqrt{(2\pi)}\sigma\}}{\prod \{\exp[-\frac{1}{2}(x_i - \mu)^2 / \sigma^2] / \sqrt{(2\pi)}\sigma\}}$$

$$= \exp[-\frac{1}{2}\{\sum(y_i - \mu)^2 - \sum(x_i - \mu)^2\} / \sigma^2]$$

$$= \exp[-\frac{1}{2}\{(\sum y_i^2 - \sum x_i^2) - 2\mu(\sum y_i - \sum x_i)\} / \sigma^2]$$

By inspection, this last does not depend on μ or σ if and only if $\sum y_i = \sum x_i$, *and* $\sum y_i^2 = \sum x_i^2$. That is, $T_1 = \sum_1^n X_i, T_2 = \sum_1^n X_i^2$ are minimal sufficient statistics.

Exercise 12. If $X_1, X_2, \ldots, X_n$ is a random sample from the regular exponential family $f(x|\theta) = \exp[a(\theta)b(x) + c(\theta) + d(x)]$, show that $\sum_1^n b(X_i)$ is minimal sufficient for θ.

Exercises 13. Show for Example (9) when $n = 3$, that fixed values of $S = (X_1, X_2 + X_3)$ divide the eight sample points into six partition sets.

Exercise 14. $X_1, X_2, \ldots, X_n$ is a random sample from the distribution with p.d.f. $f(x|\theta_1, \theta_2) = \theta_2^{-1} \exp[(\theta_1 - x)/\theta_2], x > \theta_1$. Show that $\sum X_i, \min(X_1, X_2, \ldots, X_n)$ are minimal sufficient for θ_1, θ_2. [Hint: from Equation (1.11), two samples will not be in the same partition set unless they have the same minimum.]

CHAPTER TWO

Unbiased point estimators

2.1 Introduction

We begin by revising some basic ideas. The probability density function of a random variable may contain one or more unknown parameters. One task of statistical analysis is to find 'reasonable' estimates of such parameters. This may sound coldly abstract since it springs from describing a mathematical model of a real situation. In a consignment of N articles we may wish to estimate the proportion, θ, of defectives. To this end we may draw a random sample of n articles, without replacement, and count the number, r, of defectives. The obvious estimate of θ is r/n. The theoretical model would state that the number of defectives in the sample has a hypergeometric distribution with known parameters N, n and unknown parameter θ.

Definition. A statistic $t(X_1, X_2, \ldots, X_n)$ is said to be an *unbiased estimator* of a parameter θ if $E(T) = \theta$ for all admissible values of θ. Otherwise $E(T) - \theta$ is termed the *bias*.

If the expectation of a random variable exists, then we may always estimate it without bias from the mean $\hat{X}$ of a random sample; for

$$E(\bar{X}) = E\left(\sum_1^n X_i/n \right) = \sum_1^n E(X_i)/n = n\mu/n = \mu,$$
$$\text{where } E(X_i) = \mu, \qquad i = 1, 2, \ldots, n.$$

Example 1. X has the exponential distribution with parameter λ:
$$f(x|\lambda) = \lambda \exp(-\lambda x), \qquad x > 0$$

$$E(X) = \int_0^\infty xf(x|\lambda)\mathrm{d}x = \int_0^\infty x\lambda e^{-\lambda x}\mathrm{d}x = 1/\lambda$$

If $X_1, X_2, \ldots, X_n$ is a random sample from the distribution, then $\bar{X}$ is an unbiased estimator of $1/\lambda$. It does not of course follow that $1/\bar{X}$ is an unbiased estimator of λ itself.

Example 2. X has the normal distribution $N(\mu, \sigma^2)$. Here $E(X) = \mu$. If $X_1, X_2, \ldots, X_n$ is a random sample from this distribution, $E(\bar{X}) = \mu$ for all μ. Hence $\bar{X}$ is an unbiased estimator of μ regardless of the value of the second parameter, σ.

Exercise 1.   X has probability density function $f(x|m, \lambda) = \lambda(\lambda x)^{m-1} \exp(-\lambda x)/(m-1)!, x \geqslant 0, m \geqslant 2$. Show that $E(X) = m/\lambda$ but $E(1/X) = \lambda/(m-1)$. Thus $X/m, (m-1)/X$ are unbiased estimators of $1/\lambda, \lambda$ respectively.

The value of a statistic as a point estimator is unlikely to prove very satisfying if taken in isolation. We should like some idea of its reliability. It would be very agreeable if we could claim that some estimator was better than any other in some acceptable sense. A very stiff formulation of 'best' demands that the estimator has maximum probability of being sufficiently close to the parameter. More precisely, an estimator T^* is said to be *most concentrated* if for any $\varepsilon > 0$, $\Pr[\theta - \varepsilon < T^* < \theta + \varepsilon]$ is not exceeded by any other estimator, for any θ. An estimator with such strong properties is scarcely to be found. Instead of using the entire probability distribution, we can fall back on some weaker characteristic which 'summarizes' the spread of probability. For unbiased estimators, the variance of the estimator has usually been the classical choice of summarizing measure. This measure has the following attractive features:
(a) it can readily be computed and manipulated;
(b) it plays a dominating role in large samples (approximate normality);
(c) it crudely measures the spread of probability, for by Chebychev's inequality,

$$\Pr[|T - \theta| \geqslant k] \leqslant V(T)/k^2$$

(where V is the variance). This sets an upper bound to the probability that T is more than a stated distance from $E(T) = \theta$.

Definition.   If T_1, T_2 are unbiased estimators of θ, based on the same size sample, then the *efficiency of T_2 relative to T_1* is $V(T_1)/V(T_2)$.

We must also consider the behaviour of an estimator when it is based on a large sample. A plausible requirement is that the probability of being close to the parameter of interest should then be high. Formally, an estimator Θ_n, based on a sample of size n, is said to be a *consistent* estimator of θ if for every $\varepsilon > 0$,

$$\lim_{n \to \infty} \left[\Pr(|\Theta_n - \theta| < \varepsilon) \right] = 1.$$

For example, if Y_n is the maximum value of a random sample of n from the uniform distribution over $(0, \theta)$, then

$$\Pr(|Y_n - \theta| < \varepsilon) = 1 - [(\theta - \varepsilon)/\theta]^n \to 1 \text{ as } n \to \infty.$$

Since $E(Y_n) = n\theta/(n + 1)$, we observe that a consistent estimator need not be unbiased. However, $\lim_{n \to \infty} E(Y_n) = \theta$, and Y_n is, as one might expect, asymptotically unbiased.

Direct evaluation of the relevant probability can often be avoided by using the following sufficient conditions: if Θ_n is asymptotically unbiased and $\lim_{n \to \infty} V(\Theta_n) = 0$, then Θ_n is consistent. This follows immediately from the inequalities

$$\begin{aligned} \Pr(|\Theta_n - \theta| > \varepsilon) = \Pr\left[(\Theta_n - \theta)^2 > \varepsilon^2\right] \\ \leqslant E[(\Theta_n - \theta)^2]/\varepsilon^2 \\ = \{V(\Theta_n) + [E(\Theta_n - \theta)]^2\}/\varepsilon^2 \end{aligned}$$

and if both terms in the numerator tend to zero, Θ_n must be consistent.

In contrast, an unbiased estimator need not be consistent. The first member of a random sample is an unbiased estimator of its distribution mean but is not consistent. Less trivially, if Y_1 is the minimum of a random sample of n from an exponential distribution with mean θ, then nY_1 has expectation θ but its distribution does not depend on n at all! There are 'better' unbiased estimators than nY_1 and the search for the best is one theme of this chapter.

It is now convenient to re-establish two results about variances. If $X_1, X_2, \ldots, X_n$ is a random sample from a distribution for which the variance, σ^2, exists, then:

$$(a) \quad V(\bar{X}) = V\left(\sum_1^n X_i/n\right) = V\left(\sum_1^n X_i\right)\bigg/ n^2 = \sum_1^n V(X_i)/n^2 =$$

$$= \sum_1^n \sigma^2/n^2 = \sigma^2/n$$

(b) $E\left[\sum_1^n (X_i - \bar{X})^2\right] = E\left[\sum_1^n \{X_i - \mu - (\bar{X} - \mu)\}^2\right]$

$$= E\left[\sum_1^n (X_i - \mu)^2 - n(\bar{X} - \mu)^2\right]$$

$$= \sum_1^n \{E(X_i - \mu)^2\} - nE(\bar{X} - \mu)^2$$

$$= \sum_1^n V(X_i) - nV(\bar{X})$$

$$= \sum_1^n \sigma^2 - n\sigma^2/n$$

$$= (n-1)\sigma^2$$

In (a), independence of the sample values implies $V(\sum X_i) = \sum V(X_i)$. For correlated random variables, see Exercise 2.

Exercise 2. If $X_1, X_2, \ldots, X_n$ have a joint distribution such that $V(X_i) = \sigma^2$, $\text{Cov}(X_i, X_j) = \rho\sigma^2$, $i \neq j$, show that

$$V(\bar{X}) = \frac{\sigma^2}{n}\{1 + (n-1)\rho\}$$

Calculate $E[\sum(X_i - \bar{X})^2]$.
[Ans. $(n-1)(1-\rho)\sigma^2 + \sum(\mu_i - \bar{\mu})^2$, where $E(X_i) = \mu_i$.]

Exercise 3. $X_1, X_2, \ldots, X_n$ is a random sample from the distribution $N(0, \sigma^2)$. Show that

$$\sqrt{(\pi/2)}\sum_1^n |X_i|/n$$

is an unbiased estimator of σ.

Exercise 4. If $E(T_1) = \theta = E(T_2)$, $V(T_1) = \sigma_1^2$, $V(T_2) = \sigma_2^2$ and T_1, T_2 are independent, show that $T = \lambda T_1 + (1 - \lambda)T_2$ is an unbiased estimator of θ for which the variance is minimized when $\lambda = \sigma_2^2/(\sigma_1^2 + \sigma_2^2)$.

Example 3. We now consider a more extended example. Let $X_1, X_2, \ldots, X_n$ be a random sample from the uniform distribution over $(0, \theta)$.

$$f(x|\theta) = 1/\theta, \quad 0 \leqslant x \leqslant \theta, \quad E(X) = \theta/2, \quad V(X) = \theta^2/12$$

Hence $2\bar{X}$ is an unbiased estimator of θ, $V(2\bar{X}) = 4V(\bar{X}) = 4V(X)/n = \theta^2/3n$.

An 'obvious' estimator for θ, since the distribution is symmetrical, is the sample median. For simplicity, choose $n = 2m + 1$. For any X_i, $\Pr(X_i \leqslant x) = x/\theta$, whence the probability density function of Y, the median, is

$$g(y|\theta) = (2m + 1)\binom{2m}{m}\left(\frac{y}{\theta}\right)^m\left(1 - \frac{y}{\theta}\right)^m\frac{1}{\theta}, \quad 0 \leqslant y \leqslant \theta$$

From this we derive $E(Y) = \theta/2$, $V(Y) = \theta^2/[4(2m + 3)]$. Accordingly, $2Y$ is also an unbiased estimator of θ with variance $\theta^2/(2m + 3)$.

The corresponding variance of the sample mean is $\theta^2/(6m + 3)$ and is, for every θ, smaller than that of the median. The relative efficiency is $(2m + 3)/(6m + 3)$ and tends to $1/3$ as m increases. The impression may be gained that the sample mean is 'best'. Consider, however, $Z = \max(X_i)$. For a sample of $2m + 1$, this random variable has probability density function

$$h(z|\theta) = \frac{(2m + 1)}{\theta}\left(\frac{z}{\theta}\right)^{2m}, \quad 0 \leqslant z \leqslant \theta$$

whence $\dfrac{2(m + 1)}{2m + 1}Z$ is an unbiased estimator of θ, with variance $\theta^2/[(2m + 1)(2m + 3)]$ and thus improves on the sample mean. But perhaps there exist even 'better' estimators than those already considered.

A first step towards solving the difficulty raised in Example 3 is taken by constructing an improved estimator from an existing estimator.

2.2 Rao–Blackwell theorem

Let X, Y have a joint distribution with second moments existing. $m(X)$, the conditional mean of Y given x, has the properties:
(a) $E[m(X)] = E(Y)$;
(b) $V[m(X)] \leqslant V(Y)$
The first result is immediate since the joint p.d.f. of X, Y can be factorized into the product of the conditional p.d.f. of Y given x and the p.d.f. of X.

Also
$$V(Y) = E[Y - E(Y)]^2$$
$$= E[Y - m(X) + m(X) - E(Y)]^2$$
$$= E[(Y - m(X))^2 + (m(X) - E(Y))^2 + 2(Y - m(X))$$
$$\times (m(X) - E(Y))]$$
$$= E(Y - m(X))^2 + E(m(X) - E(Y))^2 + 2E[(Y - m(X))$$
$$\times (m(X) - E(Y))]$$
$$= E[Y - m(X)]^2 + V[m(X)]$$

The cross-product vanishes on taking the expectation of $Y - m(X)$ conditional on X. Thus $V(Y) \geqslant V[m(X)]$, with in fact strict inequality unless $E[Y - m(X)]^2 = 0$. Since $[Y - m(X)]^2$ is nonnegative, it can only have zero expectation if $Y - m(X) = 0$ or $Y = m(X)$, which in turn implies that the joint distribution of X, Y is degenerate.

Example 4. Let Y_1, Y_2, Y_3 be the order statistics of a random sample of three from the uniform distribution $f(x|\theta) = 1/\theta, 0 \leqslant x \leqslant \theta$. From Example 3, $2Y_2$ is an unbiased estimator of θ with variance $\theta^2/5$. Now Y_3, Y_2 have a joint distribution and Y_3 is not just a function of Y_2. So that the Rao–Blackwell theorem assures us that the conditional mean of $2Y_2$ given Y_3 will also have mean θ and variance $< \theta^2/5$. Why then choose Y_3 instead of Y_1? It will be recalled that Y_3 is sufficient for θ, so that $E(2Y_2|Y_3)$ *will not depend on* θ, and is usable as an estimator for the unknown parameter. $E(2Y_2|Y_1)$ on the other hand, although obeying the conditions of the theorem, would contain θ and be useless as an estimator. The joint probability density function of Y_1, Y_2, Y_3 is

$$g(y_1, y_2, y_3) = 3! f(y_1|\theta) f(y_2|\theta) f(y_3|\theta)$$
$$= 6/\theta^3, \qquad 0 \leqslant y_1 \leqslant y_2 \leqslant y_3 \leqslant \theta$$

After integrating out y_1 from 0 to y_2, the joint probability density function of Y_2, Y_3 is

$$h(y_2, y_3) = 6y_2/\theta^3, \qquad 0 \leqslant y_2 \leqslant y_3 \leqslant \theta$$

The probability density function of Y_3 is thus

$$k(y_3) = \int_0^{y_3} h(y_2, y_3) dy_2 = 3y_3^2/\theta^3, \qquad 0 \leqslant y_3 \leqslant \theta$$

The conditional probability density function of Y_2 given y_3 is

$$h(y_2, y_3)/k(y_3) = 2y_2/y_3^2, \qquad 0 \leqslant y_2 \leqslant y_3$$

which does not depend on θ at all. Finally,

$$E(2Y_2|y_3) = \int_0^{y_3} \frac{4y_2^2}{y_3^2} \, dy_2 = \frac{4}{3}y_3$$

It is now readily verified that $4Y_3/3$ is an unbiased estimator of θ with variance $\theta^2/15$. [Alternatively, consider $m = 1$ in the results of Example 3.]

Exercise 5. Go round the course of Example 4 again. Show that the random variable $E(4Y_3/3 \,|\, Y_2) = (2\theta + 2Y_2)/3$ has expectation θ and variance $\theta^2/45$. This random variable is of course useless for estimation purposes.

2.3 The role of sufficient statistics

The discussion in Example 4 shows us the initial extra requirements if the Rao–Blackwell theorem is to be of service in point estimation. We require Y to be a statistic and X to be a sufficient statistic for θ. This guarantees that $E[Y|X]$ is a statistic. Suppose then we are searching for a *minimum-variance unbiased estimator* (m.v.u.e.) for θ. We now know that we must restrict attention to functions of sufficient statistics – for otherwise we may use the Rao–Blackwell theorem to improve on any other statistic.

Example 5. $X_1, X_2, \ldots, X_n$ is a random sample from the Poisson distribution with parameter λ. It is required to estimate λ starting with the trivial estimator X_1 since we know that $E(X_1) = \lambda$. But we also have seen that $\sum_1^n X_i$ is sufficient for λ (and has a Poisson distribution with parameter $n\lambda$).

$$\Pr\left(X_1 = x_1 \,\middle|\, \sum_1^n X_i = k\right)$$

$$= \frac{\Pr\left(X_1 = x_1 \text{ and } \sum_1^n X_i = k\right)}{\Pr\left(\sum_1^n X_i = k\right)}$$

$$= \frac{\Pr\left(X_1 = x_1 \text{ and } \sum_2^n X_i = k - x_1\right)}{\Pr\left(\sum_1^n X_i = k\right)}$$

$$= \frac{\Pr(X_1 = x_1)\Pr\left(\sum_2^n X_i = k - x_1\right)}{\Pr\left(\sum_1^n X_i = k\right)}$$

$$= \frac{[\lambda^{x_1} e^{-\lambda}/x_1!][\{(n-1)\lambda\}^{k-x_1} e^{-(n-1)\lambda}/(k-x_1)!]}{(n\lambda)^k e^{-n\lambda}/k!}$$

$$= \frac{k!}{x_1!(k-x_1)!}\left(\frac{1}{n}\right)^{x_1}\left(\frac{n-1}{n}\right)^{k-x_1}$$

Thus the conditional distribution of X_1 given $\sum_1^n X_i = k$ is binomial with parameters k, $1/n$, a result which, with the benefit of hindsight, may now seem obvious. The mean of this conditional distribution is $k/n = \sum_1^n X_i/n = \bar{X}$. By our standard result $E(\bar{X}) = \lambda$, $V(\bar{X}) = V(X)/n = \lambda/n$. In fact $\sum_1^n X_i$ is also *minimal* sufficient.

Not only should we restrict attention to functions of sufficient statistics, we should try also to ensure that the sufficient statistics are minimal. For if we start with a function of sufficient statistics which are not already minimal, then the minimal sufficient statistics may themselves be used to improve the estimator via the Rao–Blackwell result. The next exercise illustrates the point at issue.

Exercise 6.   Let Y_1, Y_2, Y_3 be the order statistics of a random sample of three from the uniform distribution over $(0, \theta)$. Show that Y_1, Y_3 are jointly sufficient for θ. Hence show that $E(2Y_2 | Y_1, Y_3) = Y_1 + Y_3$, and is an unbiased estimator of θ with variance $\theta^2/10$. [Warning: recall that Y_1, Y_3 are not independent when computing $V(Y_1 + Y_3)$.] The point here is that Y_1, Y_3 are not minimal sufficient. On the other hand, Y_3 is minimal sufficient for θ and $V(4Y_3/3) < V(Y_1 + Y_3)$.

It may be possible in fact to construct quite distinct unbiased estimators based on even a single sufficient statistic.

Example 6.   Consider a value X from the normal distribution $N(0, \sigma^2)$. X is sufficient for σ and $\sqrt{(\pi/2)}|X|$ is an unbiased estimator of σ. However, for this distribution, $E(X) = 0$, hence $\sqrt{(\pi/2)}|X| + aX$ is an unbiased estimator of σ for any a.

2.4 Completeness

Evidently, the further property we need is uniqueness of the unbiased estimator. That is, if $E(T_1) = E(T_2) = \theta$, we require that $T_1 = T_2$ except possibly for values which have zero probability. This requirement is formalized in the property known as *completeness*.

Definition. If the statistic T has probability density function $g(t|\theta)$ and if every statistic $s(T)$ with zero expectation for all θ implies that $s(T) \equiv 0$ almost everywhere, then the family $g(t|\theta)$ is said to be *complete*. More briefly, T is said to be complete. If the property only holds for all bounded S, then T is said to be *boundedly complete*.

Suppose then that the distribution of T is complete and both $s_1(T), s_2(T)$ are unbiased estimators of θ. Hence

$$E[s_1(T)] = E[s_2(T)] \qquad \text{for all } \theta$$
$$E[s_1(T) - s_2(T)] = 0 \qquad \text{for all } \theta$$

But since the distribution of T is complete, this implies $s_1(T) - s_2(T) = 0$ or $s_1(T) \equiv s_2(T)$, almost everywhere.

Demonstrating the completeness of a family of probability density functions in general requires mathematics beyond the level of this text. We can, however, verify it for particular families.

Example 7. Let $X_1, X_2, \ldots, X_n$ be a random sample from the uniform distribution, for which $f(x|\theta) = 1/\theta, 0 \leq x \leq \theta, \theta > 0$. Then $T = \max(X_1, X_2, \ldots, X_n)$ is shown as follows to be complete. The p.d.f. of T is $g(t|\theta) = nt^{n-1}/\theta^n, 0 \leq t \leq \theta$.

$$E[s(T)] = \int s(t)g(t|\theta)dt$$
$$= \int_0^\theta \frac{s(t)nt^{n-1}}{\theta^n} dt$$

If this integral is zero for each θ, then

$$\int_0^\theta s(t)t^{n-1} dt = 0, \qquad \theta > 0$$

Differentiating with respect to the upper limit,

$$s(\theta)\theta^{n-1} = 0, \qquad \theta > 0$$
$$s(\theta) = 0, \qquad \theta > 0$$

That is, $s(t) = 0, t > 0$. Nothing is said about $s(t)$ for $t < 0$, but then $\Pr(T < 0) = 0$. $E[\{(n + 1)/n\}T] = \theta$, hence $\{(n + 1)/n\}T$ is the m.v.u.e. of θ by virtue of the Rao–Blackwell theorem.

Our procedure, on being provided with a complete sufficient statistic for θ, is to find an unbiased estimator of θ, if possible, based on that same statistic.

Exercise 7.   A random sample $X_1, X_2, \ldots, X_n$ is drawn from the distribution with probability density function $f(x|\theta) = \exp[\theta - x]$, $\theta \leqslant x \leqslant \infty, \theta > 0$. Show that $T = \min(X_1, X_2, \ldots, X_n)$ is a complete sufficient statistic for θ and hence find the m.v.u.e. of θ.

[Ans. $T - 1/n$]

Exercise 8.   A random sample $X_1, X_2, \ldots, X_n$ is drawn from a continuous distribution with probability density function

$$f(x|\theta) = a(\theta)h(x), \qquad 0 \leqslant x \leqslant \theta, \theta > 0$$

Show that $T = \max(X_1, X_2, \ldots, X_n)$ is a complete sufficient statistic for θ.

Example 8.   Suppose X is a single value from the binomial distribution, with known parameter n and unknown parameter θ.

$$E[s(X)] = \sum_{x=0}^{n} s(x)\binom{n}{x}\theta^x(1 - \theta)^{n-x}$$

This is a polynomial in θ of degree n and if it is zero for more than n distinct values of θ (let alone the interval $0 < \theta < 1$) then all its coefficients must be zero. This implies $s(0) = s(1) = \ldots = s(n) = 0$. It is to be noted that $s(x)$ need not be zero at other points – we only require, for a discrete distribution, that it be zero at points of positive probability. Thus X is a complete sufficient statistic for θ. Since $E(X/n) = \theta, X/n$ is the m.v.u.e. of θ. Further, since

$$E(X^2) = n\theta(1 - \theta) + n^2\theta^2 = n\theta - n\theta^2 + n^2\theta^2$$

X^2/n^2 is the m.v.u.e. of $\theta/n + \{(n - 1)/n\}\theta^2$. There is no unbiased estimator of $1/\theta$.

Exercise 9. $X_1, X_2, \ldots, X_n$ is a random sample from a Poisson distribution with parameter λ. Show that $\sum_1^n X_i$ is complete.

Exercise 10. The discrete random variable X has probability density function $f(x|\theta) = (1-\theta)^2\theta^x, x = 0,1,2,\ldots, f(-1|\theta) = \theta$, and zero otherwise. Show that X is boundedly complete, but not complete.

We have spoken of a complete sufficient statistic. In fact a sufficient statistic which is complete is also necessarily minimal sufficient. On the other land, a minimal sufficient statistic need not be complete.

2.5 Joint completeness

Let $X_1, X_2, \ldots, X_n$ have a joint distribution which depends on k parameters $\theta_1, \theta_2, \ldots, \theta_k$. The statistics $t_i(X_1, X_2, \ldots, X_n)$, $i = 1, 2, \ldots, m$ are said to be *jointly complete* for the θ_i if and only if the only functions $s(T_1, T_2, \ldots, T_m)$ with zero expectation for all admissible values of the parameters are identically zero almost everywhere.

Example 9. X_1, X_2 have the joint discrete distribution

$$f(x_1, x_2|\theta_1, \theta_2) = \theta_1^{x_1}\theta_2^{x_2}(1-\theta_1-\theta_2)^{1-x_1-x_2}/x_1!x_2!$$
$$\text{for } (x_1 = x_2 = 0), (x_1 = 1, x_2 = 0),$$
$$(x_1 = 0, x_2 = 1), 0 < \theta_1 < 1, 0 < \theta_2 < 1.$$

$$E[s(X_1, X_2)] = s(0,0)(1-\theta_1-\theta_2) + s(1,0)\theta_1 + s(0,1)\theta_2$$
$$= \theta_1[s(1,0) - s(0,0)] + \theta_2[s(0,1) - s(0,0)] + s(0,0)$$

If this expression is zero for even more than two distinct pairs of values of θ_1, θ_2, then the coefficients and constant term must all be zero. That is, $s(1,0) = s(0,0) = s(0,1) = 0$ or $s(x_1,x_2)$ is zero at all points of positive probability. Thus X_1, X_2 are jointly complete for θ_1, θ_2. This trivial example can be readily extended to show that if X_1, X_2 have the trinomial distribution, with parameters n, θ_1, θ_2, then they are jointly complete.

Exercise 11. Let $X_1, X_2, \ldots, X_n$ be a random sample from the continuous distribution with probability density function $f(x) = 1/(\theta_2 - \theta_1), \theta_1 \leq x \leq \theta_2$. Show that $\min[X_1, X_2, \ldots, X_n]$, $\max[X_1, X_2, \ldots, X_n]$ are jointly complete for θ_1, θ_2.

The manner of application of joint completeness to problems of estimation for several parameters now follows a similar pattern to that employed for one parameter. In the first place if $T_1, T_2, \ldots, T_m$ are jointly complete for $\theta_1, \theta_2, \ldots, \theta_k$ and $E[s(T_1, T_2, \ldots, T_m)] =$

$\phi(\theta_1, \theta_2, \dots, \theta_k)$, then there is essentially only one *such* unbiased estimator of $\phi(\theta_1, \theta_2, \dots, \theta_k)$. For if another existed, then the difference between it and S would have zero expectation. Hence, by completeness, the estimator would have to equal S (almost everywhere). If in the second place $T_1, T_2, \dots, T_m$ are also jointly sufficient for $\theta_1, \theta_2, \dots, \theta_m$ we can apply the Rao–Blackwell theorem. That is, if $u(X_1, X_2, \dots, X_n)$ is an unbiased estimator of $\phi(\theta_1, \theta_2, \dots, \theta_k)$ which is not just a function of $T_1, T_2, \dots, T_m$, then $E[U \mid T_1, T_2, \dots, T_m]$ is a statistic, because of the joint sufficiency, with expectation $\phi(\theta_1, \theta_2, \dots, \theta_k)$. Furthermore,

$$V[U] \geqslant V[E\{U \mid T_1, T_2, \dots, T_m\}]$$

This, together with completeness, ensures that the m.v.u.e. of $\phi(\theta_1, \theta_2, \dots, \theta_k)$ must be a function of the complete sufficient statistics, if such exist. The result will apply for more than one ϕ. Thus, for a random sample from the normal distribution $N(\mu, \sigma^2)$, $T_1 = \sum_1^n X_i$, $T_2 = \sum_1^n X_i^2$ are as we have seen, jointly sufficient for μ, σ. By virtue of a general result about to be stated, they are also complete. Since $\bar{X}, \sum_1^n (X_i - \bar{X})^2/(n-1)$ are unbiased estimators of μ, σ^2 respectively, they are also m.v.u.e.

We now state (without proof) the following result for the regular exponential family of distributions.

Theorem. If $X_1, X_2, \dots, X_n$ is a random sample from a member of the regular exponential family with probability density function

$$f(x \mid \theta_1, \theta_2, \dots, \theta_k) = \exp\left[\sum_1^m a_j(\theta_1, \theta_2, \dots, \theta_k) b_j(x) + \right.$$

$$\left. c(\theta_1, \theta_2, \dots, \theta_k) + d(x) \right]$$

then (as previously observed), $T_j = \sum_{i=1}^n b_j(X_i)$, $j = 1, 2, \dots, m$ are jointly sufficient for $\theta_1, \theta_2, \dots, \theta_k$. Furthermore, if the T_j are linearly independent, and the θ_i functionally unrelated, then a necessary and sufficient condition for the T_j to be (jointly) complete for $\theta_1, \theta_2, \dots, \theta_k$ is that $m = k$.

Example 10. X has the distribution $N(\mu, \sigma^2)$.

$$f(x|\mu,\sigma) = \frac{1}{\sqrt{(2\pi)}\sigma} \exp\left[-\tfrac{1}{2}(x-\mu)^2/\sigma^2\right], \quad -\infty < x < +\infty$$

$$= \exp\left[-\frac{x^2}{2\sigma^2} + \frac{x\mu}{\sigma^2} - \frac{\mu^2}{2\sigma^2} - \log(\sqrt{(2\pi)}\sigma)\right]$$

We now identify $b_1(x)$ as x^2, $b_2(x)$ as x, $a_1(\mu,\sigma)$ as $-1/2\sigma^2$, $a_2(\mu,\sigma)$ as μ/σ^2, $c(\mu,\sigma)$ as $-\log\{\sqrt{(2\pi)}\sigma\} - \mu^2/2\sigma^2$ and $d(x)$ as identically zero. Thus, for a random sample from this distribution, $\sum_{i=1}^{n} X_i^2, \sum_{i=1}^{n} X_i$ are jointly sufficient for μ, σ. Since T_1, T_2 are not linearly dependent and σ is not a function of μ we have, since $m = 2 = k$, that $\sum_1^n X_i^2, \sum_1^n X_i$ are also jointly complete for μ, σ. Thus,

$$\frac{\sum_1^n (X_i - \bar{X})^2}{n-1} = \frac{\sum X_i^2 - (\sum X_i)^2/n}{n-1}$$

is not only an unbiased estimator of σ^2, but since it is a function of the complete sufficient statistics, it is the (unique) m.v.u.e. of σ^2 as previously claimed.

We can examine the application of the theorem to the subfamily $N(\mu, \mu^2)$

$$f(x|\mu) = \exp\left[-\frac{x^2}{2\mu^2} + \frac{x}{\mu} - \frac{1}{2} - \log\{\sqrt{(2\pi)}|\mu|\}\right], \quad -\infty < x < +\infty$$

Once again $\sum_1^n X_i^2, \sum_1^n X_i$ are jointly sufficient for μ. However, the theorem now states that they are not complete. Indeed, since

$$E\left(\sum_1^n X_i^2\right) = \sum_1^n \{V(X_i) + (E(X_i))^2\} = \sum_1^n (\mu^2 + \mu^2) = 2n\mu^2$$

and

$$E\left(\sum_1^n X_i\right)^2 = V\left[\sum_1^n X_i\right] + E\sum_1^n X_i = n\mu^2 + (n\mu)^2 = n(n+1)\mu^2$$

we have

$$E\left\{\frac{n+1}{2}\sum_1^n X_i^2 - \left(\sum_1^n X_i\right)^2\right\} \equiv 0$$

although the statistic in the curly brackets is not identically zero. [For a fuller discussion of the regular exponential family, consult Appendix 2.]

2.6 Sufficiency, completeness and independence

Let $X_1, X_2, \ldots, X_n$ be a random sample from a distribution with p.d.f. $f(x|\theta)$ and let T be a complete sufficient statistic for θ. If we can find another statistic S, not a function of T alone, which has a distribution which does not depend on θ, then S is independent of T. We adopt the approach of Hogg and Craig.

Proof (continuous case)
    If S, T have joint p.d.f. $h(s,t)$ then

$$h_1(s) = \int h(s|t)h_2(t)\mathrm{d}t$$

where $h_1(s), h_2(t), h(s|t)$ are the p.d.f.s of S, T and S given t respectively. Now:
(a) $h_1(s)$ does not depend on θ, by assumption;
(b)   since T is sufficient, the distribution of S given t does not depend on θ;
(c)   in virtue of (a), (b), for each $s, h_1(s) - h(s|T)$ is a function of T with expectation

$$\int [h_1(s) - h(s|t)]h_2(t)\mathrm{d}t$$
$$= h_1(s) - h_1(s) = 0$$

But T has a complete distribution, hence $h_1(s) \equiv h(s|t)$ which is to say, S, T are independent.

Example 11. $X_1, X_2, \ldots, X_n$ is a random sample from the distribution $N(\theta, 1)$. We have seen that $T = \sum_{i=1}^{n} X_i$ is sufficient for θ and is complete. Consider $S = \sum_{i=1}^{n} \lambda_i X_i$ where the λ_i are known constants. Then the distribution of S is $N\left(\sum_{1}^{n}\lambda_i\theta, \sum_{1}^{n}\lambda_i^2\right)$ and does not depend on θ when, and only when, $\sum_{i=1}^{n}\lambda_i = 0$, so $\sum_{i=1}^{n}\lambda_i X_i$ is independent of $\sum_{i=1}^{n} X_i$ if $\sum_{i=1}^{n}\lambda_i = 0$.

Example 12. X_1, X_2 is a random sample of two from the uniform distribution over $(0, \theta)$. We have seen that $\max[X_1, X_2] = X_{(2)}$ is a complete sufficient statistic for θ.

The random variables $Y_1 = X_1/\theta, Y_2 = X_2/\theta$ are clearly independent and uniformly distributed over $(0, 1)$. Hence $X_1/X_2 = Y_1/Y_2$ is a statistic and its distribution does not depend on θ. Thus X_1/X_2 is independent of $X_{(2)}$. This provokes the question, is $X_{(1)}/X_{(2)}$ also independent of $X_{(2)}$? The previous simple argument now fails. The random variables $Y_{(1)} = X_{(1)}/\theta, Y_{(2)} = X_{(2)}/\theta$ contain θ but their marginal distributions do not depend on θ. However $Y_{(1)}, Y_{(2)}$ are not independent and θ may have crept into their joint distribution. [It has not in fact, but see Exercise 12 for a warning example.]

Now we could revert to our previous technique of finding the joint p.d.f. of $X_{(1)}, X_{(2)}$ and derive directly the joint p.d.f. $X_{(1)}/X_{(2)}$ and $X_{(2)}$ [Exercise 14]. But we require less, namely that the distribution of $X_{(1)}/X_{(2)}$ does not depend on θ. We can sometimes confirm such a property by demonstrating that the corresponding moment generating function does not contain θ. Since the joint p.d.f. of $X_{(1)}, X_{(2)}$ is $2/\theta^2, 0 < x_{(1)} < x_{(2)} < \theta$, the m.g.f. of $X_{(1)}/X_{(2)}$ is

$$E\left[\exp\left(\frac{X_{(1)}}{X_{(2)}}t\right)\right] = \int_0^\theta \int_0^{x_{(2)}} \exp\left(\frac{x_{(1)}}{x_{(2)}}t\right)\frac{2}{\theta^2}dx_{(1)}dx_{(2)}.$$

We do not in fact have to evaluate this double integral. A formal change of variable $x_{(1)} = y_{(1)}\theta, x_{(2)} = y_{(2)}\theta$ transforms it to

$$\int_0^1 \int_0^{y_{(2)}} 2\exp\left(\frac{y_{(1)}}{y_{(2)}}t\right)dy_{(1)}dy_{(2)}$$

which clearly does not depend on θ. The reader may remark that the computation of the m.g.f. is scarcely shorter than the direct technique. This will not commonly be the case for sample sizes greater than 2.

Exercise 12. The joint distribution of X, Y is bivariate normal,

$$f(x, y) = \frac{1}{2\pi\sqrt{(1 - \rho^2)}}\exp\left\{-\frac{1}{2(1 - \rho^2)}[x^2 - 2\rho xy + y^2]\right\}.$$

Show that the distribution of X is $N(0, 1)$ and that of Y is $N(0, 1)$, neither of which depends on ρ. Nevertheless, the distribution of XY does depend on ρ. Show, for instance, that $E(XY) = \rho$.

Exercise 13. X_1, X_2 is a random sample of two from the exponential distribution $f(x|\theta) = \theta \exp(-\theta x)$. Show that X_1/X_2 is independent of $X_1 + X_2$.

Exercise 14. X_1, X_2 is a random sample of two from the uniform distribution $f(x|\theta) = 1/\theta, 0 < x < \theta$. Show by the change of variable technique that the joint p.d.f. of $S = X_{(1)}/X_{(2)}$, $T = X_{(2)}$ is $2t/\theta^2$, $0 < t < \theta, 0 < s < 1$ and deduce that S, T are independent.

Exercise 15. $X_1, X_2, \ldots, X_n$ is a random sample from the exponential distribution with parameter θ. Show that $\sum_{i=1}^{n} a_i X_i \bigg/ \sum_{i=1}^{n} X_i = S$ is independent of $\sum_{i=1}^{n} X_i$. [Hint: Write down an expression for the m.g.f. of $\sum_{1}^{n} a_i X_i \bigg/ \sum_{1}^{n} X_i$ and substitute $Y_i = \theta X_i$.]

In some instances, other parameters are present which, however, do not prevent the theorem applying. Suppose the sample is from a distribution which depends on two parameters θ_1, θ_2. If T is a complete sufficient statistic for θ_1 when θ_2 is known and S is a statistic with a distribution not involving θ_1 then S is independent of T. The proof goes through as before for each θ_2.

Example 13. $X_1, X_2, \ldots, X_n$ is a random sample from $N(\theta_1, \theta_2)$, then $\sum_{i=1}^{n} (X_i - \bar{X})^2, \bar{X}$ are independent. This well-known result can be proved in various ways but it is here intended to derive it by applying the ideas of this section.

When θ_2 is known, $\bar{X}$ is a complete sufficient statistic for θ_1. The random variables $Y_i = X_i - \theta_1$ are independent $N(0, \theta_2)$ and hence their *distribution* does not depend on θ_1. Thus $\sum_{i=1}^{n} (Y_i - \bar{Y})^2$ is a statistic and its distribution does not depend on θ_1, but $\sum_{i=1}^{n} (Y_i - \bar{Y})^2 = \sum_{i=1}^{n} (X_i - \bar{X})^2$, which is thus independent of $\bar{X}$.

Exercise 16. $X_1, X_2, \ldots, X_n$ is a random sample from $N(\theta_1, \theta_2)$. Use the result of Example 13 to explain briefly why the distribution of

$$(\bar{X} - \theta_1) \bigg/ \left[\frac{\sum(X_i - \bar{X})^2}{n(n-1)} \right]^{1/2}$$

does not depend on θ_2.

The theorem readily extends to several parameters. Without

loss of generality, we state the result for two parameters. Let $X_1, X_2, \ldots, X_n$ be a random sample of n from a distribution involving the parameters θ_1, θ_2 and T_1, T_2 be jointly sufficient complete statistics for θ_1, θ_2. If S is a statistic, not a function of (T_1, T_2) alone, and the distribution of S does not involve θ_1 or θ_2 then S is independent of (T_1, T_2).

Example 14. $X_1, X_2, \ldots, X_n$ is a random sample from the distribution $N(\theta_1, \theta_2)$. The statistics $\bar{X}, \sum_{i=1}^{n} X_i^2$ are jointly sufficient and complete for θ_1, θ_2. Consider the statistic

$$S = \sum_{i=1}^{n-1} (X_{i+1} - X_i)^2 \Big/ \sum_{i=1}^{n} (X_i - \bar{X})^2$$

Let $(X_i - \theta_1)/\sqrt{\theta_2} = Y_i$, then the Y_i are independent $N(0, 1)$, and $S = \sum_{i=1}^{n-1} (Y_{i+1} - Y_i)^2 \Big/ \sum_{i=1}^{n} (Y_i - \bar{Y})^2$ is a statistic. The expression for the m.g.f. of S (in terms of the distribution of the Y_i) involves neither θ_1 nor θ_2.

Hence S is independent of $\left(\bar{X}, \sum_{i=1}^{n} X_i^2 \right)$.

Exercise 17. $X_1, X_2, \ldots, X_n$ is a random sample from the distribution $N(\theta_1, \theta_3)$ and $Y_1, Y_2, \ldots, Y_m$ is an independent random sample from the distribution $N(\theta_2, \theta_3)$. Show that the statistics $\bar{X}, \bar{Y}, \sum_{i=1}^{n} (X_i - \bar{X})^2 + \sum_{i=1}^{m} (Y_i - \bar{Y})^2$ are jointly sufficient for $\theta_1, \theta_2, \theta_3$. The statistic

$$S = \frac{\sum_{i=1}^{n} (X_i - \bar{X})^2 / (n - 1)}{\sum_{i=1}^{m} (Y_i - \bar{Y})^2 / (m - 1)}$$

Clearly the distribution of S does not depend on $\theta_1, \theta_2, \theta_3$. Explain why in fact S has the $F(n - 1, m - 1)$ distribution. Assuming completeness, S is independently distributed of the sufficient statistics or any function of them. Deduce that in particular S is independent of

$$T = \frac{\bar{X} - \bar{Y}}{\left[\left(\frac{1}{n} + \frac{1}{m} \right) \left\{ \frac{\sum (X_i - \bar{X})^2 + \sum (Y_i - \bar{Y})^2}{n + m - 2} \right\} \right]^{1/2}}$$

Confirm that when $\theta_1 = \theta_2$, T has Student's t-distribution with

$n + m - 2$ degrees of freedom. [T is the usual statistic for testing equality of the means – a point discussed later.]

The converse to the main theorem is less restricted but without much interest. For if T is sufficient for θ then the distribution of S given t cannot perforce depend on θ. But if S is independent of T, its marginal distribution *is* the same as the aforesaid conditional distribution and hence cannot depend on θ. It should also be noted that T need not be complete. [However, for the regular exponential family, when the number of parameters equals the number of sufficient statistics then we have completeness anyway.]

2.7 Minimum-variance bounds

The method of finding a m.v.u.e. discussed earlier will fail if the sufficient statistic employed does not possess a complete distribution, since uniqueness is no longer guaranteed. Some opportunity for assessing the performance of an estimator is provided by a result due to Cramér. Under certain conditions, the result provides a lower bound for the variance of unbiased estimators of functions of the parameters. The mere existence of a lower bound, called the *minimum-variance bound* (m.v.b.), does not ensure that it is actually attained. We shall derive the result for the continuous case: the proof for the discrete only requires replacing integrations with summations.

Cramér lower bound (one parameter)

If $X_1, X_2, \ldots, X_n$ have a joint continuous distribution with probability density function $f(x_1, x_2, \ldots, x_n | \theta)$ and $t(X_1, X_2, \ldots, X_n)$ is a statistic such that $E(T) = \phi(\theta)$, then subject to the regularity conditions,

$$V[T] \geqslant [\phi'(\theta)]^2 / E\left[\frac{\partial}{\partial \theta} \{ \log f(X_1, X_2, \ldots, X_n | \theta) \} \right]^2$$

The regularity conditions shall be:

(a) integration with respect to the x_i and differentiation with respect to θ are interchangeable;
(b) the region where f is positive does not depend on θ.

By assumption

$$E[T] = \int \cdots \int t(x_1, x_2, \ldots, x_n) f(x_1, x_2, \ldots, x_n | \theta) \mathrm{d}x_1 \, \mathrm{d}x_2 \ldots \mathrm{d}x_n$$

$$= \phi(\theta) \text{ for all } \theta \tag{2.1}$$

Differentiating with respect to θ and using the regularity conditions

$$\frac{\mathrm{d}}{\mathrm{d}\theta}[E(T)] = \int \cdots \int t(x_1, x_2, \ldots, x_n) \frac{\partial}{\partial\theta} f(x_1, x_2, \ldots, x_n | \theta) \mathrm{d}x_1 \, \mathrm{d}x_2$$
$$\cdots \mathrm{d}x_n \qquad (2.2)$$

$$= \int \cdots \int t(x_1, x_2, \ldots, x_n) \frac{\partial}{\partial\theta}\{\log f(x_1, x_2 \ldots, x_n | \theta)\}$$
$$\times f(x_1, x_2, \ldots, x_n | \theta) \mathrm{d}x_1 \, \mathrm{d}x_2 \ldots \mathrm{d}x_n = \phi'(\theta) \qquad (2.3)$$

That is to say,

$$E\left[t(X_1, X_2, \ldots, X_n) \frac{\partial}{\partial\theta}\{\log f(X_1, X_2, \ldots, X_n | \theta)\} \right] = \phi'(\theta) \quad (2.4)$$

The left-hand side of Equation (2.4) is the expectation of the product of two random variables which, as it happens, is also their covariance. This is because the expectation of the second member of the product is zero. To see this, we need only choose $t(X_1, X_2, \ldots, X_n)$ as identically unity for all samples, when $\phi(\theta) = E(1) = 1$, $\phi'(\theta) = 0$, and now substitute these values in Equation (2.4). Hence we may write Equation (2.4) as

$$\mathrm{Cov}\left[T, \frac{\partial}{\partial\theta}\{\log f(X_1, X_2, \ldots, X_n | \theta) \right] = \phi'(\theta) \qquad (2.5)$$

But for any pair of random variables S, T,

$$\mathrm{Cov}^2(T, S) \leqslant V(T)V(S), \qquad (2.6)$$

with equality if and only if S is a linear function of T. So that if
$$S = \frac{\partial}{\partial\theta}\{\log f(X_1, X_2, \ldots, X_n | \theta)\},$$

$$V(T) \geqslant \frac{\mathrm{Cov}^2(T, S)}{V(S)}$$

$$= \frac{[\phi'(\theta)]^2}{V\left[\frac{\partial}{\partial\theta}\{\log f(X_1, X_2, \ldots, X_n | \theta)\} \right]}$$

$$= \frac{[\phi'(\theta)]^2}{E\left[\frac{\partial}{\partial\theta}\{\log f(X_1, X_2, \ldots, X_n | \theta)\} \right]^2} \qquad (2.7)$$

There is equality if and only if

$$\frac{\partial}{\partial\theta}\{\log f(X_1, X_2, \ldots, X_n | \theta)\} = k(\theta)T + l(\theta) \qquad (2.8)$$

Taking expectations of both sides of Equation (2.8),
$0 = k(\theta)\phi(\theta) + l(\theta)$, after substituting for $l(\theta)$ in Equation (2.8)

$$\frac{\partial}{\partial\theta}\{\log f(X_1, X_2, \ldots, X_n | \theta)\} = k(\theta)[T - \phi(\theta)] \qquad (2.9)$$

Squaring both sides of Equation (2.9) and taking expectations,

$$E\left[\frac{\partial}{\partial\theta}\{\log f(X_1, X_2, \ldots, X_n | \theta)\}\right]^2 = k^2(\theta)V(T) \qquad (2.10)$$

But when equality holds in Equation (2.7), Equation (2.10) becomes

$$\frac{[\phi'(\theta)]^2}{V(T)} = k^2(\theta)V(T) \qquad (2.11)$$

which identifies $V(T)$ as $\phi'(\theta)/k(\theta)$.
Most of our applications will be to the case when the $X_1, X_2, \ldots, X_n$ are independent random variables, each with common probability density function $f(x | \theta)$. Then

$$f(X_1, X_2, \ldots, X_n | \theta) = \prod_1^n f(X_i | \theta) \qquad (2.12)$$

and

$$V\left[\frac{\partial}{\partial\theta}\left\{\log\prod_1^n f(X_i | \theta)\right\}\right] = V\left[\frac{\partial}{\partial\theta}\left\{\sum_1^n \log f(X_i | \theta)\right\}\right]$$

$$= V\left[\sum_1^n \frac{\partial}{\partial\theta}\{\log f(X_i | \theta)\}\right], \quad \text{using the}$$
$$\text{independence,}$$

$$= \sum_1^n V\left[\frac{\partial}{\partial\theta}\{\log f(X_i | \theta)\}\right]$$

$$= nV\left[\frac{\partial}{\partial\theta}\{\log f(X | \theta)\}\right]$$

$$= nE\left[\frac{\partial}{\partial\theta}\{\log f(X | \theta)\}\right]^2 \qquad (2.13)$$

$$\text{since } E\left[\frac{\partial}{\partial\theta}\{\log f(X | \theta)\}\right] = 0 \qquad (2.14)$$

Example 15. $X_1, X_2, \ldots, X_n$ is a random sample from the Poisson distribution with parameter λ. Suppose $\phi(\lambda) = \lambda$,

$$f(x|\lambda) = \lambda^x \exp(-\lambda)/x!$$
$$\log f(x|\lambda) = x \log \lambda - \lambda - \log x!$$
$$\frac{\partial}{\partial \lambda}\{\log f(x|\lambda)\} = \frac{x}{\lambda} - 1$$

In this instance, $\phi'(\lambda) = 1$,

$$E\left[\frac{\partial}{\partial \lambda}\{\log f(X|\lambda)\}\right]^2 = E\frac{(X-\lambda)^2}{\lambda^2}$$
$$= \frac{V(X)}{\lambda^2}$$
$$= \frac{\lambda}{\lambda^2} = \frac{1}{\lambda}$$

Hence the m.v.b. is

$$\frac{[\phi'(\theta)]^2}{nE\left[\frac{\partial}{\partial \lambda}\{\log f(X|\lambda)\}\right]^2} = \frac{\lambda}{n}$$

In fact, this computation can be shortened since

$$\sum_1^n \frac{\partial}{\partial \lambda}\{\log f(X_i|\lambda)\} = \sum_1^n \left(\frac{X_i}{\lambda} - 1\right)$$
$$= \frac{n}{\lambda}(\bar{X} - \lambda)$$

which is of the form of Equation (2.9). Hence, immediately, $\bar{X}$ is an unbiased estimator of λ with variance $1/k(\theta) = \lambda/n$. Scarcely a new result! However, we can now assert further that no other unbiased estimator of λ can have smaller variance.

When the Cramér lower bound theorem is applicable, the efficiency of any unbiased estimator of a parameter is measured by the ratio of the minimum variance bound for the parameter to the variance of the estimator. An estimator with efficiency 1 is said to be *efficient*. If an unbiased estimator has efficiency 1 in the limit as the sample size increases, it is asymptotically efficient.

Exercise 18. $X_1, X_2, \ldots, X_m$ is a random sample from the binomial distribution with parameters n and θ Find the m.v.b. for unbiased estimators of θ.

$$[\text{Ans. } \theta(1-\theta)/mn]$$

Exercise 19. $X_1, X_2, \ldots, X_n$ is a random sample from the uniform distribution with probability density function $f(x|\theta) = 1/\theta$, $0 \leqslant x \leqslant \theta$. Show that the formal m.v.b. for unbiased estimators of θ is θ^2/n. Check that $(n+1)X_{\max}/n$ is an unbiased estimator of θ with variance $\theta^2/[n(n+2)] < \theta^2/n$. Is there any contradiction?

2.8 Computation of minimum variance bound

The evaluation of the m.v.b. is simplified if the distribution is such that interchanging differentiating with respect to θ and integration over the sample space is justified *for the second time*. For consider

$$E\left[\frac{\partial^2}{\partial\theta^2}\{\log f(X_1, X_2, \ldots, X_n|\theta)\}\right]$$

$$= E\left[\frac{\partial}{\partial\theta}\left\{\frac{\partial}{\partial\theta}\log f(X_1, X_2, \ldots, X_n|\theta)\right\}\right]$$

$$= E\left[\frac{\partial}{\partial\theta}\left\{\frac{1}{f(X_1, X_2, \ldots, X_n|\theta)}\frac{\partial f(X_1, X_2, \ldots, X_n|\theta)}{\partial\theta}\right\}\right]$$

$$= E\left[-\left\{\frac{1}{f(X_1, X_2, \ldots, X_n|\theta)}\frac{\partial f(X_1, X_2, \ldots, X_n|\theta)}{\partial\theta}\right\}^2\right.$$

$$\left. + \frac{1}{f(X_1, X_2, \ldots, X_n|\theta)}\frac{\partial^2 f(X_1, X_2, \ldots, X_n|\theta)}{\partial\theta^2}\right]$$

$$= -E\left[\frac{\partial}{\partial\theta}\log f(X_1, X_2, \ldots, X_n|\theta)\right]^2$$

$$+ \int \cdots \int \frac{\partial^2 f(x_1, x_2, \ldots, x_n|\theta)}{\partial\theta^2}\,dx_1\,dx_2\ldots dx_n \qquad (2.15)$$

But the second term in Equation (2.15) is

$$\frac{d^2}{d\theta^2}\left[\int \cdots \int f(x_1, x_2, \ldots, x_n|\theta)dx_1\,dx_2\ldots dx_n\right] = \frac{d^2}{d\theta^2}(1) = 0 \qquad (2.16)$$

Hence the m.v.b. may alternatively be computed as $-[\phi'(\theta)]^2/$ $E\left[\dfrac{\partial^2}{\partial\theta^2}\{\log f(X_1, X_2, \ldots, X_n|\theta)\}\right]$ or, for a random sample of n, as

$$-[\phi'(\theta)]^2/nE\left[\frac{\partial^2}{\partial\theta^2}\{\log f(X|\theta)\}\right] \qquad (2.17)$$

Thus, for Example 15,

$$E\left[\frac{\partial^2}{\partial\lambda^2}\{\log f(X|\lambda)\}\right] = E\left[\frac{\partial}{\partial\lambda}\left\{\frac{X}{\lambda} - 1\right\}\right]$$

$$= E\left[-\frac{X}{\lambda^2}\right]$$

$$= -\frac{\lambda}{\lambda^2} = -\frac{1}{\lambda}$$

Once again, the m.v.b. for unbiased estimators of λ is $-1/(n/-\lambda) = \lambda/n$

Exercise 20. $X_1, X_2, \ldots, X_n$ is a random sample from $N(\mu, \sigma_0^2)$ where σ_0 is a known constant. Show that the m.v.b. for unbiased estimators of μ is σ_0^2/n.

Exercise 21. $X_1, X_2, \ldots, X_n$ is a random sample from the distribution $N(0, \sigma^2)$. Show that the m.v.b. for unbiased estimators of σ^2 is $2\sigma^4/n$ and state an estimator which attains this bound.

[Ans. $\sum_{i=1}^{n} X_i^2/n$.]

Exercise 22. $X_1, X_2, \ldots, X_n$ is a random sample from the distribution with probability density function $f(x|\theta) = \theta^2 x \exp(-\theta x)$, $0 \leqslant x < \infty, \theta > 0$. Calculate the m.v.b. for unbiased estimators of θ and explain why it is not attained. Check that $(2n-1)/\sum_1^n X_i$ is the m.v.u.e. of θ with $V(T) = \theta^2/[2(n-1)]$.
[Ans. m.v.b. is $\theta^2/2n$]

2.9 Minimum attainable variance

The points raised in the last exercise are sufficiently important to deserve amplification. Suppose we have a random sample of n from the exponential distribution with parameter θ:

$$f(x_1, x_2, \ldots, x_n|\theta) = \prod_1^n \theta e^{-\theta x_i}$$

$$= \theta^n \exp(-\theta \sum x_i)$$

$$= \exp[-\theta \sum x_i + n \log \theta]$$

Then by the theorem on regular exponential distributions, $\sum\limits_{1}^{n} X_i$ is a complete sufficient statistic for θ. Since $E(\bar{X}) = 1/\theta$, $\bar{X}$ is the m.v.u.e. of $1/\theta$ with variance $1/n\theta^2$. Also, $\sum\limits_{1}^{n} X_i$ has a $\Gamma(n,\theta)$ distribution whence, easily, $E[(n-1)/\sum x_i] = \theta$. Again by complete sufficiency, $(n-1)/\sum X_i$ is the m.v.u.e. of θ. Alternatively,

$$\frac{\partial}{\partial\theta}\{\log f(x_1, x_2, \ldots, x_n \,|\, \theta)\} = \frac{\partial}{\partial\theta}[\log\{\theta^n \exp(-\theta\sum x_i)\}$$

$$= \frac{\partial}{\partial\theta}[n\log\theta - \theta\sum x_i]$$

$$= \frac{n}{\theta} - \sum_{1}^{n} x_i$$

$$= -n\left[\bar{x} - \frac{1}{\theta}\right]$$

and the last step is in the linear form which admits $\bar{X}$ to be an unbiased estimator of $\phi(\theta) = 1/\theta$ attaining the m.v.b., which from Equation (2.11) with $\phi'(\theta) = -1/\theta^2$, $k(\theta) = -n$, is $\phi'(\theta)/k(\theta) = 1/n\theta^2$. On the other hand, the aforementioned last step is *not* linear in $1/\bar{x}$. The m.v.b. for θ may be found, with $\phi(\theta) = \theta$, from Equation (2.17):

$$-[\phi'(\theta)]^2/nE\left[\frac{\partial^2}{\partial\theta^2}\{\log f(X\,|\,\theta)\}\right]$$

$$= -n^{-1}/E\left[\frac{\partial^2}{\partial\theta^2}\{\log(\theta) - \theta X\}\right]$$

$$= -n^{-1}/E\left[\frac{\partial}{\partial\theta}\left\{\frac{1}{\theta} - X\right\}\right]$$

$$= -n^{-1}/E[-1/\theta^2]$$

$$= \theta^2/n$$

However, no unbiased estimator attains this m.v.b. When the m.v.b. for a parameter is not attainable, then the measure of efficiency given in 2.7 under-rates the performance of other unbiased estimators, since they cannot improve on the m.v.u.e. However, the m.v.u.e. may be asymptotically efficient. In the present example $(n-1)/\sum X_i$ is the m.v.u.e. of θ with variance $\theta^2/(n-2)$. The limit of the ratio of the m.v.b. to this variance is 1.

Exercise 23. $X_1, X_2, \ldots, X_n$ is a random sample from the Cauchy distribution with probability density function $f(x|\theta) = \dfrac{1}{\pi[1 + (x - \theta)^2]}$, $-\infty < x < \infty$. Show that the m.v.b. for unbiased estimation of θ is $2/n$ and is not attainable. [This is a case where taking the second derivative does *not* advance matters.] The sample median is an unbiased estimator of θ (from symmetry) and for large n has approximate variance $\pi^2/4n$.

In general, if T *attains* the m.v.b. for unbiased estimators of $\phi(\theta)$, then the unbiased estimators of, say, $\chi(\theta)$ do *not* attain the m.v.b. except for the trivial class of instances $\chi(\theta) = a\phi(\theta) + b$.

Exercise 24. $X_1, X_2, \ldots, X_n$ is a random sample from $N(0, \sigma^2)$. From Exercise 21, there is an unbiased estimator of σ^2 which attains the corresponding m.v.b. Explain why there is no m.v.b. estimator for σ and calculate the appropriate m.v.b. [Ans. $\sigma^2/2n$]

Exercise 25. $X_1, X_2, \ldots, X_n$ is a random sample from a continuous distribution with probability density function $f(x|\theta)$. Show that if T is unbiased for $\phi(\theta)$ *and* attains the m.v.b., then T is sufficient for θ.

2.10 Mean square error

The strong emphasis on unbiased estimators to be found in the orthodox approach has often been criticized. It has been asserted that a small bias is tolerable if there is a corresponding saving in mean square error (m.s.e.). Suppose then the statistic T is used as an estimator for $\phi(\theta)$. The mean square error of T (about $\phi(\theta)$) is

$$\begin{aligned}
E[T - \phi(\theta)]^2 &= E[T - E(T) + E(T) - \phi(\theta)]^2 \\
&= E[T - E(T)]^2 + [E(T) - \phi(\theta)]^2, \text{ since the} \\
&\qquad \text{cross-product term vanishes} \\
&= V(T) + [b(\theta)]^2
\end{aligned}$$

where $b(\theta)$ is the bias. Thus the m.s.e. is the sum of the variance and the square of the bias. Instead of minimizing $V[T]$ subject to those T such that $b(\theta) = 0$, it has been suggested that the m.s.e. be minimized within other restricted classes of statistics T.

Example 16. $X_1, X_2, \ldots, X_n$ is a random sample from $N(0, \sigma^2)$. We have already seen that $\sum X_i^2/n$ is an unbiased estimator of σ^2

that attains the m.v.b., which is $2\sigma^4/n$. Since it is unbiased, $2\sigma^4/n$ is also the m.s.e. for this estimator. Consider the class of estimators $T = a\sum_1^n X_i^2$. We have

$$E(T) = a\sum_1^n E(X_i^2) = an\sigma^2$$

Hence the bias is

$$an\sigma^2 - \sigma^2 = \sigma^2(an - 1),$$

$$V[T] = V\left[a\sum_1^n X_i^2\right] = a^2 V\left[\sum_1^n X_i^2\right] = a^2 \sum_1^n V(X_i^2) = a^2 n(2\sigma^4)$$

Hence the m.s.e. of T is

$$2na^2\sigma^4 + \sigma^4(an - 1)^2 = \sigma^4[2na^2 + (an - 1)^2]$$

If this expression is minimized with respect to a, then $a = 1/(n + 2)$, the minimum m.s.e. being $2\sigma^4/(n + 2)$. The bias is $-2\sigma^2/(n + 2)$.

It is to be noted that we cannot hope for a statistic T which has unrestricted minimum m.s.e. for all θ. If in fact $\theta = \theta_0$, an estimator with small m.s.e. should be highly concentrated near θ_0. But then such an estimator will have correspondingly large m.s.e. for other values of θ far from θ_0.

More wholesale criticisms of the position adopted in this chapter include the following complaints:

(a) No account is taken of any likely prior distribution of the parameter.

(b) The mean square error, subject to whatever restriction, is not necessarily the soundest principle for judging estimators. Due account should be taken of the costs involved.

Both these points will be taken up in the next chapter.

2.11 Two parameters

We close with some brief further remarks for the case when more than one parameter is involved. In particular, we have to consider the effect on the Cramér lower bound, which will be sufficiently illustrated by the case of two parameters. But first a brief lemma.

Lemma. If the random variable T, S_1, S_2 have a joint distribution, then perforce

$$V[T - a_1 S_1 - a_2 S_2] \geq 0, \qquad a_1, a_2 \text{ real} \qquad (2.18)$$

Expanding the left-hand side of Equation (2.18),

$$V(T) + a_1^2 V(S_1) + a_2^2 V(S_2) - 2a_1 \text{Cov}(T, S_1) - 2a_2 \text{Cov}(T, S_2)$$
$$+ 2a_1 a_2 \text{Cov}(S_1, S_2) \geq 0 \qquad (2.19)$$

Since Equation (2.19) is to hold for all real a_1, a_2, we can minimize the expression subject to various restrictions on the other quantities. Thus suppose we require $\text{Cov}(T, S_1) = 1$, and $\text{Cov}(T, S_2) = 0$. Then differentiating with respect to a_1, a_2 in turn,

$$2a_1 V(S_1) - 2 + 2a_2 \text{Cov}(S_1, S_2) = 0$$
$$2a_2 V(S_2) \qquad + 2a_1 \text{Cov}(S_1, S_2) = 0$$

Solving simultaneously for a_1, a_2, leads to

$$a_1 = \frac{V(S_2)}{V(S_1) V(S_2) - \text{Cov}^2(S_1, S_2)}$$

$$a_2 = \frac{-\text{Cov}(S_1, S_2)}{V(S_1) V(S_2) - \text{Cov}^2(S_1, S_2)}$$

After substituting these values of a_1, a_2 in Equation (2.19) and after some elementary manipulation, we obtain

$$V(T) \geq \frac{V(S_2)}{V(S_1) V(S_2) - \text{Cov}^2(S_1, S_2)} \qquad (2.20)$$

Of the form of Equation (2.20) we may remark that if we consider the covariance matrix of the joint distribution of S_1, S_2,

$$\begin{pmatrix} V(S_1) & \text{Cov}(S_1, S_2) \\ \text{Cov}(S_1, S_2) & V(S_2) \end{pmatrix} \qquad (2.21)$$

then the right-hand side of Equation (2.20) is just the element in the first row and first column of the inverse matrix.

We now return to our main theme. Let $X_1, X_2, \ldots, X_n$ have a joint continuous distribution with probability density function $f(x_1, x_2, \ldots, x_n | \theta_1, \theta_2)$, and assume that $t_1(X_1, X_2, \ldots, X_n)$, $t_2(X_1, X_2, \ldots, X_n)$ are unbiased estimators of θ_1, θ_2 respectively. Suppose also the regularity conditions obtain for both parameters.

$$E[T_1] = \int \cdots \int t_1(x_1, x_2, \ldots, x_n) f(x_1, x_2, \ldots, x_n | \theta_1, \theta_2)$$
$$\times \, dx_1 \, dx_2 \ldots dx_n = \theta_1 \qquad (2.22)$$

Differentiating with respect to θ_1, we have

$$E\left[T_1\frac{\partial}{\partial\theta_1}\{\log f(X_1,X_2,\ldots,X_n|\theta_1,\theta_2)\}\right]=E[T_1S_1]=1$$

or

$$\mathrm{Cov}(T_1,S_1)=1 \tag{2.23}$$

Differentiating with respect to θ_2, we have

$$E\left[T_1\frac{\partial}{\partial\theta_2}\log f(X_1,X_2,\ldots,X_n|\theta_1,\theta_2)\}\right]=E[T_1S_2)=0$$

or

$$\mathrm{Cov}(T_1,S_2)=0. \tag{2.24}$$

But these are precisely the restrictions envisaged in the lemma; hence

$$V(T_1)\geqslant\frac{V(S_2)}{V(S_1)V(S_2)-\mathrm{Cov}^2(S_1,S_2)} \tag{2.25}$$

In a similar way

$$V(T_2)\geqslant\frac{V(S_1)}{V(S_1)V(S_2)-\mathrm{Cov}^2(S_1,S_2)} \tag{2.26}$$

Exercise 26. If $S_i=\dfrac{\partial}{\partial\theta_i}[\log f(X_1,X_2,\ldots,X_n|\theta_1,\theta_2)]$, $i=1,2$, show that:

$$V[S_i]=-E\left[\frac{\partial S_i}{\partial\theta_i}\right],i=1,2,\mathrm{Cov}(S_1,S_2)=-E\left(\frac{\partial S_1}{\partial\theta_2}\right)=-E\left(\frac{\partial S_2}{\partial\theta_1}\right).$$

[Assuming second-order differentiation with respect to the parameters and integration over the sample space to be interchangeable.]

Example 17. $X_1,X_2,\ldots,X_n$ is a random sample from the distribution $N(\mu,\sigma^2)$. It is required to find the minimum variance bounds for unbiased estimators of $\theta_1=\mu,\theta_2=\sigma^2$.

$$f(x_1,x_2,\ldots,x_n|\theta_1,\theta_2)=\prod_1^n\frac{1}{\sqrt{(2\pi\theta_2)}}\exp\left[-\frac{1}{2}(x_i-\theta_1)^2/\theta_2\right]$$

$$S_1=\frac{\partial}{\partial\theta_1}\{\log f(X_1,X_2,\ldots,X_n|\theta_1,\theta_2)\}=\frac{n}{\theta_2}(\bar{X}-\theta_1)$$

$$S_2=\frac{\partial}{\partial\theta_2}\{\log f(X_1,X_2,\ldots,X_n|\theta_1,\theta_2)\}=-\frac{n}{2\theta_2}+\frac{1}{2\theta_2^2}\sum(X_i-\theta_1)^2$$

For the normal distribution, $E(X_i) = \theta_1, E(X_i - \theta_1)^2 = \theta_2$, whence it is easily confirmed that $E(S_1) = E(S_2) = 0$.

$$V(S_1) = -E\left[\frac{\partial S_1}{\partial \theta_1}\right] = \frac{n}{\theta_2}$$

$$V(S_2) = -E\left[\frac{\partial S_2}{\partial \theta_2}\right] = \frac{n}{2\theta_2^2}$$

$$\text{Cov}(S_1, S_2) = -E\left[\frac{\partial S_1}{\partial \theta_2}\right] = 0$$

The covariance matrix of S_1, S_2 is

$$\begin{pmatrix} n/\theta_2 & 0 \\ 0 & n/2\theta_2^2 \end{pmatrix}$$

which has inverse

$$\begin{pmatrix} \theta_2/n & 0 \\ 0 & 2\theta_2^2/n \end{pmatrix}.$$

Finally, if $E(T_1) = \theta_1$, then $V(T_1) \geqslant \theta_2/n$, and if $E(T_2) = \theta_2$, then $V(T_2) \geqslant 2\theta_2^2/n$.

Exercise 27. $(X_1, Y_1), (X_2, Y_2), \ldots, (X_m, Y_m)$ is a random sample of m pairs from the trinomial distribution with parameters n, θ_1, θ_2. Show that the minimum variance bounds for unbiased estimators of θ_1, θ_2 are $\theta_1(1 - \theta_1)/mn, \theta_2(1 - \theta_2)/mn$, respectively.

The method outlined for two parameters can be extended to parameters $\theta_1, \theta_2, \ldots, \theta_k$. Suppose

$$S_i = \frac{\partial}{\partial \theta_i}\{\log f(X_1, X_2, \ldots, X_n | \theta_1, \theta_2, \ldots, \theta_k)\} \text{ and } t_j(X_1, X_2, \ldots, X_n)$$

is an unbiased estimator of $\theta_j, j = 1, 2, \ldots, k$. Define $c_{ij} = \text{Cov}(S_i, S_j)$ to be the element in the ith row and jth column of a matrix **C**. Then, subject to the regularity conditions,

$$V[T_i] \geqslant c^{ii}$$

where c^{ii} is the ith diagonal element in the inverse matrix, $\mathbf{C}^{-1}$. Although $c_{ij} = E(S_i S_j)$, if a second differentiation with respect to the parameter may be transposed with 'summations' over the sample values, then c_{ij} may also be computed as $-E\left(\frac{\partial}{\partial \theta_i} S_j\right)$.

CHAPTER THREE

Elementary decision theory and Bayesian methods

3.1 Comments on classical techniques

Considerable effort has gone into the study of minimum variance unbiased estimators, though it has been complained that the search for such 'paragons' has been largely misguided. In particular instances, such estimators may have unacceptable, not to say ridiculous, properties.

Example 1. $X_1, X_2, \ldots, X_n$ is a random sample from the distribution with p.d.f. $f(x|\theta) = \exp(\theta - x), x > \theta \geqslant 0$. Then $Y = \min[X_1, X_2, \ldots, X_n]$ is a complete sufficient statistic for θ and since $E[Y] = \theta + 1/n$, $Y - 1/n$ is the m.v.u.e. for θ. However, if $\theta < 1/n$, the estimate may be negative although $\theta \geqslant 0$. To remove this absurdity, we may replace $Y - 1/n$ by zero whenever $Y < 1/n$. The estimator, $\max[0, Y - 1/n]$ is no longer unbiased.

Example 2. If X has the Poisson distribution with parameter λ, the only unbiased estimator of $\exp(-2\lambda)$ is $(-1)^X$ which is negative if X is odd. [Incidentally, there is *no* exactly unbiased estimator of $1/\lambda$ for any sample size.]

Exercise 1. $X_1, X_2, \ldots, X_n$ is a random sample from $N(\theta, 1)$. Find the m.v.u.e. of θ^2. Is this estimator sensible? [Ans. $\bar{X}^2 - 1/n$]

In a more general way it has been remarked that an unbiased estimator enjoys but a hollow optimal property if it is the sole member in its class! If bias is permitted and performance is measured by m.s.e., then we will be forced to restrict the class of estimators in some other way. (2.10)

52

Exercise 2. If $E(X|\theta) = \theta, V(X|\theta) = \sigma^2$, show that

$$E[(aX + b - \theta)^2|\theta] = \psi(\theta) = \theta^2(a-1)^2 + 2b(a-1)\theta + a^2\sigma^2 + b^2.$$

Show further that if θ is regarded as a realization of a random variable Θ with mean μ and variance τ^2, then the mean of $\chi(\Theta)$ is minimized when $a = \tau^2/(\tau^2 + \sigma^2)$ and $b = \mu\sigma^2/(\tau^2 + \sigma^2)$.

3.2 Loss functions

An initial objection to the mean square error is the difficulty of interpretation. We shall see it has a role in another, broader assessment of estimators. It may be claimed that the merit of an estimator should be judged by the average cost of its use. Thus if T is an estimator of $\phi(\theta)$, one should be able to identify a penalty as some function of $T - \phi(\theta)$. Such a *loss function* should ideally be strongly shaped by practical experience, but its form is also likely to be influenced by considerations of mathematical convenience. A popular choice is the quadratic loss function, $[T - \phi(\theta)]^2$, which is zero if indeed $T = \phi(\theta)$, and is increasingly expensive for large errors. With this loss function, let us compare the estimators $X, \frac{1}{2}X$ for estimating $\phi(\theta) = 1/\theta$ when X has the exponential distribution with parameter θ. In fact, X will be 'cheaper' than $X/2$ when

$$(x - 1/\theta)^2 < (x/2 - 1/\theta)^2 \text{ or } x \leqslant 4/3\theta$$

We can measure the chance that X is cheaper from $\Pr(X \leqslant 4/3\theta)$ which is

$$\int_0^{4/3\theta} \theta\exp(-\theta x)\mathrm{d}x = 1 - \exp(-4/3) \approx 0.74 \text{ for all } \theta.$$

The result does not decisively favour X, since the penalty for using $X/2$ for large x is markedly less. Evidently, an overall measure of loss is required and we shall take it as fundamental that this shall be the *expected loss*. This expectation is over the sample values given the parameter and is called the *risk function* of the estimator. Thus the risk functions for $X, X/2$, in the present example are

$$E[(X - 1/\theta)^2|\theta] = \int_0^\infty (x - 1/\theta)^2 \theta\mathrm{e}^{-\theta x}\mathrm{d}x = 1/\theta^2$$

$$E[(X/2 - 1/\theta)^2|\theta] = \int_0^\infty (x/2 - 1/\theta)^2 \theta\mathrm{e}^{-\theta x}\mathrm{d}x = 1/2\theta^2$$

Hence, in terms of risk, $X/2$ is better than X for any θ. In that sense, X is 'disqualified' or *inadmissible*. We hasten to add that this conclusion is dependent on the form of the loss function employed. In this limited initial discussion, several matters are left untouched. For instance we have not shown that $X/2$ is the best possible estimator even in the restricted class of estimators $T = aX$.

Exercise 3. If X has the distribution $f(x|\theta) = \theta \exp(-\theta x)$, show that $E(aX - 1/\theta)^2 = (2a^2 - 2a + 1)/\theta^2$, and is minimized when $a = 1/2$.

It may not be possible to make unequivocal comparisons for the estimators via their risk functions, as the following example illustrates.

Example 3. X has the distribution $N(\theta, 1)$ and it is required to estimate θ subject to the loss function $(T - \theta)^2$. Then, for a sample of one value, the risk of estimators in the class $T = aX$ is

$$E[(aX - \theta)^2 | \theta] = a^2 E(X^2 | \theta) - 2a\theta E(X|\theta) + \theta^2$$
$$= a^2(\theta^2 + 1) - 2a\theta^2 + \theta^2$$
$$= \theta^2(a - 1)^2 + a^2$$

Now for the 'usual' unbiased estimator, $a = 1$, for which the risk is 1 for all θ. Whereas for $a = 1/2$, the risk is

$$(\theta^2 + 1)/4 < 1 \text{ when } \theta^2 < 3$$
$$> 1 \text{ when } \theta^2 > 3$$

When the comparisons between the risk functions are not favourable to one estimator for all permissible values, some fresh consideration or principle must be invoked. It can be remarked that, in Example 3, the risk function is unbounded for all $a \neq 1$. So, in this rather crude ordering of the estimators aX, it can be claimed that $T = X$ has the smallest maximum for the risk function. Alternatively, if the value of θ may be regarded as a value of a random variable, we can average the risk over its distribution. Thus, if Θ has a known distribution possessing a second moment then, in Example 3, the average risk is $(a - 1)^2 E(\Theta^2) + a^2$ and is readily minimized with respect to a. By neither criterion is it to be supposed that estimators in the class aX have the last word. The enlarged class $T = aX + b$ may lead to yet further improvement.

3.3 Decision theory

Decision theory is the name given to that study of statistical problems which pays particular attention to the costs of any particular procedure. Indeed, the ideas suggested are applicable to situations where initially there *are* no data. A feature of insurance schemes is that there are several levels of premium available, where the effect of a larger premium is to reduce the loss suffered in case of an accident. Even if no accident is experienced, the premium is lost, though there may be a delayed reward in the form of a lower premium at the next renewal. Suppose then the losses for such a scheme are as in Table 3.1.

Table 3.1

Premium	(£)	Accident	No accident
Super	80	80	80
Standard	40	240	40
Basic	20	560	20

In line with our previous discussion, we consider two principles which may be invoked in selecting a premium:

(a) Regardless of the probability of an accident, it is desired to avoid a large penalty. The maximum loss for each premium is £80, £240, £560 and the minimum of these is £80. Hence the super premium will be taken. This is to act in accordance with the *minimax principle*.

(b) Due account is taken of the probability of having an accident — which is certainly the platform from which insurance companies construct their tariffs. If the subscriber takes this to be one-eighth, then for him the anticipated average losses are $\frac{1}{8}(80) + \frac{7}{8}(80) = 80$, $\frac{1}{8}(240) + \frac{7}{8}(40) = 65$, $\frac{1}{8}(560) + \frac{7}{8}(20) = 87.50$ and this suggests that he should take the 'standard' premium.

It can be objected that it is not the absolute losses but rather the additional losses contingent on not having taken the best action which should count. These additional losses (which are a disappointment to us all) are termed *regrets*. Thus if in fact there is no accident anything in excess of £20 is 'regretted'. A similar emotion is expressed towards anything over £80 in case there is an accident. The table of regrets is then as shown in Table 3.2

Table 3.2

Premium (£)	Accident	No accident	Maximum
Super	0	60	60
Standard	160	20	160
Basic	480	0	480

The minimax adherent still picks, as it happens, the 'super' premium which has a maximum regret of £60. In general, the choice which minimizes the maximum regret is not necessarily that which minimizes the maximum loss, since a different amount is subtracted from the losses to find the regrets. If the probability of an accident is judged to be one-eighth, then the average regrets will be $\frac{1}{8}(0) + \frac{7}{8}(60) = 52.5$, $\frac{1}{8}(160) + \frac{7}{8}(20) = 37.5$, $\frac{1}{8}(480) + \frac{7}{8}(0) = 60$ and the minimum of these, 37.5, corresponds again to the 'standard' premium. This is not a case of 'as it happens' since the average losses are all reduced by the same amount, $\frac{1}{8}(80) + \frac{7}{8}(20) = 27.5$.

One other feature of this example calls for consideration. Suppose the subscriber permits himself to use a table of random numbers. Can he use chance to improve his situation? Suppose he selects the super premium with probability p and the standard premium with probability $1 - p$. His average regret in case there is an accident is $0 \times p + 160(1 - p) = 160 - 160p$ and when not, $60 \times p + 20(1 - p) = 20 + 40p$. Recall that we are trying to improve on £60, hence we require

$$\max(160 - 160p, 20 + 40p] < 60$$

which will hold only if both regrets are less than 60. But $160 - 160p < 60$ implies $p > 5/8$, and $20 + 40p < 60$ when $p < 1$, so that any randomized choice with $5/8 < p < 1$ will have an average maximum regret less than 60. Since one component is increasing with p and the other decreasing, the optimum choice of p is when the two are equal, or

$$160 - 160p = 20 + 40p, \text{ that is, } p = 7/10$$

in which case both regrets are 48. No such improvement by randomizing the choice is possible when the criterion for selection is the least *expected* regret for the given probability, 1/8, of an accident. This has been computed as 37.5 for the standard premium, and to chose this option with less than certainty will only give, on average, a poorer result (see Exercise 4).

Exercise 4. Show that $\theta(160 - 160p) + (1 - \theta)(20 + 40p)$, $0 < \theta < 1$, is minimized by choosing $p = 1$ when $\theta > 1/5$ and by choosing $p = 0$ when $\theta < 1/5$.

We now seek to formalize some of the ideas thrown up in the above discussion. Behind such a formal framework there lie, of course, serious practical problems of great variety and complexity. The proportion of defectives in a batch of articles, the amount of oil in a prospecting area, the life expectancy of a person, are typical subjects of enquiry. Such 'states of nature' are indexed by one or more parameters and it is the business of the investigator to propose some action on the basis of relevant data. For this task he must have a working model of how the data are related to the parameters, and of the consequences of any proposed action. In the formal framework we are obliged to estimate the parameters and prescribe efficient rules for so doing.

Suppose the state of nature is indexed by a single parameter θ which is known to be one of the values $\theta_1, \theta_2, \ldots, \theta_k$. The investigator has at his disposal one of a finite number of actions $a_1, a_2, \ldots, a_m$, and if action a_i is proposed when θ_j is the case, then a 'loss' $l(a_i, \theta_j)$ is incurred. We restrict our attention to losses which are monetary and remark that a negative loss is a gain. It is permitted to make random choices between the actions and if the probability of selecting a_i is $p_i \left(\sum\limits_{i=1}^{m} p_i = 1 \right)$ then, since a loss of $l(a_i, \theta_j)$ is incurred with probability p_i, the appropriate loss is

$$\sum_{i=1}^{m} l(a_i, \theta_j) p_i = l(p_1, p_2, \ldots, p_m, \theta_j)$$

Allocating $p_i = 1$ recovers the non-randomized action a_i. The facility of making randomized actions generates a vast number of possibilities, but many will be eliminated by commonsense considerations. Who would employ a particular action when another can be found which is never dearer and sometimes cheaper? That is, if

$$l(a_i, \theta_j) \leqslant l(a_r, \theta_j), \qquad j = 1, 2, \ldots, k$$

with strict inequality for at least one value of j, then action a_r is said to be inadmissible (and is dominated by a_i). More generally, if there exist $p_1, p_2, \ldots, p_m$ such that

$$\sum_{1}^{m} l(a_i, \theta_j) p_i \leqslant \sum_{1}^{m} l(a_i, \theta_j) p_i', \qquad j = 1, 2, \ldots, k$$

with strict inequality for at least one value of j, then the randomized action which employs the p_i' is said to be *inadmissible* – otherwise it is said to be *admissible*.

With this meagre amount of information, a defensive choice is the *minimax* action for which

$$\max_{\theta_j}\left[\sum_{i=1}^{m} l(a_i, \theta_j)p_i\right]$$

is a minimum. The above basic structure has a geometrical representation. The non-randomized action a_i may be thought of as a point in k-dimensional Euclidean space for which the jth co-ordinate is $l(a_i, \theta_j)$. Figure 3.1 and 3.2 illustrate two possibilities when $m = 5, k = 2$.

In Fig. 3.1, the five non-randomized actions lie at the vertices of the convex pentagon CDEFG. The randomized actions are represented by points in the interior and on the boundary. However, the only admissible ones lie on the 'south-west' boundary CDE (why?). Consider the line of points for which the losses are equal. The maximum loss is against θ_2 or θ_1 according as any other point is above or below this line. A contour for which

$$\max\left[l(p_1, p_2, \ldots, p_m, \theta_1), l(p_1, p_2, \ldots, p_m, \theta_2)\right] = \text{constant} = h$$

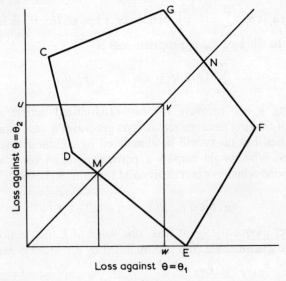

Fig. 3.1

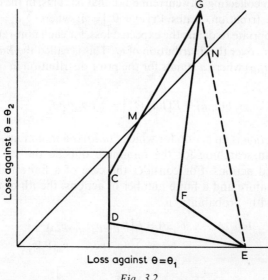

Fig. 3.2

lies along lines such as uv, vw, as in Fig. 3.1. So to find the minimax action we must find the admissible point on that contour for which h is a minimum. More picturesquely, find where a square, moving from the south-west, first hits the loss set. In Fig. 3.1, this happens at M and is admissible. But this point corresponds to selecting D (d_1, d_2) with probability p and E (e_1, e_2) with probability $1 - p$, so that the losses are equalized. That is,

$$pd_1 + (1 - p)e_1 = pd_2 + (1 - p)e_2$$

which may be solved for p. In Fig. 3.2, the non-randomized actions do not themselves form a convex polygon but the complete set of randomized actions fills out the convex quadrilateral CDEG. If CD is parallel to the θ_2 axis, the only admissible points are on DE. None of the points with equal losses is admissible and the square first hits the loss set along the edge CD on which D alone is admissible. We summarize: the minimax action is an equalizer rule, if any such be admissible, otherwise it is minimax in the set of non-randomized actions.

3.4 Bayes decisions

There are other considerations if further information is available about θ. Typically this will be in the form of a prior distribution for

Θ (prior to collecting any current data, that is). This, in the case of a discrete distribution, states $\Pr[\Theta = \theta_j] = g_j$ where $\sum g_j = 1$. It is then appropriate to define the expected loss, for each non-randomized action a_i, over the distribution of Θ. This is called the *Bayes loss*, written $b(a_i, g)$ where g stands for the prior distribution in question. Thus

$$b(a_i, g) = E[l(a_i, \Theta)] = \sum_j l(a_i, \theta_j) g_j$$

A *Bayes action* is an action for which $b(a_i, g)$ is a minimum. There is no point in searching for the minimum outside the set of non-randomized actions. For consider the case of a finite number of states of nature and a finite number of actions, the ith of which is selected with probability p_i:

$$
\begin{aligned}
b(p_1, p_2, \ldots, p_m, g) &= E[l(p_1, p_2, \ldots, p_m, \Theta)] \\
&= \sum_j l(p_1, p_2, \ldots, p_m, \theta_j) g_j \\
&= \sum_j \left[\sum_i l(a_i, \theta_j) p_i \right] g_j \\
&= \sum_i \left[\sum_j l(a_i, \theta_j) g_j \right] p_i \\
&= \sum_i b(a_i, g) p_i \\
&\geqslant \sum_i p_i [\min b(a_i, g)] \\
&= \min b(a_i, g)
\end{aligned}
$$

Now the minimum Bayes loss may be attained by more than one non-randomized action, though some of these may be inadmissible. A sufficient condition for a Bayes action to be admissible is that the prior distribution of Θ assigns positive probability to each possible θ_i. For suppose a_i is a Bayes action but is not admissible. Then there exists another action, possibly randomized, such that

$$l(p_1, p_2, \ldots, p_m, \theta_j) \leqslant l(a_i, \theta_j), \qquad j = 1, 2, \ldots, k$$

Multiplying both sides by g_j and summing over j,

$$
\begin{aligned}
b(p_1, p_2, \ldots, p_m, g) &= \sum_j l(p_1, p_2, \ldots, p_m, \theta_j) g_j \\
&< \sum_j l(a_1, \theta_j) g_j = b(a_i, g)
\end{aligned}
$$

(since there is strict inequality for at least one j). But the result is a

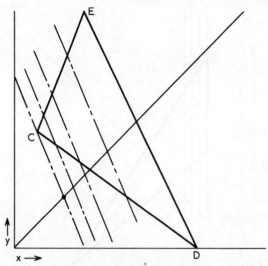

Fig. 3.3 The dashed lines have constant slope $-g/(1-g)$ and C corresponds to the Bayes action.

contradiction. The argument fails when those θ_j for which strict inequality holds are assigned zero probability.

We now illustrate some further geometrical aspects when there are two states of nature and $\Pr[\Theta = \theta_1] = g$, $\Pr[\Theta = \theta_2] = 1 - g$. A point with co-ordinates $x = $ loss against θ_1, $y = $ loss against θ_2, has an associated Bayes loss $xg + (1-g)y$. The set of points for which the Bayes risk is a constant, b, lies on a line with slope $-g/(1-g)$. We can keep b 'in sight' by observing that such a line intersects the line $y = x$ at (b,b). The Bayes principle requires these co-ordinates to be minimized. The sought line will either:

(a) pass through just one vertex of the loss polygon which then corresponds to a unique Bayes action (as in Fig. 3.3); or

(b) lie along a side of the loss polygon. Provided $0 < g < 1$, every point on the side represents a Bayes action and is admissible. But if $g = 0$ or $g = 1$, only one of the points will be admissible (Fig. 3.4).

By looking at Fig. 3.3 we can observe that C will correspond to the Bayes action for a range of values of g, in fact all those g such that the slope of a line of constant Bayes loss is less than the slope, m, of CD. That is, when $-g/(1-g) < m$, C is Bayes; when $-g/(1-g) > m$, D is Bayes; while if $-g/(1-g) = m$, every point

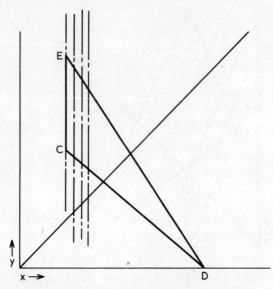

Fig. 3.4 The dashed lines are parallel to the vertical axis corresponding to $g = 1$ and C is the Bayes action.

on CD inclusive is Bayes. In the case of a finite number of non-randomized actions, each *admissible* action will be Bayes for some interval for g. There will evidently be a prior distribution for which the minimum Bayes loss will be a maximum, and this prior distribution earns the description *least favourable*. In fact, for the least favourable distribution, the Bayes action is the same as the minimax action.

Example 4. Suppose we are to find Bayes actions for the loss table in Fig. 3.5.

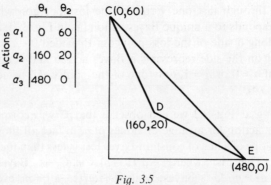

	θ_1	θ_2
a_1	0	60
a_2	160	20
a_3	480	0

Actions

C(0,60)

D
(160,20)

E
(480,0)

Fig. 3.5

The slope of CD is $(60 - 20)/(0 - 160) = -1/4$. Hence if $-g/(1-g) < -1/4$ then $g > 1/5$, C is the Bayes action. The slope of DE is $(20-0)/(160-480) = -1/16$. Hence if $-1/4 < -g/(1-g) < -1/16$ then $1/17 < g < 1/5$, D is the Bayes action; while if $g < 1/17$, E is the Bayes action. The Bayes loss for action a_1 is $0 \times g + 60(1-g)$, $1/5 < g < 1$, and is a maximum when $g = 1/5$, its value then being 48. It is readily checked that this is the maximum for any Bayes action and equals the loss due to the minimax action, which is to take a_1 with probability $7/10$ and a_2 with probability $3/10$. We recognize that this short solution has rested heavily on arguing from the geometry. An alternative algebraic solution is pursued in the following exercise.

Exercise 5. Show for Example 4 that $b(a_1,g) = 60 - 60g, b(a_2,g) = 20 + 140g, b(a_3,g) = 480g$. By considering the values of g for which $b(a_i,g) = b(a_j,g), i \neq j$, show that:

When $\qquad 0 < g < 1/17, \qquad b(a_3,g) < b(a_2,g) < b(a_1,g)$

$\qquad\qquad 1/17 < g < 1/9, \qquad b(a_2,g) < b(a_3,g) < b(a_1,g)$

$1/9 < g < 1/5$ $1/17 < g < 1/9, \qquad b(a_2,g) < b(a_1,g) < b(a_3,g)$

$\qquad\qquad 1/5 < g < 1, \qquad b(a_1,g) < b(a_2,g) < b(a_3,g)$

Draw the graphs of $b(a_i,g)$ against g.

3.5 Using data

The most glaring omission in the foregoing discussion relates to the use of current data. It is rather as though, in deciding whether or not to plant at a certain time, we had an estimate of the crop lost through frost, of yield lost through delay, were even armed with previous seasonal records but had failed to consult the immediate weather forecast. Provided we have a clear model relating the data to nature and a prior distribution for the parameters in the model, we shall proceed by recalculating the probability distribution of the parameters *conditional on the data*, which is then called the *posterior distribution*. This method effectively reduces the situation to a no-data problem and our previous techniques may be applied. Our illustrative example this time relates to profits rather than losses.

Example 5. A manufacturer delivers articles which if found by the customer to be satisfactory (S) give him a profit of £50 per article, while if unsatisfactory ($\bar{S}$) give only a profit of £20 per article. Past production records show that 90 per cent of the articles are S. Thus if no quality control is exercised, the expected profit per article is $50 \times 9/10 + 20 \times 1/10 = 47$. It is possible to prevent entirely the delivery of $\bar{S}$ articles by a severe inspection which costs the manufacturer £10 per article and thus if carried out on every article would guarantee him a profit of £40 per article. Alternatively, the manufacturer can make a relatively superficial test costing £1 per article. This test is not entirely reliable; the probability that it indicates a 'defect' (D) given it *is* unsatisfactory is 0.99 while the probability it indicates 'no defect' ($\bar{D}$) given it *is* satisfactory is also 0.99. How should the manufacturer maximize his expected profit? The 'obvious' strategy, to test and inspect the article only if D is indicated, is confirmed by a narrow margin. Suppose an article is tested and the test indicates D. We use the standard formulae for conditional probabilities.

$$\Pr[\bar{S}|D] = \frac{\Pr[\bar{S} \text{ and } D]}{\Pr[D]} = \frac{\Pr[D|\bar{S}]\Pr[\bar{S}]}{\Pr[D]}, \qquad (3.1)$$

$$\Pr[D] = \Pr[D|S]\Pr[S] + \Pr[D|\bar{S}]\Pr[\bar{S}] \qquad (3.2)$$

In Equation (3.2) we insert the figures for the performance of the instrument and the prior probabilities for $S, \bar{S}$,

$$\Pr[D] = \frac{1}{100} \times \frac{9}{10} + \frac{99}{100} \times \frac{1}{10} = \frac{108}{1000} \qquad (3.3)$$

$$\Rightarrow \Pr[\bar{S}|D] = \left(\frac{99}{100} \times \frac{1}{10} \right) \Big/ \frac{108}{1000} = \frac{11}{12} \qquad (3.4)$$

so that 11/12 is the posterior probability of $\bar{S}$ (given D).

$$\Pr[S|D] = 1 - \Pr[\bar{S}|D] = 1 - \frac{11}{12} = \frac{1}{12}$$

If $\bar{D}$ indicated,

$$\Pr[\bar{S}|\bar{D}] = \frac{\Pr[\bar{D}|\bar{S}]\Pr[\bar{S}]}{\Pr[\bar{D}]}$$

$$= \left(\frac{1}{100} \times \frac{1}{10} \right) \Big/ \left(1 - \frac{108}{1000} \right) = \frac{1}{892}$$

$$\Rightarrow \Pr[S|\bar{D}] = 1 - \Pr[\bar{S}|\bar{D}] = \frac{891}{892}$$

so that 1/892 is the posterior probability of $\bar{S}$ (given $\bar{D}$). If D is indicated and the full inspection is carried out, the expected profit is, since faulty articles are repaired at no extra cost,

$$39 \times \frac{11}{12} + 39 \times \frac{1}{12} = 39.$$

[The profit is reduced by test and inspection costs.]

On the other hand, if D is indicated, and the full inspection is not carried out, the expected profit is

$$19 \times \frac{11}{12} + 49 \times \frac{1}{12} = \frac{258}{12} = 21.5 < 39$$

So that it is better to carry out the inspection. On the other hand, if $\bar{D}$ is indicated, the corresponding expected profits are

$$39 \times \frac{891}{892} + 39 \times \frac{1}{892} = 39$$

$$49 \times \frac{891}{892} + 19 \times \frac{1}{892} = \frac{43\,678}{892} = 48.97 > 39$$

So in this case, if no defect is indicated, do not carry out the full inspection. The overall expected profit from the best strategy depends on the proportion of times that $D, \bar{D}$ are observed and is

$$39 \times \text{Pr}[D] + \frac{43\,678}{892} \times \text{Pr}[\bar{D}]$$

$$= 39 \times \frac{108}{1000} + \frac{43\,678}{892} \times \frac{892}{1000} = 47.89$$

At this exceeds 47, the cost of the test is a profitable investment.

The method employed to solve the example is called the *extensive form*. Although we have considered the situation for either type of observation, one of its attractions is that in practice we are able to restrict our attention to choosing an action in the light of the data actually obtained. In Example 7, we look at the same problem from another perspective. Instead of fixing the observation(s) we fix the state of nature. For each sample of data that can be observed we must decide which action to take. It is appropriate to call any such rule a decision function. We shall denote a non-randomized decision function by $d(x)$, where x is the observation. Any particular decision function will entail a 'loss', $l[d(x), \theta]$, when x is the observation, but we measure the effectiveness of any particular d by computing the expected loss over the distribution of X given θ. This is called the *risk*, denoted $R(d,\theta)$, and is calculated as

$$R(d,\theta) = E\{l[d(x),\theta]\,|\,\theta\}$$

Lacking the benefit of a prior distribution for Θ, we may fall back on the minimax decision function which has the smallest maximum risk. If a prior distribution g for Θ is available, we can order the decision functions by finding the expectation of their risks over the prior distribution of Θ. This is called the *Bayes risk* of the decision function, denoted $b(d,g)$, and is calculated as

$$b(d,g) = E[R(d,\Theta)]$$

A Bayes decision function has minimum Bayes risk.

Example 6.   (Being Example 5 revisited.)
The data can only be D or $\bar{D}$ and the only actions possible are inspect, do not inspect. Hence there are only four non-randomized decision functions:

$$d_1(D) = \text{inspect}, \qquad d_1(\bar{D}) = \text{do not inspect}$$
$$d_2(D) = \text{do not inspect}, \qquad d_2(\bar{D}) = \text{inspect}$$
$$d_3(D) = \text{do not inspect}, \qquad d_3(\bar{D}) = \text{do not inspect}$$
$$d_4(D) = \text{inspect}, \qquad d_4(\bar{D}) = \text{inspect}.$$

Consider d_1. When $\bar{S}$ is the state of the article, D is indicated with probability $99/100$, inspection is carried out and a gain of 39 made. When $\bar{D}$ is indicated, with probability $1/100$, there is no inspection – entailing a gain of 19. Hence the risk for d_1, when $\bar{S}$ is the case, is

$$39 \times \frac{99}{100} + 19 \times \frac{1}{100} = 38.8$$

Similarly, when S is the state of the article, the risk is

$$39 \times \frac{1}{100} + 49 \times \frac{99}{100} = 48.9$$

Since the respective prior probabilities of $\bar{S}, S$ are $1/10$, $9/10$, the Bayes risk is

$$\frac{1}{10}(38.8) + \frac{9}{10}(48.9) = 47.89$$

The corresponding results for the other decision functions are:

	$\bar{S}$	S
d_2	19.20	39.1
d_3	19	49	$\dfrac{1}{10} \times 19 + \dfrac{9}{10} \times 49 = 46 < 47.89$
d_4	39	39	$\dfrac{1}{10} \times 39 + \dfrac{9}{10} \times 39 = 39 < 47.89$

By comparison with d_1, it is seen that d_2 is not admissible, and clearly d_1 is the best decision function, in agreement with the calculation in Example 5.

3.6 Computing posterior distributions

The analysis in Example 6 is called the *normal form*. Here the posterior distribution is not calculated, but the labour saved is more than expended in calculating the risks for all possible decision functions. We therefore pay more attention to the extensive form in which only the data actually obtained need be considered. The derivation of the posterior distribution of a parameter conditional on the sample value(s) is, in the extensive form, of prime importance. In this connection we return to the problem of estimating a parameter, θ, when a prior distribution is available for Θ. We touch only lightly on the grounds leading to the choice of a particular prior distribution. Results from situations similar to the one presently under study may give a firm hint. In contrast, a paucity of previous data suggests using a prior distribution which reflects relative ignorance about the parameter. In both cases, there is considerable manipulative advantage to be enjoyed should the posterior distribution, given the sample values, belong to the same family as the prior distribution. Before turning to some (standard) examples we remind the reader of the formulae for recovering the posterior distribution of Θ given the sample values. Suppose X, Θ have a joint probability density function $f(x, \theta)$, Θ is continuous, with probability density function $g(\theta)$, while the marginal distribution of X has p.d.f. $f_1(x)$. Then the posterior distribution of Θ given x, has probability density function $g(\theta|x)$

such that, where $f_1(x) \neq 0$,

$$g(\theta \mid x) = \frac{f(x, \theta)}{f_1(x)} = \frac{f(x \mid \theta)g(\theta)}{f_1(x)},$$

$$f_1(x) = \int_{-\infty}^{+\infty} f(x, \theta) d\theta$$

Example 7. The distribution of X given θ is binomial with parameters n and θ. The prior distribution of Θ is beta (α, β), so that

$$g(\theta) = \frac{\Gamma(\alpha + \beta)}{\Gamma(\alpha)\Gamma(\beta)} \theta^{\alpha-1}(1-\theta)^{\beta-1}, \qquad 0 < \theta < 1, \alpha > 0, \beta > 0$$

$$f(x \mid \theta) = \binom{n}{x} \theta^x (1-\theta)^{n-x}, \qquad x = 0, 1, \ldots, n$$

$$\begin{aligned}
f(x, \theta) &= f(x \mid \theta)g(\theta) \\
&= \binom{n}{x} \theta^x (1-\theta)^{n-x} \frac{\Gamma(\alpha + \beta)}{\Gamma(\alpha)\Gamma(\beta)} \theta^{\alpha-1}(1-\theta)^{\beta-1} \\
&= \binom{n}{x} \frac{\Gamma(\alpha + \beta)}{\Gamma(\alpha)\Gamma(\beta)} \theta^{x+\alpha-1}(1-\theta)^{n-x+\beta-1}
\end{aligned}$$

$$\begin{aligned}
f_1(x) &= \binom{n}{x} \frac{\Gamma(\alpha + \beta)}{\Gamma(\alpha)\Gamma(\beta)} \int_0^1 \theta^{x+\alpha-1}(1-\theta)^{n-x+\beta-1} d\theta \\
&= \binom{n}{x} \frac{\Gamma(\alpha + \beta)}{\Gamma(\alpha)\Gamma(\beta)} \frac{\Gamma(x+\alpha)\Gamma(n-x+\beta)}{\Gamma(\alpha+\beta+n)}
\end{aligned}$$

Whence $g(\theta \mid x) = \dfrac{f(x \mid \theta)g(\theta)}{f_1(x)}$

$$= \frac{\Gamma(\alpha + \beta + n)}{\Gamma(\alpha + x)\Gamma(n - x + \beta)} \theta^{\alpha+x-1}(1-\theta)^{n-x+\beta-1}$$

which we identify as corresponding to a beta distribution $(\alpha + x, \beta + n - x)$.

We see in Example 7 that indeed the posterior distribution of Θ given x belongs to the same family as the prior distribution, the known parameters α, β being 'advanced' to $\alpha + x, \beta + n - x$. This (correctly) suggests that if a random sample $X_1, X_2, \ldots, X_m$ is drawn from the common binomial distribution of X given θ, then with a beta (α, β) prior distribution, the posterior distribution will be beta $(\alpha + \sum x_i, \beta + nm - \sum x_i)$. Moreover, the prior distribution is 'rich' in the sense that different choices of α, β provide a wide variety of shapes in the prior distribution. One choice is $\alpha = 1, \beta = 1$, when $g(\theta) = 1, 0 < \theta < 1$, and this prior may be said to represent 'ignorance about θ'. While this has its attractions, since it corresponds to equal intervals being equi-probable for Θ, it follows that other functions of θ cannot have this fetching property. Does, then, some particular function of Θ have first claim in this respect? It has been pointed out that as the probability density function of the binomial distribution can be written

$$\binom{n}{x}\theta^x(1-\theta)^{n-x} = \exp\left[x\log\{\theta/(1-\theta)\} + n\log(1-\theta) + \log\binom{n}{x}\right],$$

a member of the regular exponential family, $\phi = \log[\theta/(1-\theta)]$ should be regarded as the 'natural' parameter. Since $0 < \theta < 1$, $-\infty < \phi < +\infty$, so that if the natural parameter is to have a uniform distribution, it must be an improper one. This topic is followed up in the next exercise.

Exercise 6. For Example 7, show that, if $x \neq 0, x \neq n$, then the limit of $g(\theta|x)$ as $\alpha \to 0, \beta \to 0$ is proper. Compare the result with the posterior distribution of Θ given x when Θ has the improper prior distribution with 'density' $\theta^{-1}(1-\theta)^{-1}$. By making a formal change of variable, show that if Θ has the improper prior density $\theta^{-1}(1-\theta)^{-1}$, then $\phi(\Theta) = \log[\Theta/(1-\Theta)]$ has an improper uniform distribution over the real line.

Exercise 7. For Example 7, show that if $\alpha = \beta = \frac{1}{2}$, then the distribution of $\sin^{-1}(\Theta^{1/2})$ is uniform over $(0, \pi/2)$.

In Example 7, we showed every step of the working, although the marginal distribution of the observations was not really required. The argument may be shortened as follows:

$$f(x|\theta) \propto \theta^x(1-\theta)^{n-x}$$
$$g(\theta) \propto \theta^{\alpha-1}(1-\theta)^{\beta-1}$$
$$\Rightarrow f(x,\theta) \propto \theta^{\alpha+x-1}(1-\theta)^{\beta+n-x-1}$$
$$\Rightarrow g(\theta|x) \propto \theta^{\alpha+x-1}(1-\theta)^{\beta+n-x-1}$$

where the constant of proportionality is found by integrating θ over $(0,1)$ but also may be obtained by recognizing $g(\theta|x)$ as a beta $(\alpha+x, \beta+n-x)$ distribution.

Exercise 8.   The distribution of X given θ is Poisson with parameter θ and the prior distribution of Θ is gamma (α, λ), that is,

$$g(\theta) = \lambda(\lambda\theta)^{\alpha-1} \exp(-\lambda\theta)/\Gamma(\alpha), \qquad 0 < \theta < \infty.$$

Show that the marginal distribution of X has probability density function

$$\frac{\Gamma(\alpha + x)}{x!\,\Gamma(\alpha)} \frac{\lambda^{\alpha}}{(\lambda + 1)^{x+\alpha}}, \qquad x = 0, 1, 2, \ldots$$

and that the posterior distribution of Θ given x is gamma $(\alpha + x, \lambda + 1)$. Hence deduce the posterior distribution of Θ given the values $x_1, x_2, \ldots, x_n$ of a random sample of n from the same Poisson distribution.

We next give an example where the distribution of X given θ is continuous and the prior distribution of Θ happens to be improper.

Example 8.   The distribution of X given θ is $N(\theta, \sigma_0^2)$, σ_0^2 known, where the (improper) prior distribution of Θ is uniform over $(-\infty, +\infty)$.

$$f(x|\theta) = \frac{1}{\sqrt{(2\pi)}\sigma_0} \exp\left[-\tfrac{1}{2}(x-\theta)^2/\sigma_0^2\right], \qquad -\infty < x < +\infty$$

$$f(x,\theta) = \frac{1}{\sqrt{(2\pi)}\sigma_0} \exp\left[-\tfrac{1}{2}(x-\theta)^2/\sigma_0^2\right] \times 1, \qquad \text{since } g(\theta) = 1.$$

Now the integral of $f(x,\theta)$ over θ is in fact unity since we may regard it as a probability density function $N(x, \sigma_0^2)$. Finally,

$$g(\theta|x) = \frac{1}{\sqrt{(2\pi)}\sigma_0} \exp\left[-\tfrac{1}{2}(\theta - x)^2/\sigma_0^2\right].$$

Thus the posterior distribution of Θ given x is $N(x, \sigma_0^2)$ (and is proper).

Exercise 9.   The distribution of X given θ is uniform over $(0, \theta)$ while the prior distribution of Θ is Pareto with parameters α, θ_0, that is $g(\theta) = \alpha\theta_0^{\alpha}/\theta^{\alpha+1}, \theta > \theta_0$. Show that the posterior distribution of Θ given $X = x$ is again Pareto with parameters $\alpha + 1, t$, where $t = \max(\theta_0, x)$.

Exercise 10. $X_1, X_2, \ldots, X_n$ is a random sample from the exponential distribution with unknown parameter λ, i.e., $f(x_i|\lambda) = \lambda$

$\exp(-\lambda x_i)$. The prior distribution of Λ is gamma with known parameters α, β. Show that the posterior distribution of Λ given $x_1, x_2, \ldots, x_n$ is gamma $(\alpha + n, \beta + \sum x_i)$.

Example 9. (The normal distribution with known variance revisited.)

$X_1, X_2, \ldots, X_n$ is a random sample from the distribution $N(\theta, \sigma_0^2)$ where σ_0^2 is known. The prior distribution of Θ is $N(\mu, \tau^2)$. (Generalization from a sample of one observation is not obvious and the 'proportional' notation is used with advantage.)

$$f(x_1, x_2, \ldots, x_n | \theta) \propto \exp\left[-\frac{1}{2}\sum(x_i - \theta)^2 / \sigma_0^2\right]$$

$$= \exp\left\{\left[-\frac{1}{2}\sum(x_i - \bar{x})^2 - \frac{n}{2}(\bar{x} - \theta)^2\right] / \sigma_0^2\right\}$$

$$\propto \exp\left[-\frac{n}{2}(\bar{x} - \theta)^2 / \sigma_0^2\right]$$

$$g(\theta) \propto \exp\left[-\frac{1}{2}(\theta - \mu)^2 / \tau^2\right]$$

$$f(x_1, x_2, \ldots, x_n, \theta) \propto \exp\left[-\frac{n}{2}\left(\frac{\bar{x} - \theta}{\sigma_0}\right)^2 - \frac{1}{2}\left(\frac{\theta - \mu}{\tau}\right)^2\right]$$

(squaring out and omitting terms not involving θ)

$$\propto \exp\left[-\frac{\theta^2}{2}\left(\frac{n}{\sigma_0^2} + \frac{1}{\tau^2}\right) + \frac{1}{2}2\theta\left(\frac{n\bar{x}}{\sigma_0^2} + \frac{\mu}{\tau^2}\right)\right]$$

(completing the square on θ)

$$\propto \exp\left[-\frac{1}{2}\left(\theta - \frac{(n\bar{x}/\sigma_0^2) + \mu/\tau^2}{(n/\sigma_0^2) + 1/\tau^2}\right)^2\left(\frac{n}{\sigma_0^2} + \frac{1}{\tau^2}\right)\right]$$

$$= \exp\left[-\frac{1}{2}(\theta - m)^2 / \sigma^2\right]$$

So that the posterior distribution of Θ, given the sample values, is normal with mean

$$m = \frac{(n\bar{x}/\sigma_0^2) + \mu/\tau^2}{(n/\sigma_0^2) + 1/\tau^2} = \frac{\bar{x}\tau^2 + \mu\sigma_0^2/n}{\tau^2 + \sigma_0^2/n}$$

and variance

$$\sigma^2 = \frac{1}{(n/\sigma_0^2) + 1/\tau^2} = \frac{\tau^2\sigma_0^2/n}{\tau^2 + \sigma_0^2/n}$$

Thus the mean is a weighted combination of the sample mean $\bar{x}$ and that of the prior distribution, and is concentrated at $\bar{x}$ as n increases. A special case of interest is when τ is large, when again m tends to $\bar{x}$ and σ^2 to σ_0^2/n. This might be said to correspond to 'vague' prior knowledge about θ and is effectively Example 8 when $n = 1$.

3.7 Conjugate distributions

Our examples have nominated prior distributions which combine with the joint p.d.f. of the observations to produce a posterior distribution for the parameter which belongs to the same family as the prior distribution. Such a family is said to be (naturally) *conjugate* to the distribution yielding the observations. What are the properties which qualify a family of distributions to be conjugate? A glance back at Exercise 8 shows the main features. Since the observations there have independent Poisson distributions, their joint p.d.f., given the parameter, is proportional to

$$\theta^{\Sigma x_i} \exp(-n\theta) \tag{3.5}$$

But the prior distribution proposed is proportional to

$$\theta^{\alpha-1} \exp(-\lambda\theta) \tag{3.6}$$

So that, *regarded as a function of* θ, Equation (3.5) is similar to Equation (3.6), and the product of Equation (3.5) and (3.6), on which the posterior distribution is based, is

$$\theta^{\Sigma x_i + \alpha - 1} \exp[-(\lambda + n)\theta] \tag{3.7}$$

which is *again* similar to Equation (3.5). But how do we know that Equation (3.5) will hold whatever the sample size? We know this because $\sum_1^n X_i$ is a sufficient statistic for θ and hence the joint p.d.f. is always proportional to Equation (3.5). The key step then is to base the family of prior distributions on the joint p.d.f. regarded as a function of θ.

Exercise 11. $\theta^{\Sigma x_i} \exp(-n\theta)$ is not a probability density function for a random variable Θ. Show that the integral of the expression with respect to θ $(0, \infty)$ is $(\sum x_i)!/n^{\Sigma x_i + 1}$.

Example 10. $X_1, X_2, \ldots, X_n$ is a random sample from the distribution $N(\mu, \theta)$ where μ is a known constant.

$$f(x_1, x_2, \ldots, x_n | \mu, \theta) = \prod_1^n f(x_i | \mu, \theta)$$

$$= \prod_1^n \frac{1}{\sqrt{(2\pi\theta)}} \exp\left[-\tfrac{1}{2}(x_i - \mu)^2/\theta\right]$$

$$\propto \frac{1}{\theta^{n/2}} \exp\left[-\tfrac{1}{2}t/\theta\right]$$

(where $T = \sum_1^n (X_i - \mu)^2$ is a sufficient statistic for θ), and we recognize that for fixed $T = t$, this is proportional to a gamma density for $1/\Theta$. Thus, if the prior distribution for $1/\Theta$ is $\Gamma(\alpha, \lambda)$, then since

$$\frac{1}{\theta^{n/2}} \exp\left[-\tfrac{1}{2}t/\theta\right] \left(\frac{1}{\theta}\right)^{\alpha-1} \exp\left[-\lambda/\theta\right]$$

$$= \left(\frac{1}{\theta}\right)^{n/2+\alpha-1} \exp\left[-(\lambda + \tfrac{1}{2}t)/\theta\right]$$

the posterior distribution of $1/\Theta$ given $x_1, x_2, \ldots, x_n$ is $\Gamma(\alpha + n/2, \lambda + \tfrac{1}{2}\sum(x_i - \mu)^2)$. The prior distribution of Θ itself may be easily recovered if required.

We can now see more clearly the role of a statistic $t(X_1, X_2, \ldots, X_n)$ which is single sufficient for θ whatever the sample size. For if such exists, we must have a factorization of the joint p.d.f.,

$$f(x_1, x_2, \ldots, x_n | \theta) = h(t | \theta)g(x_1, x_2, \ldots, x_n).$$

It is true that $h(t | \theta)$ is a p.d.f. for T given θ and not for Θ. If, however, $\int h(t | \theta) d\theta$ exists, we can normalize, and we take the family of prior distribution for Θ as proportional to $h(t | \theta)$. How about the 'closure' property which ensures that we remain in the family? T remains single sufficient, so if we have two independent samples $(X_1, X_2, \ldots, X_n), (Y_1, Y_2, \ldots, Y_m)$, we have

$$f(x_1, \ldots, x_n, y_1, \ldots, y_m | \theta) = f(x_1, \ldots, x_n | \theta)f(y_1, \ldots, y_m | \theta)$$
$$h[t(x_1, \ldots, y_m) | \theta]g(x_1, \ldots, y_m) = h[t(x_1, \ldots, x_n) | \theta]g(x_1, \ldots, x_n)$$
$$\times h[t(y_1, \ldots, y_m) | \theta]g(y_1, \ldots, y_m)$$

or $$h[t_{m+n} | \theta] \propto h(t_n | \theta)h(t_m | \theta)$$

Exercise 12. $X_1, X_2, \ldots, X_n$ is a random sample from the uniform distribution over $(0, \theta)$. It has been shown that $\max[X_1, \ldots, X_n] = T$ is sufficient for θ. Check that $f(x_1, x_2, \ldots, x_n | \theta)$ can hence be factorized in the form

$$h(t|\theta)g(x_1, \ldots, x_n) = \left(\frac{nt^{n-1}}{\theta^n}\right)\frac{1}{nt^{n-1}}, \qquad 0 < t < \theta$$

Show that $\int_t^\infty h(t|\theta)\,d\theta = n/(n-1)$, $n \geq 2$, and hence the conjugate family of prior distributions is the family with p.d.f. $\alpha\theta_0/\theta^{\alpha+1}$, $\theta > \theta_0$.

3.8 Distribution of the next observation

Having drawn a sample of data, we may be interested in the distribution of a new value, conditional on the data drawn but regardless of the value of the (unknown) parameter. We shall quote few general formulae since the general idea is clear.

The least fatiguing method appears to consist of first computing the posterior distribution of Θ, given the existing data, and then finding the marginal distribution of the new observation by averaging its p.d.f. with respect to θ, over this same posterior distribution. If the data consist of one value x, and the new value is y, this means evaluating

$$\int f(y|\theta)g(\theta|x)\,d\theta$$

Example 11. The distribution of X given θ is exponential with parameter θ, while the prior distribution of Θ is $\Gamma(1, 1)$. Hence (by Exercise 10), the posterior distribution of Θ given x is $\Gamma(2, 1 + x)$. The p.d.f. for a new value Y, given x, is thus

$$\int_0^\infty \theta\exp(-\theta y) \times (1+x)^2\,\theta\exp[-(1+x)\theta]\,d\theta$$

$$= \int_0^\infty (1+x)^2\theta^2\exp[-(1+x+y)\theta]\,d\theta$$

$$= \frac{2(1+x)^2}{(1+x+y)^3}, \qquad y > 0$$

Exercise 13. Show that in Example 11, that although X given θ, and Y given θ, are independent, X and Y are *not* independent unconditionally.

3.9 More than one parameter

We shall not explore this topic very far. Provided the full joint prior distribution of the several parameters is supplied, we may use the same technique to find the joint posterior distribution. We may then, in principle, find the posterior distribution of subsets of these same parameters by 'integrating out' the remainder.

Example 12. The distribution of X given θ is Poisson with parameter θ and the independent distribution of Y given ϕ is Poisson with parameter ϕ.

If Θ, Φ have independent prior $\Gamma(1, 1)$ distributions, find the posterior distribution of Θ/Φ given x and y.

The joint p.d.f. of X, Y, Θ, Φ is

$$\frac{\theta^x \exp(-\theta)}{x!} \frac{\phi^y \exp(-\phi)}{y!} \exp(-\theta) \exp(-\phi)$$

$$= \frac{1}{x! y!} \theta^x \exp(-2\theta) \phi^y \exp(-2\phi) \tag{3.8}$$

Hence the marginal joint probability density function of X and Y is

$$\frac{1}{x! y!} \int_0^\infty \int_0^\infty \theta^x \exp(-2\theta) \phi^y \exp(-2\phi) \mathrm{d}\theta \mathrm{d}\phi$$

$$= \frac{1}{2^{x+1} 2^{y+1}} \tag{3.9}$$

So the joint posterior distribution of Θ, Φ given x, y (found by dividing Equation (3.8) by Equation (3.9)) is

$$\frac{2(2\theta)^x \exp(-2\theta)}{x!} \frac{2(2\phi)^y \exp(-2\phi)}{y!} \tag{3.10}$$

As might have been anticipated, Θ, Φ have independent posterior distributions, being $\Gamma(x+1, 2), \Gamma(y+1, 2)$ respectively. Now change the variables to $\psi = \theta/\phi$, $\omega = \theta + \phi$. The Jacobian of the transformation is $\omega/(\psi + 1)^2$ and, by substitution in Equation (3.10), we have for the joint posterior density for the transformed parameters

$$\frac{2^{x+y+2}}{x! y!} \left(\frac{\psi \omega}{\psi + 1} \right)^x \left(\frac{\omega}{\psi + 1} \right)^y \exp(-2\omega) \times \frac{\omega}{(\psi + 1)^2} \tag{3.11}$$

We may factorize Equation (3.11), by inspection, as

$$\left[\frac{2(2\omega)^{x+y+1}\exp(-2\omega)}{(x+y+1)!}\right]\frac{(x+y+1)!}{x!y!}\left(\frac{\psi}{\psi+1}\right)^{x}\left(\frac{1}{1+\psi}\right)^{y+2} \quad (3.12)$$

so that $\Theta + \Phi, \Theta/\Phi$ are independent, given x, y. As an exercise, show that $1/(1 + \Theta/\Phi)$ has a beta $(x + 1, y + 1)$ distribution, given x, y.

Exercise 14. The distribution of X given θ_1 is $N(\theta_1, \sigma_1^2)$ and the independent distribution of Y given θ_2 is $N(\theta_2, \sigma_2^2)$, where σ_1, σ_2 are known. The Θ_i have independent prior distributions $N(\mu_i, \tau_i^2)$, $i = 1, 2$. Show that the posterior distributions of Θ_1, Θ_2 given x, y are independent and use the result of Example 10 to deduce the posterior distribution of $\Theta_1 + \Theta_2$.

Our final topic in this section relates to sampling a normal distribution for which both the mean, θ_1, and the variance, θ_2, are unknown. We are obliged to state a joint prior distribution for the random variables Θ_1, Θ_2. Example 10 suggests that Θ_1 should have a normal distribution as its prior distribution and Example 10 suggests that $1/\Theta_2$ should have a gamma distribution. The mathematical details reach about the limit of complexity envisaged for this text, but are laid out in the next (optional) exercise. With a simple assumption about the joint prior distribution, it is found that the unconditional posterior distribution of Θ_1 is related to Student's t-distribution: a satisfactory outcome in view of certain standard results concerning sampling a normal distribution.

Exercise 15. (Optional.) $X_1, X_2, \ldots, X_n$ is a random sample from the distribution $N(\theta_1, \theta_2)$. The prior distribution of Θ_1, given θ_2, is $N(\mu, a\theta_2), a > 0$. The prior distribution of $1/\Theta_2$ is $\Gamma(\alpha, \lambda)$. Verify that

$$f(x_1, x_2, \ldots, x_n | \theta_1, \theta_2) \propto \frac{1}{\theta_2^{n/2}}\exp\left[-\tfrac{1}{2}\sum(x_i - \theta_1)^2/\theta_2\right]$$

$$g(\theta_1 | \theta_2) \propto \frac{1}{\theta_2^{1/2}}\exp\left[-\tfrac{1}{2}(\theta_1 - \mu)^2/a\theta_2\right]$$

But the density of $1/\Theta_2$ is proportional to

$$\left(\frac{1}{\theta_2}\right)^{\alpha-1}\exp\left[-\lambda/\theta_2\right]$$

hence the joint p.d.f. of $X_1, X_2, \ldots, X_n, \Theta_1, 1/\Theta_2$ is proportional to

$$\frac{1}{\theta_2^{\alpha + (n-1)/2}} \exp\left[-\frac{1}{2}\left\{ \sum(x_i - \bar{x})^2 + n(\bar{x} - \theta_1)^2 + \frac{(\theta_1 - \mu)^2}{a} + 2\lambda \right\} \middle/ \theta_2 \right]$$

By expanding the terms $n(\bar{x} - \theta_1)^2 + (\theta_1 - \mu)^2/a$, rearranging as a quadratic in θ_1, and completing the square on θ_1, show the posterior distribution of Θ_1 given θ_2 is $N(m, \sigma^2)$ where

$$m = \frac{\mu + na\bar{x}}{1 + na} \qquad \text{(a weighted mean of } \mu, \bar{x})$$

$$\sigma^2 = \frac{a\theta_2}{1 + na}$$

Deduce that posterior distribution of $1/\Theta_2$ is $\Gamma(\alpha', \lambda')$ where

$$\alpha' = \alpha + n/2,$$
$$\lambda' = \lambda + \tfrac{1}{2}\sum(x_i - \bar{x})^2 + \tfrac{1}{2}n(\bar{x} - \mu)^2/(an + 1)$$

Exercise 16. In Exercise 15, Θ_1 given θ_2 is $N(\mu, a\theta_2)$ while the marginal distribution of $1/\Theta_2$ is $\Gamma(\alpha, \lambda)$. Show that the distribution of Θ_1 (*not* conditional on θ_2) has a density proportional to $[\lambda + (\theta_1 - \mu)^2/2a]^{-\alpha - 1/2}$. Compare this density with that of a t-distribution.

3.10 Decision functions

We now apply the technique of Example 6 to the problem of point estimation. We confine our discussion to non-negative loss functions which can assume the value zero, and thus the distinction between losses and regrets no longer applies. For each sample we may choose a decision function $d(x_1, x_2, \ldots, x_n)$, being a function of the sample values, which is to be the estimate of the parameter.

Example 13. The distribution of X given θ is binomial with parameters n and θ. Suppose the loss function has the form $l[d(x), \theta] = [d(x) - \theta]^2$ and we require the risk function for the class of estimators $d(X) = aX + b$. The loss for any particular x is

$$(ax + b - \theta)^2 = a^2 x^2 + 2a(b - \theta)x + (b - \theta)^2$$

The risk is the conditional expectation of the loss over the distribution of X given θ.

$$R(d,\theta) = E[(aX + b - \theta)^2 | \theta]$$
$$= a^2 E(X^2 | \theta) + 2a(b - \theta)E(X | \theta) + (b - \theta)^2$$

Now for the binomial distribution, $E(X | \theta) = n\theta$, $E(X^2 | \theta) = n\theta(1 - \theta)$ $+ n^2\theta^2$, and after rearranging, $R(d,\theta) = \theta^2[a^2 n(n - 1) - 2an + 1]$ $+ \theta(2abn - 2b + a^2 n) + b^2$. To choose d here means to select a, b. The risk will depend on the value of the parameter. For instance, when $n = 2$, $a = 1$, $b = 0$, we have $E[(X - \theta)^2 | \theta] = 2\theta - \theta^2$, while if $a = 0$, $b = 1$, then $E[(1 - \theta)^2 | \theta] = (1 - \theta)^2$. Yet $(1 - \theta)^2 < 2\theta - \theta^2$ if $2\theta^2 - 4\theta + 1 < 0$, i.e., if $\theta > 1 - 1/\sqrt{2}$. That is, the seemingly arbitrary choice that $\theta = 1$ may, for some values of θ, be less expensive on average than another rule which takes some account of the data. As before, some additional criterion is needed to order the decision functions. The minimax estimate, for instance, will have the smallest maximum risk. A decision function which is admissible and has constant risk is minimax. We can find a decision which has constant risk by equating the coefficients of θ^2, θ to zero and solving for a, b. Thus, when $n = 4$, $a = b = 1/6$ is such a choice and the constant risk is $b^2 = 1/36$. [$n = 4$, $a = -b = \frac{1}{2}$ is the other possibility; why is it not acceptable?] For the moment we can claim only that $d(X) = (X + 1)/6$ is minimax in the class $aX + b$. We defer considering why the decision function is admissible.

Exercise 17.   Show that, for Example 13, the solutions to the equations

$$a^2 n(n - 1) - 2an + 1 = 0, \qquad 2abn - 2b + a^2 n = 0$$

are $a = 1/(n + \sqrt{n})$, $b = 1/[2(\sqrt{n} + 1)]$. Check that $0 < ax + b < 1$.

Further progress is possible in Example 14 if there is a known prior distribution for Θ. For then we may compute the Bayes risk for a decision function as the expected value of the risk over the distribution of Θ. For decision functions in the class $aX + b$, the risk is

$$\theta^2[a^2 n(n - 1) - 2an + 1] + \theta[2abn - 2b + a^2 n] + b^2$$

Suppose now that Θ has a uniform distribution over $(0,1)$, then $E(\Theta) = \frac{1}{2}$, $E(\Theta^2) = \frac{1}{3}$, so that the Bayes risk is

$$\tfrac{1}{3}[a^2 n(n - 1) - 2an + 1] + \tfrac{1}{2}[2abn - 2b + a^2 n] + b^2$$

By the usual calculus method, this is minimized when $a = b = 1/(n + 2)$. Hence $(X + 1)/(n + 2)$ has minimum Bayes risk. The result is extended in Exercise 18.

Exercise 18.   Show for Example 13 that if the prior distribution of Θ is beta (α, β), then for $d(X) = aX + b$, the Bayes risk is minimized when $a = 1/(\alpha + \beta + n), b = \alpha/(\alpha + \beta + n)$.
[Note: $E(\Theta) = \alpha/(\alpha + \beta), E(\Theta^2) = \alpha(\alpha + 1)/[(\alpha + \beta)(\alpha + \beta + 1)]$]

Exercise 19.   The distribution of X given θ is Poisson with parameter θ. Show that the risk for $aX + b$ when $l[d(x), \theta] = [d(x) - \theta]^2$ is

$$E[(aX + b - \theta)^2 | \theta] = \theta^2(a - 1)^2 + \theta(a^2 + 2ab - 2b) + b^2.$$

Show further, that if Θ has a $\Gamma(\alpha, \lambda)$ prior distribution, then the Bayes risk is

$$[\alpha(1 + \alpha)(a - 1)^2/\lambda^2] + [\alpha(a^2 + 2ab - 2b)/\lambda] + b^2,$$

and is minimized when $a = 1/(1 + \lambda), b = \alpha/(1 + \lambda)$.

Example 14.   The lengthy discussion of Example 13 was in terms of the restricted class $d(X) = aX + b$. If the prior distribution is uniform, can we find the unrestricted $d(X)$ which has minimum Bayes risk for the loss function $[d(x) - \theta]^2$?

$$R(d, \theta) = E[(d(X) - \theta)^2 | \theta]$$

$$= \sum_{x=0}^{n} [d(x) - \theta]^2 \binom{n}{x} \theta^x (1 - \theta)^{n-x}$$

$$b(d, g) = E[R(d, \Theta)] = \int_0^1 R(d, \theta) d\theta$$

$$= \int_0^1 \sum [d(x) - \theta]^2 \binom{n}{x} \theta^x (1 - \theta)^{n-x} d\theta$$

The trick is to interchange summation with integration:

$$b(d, g) = \sum \binom{n}{x} \int_0^1 [d^2(x) - 2d(x)\theta + \theta^2] \theta^x (1 - \theta)^{n-x} d\theta$$

(using standard results for beta integrals)

$$= \frac{1}{n + 1} \left[\sum d^2(x) - 2\sum \frac{d(x)(x + 1)}{n + 2} + \sum \frac{(x + 1)(x + 2)}{(n + 2)(n + 3)} \right]$$

$$= \frac{1}{n + 1} \left[\sum \left[d(x) - \frac{x + 1}{n + 2} \right]^2 + \sum \frac{(x + 1)(x + 2)}{(n + 2)(n + 3)} - \sum \frac{(x + 1)^2}{(n + 2)^2} \right]$$

Only the first term depends on $d(x)$, and it is minimized when $d(x) = (x+1)/(n+2)$. Since this has minimum Bayes risk, we call it the *Bayes estimate for* θ. [But of course only for this particular prior distribution and loss function.]

3.11 Bayes estimators

What we evidently need is some generalization of the advantage gained by the interchange of operations used in Example 15. This is provided by a theorem which states that the Bayes estimate minimizes the expectation of the loss function over the *posterior distribution of* Θ. We prove the result when (without loss of generality) the distribution of X given θ is discrete and the prior distribution is continuous. The Bayes risk for d is then

$$b(d,g) = \int \sum_x l[d(x),\theta] f(x|\theta) g(\theta) \mathrm{d}\theta$$

Substituting $f(x|\theta)g(\theta) = g(\theta|x) f_1(x)$, and interchanging integration and summation,

$$b(d,g) = \sum_x \left\{ f_1(x) \int l[d(x),\theta] g(\theta|x) \mathrm{d}\theta \right\}$$

Since $f_1(x) \geqslant 0$, $l[d(x),\theta] \geqslant 0$, the d which minimizes $b(d,g)$ must, for each x, minimize

$$\int l[d(x),\theta] g(\theta|x) \mathrm{d}\theta = E\{l[d(x),\Theta]|x\}$$

The quadratic loss function $l[d(x),\theta] = [d(x) - \theta]^2$ is frequently used and we may then further specialize the result.

$$E\{[d(x) - \Theta]^2 | x\} = E\{[\Theta - E(\Theta|x)]^2 | x\} + [d(x) - E(\Theta|x)]^2$$

and is clearly minimized when $d(x) = E(\Theta|x)$. That is, *the Bayes estimate is the mean of the posterior distribution of* Θ. Further, the minimum Bayes risk is the expected variance of the posterior distribution of Θ.

Example 15. The distribution of X given θ is binomial with parameters n and θ. The prior distribution for Θ is beta (α, β) and the loss function quadratic. We have shown (Example 7) that the posterior distribution of Θ given x is beta $(\alpha + x, \beta + n - x)$. Hence the Bayes estimate of θ is the mean of a beta $(\alpha + x, \beta + n - x)$

distribution, i.e., $(\alpha + x)/(\alpha + x + \beta + n - x) = (\alpha + x)/(\alpha + \beta + n)$. Since the (conjugate) posterior becomes the prior distribution for the next observation we have, by repeated application, that for a random sample $X_1, X_2, \ldots, X_m$, the Bayes estimator for θ is

$$\frac{\alpha + \sum X_i}{\alpha + \beta + nm}$$

Exercise 20. The distribution of X given θ is Poisson with parameter θ and the prior distribution of Θ is gamma (α, λ). For the quadratic loss function, show that the Bayes estimator of θ is $(X + \alpha)/(\lambda + 1)$. State the Bayes estimator for a random sample of size n.

One loss function which does not penalize estimates far from θ so severely as does the quadratic, is $l(d(x), \theta) = |d(x) - \theta|$. The Bayes estimate minimizes $E[|d(x) - \Theta\,\|\,x]$ and this is accomplished by choosing $d(x)$ as a median of the posterior distribution of Θ given x. A proof is outlined, for the continuous case, in the next exercise.

Exercise 21. If m is the median of a continuous probability density function $f(y)$, then

$$\int_{-\infty}^{m} f(y)\mathrm{d}y = \int_{m}^{\infty} f(y)\mathrm{d}y = \tfrac{1}{2}$$

For any $b \leqslant m$, verify the following steps:

$$
\begin{aligned}
E[\,|Y - b|\,] &= \int_{-\infty}^{b} (b - y)f(y)\mathrm{d}y + \int_{b}^{\infty} (y - b)f(y)\mathrm{d}y \\
&= \int_{-\infty}^{m} (m - y)f(y)\mathrm{d}y + \int_{m}^{\infty} (y - m)f(y)\mathrm{d}y \\
&\quad + 2\int_{b}^{m} (y - b)f(y)\mathrm{d}y \\
&= \int_{-\infty}^{+\infty} |y - m|f(y)\mathrm{d}y + 2\int_{b}^{m} (y - b)f(y)\mathrm{d}y \\
&= E[\,|Y - m|\,] + 2\int_{b}^{m} (y - b)f(y)\mathrm{d}y \\
&\geqslant E[\,|Y - m|\,], \qquad \text{with equality when } b = m.
\end{aligned}
$$

Example 16. The distribution of X given θ is uniform over $(0, \theta)$, while the prior distribution of Θ is Pareto with parameters α, θ_0. We have shown that the posterior distribution of Θ given x is also Pareto with parameters $\alpha + 1, t$, where $t = \max (\theta_0, x)$. Hence, if the loss function is $|d(x) - \theta|$, the Bayes estimate is the median, m, of $g(\theta|x) = (\alpha + 1)t^{\alpha+1}/\theta^{\alpha+2}, \theta > t$.

$$\int_t^m \frac{(\alpha + 1)t^{\alpha+1}}{\theta^{\alpha+2}} d\theta = \frac{1}{2}, \text{ hence}$$

$$1 - (t/m)^{\alpha+1} = \tfrac{1}{2} \quad \text{or} \quad m = [2^{1/(\alpha+1)}]t$$

Suppose we require the Bayes estimator of $\phi(\theta)$. We need not trouble to compute the posterior distribution of $\phi(\Theta)$. The Bayes estimate will be that function d which minimizes $E\{l[d(x), (\phi\Theta)]|x\}$, where the expectation is with respect to the posterior distribution of Θ given x and l is the appropriate loss function for the $\phi(\theta)$ in question.

Example 17.   The distribution of X given (θ) is Poisson and the prior distribution is $\Gamma(\alpha, \lambda)$. Then the posterior distribution of Θ is $\Gamma(\alpha + x, \lambda + 1)$. If the loss function for $\phi(\theta) = 1/\theta$ is $[d(x) - 1/\theta]^2$, then the Bayes estimator is the mean of the posterior distribution of $1/\Theta$. But this we compute as

$$E\left[\frac{1}{\Theta}\Big|x\right] = \int \frac{1}{\theta} g(\theta|x) d\theta$$

$$= \int_0^\infty \frac{1}{\theta} \frac{(\lambda + 1)[(\lambda + 1)\theta]^{\chi+x-1}}{\Gamma(\alpha + x)} \exp[-(\lambda + 1)\theta] d\theta$$

$$= (\lambda + 1)/(\alpha + x - 1) \quad (\alpha > 1)$$

3.12 Admissibility

We have evaded asking so far whether Bayes estimators are admissible. We cannot rely on our earlier result which guarantees this when there is a finite number of states of nature and each of these receives positive prior probability. We do not offer a rigorous proof when Θ has a continuous distribution over an interval, though admissibility here seems plausible enough. For suppose d is Bayes but is not admissible, then there must exist d^* such that

$$R(d^*, \theta) \leqslant R(d, \theta)$$

with strict inequality for at least one value of θ. Now providing that, for every decision function, the risk function is continuous in θ, if $R(d^*,\theta_0) < R(d,\theta_0)$, then $R(d^*,\theta) < R(d,\theta_0)$ in a sufficiently small interval about θ_0. This is enough to force

$$b(d^*,g) = \int R(d^*,\theta)g(\theta)\mathrm{d}\theta < \int R(d,\theta)g(\theta)\mathrm{d}\theta = b(d,g)$$

and contradicts the fact that d is Bayes and hence has the minimum Bayes risk. If the result is accepted then we have a method for confirming an estimator as minimax. Suppose we have an estimator which has constant risk against each value of the parameter *and* we can show that it is a Bayes estimator against *some* suitable continuous prior distribution for Θ, then it will be admissible and hence minimax.

Example 18. The distribution of X given θ is binomial with parameters n and θ, and the loss function is $[d(x) - \theta]^2$. Then by Exercise 17, $d(X) = X/(n+\sqrt{n}) + 1/2(\sqrt{n}+1)$ has constant risk against each θ. Furthermore, if Θ has a beta (α, β) prior distribution, then by Example 15, $d_0(X) = (\alpha + x)/(n + \alpha + \beta)$ is a Bayes estimator. By equating coefficients

$$\frac{1}{n+\alpha+\beta} = \frac{1}{n+\sqrt{n}}, \quad \frac{\alpha}{n+\alpha+\beta} = \frac{1}{2(\sqrt{n}+1)} \quad \text{or} \quad \alpha = \beta = \tfrac{1}{2}\sqrt{n}.$$

So that, for a prior distribution beta $(\tfrac{1}{2}\sqrt{n}, \tfrac{1}{2}\sqrt{n})$, $d_0(X)$ is Bayes, has constant risk, and hence is minimax.

Exercise 22. The distribution of X given θ has p.d.f.

$$f(x|\theta) = \theta^x(1+\theta)^{-(1+x)}, x = 0, 1, \dots, \theta > 0.$$

If the loss function is

$$l[d(x),\theta] = [d(x) - \theta]^2/[\theta(1+\theta)]$$

show that $d_1(X) = X$ has constant risk for all θ. By considering $d_2(X) = X/2$, show however that d_1 is not minimax.

The computation of the actual Bayes risk is apt to prove tedious.

Example 19. To compute the Bayes risk for $d(X) = (\alpha + X)/(\alpha + \beta + n)$ in Example 15 we require first the risk, which is

$$E\left[\left(\frac{\alpha + X}{\alpha + \beta + n} - \theta\right)^2 \Big| \theta\right] = \frac{1}{(\alpha + \beta + n)^2} E(\alpha + X - \alpha\theta - \beta\theta - n\theta)^2 | \theta]$$

$$= \frac{1}{(\alpha + \beta + n)^2} E[(X - n\theta)$$

$$+ (\alpha - \alpha\theta - \beta\theta) | \theta]^2$$

$$= \frac{1}{(\alpha + \beta + n)^2} \{E[(X - n\theta)^2 | \theta]$$

$$+ (\alpha - \alpha\theta - \beta\theta)^2\}$$

Since $E[X | \theta] = n\theta, V(X | \theta) = n\theta(1 - \theta)$, the risk is

$$\frac{1}{(\alpha + \beta + n)^2} \{\alpha^2 + \theta[n - 2\alpha(\alpha + \beta)] + \theta^2[(\alpha + \beta)^2 - n]\}$$

To compute the Bayes risk, we must now take the expectation of this risk over the distribution of Θ. The Bayes risk may also be found by reversing the order of the operations.

CHAPTER FOUR

Methods of estimation

4.1 Introduction

The practical man may entertain some misgivings about the methods discussed in the last two chapters. Bayesian point estimation appears to be very flexible, but if there is no secure basis for a particular prior distribution and only a sketchy idea of the loss function, is there not a danger of drawing misleading conclusions? As to the principle of best unbiased estimation, he might complain that sufficient statistics are sometimes excessively numerous or possess incomplete distributions (these last objections are illustrated in the following two examples). There is a clear demand for routine procedures, of wide applicability, which will (generally) produce unique estimators. Such estimators should, in some sense, be 'good'. However, we might be prepared to sacrifice some degree of optimality in small samples, provided efficiency tended to be high in large samples. Two well-established routines are discussed in this chapter.

Example 1. For the Cauchy distribution, $f(x|\theta) = \dfrac{1}{\pi[1 + (x - \theta)^2]}$, there is only one parameter to estimate for which there is no single sufficient statistic. The distribution is symmetric about θ, which is its median. The sample median is an unbiased estimator of θ with variance approximately $\pi^2/4n, n > 1$. The Cramér lower bound is $2/n$, so that the efficiency is about 80 per cent.

Example 2. A multinomial distribution has four categories for which the probabilities are

$$p_1 = (2 + \theta)/4, \qquad p_2 = p_3 = (1 - \theta)/4, \qquad p_4 = \theta/4$$

The sample yields a_i in category $i (i = 1, \ldots, 4)$ the probability of which is

$$\frac{n!}{a_1! a_2! a_3! a_4!} \left(\frac{2 + \theta}{4}\right)^{a_1} \left(\frac{1 - \theta}{4}\right)^{a_2 + a_3} \left(\frac{\theta}{4}\right)^{a_4},$$

$$a_4 = n - a_1 - a_2 - a_3$$

This is a function of $\theta, a_1, a_2 + a_3$, so $(A_1, A_2 + A_3)$ are jointly sufficient for θ. It is readily verified that $(4A_1/n) - 2, 1 - 2(A_2 + A_3)/n$ are different unbiased estimators of θ.

4.2 Maximum likelihood estimation

The *method of maximum likelihood* is of wide applicability and is relatively unhindered by the considerations raised in Examples 1 and 2. Suppose then that X has probability density function $f(x | \theta)$. For a random sample the joint density is

$$f(x_1, x_2, \ldots, x_n | \theta) = \prod_1^n f(x_i | \theta)$$

For fixed $x_1, x_2, \ldots, x_n$, the joint density, regarded as a function of θ, will be termed the *likelihood* and denoted $L(x_1, x_2, \ldots, x_n, \theta)$. The maximum likelihood estimate (m.l.e) of θ is that value, $\hat{\theta}$, such that

$$L(x_1, x_2, \ldots, x_n, \hat{\theta}) \geqslant L(x_1, x_2, \ldots, x_n, \theta)$$

for all other values of θ.

It is hard to pin down the intuitive basis for this estimator. Its merits ultimately are seen in large samples. For a discrete distribution we appear to say 'choose that value of θ which maximizes the probability of drawing just the sample actually obtained'.

For a continuous distribution, roughly speaking, θ is chosen to maximize the probability that the sample values are simultaneously close to the obtained values. Now the Bayesian is itching to turn the argument the other way up. It is not, he might declare, a matter for maximizing the (local) probability of the sample values but rather of seeking the most probable values of θ in the light of the sample. The points of view are not totally in conflict – for the posterior distribution of Θ is related to the likelihood through the equation (where x denotes the sample values)

$$g(\theta | x) \propto L(x | \theta) g(\theta)$$

To maximize $g(\theta | x)$ for fixed x we should maximize the product $L(x | \theta) g(\theta)$. But it may be that either:

(a) the prior distribution varies little with θ – corresponding to vague prior information; or

(b) the sample is so large that its contribution swamps the prior information. In such cases we are effectively maximizing $L(x|\theta)$.

Example 3. If $X_1, X_2, \ldots, X_n$ is a random sample from $N(\theta, \sigma_0^2)$ and Θ has the prior distribution $N(\mu, \sigma_1^2)$, then the posterior distribution of Θ is also normal with mean

$$\frac{\mu\sigma_0^2 + n\bar{x}\sigma_1^2}{\sigma_0^2 + n\sigma_1^2}, \qquad \sigma_0, \sigma_1, \mu \text{ known}$$

and from symmetry, this is the point of highest posterior density.

(a) If $\sigma_1 \to \infty$, corresponding to vague prior information, the mean $\to \bar{x}$.

(b) Even if σ_1 is not large, if $n \to \infty$, the posterior mean $\to \bar{x}$.

But $L(x|\theta) = \prod_1^n \frac{1}{\sqrt{(2\pi)}\sigma_0} \exp[-\tfrac{1}{2}(x_i - \theta)^2/\sigma_0^2]$

$$= \left(\frac{1}{\sqrt{(2\pi)}\sigma_0}\right)^n \exp\left\{-\tfrac{1}{2}\left[\sum_1^n (x_i - \bar{x})^2 + n(\bar{x} - \theta)^2\right]\bigg/\sigma_0^2\right\}$$

and is clearly maximized when $\theta = \bar{x}$.

4.3 Locating the maximum likelihood estimator

In many instances, the ordinary calculus methods will serve. The problems of manipulation are generally eased by examining the logarithm of the likelihood. The equation

$$\frac{\partial \log L}{\partial \theta} = 0$$

is the *likelihood equation*.

Example 4. $X_1, X_2, \ldots, X_n$ is a random sample from the Poisson distribution with parameter θ.

$$L(x_1, x_2, \ldots, x_n, \theta) = \prod_1^n \theta^{x_i} \exp(-\theta)/x_i!$$

$$\log L = \sum_1^n x_i \log \theta - n\theta - \sum_1^n \log x_i!$$

$$\frac{\partial \log L}{\partial \theta} = \frac{\sum_1^n x_i}{\theta} - n = \frac{n}{\theta}(\bar{x} - \theta)$$

There is one turning value, at $\theta = \bar{x}$, which is clearly a maximum. Thus $\bar{X}$ is the maximum likelihood estimator. It happens to be unbiased – in fact, it is an m.v.u.e.

Exercise 1.   Confirm the maximum likelihood estimate (m.l.e.) for θ, given a random sample of n from the following distributions:

(a) $f(x|\theta) = (1 - \theta)^{x-1}\theta$, $x = 1, 2, \ldots, 0 < \theta < 1$.

$\hat{\theta} = \dfrac{1}{\bar{x}}$.   Show that $\hat{\Theta}$ is biased.

(b) $f(x|\theta) = \dfrac{1}{\sqrt{(2\pi)}\sigma_0} \exp\left[-\tfrac{1}{2}(x - \theta)^2/\sigma_0^2\right]$, σ_0 known.

$\hat{\theta} = \bar{x}$.   State the distribution of $\hat{\Theta}$.

(c) $f(x|\theta) = \dfrac{1}{\sqrt{(2\pi\theta)}} \exp\left[-\tfrac{1}{2}(x - \mu_0)^2/\theta\right]$, μ_0 known.

$\hat{\theta} = \displaystyle\sum_1^n (x_i - \mu_0)^2/n$

(d) $f(x|\theta) = \theta(\theta x)^{\alpha - 1} \exp(-\theta x)/\Gamma(\alpha)$,

$\hat{\theta} = \dfrac{n\alpha}{\sum x_i}$. Show that $E(\hat{\Theta}) = n\alpha\theta/(n\alpha - 1)$

(e) $f(x|\theta) = \theta x^{\theta - 1}$, $0 < x < 1$.

$1/\hat{\theta} = -\displaystyle\sum_1^n (\log x_i)/n$.   Calculate $E(1/\hat{\Theta})$.

4.4 Estimation of a function of a parameter

If $\hat{\theta}$ is the m.l.e. of θ, what is the m.l.e. of $\phi(\theta)$? If $\phi(\theta)$ has a unique inverse, then clearly the likelihood given $\phi(\theta)$ is the likelihood given θ and the maximum likelihood estimator of $\phi(\theta)$ is that same function of the maximum likelihood estimator of θ. If, however, ϕ does *not* have a unique inverse, it is no longer clear how the likelihood, given $\phi(\theta) = \tau$, is to be defined. If we insist that this is to be the maximum of the likelihood over those θ such that $\phi(\theta) = \tau$, then once again the m.l.e. of $\phi(\theta)$ is $\phi(\hat{\theta})$.

Example 5. In Exercise 1(*b*), the m.l.e. of θ^2 is $\bar{x}^2$. In (*d*), the m.l.e. of $1/\theta$ is $\sum x_i/n\alpha$.

If a single sufficient statistic, T, exists for θ, then the likelihood must factorize in the form $h(t\,|\,\theta)g(x_1,x_2,\ldots,x_n)$. Since $g(x_1,x_2,\ldots,x_n)$ does not contain θ, we have to maximize $h(t\,|\,\theta)$ for variation in θ and $\hat{\theta}$ is a function of t.

Exercise 2. If the regularity conditions for the Cramér lower bound are satisfied for some $\phi(\theta)$, then (see Chapter 2),

$$\frac{\partial \log L}{\partial \theta} = k(\theta)[t - \phi(\theta)]$$

where $V(T) = \phi'(\theta)/k(\theta)$. Show that

$$\left[\frac{\partial^2 \log L}{\partial \theta^2}\right]_{\hat{\theta}} = \left[- k^2(\theta)V(T)\right]_{\hat{\theta}}.$$

Deduce that any turning value is a local maximum and hence there is only one such.

If the domain in which the probability density function is positive actually depends on the parameter, then the maximum of the likelihood may not occur at a turning value.

Example 6. If X is uniformly distributed over $[k\theta, (k+1)\theta]$, $k > 0, \theta > 0$, then for a random sample of size n the likelihood is $1/\theta^n$, $k\theta < x_i < (k+1)\theta$. It is decreasing with θ, hence the likelihood is a maximum when θ is a minimum. But $k\theta \leqslant \min[x_1,x_2,\ldots,x_n] \leqslant \max[x_1,x_2,\ldots,x_n] \leqslant (k+1)\theta$, or

$$\frac{y_n}{k+1} < \theta < \frac{y_1}{k} \qquad y_1 = \min(x_i), y_n = \max(x_i)$$

so that $\hat{\theta} = y_n/(k+1)$. In this case $\hat{\Theta}$ is not sufficient for θ. The limiting case $k \to 0$ yields y_n as the m.l.e.

Exercise 3. For a random sample of size n from the distribution with p.d.f. $f(x\,|\,\theta) = \exp(\theta - x), x > \theta$, the m.l.e. is $\min[x_1,x_2,\ldots,x_n]$.

Exercise 4. For a random sample, from the uniform distribution over $(\theta - \frac{1}{2}, \theta + \frac{1}{2})$, show that the likelihood is constant. Any statistic which satisfies the boundary conditions is a m.l.e. That is, $\max(x_i) - \frac{1}{2} < \hat{\theta} < \min(x_i) + \frac{1}{2}$.

There may also be a restriction on the domain of the parameter so that the statistic which is to be the estimator is not always the same function of the observations.

Example 7. For a random sample of size n from the distribution $N(\theta, 1)$, when it is known that $\theta \geq 0$, we have

$$\frac{\partial \log L}{d\theta} = n(\bar{x} - \theta)$$

Thus, if $\bar{x} > 0$, there is a turning value at $\theta = \bar{x}$ but if $\bar{x} < 0$ the slope is negative and θ is chosen to be a minimum, i.e., zero. Hence $\hat{\theta} = \max(0, \bar{x})$.

Further difficulties arise if the likelihood is continuous but its derivative is not. The maximum then may occur at a 'spike'. Such a case is outlined in the next exercise.

Exercise 5. Consider a random sample of three from the distribution for which $f(x|\theta) = \frac{1}{2}\exp[-|x-\theta|]$, $-\infty < x < +\infty$. Show that for the log-likelihood, the slope is $+3$ if $\theta < x_{(1)}$, $+1$ if $x_{(1)} < \theta < x_{(2)}$, -1 if $x_{(2)} < \theta < x_{(3)}$, -3 if $x_{(3)} < \theta$. So the maximum is attained for $\theta = x_{(2)}$. In general, for a sample of n, the maximum likelihood estimate is the sample median. For $n = 2m$, this is not unique, by convention the average of $x_{(m)}, x_{(m+1)}$ is taken.

4.5 Truncation and censoring

It may happen, either by accident or design, that information about some of the sample values is incomplete.

In *truncation*, values which fall outside the interval (a, b) cannot be observed. We are obliged to argue conditionally on the n observations which fall in the interval. The p.d.f. of the truncated distribution is $f(x|\theta)/[\Pr(a \leq X \leq b)]$ where $f(x|\theta)$ is the original p.d.f.

Example 8. A random sample is drawn from a Poisson distribution but the zero values are not recorded. The distribution is said to be truncated at the origin and has accordingly p.d.f.

$$\frac{\theta^x \exp(-\theta)}{x![1 - \exp(-\theta)]}, \qquad x = 1, 2, \ldots$$

whence $L(x_1, x_2, \ldots, x_n, \theta) = \dfrac{\theta^{\Sigma x_i} \exp(-n\theta)}{\prod_1^n x_i! [1 - \exp(-\theta)]^n}$

$\dfrac{\partial \log L}{\partial \theta} = \dfrac{n\bar{x}}{\theta} - \dfrac{n}{1 - \exp(-\theta)}$, and $\hat{\theta}$ satisfies

$\dfrac{\hat{\theta}}{1 - \exp(-\hat{\theta})} = \bar{x}$

Exercise 6. A random sample is drawn from the exponential distribution, with parameter θ, which is truncated on the right at x_0. That is, n values less than x_o are recorded, but the number in excess of x_0 is not known. Show that the m.l.e. of θ satisfies

$$\frac{1}{\hat{\theta}} = \bar{x} + \frac{x_0 \exp(-\hat{\theta} x_0)}{1 - \exp(-\hat{\theta} x_0)}$$

A closely related practice is to *censor* the sample values and record the number which fall outside the censoring points. This process may be carried out either with fixed censoring points or points determined by a fixed proportion of the observations.

Example 9. The time to failure of an electric lamp is exponential with parameter θ. A sample of $n + m$ such new lamps are switched on at time $x = 0$ and the actual failure times are recorded provided they fail before the fixed time x_0, when it is noticed that m lamps are still burning. The likelihood consists of the product of two parts. The first part corresponds to the probability density of the first n order statistics, $Y_1, Y_2, \ldots, Y_n$, from an exponential distribution truncated at x_0. The second part corresponds to the probability that precisely m out of $n + m$ lamps last longer than x_0.

$$L = \frac{n! \, \theta^n \exp\left(-\theta \sum_1^n y_i\right)}{[1 - \exp(-\theta x_0)]^n} \times \binom{n+m}{n} [1 - \exp(-\theta x_0)]^n \exp(-m\theta x_0)$$

$$\frac{\partial \log L}{\partial \theta} = \frac{n}{\theta} - \sum_1^n y_i - m x_0$$

$$\hat{\theta} = \frac{n}{\sum_1^n y_i + m x_0}$$

In this form of censoring, n is a random variable.

Exercise 7. In Example 9, let the censoring time be the instant that the nth lamp fails. Show that the maximum likelihood estimate of θ is

$$\frac{n}{\sum\limits_1^n y_i + m y_n}$$

In this form, the censoring point is a random variable.

4.6 Estimation of several parameters

More generally if $X_1, X_2, \ldots, X_n$ is a random sample from a distribution with probability density function $f(x \mid \theta_1, \theta_2, \ldots, \theta_k)$ then the maximum likelihood estimators $\hat{\theta}_i$, $i = 1, 2, \ldots, k$ satisfy

$$L(x_1, x_2, \ldots, x_n, \hat{\theta}_1, \hat{\theta}_2, \ldots, \hat{\theta}_k) \geqslant L(x_1, x_2, \ldots, x_n, \theta_1, \theta_2, \ldots, \theta_k),$$

in which the sample values are permitted to be vectors of observations. We record, from standard results in the calculus, that if $\hat{\theta}_1, \hat{\theta}_2, \ldots, \hat{\theta}_k$ determine a turning value in $\log L$, that is, if

$$\left[\frac{\partial \log L}{\partial \theta_i}\right]_{\theta_1, \theta_2, \ldots, \hat{\theta}_k} = 0, \qquad i = 1, 2, \ldots k,$$

then the turning value will be a maximum if the matrix with entries

$$\left[-\frac{\partial^2 \log L}{\partial \theta_i \partial \theta_j}\right]_{\hat{\theta}_1, \hat{\theta}_2, \ldots, \hat{\theta}_k} \qquad , i, j = 1, 2, \ldots, k$$

is positive definite. In the frequent case when $k = 2$ this requires

$$\left[\frac{\partial^2 \log L}{\partial \theta_1^2}\right]_{\hat{\theta}_1, \hat{\theta}_2} < 0,$$

$$\left[\frac{\partial^2 \log L}{\partial \theta_2^2}\right]_{\hat{\theta}_1, \hat{\theta}_2} < 0$$

$$\left[\left(\frac{\partial^2 \log L}{\partial \theta_1^2}\right)\left(\frac{\partial^2 \log L}{\partial \theta_2^2}\right)\right]_{\hat{\theta}_1, \hat{\theta}_2} > \left(\frac{\partial^2 \log L}{\partial \theta_1 \partial \theta_2}\right)^2_{\hat{\theta}_1, \hat{\theta}_2}$$

Example 10. $X_1, X_2, \ldots, X_n$ is a random sample from the distribution $N(\theta_1, \theta_2)$

$$L(x_1, x_2, \ldots, x_n, \theta_1, \theta_2) = \frac{1}{(2\pi\theta_2)^{n/2}} \exp\left[-\frac{1}{2}\sum_1^n (x_i - \theta_1)^2/\theta_2\right]$$

$$\log L = -n\log\sqrt{(2\pi\theta_2)} - \frac{1}{2}\sum_1^n (x_i - \theta_1)^2/\theta_2$$

$$\frac{\partial \log L}{\partial \theta_1} = \frac{n(\bar{x} - \theta_1)}{\theta_2}$$

$$\frac{\partial \log L}{\partial \theta_2} = -\frac{n}{2\theta_2} + \frac{\sum(x_i - \theta_1)^2}{2\theta_2^2}$$

The only turning value happens at $\hat{\theta}_1 = \bar{x}, \hat{\theta}_2 = \sum(x_i - \bar{x})^2/n$.

Now $\dfrac{\partial^2 \log L}{\partial \theta_1^2} = -\dfrac{n}{\theta_2} < 0$, $\dfrac{\partial^2 \log L}{\partial \theta_2^2}\bigg]_{\hat{\theta}_1, \hat{\theta}_2} = \left[+\dfrac{n}{2\theta_2^2} - \dfrac{\sum(x_i - \theta_1)}{\theta_2^3}\right]_{\hat{\theta}_1, \hat{\theta}_2}$

$= -\dfrac{n}{2\hat{\theta}_2^2} < 0$, while $\left[\dfrac{\partial^2 \log L}{\partial \theta_1 \partial \theta_2}\right]_{\hat{\theta}_1, \hat{\theta}_2} = 0$

So that $\hat{\theta}_1, \hat{\theta}_2$ are indeed the maximum likelihood estimates.

Example 11. The joint distribution of the discrete random variables U, V is trinomial with parameters m, θ_1, θ_2. If (U_1, V_1), $(U_2, V_2), \ldots, (U_n, V_n)$ is a random sample of n pairs of values from this distribution, find the maximum likelihood estimates of θ_1, θ_2.

$$L[(u_1, v_1), (u_2, v_2), \ldots, (u_n, v_n), \theta_1, \theta_2]$$

$$= \prod_1^n \frac{m!}{u_i!\,v_i!\,(m - u_i - v_i)!}\theta_1^{u_i}\theta_2^{v_i}(1 - \theta_1 - \theta_2)^{m - u_i - v_i}$$

$$\propto \theta_1^{\Sigma u_i}\theta_2^{\Sigma v_i}(1 - \theta_1 - \theta_2)^{nm - \Sigma u_i - \Sigma v_i}$$

$$\frac{\partial \log L}{\partial \theta_1} = \frac{\sum u_i}{\theta_1} - \frac{nm - \sum u_i - \sum v_i}{1 - \theta_1 - \theta_2}$$

$$\frac{\partial \log L}{\partial \theta_2} = \frac{\sum v_i}{\theta_2} - \frac{nm - \sum u_i - \sum v_i}{1 - \theta_1 - \theta_2}$$

Hence at a turning value, $\dfrac{\sum u_i}{\hat{\theta}_1} = \dfrac{\sum v_i}{\hat{\theta}_2}$,

whence $\hat{\theta}_1 = \sum_1^n u_i/nm$, $\qquad \hat{\theta}_2 = \sum_1^n v_i/nm$.

Exercise 8. For Example 11, verify that the turning value corresponds to a maximum. Show that the estimators are unbiased and consistent.

Exercise 9. If $(U_1, V_1), (U_2, V_2), \ldots, (U_n, V_n)$ is a random sample of n pairs from the bivariate normal distribution $N(0, 0, \sigma_1^2, \sigma_2^2, \rho)$, show that $\hat{\sigma}_1^2 = \sum u_i^2/n$, $\hat{\sigma}_2^2 = \sum v_i^2/n$, $\hat{\rho} = \sum u_i v_i / n \hat{\sigma}_1 \hat{\sigma}_2$.

Exercise 10. Given a random sample of size n from the exponential distribution with parameter θ_1 and an independent random sample of n from another exponential distribution with parameter $\theta_1 \theta_2$, find the maximum likelihood estimates of θ_1, θ_2. [Ans. $\hat{\theta}_1 = 1/\bar{x}, \hat{\theta}_2 = \bar{x}/\bar{y}$.]

Example 12. For a random sample from the uniform distribution over $(\theta_1 - \theta_2, \theta_1 + \theta_2), \theta_2 > 0$, the likelihood is

$$\left(\frac{1}{2\theta_2}\right)^n$$

and is large when θ_2 is small. However, since

$$\theta_1 - \theta_2 \leqslant x_i \leqslant \theta_1 + \theta_2, \qquad i = 1, 2, \ldots, n$$

then $\qquad \theta_1 - \theta_2 \leqslant y_1 \leqslant y_n \leqslant \theta_1 + \theta_2$

where $\qquad y_1 = \min[x_i], y_n = \max[x_i]$. That is,

$$\theta_2 \geqslant \theta_1 - y_1 \text{ and } \theta_2 \geqslant y_n - \theta_1$$

$$\Rightarrow \theta_2 \geqslant \max[\theta_1 - y_1, y_n - \theta_1]$$

$$\hat{\theta}_2 = \min_{\theta_1}[\max(\theta_1 - y_1, y_n - \theta_1)]$$

$\max[\theta_1 - y_1, y_n - \theta_1]$ is minimized when $\theta_1 - y_1 = y_n - \theta_1$ or $\hat{\theta}_1 = (y_1 + y_n)/2$, whence $\hat{\theta}_2 = (y_n - y_1)/2$.

4.7 Approximation techniques

Our remarks in this section will be brief, since the subject matter really belongs to the field of numerical analysis. On some occasions, the likelihood equation has not yielded an explicit solution for the maximum likelihood estimator. Thus for the truncated Poisson distribution, $\hat{\theta}$ must satisfy $\theta = \bar{x}[1 - \exp(-\theta)]$. Either tables or graphical techniques will provide a good approximate root, but we may be willing to put some effort into improving it. One standard method for solving $\theta = g(\theta)$ is the iteration process, in which if θ_r is the rth approximation, then θ_{r+1} is defined as $g(\theta_r)$. If this sequence converges, then it does so to one of the roots. If in an interval containing a root, we have $|g'(\theta)| < 1$, then provided the first approximate root, θ_1, lies in that interval, the process will converge to that particular root. For the truncated Poisson distribution with $g(\theta) = \bar{x}[1 - \exp(-\theta)]$, we have $g'(\theta) = \bar{x}e^{-\theta}$. Since $\bar{x} \geqslant 1$, if $\theta_1 = \bar{x}, |\bar{x}\exp(-\bar{x})| < 1$ and the sequence converges to $\hat{\theta}$ (and not to the unwanted second root, $\theta = 0$).

Suppose it is required to find a root of $g(\theta) = 0$. A popular iteration process for this problem defines θ_{r+1}, the $(r+1)$th approximation, as

$$\theta_r - g(\theta_r)/g'(\theta_r)$$

If the sequence converges, say, to θ^* and $g'(\theta^*) \neq 0$, then evidently $g(\theta^*) = 0$.

Exercise 11. Find the equation of the tangent to the curve $g(\theta)$ at the point $[\theta_r, g(\theta_r)]$. Show that the tangent meets the θ axis at the point $[\theta_{r+1}, 0]$, where

$$\theta_{r+1} = \theta_r - g(\theta_r)/g'(\theta_r)$$

In maximum likelihood estimation, we are trying to solve the likelihood equation $\partial \log L/\partial \theta = 0$. Using the above iteration formula we have

$$\hat{\theta}_{r+1} = \hat{\theta}_r - \left[\frac{\partial \log L}{\partial \theta}\right]_{\hat{\theta}_r} \Big/ \left[\frac{\partial^2 \log L}{\partial \theta^2}\right]_{\hat{\theta}_r}$$

The iteration is not likely to converge to the wrong root, since for a large sample, the likelihood tends to a unique solution (which is consistent). This is little consolation if we do not start near enough to the root, for then the processes may not converge at all. One possibility is to commence with the value of a consistent estimator.

Example 13. For the Poisson distribution truncated at the origin, the initial estimator $\bar{X}$ is not consistent; indeed $E(\bar{X}) = \theta / [1 - \exp(-\theta)]$. Let N_1 be the number of sample values which are equal to 1. Then $E[N_1/n] = \Pr[X = 1 | X \geqslant 1] = \theta \exp(-\theta) / [1 - \exp(-\theta)]$. Hence $E(\bar{X} - N_1/n) = \theta$. We take $\hat{\theta}_1 = \bar{x} - n_1/n$.

The variance of the estimator tends to zero for large n.

$$\left[\frac{\partial \log L}{\partial \theta} \right]_{\hat{\theta}_1} = \left[\frac{n\bar{x}}{\theta} - \frac{n}{1 - \exp(-\theta)} \right]_{\hat{\theta}_1}$$

$$\left[\frac{\partial^2 \log L}{\partial \theta^2} \right]_{\hat{\theta}_1} = \left[-\frac{n\bar{x}}{\theta^2} + \frac{n \exp(-\theta)}{[1 - \exp(-\theta)]^2} \right]_{\hat{\theta}_1}$$

the results are then substituted to obtain $\hat{\theta}_2$.

In some cases, $\left[\dfrac{\partial^2 \log L}{\partial \theta^2} \right]_{\hat{\theta}_r}$ will prove a cumbersome calculation. But, for a random sample of size n,

$$\frac{\partial^2 \log L}{\partial \theta^2} = n \left[\frac{\sum \dfrac{\partial^2}{\partial \theta^2} \log f(X_i | \theta)}{n} \right]$$

For large n, the sample mean of the $\dfrac{\partial^2}{\partial \theta^2} \log f(X_i | \theta)$ tends to $E\left[\dfrac{\partial^2}{\partial \theta^2} \log f(X | \theta) \right]$. Hence, for a large sample, we approximate $-1 \Big/ \dfrac{\partial^2 \log L}{\partial \theta^2}$ by $-1 \Big/ E\left[\dfrac{\partial^2 \log L}{\partial \theta^2} \right]$.

Under suitable regularity conditions, the last expression is the minimum-variance bound for unbiased estimators of θ. It may be that the m.v.b. does not depend on θ at all. This is the happy circumstance in Example 14. Generally the m.v.b. will contain θ and will have to be replaced by the current trial value. The resulting expression will be simpler then $-1 \Big/ \left[\dfrac{\partial^2 \log L}{\partial \theta^2} \right]_{\hat{\theta}_r}$ itself [see Exercise 12].

Example 14.   For a random sample from the Cauchy distribution, $f(x | \theta) = 1/\pi\{1 + (x - \theta)^2\}$, the likelihood equation is

$$\frac{\partial \log L}{\partial \theta} = 2 \sum_1^n \left[\frac{x_i - \theta}{1 + (x_i - \theta)^2} \right] = 0$$

The minimum-variance bound for unbiased estimators of θ is $2/n$. The sample median, M, is a consistent estimator of θ with fairly high efficiency, so if $\hat{\theta}_1 = m$,

$$\hat{\theta}_2 = m + \frac{2}{n} \left[\frac{\partial \log L}{\partial \theta} \right]_{\theta = m}$$

Exercise 12. For Example 2, show that:
(a) the maximum likelihood estimate satisfies

$$\frac{a_1}{2+\hat{\theta}} - \frac{(a_1+a_2)}{1-\hat{\theta}} + \frac{a_4}{\hat{\theta}} = 0;$$

(b) the m.v.b. for unbiased estimators of θ is

$$\frac{2\theta(1-\theta)(2+\theta)}{n(1+2\theta)};$$

(c) $(A_1 + A_4 - A_2 - A_3)/n$ is a consistent estimator of θ.
  Hence set up an iterative process for computing the maximum likelihood estimate.

4.8 Large-sample properties

First a few remarks about limiting distributions. If $\bar{X}_n$ is the mean of a random sample from the distribution $N(\mu,\sigma^2)$, then $\bar{X}_n$ is itself exactly distributed $N(\mu,\sigma^2/n)$. As $n \to \infty$, $\bar{X}_n$ has a limiting distribution which is degenerate. However $Z_n = \sqrt{n}(\bar{X}_n - \mu)/\sigma$ has exactly the distribution $N(0,1)$ for every n. If $\bar{X}_n$ is the mean of a random sample from any distribution with expectation μ and variance σ^2, then $Z_n = \sqrt{n}(\bar{X}_n - \mu)/\sigma$ has expectation zero and variance one for every n. Moreover, by the central limit theorem, the limiting distribution of Z_n is $N(0,1)$. We shall say that $\bar{X}_n$ is asymptotically distributed $N(\mu,\sigma^2/n)$, or, with a slight abuse of language, that $\bar{X}_n$ is approximately distributed $N(\mu,\sigma^2/n)$ for large n. For the exponential distribution with parameter θ, $E(\bar{X}_n) = 1/\theta$, $V(\bar{X}_n) = 1/(n\theta^2)$, hence $\bar{X}_n$ is asymptotically distributed $N[1/\theta, 1/(n\theta^2)]$. Now for the same distribution, $1/\bar{X}_n$ has expectation $n\theta/(n-1)$ and variance $(n\theta)^2/[(n-2)(n-1)^2]$ so that we (correctly) suppose that

$$\frac{\dfrac{1}{\bar{X}_n} - \dfrac{n\theta}{n-1}}{\dfrac{n\theta}{(n-1)\sqrt{(n-2)}}} = \frac{\dfrac{n-1}{n\bar{X}_n} - \theta}{\dfrac{\theta}{\sqrt{(n-2)}}}$$

has the limiting distribution $N(0,1)$. However it is also the case that

$$\frac{\dfrac{1}{\bar{X}_n} - \theta}{\dfrac{\theta}{\sqrt{(n)}}}$$

has the limiting distribution $N(0, 1)$ and we should then claim that $1/\bar{X}_n$ is asymptotically distributed $N(\theta, \theta^2/n)$. There is no contradiction, only a reflection of the fact that the limit of the expectation of $1/\bar{X}$ is θ and that the ratio of the variance of $1/\bar{X}_n$ to $\theta^2/n \to 1$ as $n \to \infty$. Not all limiting distributions are normal. For instance, if Y_1 is the minimum of a random sample from the uniform distribution over $(0, 1)$ then

$$\Pr(nY_1 > t) = \Pr(Y_1 > t/n) = (1 - t/n)^n \to \exp(-t) \text{ as } n \to \infty.$$

Hence the asymptotic distribution of nY_1 is exponential. (For further comment on these and other vexing points, consult *Theoretical Statistics* by Cox and Hinkley).

The chief justification for the method of maximum likelihood lies in its near-optimal properties for large samples. For a random sample from a distribution which satisfies certain conditions, the maximum likelihood estimators are consistent, asymptotically efficient and have a joint distribution which is asymptotically multivariate normal. The discussion of the analytic details lies outside the level of this text. (Kendall and Stuart, *The Advanced Theory of Statistics*, should be consulted for further details — see 'Further readings'.)

The multivariate normal distribution in question has the following properties:

(*a*) Its vector of means is equal to the vector of the true parameter values.

(*b*) Its covariance matrix, **V**, is such that the (i, j)th element of the inverse matrix, $\mathbf{V}^{-1}$, is

$$- E\left[\frac{\partial^2 \log L}{\partial \theta_i \partial \theta_j} \right], \; i, j = 1, 2, \ldots, k$$

where k is the number of parameters.

Thus if there is only one parameter, θ, then $\hat{\Theta}$ is approximately normally distributed with mean θ, the true value of the parameter, and variance

$$- 1 \bigg/ E\left[\frac{\partial^2 \log L}{\partial \theta^2} \right]$$

If there are two parameters, θ_1, θ_2, then $\hat{\Theta}_1, \hat{\Theta}_2$ have an approximate bivariate normal distribution with means θ_1, θ_2, the true values of the parameters, and matrix of covariances

$$\begin{pmatrix} v_{11} & v_{12} \\ v_{21} & v_{22} \end{pmatrix} = \begin{pmatrix} -E\left[\dfrac{\partial^2 \log L}{\partial \theta_1^2}\right] & -E\left[\dfrac{\partial^2 \log L}{\partial \theta_1 \partial \theta_2}\right] \\ -E\left[\dfrac{\partial^2 \log L}{\partial \theta_2 \partial \theta_1}\right] & -E\left[\dfrac{\partial^2 \log L}{\partial \theta_2^2}\right] \end{pmatrix}^{-1}$$

Example 15. $X_1, X_2, \ldots, X_n$ is a random sample from $N(0, \sigma^2)$.

$$\frac{\partial \log L}{\partial \sigma} = -\frac{n}{\sigma} + \frac{\sum x_i^2}{\sigma^3}, \qquad \text{whence } \hat{\sigma} = \sqrt{\left[\frac{\sum x_i^2}{n}\right]}$$

$$\frac{\partial^2 \log L}{\partial \sigma^2} = \frac{n}{\sigma^2} - \frac{3\sum x_i^2}{\sigma^4}, \qquad -E\left[\frac{\partial^2 \log L}{\partial \sigma^2}\right] = \frac{2n}{\sigma^2}$$

Thus, for large n, the estimator is approximately distributed $N(\sigma, \sigma^2/2n)$. On the other hand, if we regard $\sigma^2 = \theta$ as the parameter,

$$\frac{\partial \log L}{\partial \theta} = -\frac{n}{2\theta} + \frac{\sum x_i^2}{2\theta^2}, \qquad \text{whence } \hat{\theta} = \frac{\sum x_i^2}{n}$$

$$\frac{\partial^2 \log L}{\partial \theta^2} = \frac{n}{2\theta^2} - \frac{\sum x_i^2}{\theta^3}, \qquad -E\left[\frac{\partial^2 \log L}{\partial \theta^2}\right] = -\frac{n}{2\theta^2} + \frac{n\theta}{\theta^3} = \frac{n}{2\theta^2}$$

So that, for large n, the estimator is approximately distributed $N(\sigma^2, 2\sigma^4/n)$.

Example 16. $X_1, X_2, \ldots, X_n$ is a random sample from $N(\theta_1, \theta_2)$.

$$\frac{\partial \log L}{\partial \theta_1} = \frac{n(\bar{x} - \theta_1)}{\theta_2}, \qquad \frac{\partial \log L}{\partial \theta_2} = -\frac{n}{2\theta_2} + \frac{\sum(x_i - \theta_1)^2}{2\theta_2^2}$$

$$\frac{\partial^2 \log L}{\partial \theta_1^2} = -\frac{n}{\theta_2}, \qquad \frac{\partial^2 \log L}{\partial \theta_2^2} = \frac{n}{2\theta_2^2} - \frac{\sum(x_i - \theta_1)^2}{\theta_2^3}$$

$$-E\left[\frac{\partial^2 \log L}{\partial \theta_1^2}\right] = \frac{n}{\theta_2}, \qquad -E\left[\frac{\partial^2 \log L}{\partial \theta_2^2}\right] = \frac{n}{2\theta_2^2}$$

$$-E\left[\frac{\partial^2 \log L}{\partial \theta_2 \partial \theta_1}\right] = +E\left[\frac{n(\bar{X} - \theta_1)}{\theta_2^2}\right] = 0$$

$$\mathbf{V} = \begin{pmatrix} n/\theta_2 & 0 \\ 0 & n/2\theta_2^2 \end{pmatrix}^{-1} = \begin{pmatrix} \theta_2/n & 0 \\ 0 & 2\theta_2^2/n \end{pmatrix}$$

Hence in the asymptotic distribution of

$$\hat{\Theta}_1 = \bar{X}, \hat{\Theta}_2 = \frac{\sum (X_i - \bar{X})^2}{n}, v_{11} = \theta_2/n, v_{22} = 2\theta_2^2/n, v_{12} = 0.$$

The regularity conditions will not obtain if the region in which the distribution has positive probability density depends on the parameters.

Example 17. For a random sample of size n from the distribution for which $f(x|\theta) = \exp(\theta - x)$, $x \geqslant \theta$, the maximum likelihood estimator is $T = \min[X_1, X_2, \ldots, X_n]$. Now the density of T is $g(t|\theta) = n\exp(n\theta - nt)$, $t \geqslant \theta$. It is true that $E[T] = \theta - 1/n \to \theta$, but the distribution of $T - \theta$ is exponential with parameter n and there is no approach to normality.

4.9 Method of least squares

The method of maximum likelihood chooses a distribution which makes the obtained sample values (locally) most probable. A weaker alternative is to suggest that the sample values are as near as possible, in some sense, to their expected values. The usual sense (classically) has been based on the ordinary Euclidean distance. Think of the sample values $x_1, x_2, \ldots, x_n$ as the co-ordinates of one point and their expected values $\mu_1, \mu_2, \ldots, \mu_n$ as the co-ordinates of another point, then the square of the distance between them is $\sum_{i=1}^{n} (x_i - \mu_i)^2$. If the μ_i can all be varied independently then this distance is zero when $\mu_i = x_i$. Much more interesting is any situation involving dependences between the μ_i. Not surprisingly, the process of minimizing $\sum_{i=1}^{n} (x_i - \mu_i)^2$, subject to any such constraints, is known as the *method of least squares*. The corresponding estimates are then *the least-squares estimates*. We shall assume, initially, that the random variables X_i are uncorrelated and each has variance σ^2. It is then natural that each term, $(x_i - \mu_i)^2$, should be given equal weight in the total sum of squares, $\sum_{i=1}^{n} (x_i - \mu_i)^2$.

Example 18. The strictest dependence between the μ_i is that they are all equal, say to θ. Since

$$\sum_{i=1}^{n} (x_i - \theta)^2 = \sum_{i=1}^{n} (x_i - \bar{x})^2 + n(\bar{x} - \theta)^2$$

the sum of squares is minimized when $\hat{\theta} = \bar{x}$. From elementary results, $E(\bar{X}) = \theta$, $V(\bar{X}) = \sigma^2/n$ and the expected minimum distance squared is $E\left[\sum_{i=1}^{n}(X_i - \bar{X})^2\right] = (n-1)\sigma^2$.

Without knowing the joint distribution of the sample values, the least-squares estimators have no claim on such properties as sufficiency and minimum variance. In Example 18, $\bar{X}$ is the best *linear* unbiased estimator (b.l.u.e.). For suppose $\sum_{i=1}^{n} a_i X_i$ is a linear combination of the sample values unbiased for θ. Then $E\left(\sum_{i=1}^{n} a_i X_i\right) = \theta \sum_{i=1}^{n} a_i \equiv \theta$ requires $\sum_{i=1}^{n} a_i = 1$. But $V\left[\sum_{i=1}^{n} a_i X_i\right] = \sigma^2 \sum_{i=1}^{n} a_i^2$ and since $\sum_{i=1}^{n}(a_i - \bar{a})^2 \geqslant 0$, $\sum_{i=1}^{n} a_i^2 \geqslant n\bar{a}^2$, with equality if and only if $a_i = \bar{a} = 1/n$. In general, calculus methods will be employed to effect any minimizations.

Example 19. $X_1, X_2, \ldots, X_n$ is a random sample from a distribution for which $E(X_i) = k_i\theta$, $V(X_i) = \sigma^2$. It is required to find the least-squares estimator of θ, if the k_i are known real constants.

$$d^2 = \sum_{i=1}^{n}(x_i - k_i\theta)^2$$

$$\frac{\partial d^2}{\partial \theta} = -2\sum_{i=1}^{n}(x_i - k_i\theta)k_i$$

There is a turning value at $\hat{\theta} = \sum_{i=1}^{n} k_i x_i \bigg/ \sum_{i=1}^{n} k_i^2$ corresponding to a minimum since the second derivative is $2\sum_{i=1}^{n} k_i^2 > 0$.

It is readily shown that $\hat{\Theta}$ is unbiased and has variance $\sigma^2 \bigg/ \sum_{i=1}^{n} k_i^2$. The next exercise shows that it is also a b.l.u.e.

Exercise 13. For Example 19, show that if $\sum_{i=1}^{n} a_i X_i = T$ is such that $E(T) = \theta$, then $\sum_{i=1}^{n} k_i a_i = 1$.

Apply Cauchy's inequality to show that

$$\left(\sum_{i=1}^{n} a_i^2\right)\left(\sum_{i=1}^{n} k_i^2\right) \geqslant 1$$

with equality if and only if $a_i = k_i \Big/ \sum_{i=1}^{n} k_i^2$.

Exercise 14. For Example 19, show that

$$\sum_{i=1}^{n} (x_i - k_i\theta)^2 = \sum_{i=1}^{n} (x_i - k_i\hat{\theta})^2 + \sum_{i=1}^{n} k_i^2(\hat{\theta} - \theta)^2.$$

Deduce that $E\left[\sum_{i=1}^{n} (X_i - k_i\hat{\Theta})^2\right] = (n-1)\sigma^2.$

Check that $\text{Cov}[X_i - k_i\hat{\Theta}, \hat{\Theta} - \theta] = 0.$

Exercise 15. For Example 19, if additionally it is known that the X_i are normally distributed, show that $\hat{\Theta}$ is also the maximum likelihood estimator of θ and is sufficient for θ. Show that the distribution of $X_i - k_i\hat{\Theta}$ is normal and does not depend on θ. Assume that $\sum_{i=1}^{n} (X_i - k_i\hat{\Theta})^2/\sigma^2$ is independent of $\hat{\Theta}$, and hence or otherwise has the χ_{n-1}^2 distribution. [Hint: consider the first equation in Exercise 14.] Finally, $(\hat{\Theta} - \theta)/\sqrt{[\sum(X_i - \hat{\Theta}k_i)^2/(n-1)\sum k_i^2]}$ has Student's t-distribution with n-1 degrees of freedom.

There are two ways of 'picturing' the method of least squares. If X_1, X_2, X_3 have expectations $k_1\theta, k_2\theta, k_3\theta$, then, in three-dimensional space, the points with co-ordinates $(k_1\theta, k_2\theta, k_3\theta)$ lie on a line through the origin. The shortest distance from the sample point (x_1, x_2, x_3) to the aforementioned line is attained by the foot of the perpendicular, with co-ordinates $(k_1\hat{\theta}, k_2\hat{\theta}, k_3\hat{\theta})$. The 'perpendicularity' is immediately expressible as

$$\sum_{1}^{3}(x_i - k_i\hat{\theta})k_i = 0$$

which is precisely the least-squares equation.

Alternatively, in two dimensions, let the ith sample value be represented by a point with co-ordinates $[k_i, x_i]$. The set of points $[k_i, k_i\theta]$ lie on a line through the origin with slope θ, and $\sum_{i=1}^{3} (x_i - k_i\theta)^2$ measures the sum of the squares of the vertical distances of the individual sample values from this line.

Thus, we may legitimately think of the process as finding the line of closest fit to the points (k_i, x_i) which passes through the origin. This latter restriction may be removed by considering a distribution such that $E(X_i) = \theta_1 + k_i \theta_2$. The sum of squares is

$$d^2 = \sum_{i=1}^{n} (x_i - \theta_1 - \theta_2 k_i)^2$$

which may be minimized with respect to θ_1, θ_2 by partial differentiation:

$$\frac{\partial d^2}{\partial \theta_1} = -2 \sum_{i=1}^{n} (x_i - \theta_1 - \theta_2 k_i)$$

$$\frac{\partial d^2}{\partial \theta_2} = -2 \sum_{i=1}^{n} (x_i - \theta_1 - \theta_2 k_i) k_i$$

After equating to zero and solving simultaneously we obtain

$$\hat{\theta}_2 = \frac{\sum_{i=1}^{n} [(x_i - \bar{x}) k_i]}{\sum_{i=1}^{n} [(k_i - \bar{k}) k_i]}$$

$$\hat{\theta}_1 = \bar{x} - \hat{\theta}_2 \bar{k}$$

Exercise 16. If the random variables $X_1, X_2, \ldots, X_n$ are uncorrelated, have common variance σ^2, and $E(X_i) = \theta_1 + k_i \theta_2$, then the least-squares estimators of θ_1, θ_2 can be written

$$\hat{\Theta}_2 = \frac{\sum_{i=1}^{n} (X_i - \bar{X})(k_i - \bar{k})}{\sum_{i=1}^{n} (k_i - \bar{k})^2}$$

$$\hat{\Theta}_1 = \bar{X} - \hat{\Theta}_2 \bar{k}$$

Show that:

(a) $E(\hat{\Theta}_2) = \theta_2, \quad V(\hat{\Theta}_2) = \sigma^2 \left/ \left[\sum_{i=1}^{n} (k_i - \bar{k})^2 \right] \right.$

(b) $E(\hat{\Theta}_1) = \theta_1, \quad V(\hat{\Theta}_1) = \sigma^2 \sum_{i=1}^{n} k_i^2 \left/ \left[n \sum_{i=1}^{n} (k_i - \bar{k})^2 \right] \right.$

(c) $\text{Cov}(\hat{\Theta}_1, \hat{\Theta}_2) = -\bar{k}\sigma^2 \Big/ \left[\sum_{i=1}^{n} (k_i - \bar{k})^2 \right]$

(d) $\sum_{i=1}^{n} (X_i - \theta_1 - \theta_2 k_i)^2$

$$= \sum_{i=1}^{n} (X_i - \hat{\Theta}_1 - \hat{\Theta}_2 k_i)^2 + \sum_{i=1}^{n} [(\hat{\Theta}_1 - \theta_1) + (\hat{\Theta}_2 - \theta_2)k_i]^2$$

(e)   By taking expectations of both sides in (d),

$$E \sum_{i=1}^{n} (X_i - \hat{\Theta}_1 - \hat{\Theta}_2 k_i)^2 = (n - 2)\sigma^2.$$

[Hint: expand the final term in (d) and use (a), (b), (c)]

Example 20. Let X_1, X_2, X_3 be uncorrelated and have common variance σ^2. If $E(X_1) = \theta_1 + \theta_2$, $E(X_2) = 2\theta_1 + \theta_2$, $E(X_3) = \theta_1 + 2\theta_2$, then the least-square estimates $\hat{\theta}_1, \hat{\theta}_2$, satisfy the equations

$$6\hat{\theta}_1 + 5\hat{\theta}_2 = x_1 + 2x_2 + x_3$$
$$5\hat{\theta}_1 + 6\hat{\theta}_2 = x_1 + x_2 + 2x_3$$

Hence $\hat{\theta}_1 = (x_1 + 7x_2 - 4x_3)/11$, $\hat{\theta}_2 = (x_1 - 4x_2 + 7x_3)/11$. It is easily verified that $E(\hat{\Theta}_1) = \theta_1$, $E(\hat{\Theta}_2) = \theta_2$, $V(\hat{\Theta}_1) = V(\hat{\Theta}_2) = 6\sigma^2/11$, $\text{Cov}(\hat{\Theta}_1, \hat{\Theta}_2) = -5\sigma^2/11$.

We now examine a related question. What is the best linear unbiased estimator of $a_1\theta_1 + a_2\theta_2$?

The linear expression $b_1 X_1 + b_2 X_2 + b_3 X_3$ has expectation, after collecting terms, $(b_1 + 2b_2 + b_3)\theta_1 + (b_1 + b_2 + 2b_3)\theta_2$. If this is to be $a_1\theta_1 + a_2\theta_2$ for all θ_1, θ_2, then we must have

$$b_1 + 2b_2 + b_3 = a_1$$
$$b_1 + b_2 + 2b_3 = a_2$$

Now the variance of the estimator is $(b_1^2 + b_2^2 + b_3^2)\sigma^2$. Although not recommended for general use, this can be easily minimized by substituting for b_1, b_2 in terms of b_3 using the restrictions. Minimizing with respect to the resultant expression in b_3 leads to $b_3 = -(4a_1 - 7a_2)/11$. But this is precisely the coefficient of x_3 in $a_1\hat{\theta}_1 + a_2\hat{\theta}_2$. That is to say, the b.l.u.e. of $a_1\theta_1 + a_2\theta_2$ is $a_1\hat{\Theta}_1 + a_2\hat{\Theta}_2$.

4.10 Normal equations

We now proceed to a more general discussion. While retaining the properties that the random variables are uncorrelated and have equal variance σ^2, we now propose that

$$E(X_i) = \sum_{k=1}^{m} a_{ik}\theta_k, \qquad i = 1, 2, \dots, n \tag{4.1}$$

That is, all the means are expressible as linear combinations of m unknown parameters, $\theta_1, \theta_2, \dots, \theta_m$. The sum of squares of the distances of the observed values from their expected values is

$$d^2 = \sum_{i=1}^{n} \left(x_i - \sum_{k=1}^{m} a_{ik}\theta_k \right)^2$$

$$\frac{\partial d^2}{\partial \theta_j} = -2 \sum_{i=1}^{n} \left[a_{ij} \left(x_i - \sum_{k=1}^{m} a_{ik}\theta_k \right) \right], \qquad j = 1, 2, \dots, m$$

Hence the least-squares estimates satisfy the *normal* equations

$$\sum_{i=1}^{n} \left[a_{ij} \left(\sum_{k=1}^{m} a_{ik}\hat{\theta}_k \right) \right] = \sum_{i=1}^{n} a_{ij}x_i, \qquad j = 1, 2, \dots, m \tag{4.2}$$

Without solving for the $\hat{\theta}_k$, we have

$$\sum_{i=1}^{n} \left(x_i - \sum_{k=1}^{m} a_{ik}\theta_k \right)^2 = \sum_{i=1}^{n} \left[x_i - \sum_{k=1}^{m} a_{ik}\hat{\theta}_k + \left\{ \sum_{k=1}^{m} a_{ik}(\hat{\theta}_k - \theta_k) \right\} \right]^2$$

$$= \sum_{i=1}^{n} \left(x_i - \sum_{k=1}^{m} a_{ik}\hat{\theta}_k \right)^2 + \sum_{i=1}^{n} \left[\sum_{k=1}^{m} a_{ik} \right.$$

$$\left. \times (\hat{\theta}_k - \theta_k) \right]^2 \tag{4.3}$$

In this identity, the cross-product term vanishes in virtue of Equation (4.2). From Equation (4.3), it is evident that the $\hat{\theta}_k$ correspond to a minimum. That is to say, any solution of the normal equations satisfies

$$\sum_{i=1}^{n} \left(x_i - \sum_{k=1}^{m} a_{ik}\theta_k \right)^2 \geq \sum_{i=1}^{n} \left(x_i - \sum_{k=1}^{m} a_{ik}\hat{\theta}_k \right)^2 \tag{4.4}$$

with equality, if and only if

$$\sum_{k=1}^{m} a_{ik}\theta_k = \sum_{k=1}^{m} a_{ik}\hat{\theta}_k, \qquad i = 1, 2, \dots, n \tag{4.5}$$

So that if there exists *another* different solution, say $\hat{\phi}_1, \hat{\phi}_2, \dots, \hat{\phi}_k$, of the normal equations, then a double application of Equations (4.4) and (4.5) forces

$$\sum_{k=1}^{m} a_{ik}\hat{\theta}_k = \sum_{k=1}^{m} a_{ik}\hat{\phi}_k, \qquad i = 1, 2, \ldots, n \tag{4.6}$$

That is to say, in terms of the first representation (advanced in Section 4.9), the co-ordinates of the foot of the perpendicular are unique.

4.11 Solution of the normal equations (non-singular case)

We rewrite Equation (4.2), after interchanging the order of summation,

$$\sum_{k=1}^{m} \left[\left(\sum_{i=1}^{n} a_{ij}a_{ik} \right) \hat{\theta}_k \right] = \sum_{i=1}^{n} a_{ij}x_i, \qquad j = 1, 2,, \ldots, m \tag{4.7}$$

or

$$\sum_{k=1}^{m} b_{jk}\hat{\theta}_k = c_j, \qquad j = 1, 2, \ldots, m \tag{4.8}$$

In Equation (4.8), the reader will recognize a set of m linear equations in m unknowns, $\hat{\theta}_1, \ldots, \hat{\theta}_m$. A necessary and sufficient condition for a *unique* solution is that the $m \times m$ matrix (b_{jk}) be non-singular. In that case, the $\hat{\theta}_k$ are linear combinations of the c_j and hence of the x_i. Furthermore, taking expectations in Equation (4.8)

$$\sum_{k=1}^{m} b_{jk}E(\hat{\Theta}_k) = E(C_j)$$

$$= E\left(\sum_{i=1}^{n} a_{ij}X_i \right)$$

$$= \sum_{i=1}^{n} [a_{ij}E(X_i)]$$

$$= \sum_{i=1}^{n} \left[a_{ij} \left(\sum_{k=1}^{m} a_{ik}\theta_k \right) \right]$$

$$= \sum_{k=1}^{m} b_{jk}\theta_k$$

That is,

$$\sum_{k=1}^{m} b_{jk}[E(\hat{\Theta}_k) - \theta_k] = 0, \qquad j = 1, \ldots, m \tag{4.9}$$

In virtue of the non-singularity of the matrix (b_{jk}), the only solution to *this* set of equations is

$$E(\hat{\Theta}_k) - \theta_k = 0 \tag{4.10}$$

so that the least-squares estimators are unbiased

4.12 Use of matrices

Let a_{ik} be the element in the ith row and kth column of the $n \times m$ matrix $\mathbf{A}$. Let $\theta_1, \theta_2, \ldots, \theta_m$ be the elements in the $m \times 1$ column vector θ and $x_1, x_2, \ldots, x_n$ be the elements in the $n \times 1$ column vector $\mathbf{x}$. Then Equation (4.1) may be summarized as

$$E(\mathbf{X}) = \mathbf{A}\theta \qquad (4.1')$$

Since $\sum\limits_{i=1}^{n} a_{ij}a_{ik}$ is the product of the jth row of the transpose $\mathbf{A}'$ and the kth column of $\mathbf{A}$, we can summarize Equation (4.2) as

$$\mathbf{A}'\mathbf{A}\hat{\theta} = \mathbf{A}'\mathbf{x} \qquad (4.2')$$

whence the equivalent of Equation (4.3) is

$$(\mathbf{x} - \mathbf{A}\theta)'(\mathbf{x} - \mathbf{A}\theta) = (\mathbf{x} - \mathbf{A}\hat{\theta})'(\mathbf{x} - \mathbf{A}\hat{\theta}) + (\hat{\theta} - \theta)'\mathbf{A}'\mathbf{A}(\hat{\theta} - \theta) \qquad (4.3')$$

Since for real elements each expression is a non-negative sum of squares,

$$(\mathbf{x} - \mathbf{A}\theta)'(\mathbf{x} - \mathbf{A}\theta) \geqslant (\mathbf{x} - \mathbf{A}\hat{\theta})'(\mathbf{x} - \mathbf{A}\hat{\theta}) \qquad (4.4')$$

$\mathbf{A}'\mathbf{A}$ is an $(m \times m)$ matrix which has the same rank as $\mathbf{A}$. If the rank of $\mathbf{A}$ is m, then $\mathbf{A}'\mathbf{A}$ has an inverse and Equation (4.2') may be solved for $\hat{\theta}$ uniquely:

$$\hat{\theta} = (\mathbf{A}'\mathbf{A})^{-1}\mathbf{A}'\mathbf{x} \qquad (4.8')$$

In this case, $E(\hat{\theta}) = (\mathbf{A}'\mathbf{A})^{-1}\mathbf{A}' E(\mathbf{X})$
$$= (\mathbf{A}'\mathbf{A})^{-1}\mathbf{A}'\mathbf{A}\theta$$
$$= \theta$$

so that $\hat{\Theta}$ is an unbiased estimator of θ.

Exercise 17. Show that

$(\mathbf{x} - \mathbf{A}\hat{\theta})'(\mathbf{x} - \mathbf{A}\hat{\theta}) = \mathbf{x}'\mathbf{x} - \mathbf{x}'\mathbf{A}\hat{\theta} = \mathbf{x}'\mathbf{x} - \hat{\theta}'\mathbf{A}'\mathbf{A}\hat{\theta}$, and is $\mathbf{x}'[\mathbf{I} - \mathbf{A}(\mathbf{A}'\mathbf{A})^{-1}\mathbf{A}']\mathbf{x}$, if $(\mathbf{A}'\mathbf{A})^{-1}$ exists.

Example 21. (Being Example 20 revisited in terms of matrix notation.)

$$\mathbf{x} = \begin{pmatrix} x_1 \\ x_2 \\ x_3 \end{pmatrix}, \qquad \theta = \begin{pmatrix} \theta_1 \\ \theta_2 \end{pmatrix}, \qquad \mathbf{A} = \begin{pmatrix} 1 & 1 \\ 2 & 1 \\ 1 & 2 \end{pmatrix}$$

$$\mathbf{A}'\mathbf{A} = \begin{pmatrix} 6 & 5 \\ 5 & 6 \end{pmatrix}, \qquad \det(\mathbf{A}'\mathbf{A}) = 11$$

$$(\mathbf{A}'\mathbf{A})^{-1} = \begin{pmatrix} 6/11 & -5/11 \\ -5/11 & 6/11 \end{pmatrix}, \qquad \mathbf{A}'\mathbf{x} = \begin{pmatrix} x_1 + 2x_2 + x_3 \\ x_1 + x_2 + 2x_3 \end{pmatrix}$$

$$\hat{\boldsymbol{\theta}} = \begin{pmatrix} 6/11 & -5/11 \\ -5/11 & 6/11 \end{pmatrix} \begin{pmatrix} x_1 + 2x_2 + x_3 \\ x_1 + x_2 + 2x_3 \end{pmatrix}$$

$$= \begin{pmatrix} [x_1 + 7x_2 - 4x_3]/11 \\ [x_i - 4x_2 + 7x_3]/11 \end{pmatrix}$$

Exercise 18. Show for Example 21, that the minimum sum of squares, $\mathbf{x}'\mathbf{x} - \mathbf{x}'\mathbf{A}\hat{\boldsymbol{\theta}}$, can be written as $(3x_1 - x_2 - x_3)^2/11$. Deduce that if X_1, X_2, X_3 are also normally distributed, then $(3X_1 - X_2 - X_3)^2/11\sigma^2$ has the χ_1^2 distribution.

4.13 Best unbiased linear estimation

It would appear from Example 20 that there must be a close relation between least-squares estimators and best linear unbiased estimators. Suppose, then, we have the present model of uncorrelated random variables with equal variances, and

$$E(X_i) = \sum_{j=1}^{m} a_{ij}\theta_j, \qquad i = 1, 2, \dots, n$$

Among the unbiased linear estimators, if any such exist, of $\sum_{j=1}^{m} \mu_j \theta_j$, we seek one which has minimum variance. The guarded nature of this remark betrays the fact that there may not exist 'any such'. If

$$E\left[\sum_{i=1}^{n} d_i X_i \right] = \sum_{j=1}^{m} \mu_j \theta_j \tag{4.11}$$

then

$$\sum_{i=1}^{n} \left[d_i \left(\sum_{j=1}^{m} a_{ij}\theta_j \right) \right] = \sum_{j=1}^{m} \mu_j \theta_j \tag{4.12}$$

Absence of bias for all θ_j requires

$$\sum_{i=1}^{n} d_i a_{ij} = \mu_j, \qquad j = 1, 2, \dots, m \tag{4.13}$$

We are to minimize $V\left[\sum_{i=1}^{n} d_i X_i \right] = \sigma^2 \sum_{i=1}^{n} d_i^2$, subject to the constraints of Equation (4.13). To this end we use the method of Lagrange, which consists of minimizing

$$\sum_{i=1}^{n} d_i^2 + \sum_{j=1}^{m} \lambda_j \left[\sum_{i=1}^{n} d_i a_{ij} - \mu_j \right] \tag{4.14}$$

with respect to the d_i. Differentiating partially with respect to d_i produces

$$2d_i + \sum_{j=1}^{m} \lambda_j a_{ij} = 0, \qquad i = 1, 2, \dots, n \tag{4.15}$$

Multiply Equation (4.15) by x_i and sum over i:

$$2 \sum_{i=1}^{n} d_i x_i + \sum_{i=1}^{n} \left(\sum_{j=1}^{m} \lambda_j a_{ij} \right) x_i = 0 \tag{4.16}$$

that is,

$$2 \sum_{i=1}^{n} d_i x_i + \sum_{j=1}^{m} \lambda_j \left[\sum_{i=1}^{n} a_{ij} x_i \right] = 0 \tag{4.17}$$

But in Equation (4.17) we recognize $\sum_{i=1}^{n} a_{ij} x_i$ as belonging to the jth normal equation, and on substituting in Equation (4.17) we have

$$2 \sum_{i=1}^{n} d_i x_i + \sum_{j=1}^{m} \lambda_j \left[\sum_{i=1}^{n} \sum_{k=1}^{m} a_{ij} a_{ik} \hat{\theta}_k \right] = 0 \tag{4.18}$$

$$2 \sum_{i=1}^{n} d_i x_i + \sum_{k=1}^{m} \hat{\theta}_k \left[\sum_{j=1}^{m} \left(\lambda_j \sum_{i=1}^{n} a_{ij} a_{ik} \right) \right] = 0 \tag{4.19}$$

The term in the square brackets can be simplified. If Equation (4.15) is multiplied by a_{ik} and summed over i,

$$2 \sum_{i=1}^{n} d_i a_{ik} + \sum_{i=1}^{n} \sum_{j=1}^{m} \lambda_j a_{ij} a_{ik} = 0 \tag{4.20}$$

and Equation (4.13) requires $\sum_{i=1}^{n} d_i a_{ik} = \mu_k$, which together with Equation (4.20) allows us to write Equation (4.19) as

$$\sum_{i=1}^{n} d_i x_i = \sum_{k=1}^{m} \mu_k \hat{\theta}_k \tag{4.21}$$

So if there are linear unbiased estimators of $\sum_{k=1}^{m} \mu_k \theta_k$, then $\sum_{k=1}^{m} \mu_k \hat{\Theta}_k$ is one such having minimum variance. On consideration, it does not matter which solution of the normal equations is taken. It is not claimed that the $\hat{\Theta}_k$ are *individually* unbiased estimators of the θ_k — though this *is* the case when there is a unique solution.

Example 22. $E(X_1) = E(X_2) = \theta_1 + \theta_2,\ \ E(X_3) = E(X_4) = \theta_1 + \theta_3.$
The normal equations are

$$4\hat{\theta}_1 + 2\hat{\theta}_2 + 2\hat{\theta}_3 = x_1 + x_2 + x_3 + x_4$$
$$2\hat{\theta}_1 + 2\hat{\theta}_2 \qquad\quad = x_1 + x_2$$
$$2\hat{\theta}_1 \qquad\quad + 2\hat{\theta}_3 = \qquad\qquad x_3 + x_4$$

The equations are clearly not independent, and do not have an unique solution. Suppose we attempt to find an unbiased estimator of θ_1. Then the conditions of Equation (4.13) become

$$\sum_{i=1}^{4} d_i a_{i1} = d_1 + d_2 + d_3 + d_4 = \mu_1 = 1$$

$$\sum_{i=1}^{4} d_i a_{i2} = d_1 + d_2 \qquad\qquad = \mu_3 = 0$$

$$\sum_{i=1}^{4} d_i a_{i3} = \qquad\qquad d_3 + d_4 = \mu_3 = 0$$

These equations are inconsistent (substitute the last two in the first). We conclude that there are *no* linear unbiased estimators of θ_1 (nor θ_2, θ_3). Now consider the linear combination $\theta_3 - \theta_2$. Applying Equation (4.13) to the linear estimator $\sum d_i X_i$ yields

$$d_1 + d_2 + d_3 + d_4 = \mu_1 = 0$$
$$d_1 + d_2 \qquad\qquad = \mu_2 = -1$$
$$d_3 + d_4 = \mu_3 = +1$$

These equations are consistent and solutions include $d_1 = 0$, $d_2 = -1, d_3 = 1, d_4 = 0$. For the best (minimum variance) estimator we require $\mu_1 \hat{\theta}_1 + \mu_2 \hat{\theta}_2 + \mu_3 \hat{\theta}_3 = -\hat{\theta}_2 + \hat{\theta}_3$, where $\hat{\theta}_1, \hat{\theta}_2, \hat{\theta}_3$ are any values satisfying the normal equations. But from these equations we have immediately

$$\hat{\theta}_3 - \hat{\theta}_2 = (x_4 + x_3 - x_2 - x_1)/2$$

A combination of the parameters which can be estimated without bias from a linear function of the observations is said to be *estimable*. In Example 22, we checked that θ_1 was non-estimable but that $\theta_3 - \theta_2$ was estimable. That same example sheds no general light on which linear functions are estimable. One case is straightforward, namely when the normal equations have a unique solution. In that circumstance, the $\theta_k, k = 1, 2, \ldots m$, *are* individually estimable by Equation (4.10), and from Equation (4.21), each $\hat{\Theta}_k$ is the b.l.u.e. of θ_k. If the normal equations have been explicitly solved in terms of the observations, then all variances and covariances may be readily computed.

Exercise 19. An interesting result may be derived via the normal equations, when they have a unique solution.

Consider the *j*th normal equation from Equation (4.7).

$$\sum_{k=1}^{m}\left[\left(\sum_{i=1}^{n} a_{ij}a_{ik}\right)\hat{\Theta}_k\right] = \sum_{i=1}^{n} a_{ij}X_i \qquad (4.22)$$

Take the covariance of both sides with $\hat{\Theta}_t$ and denote $\mathrm{Cov}(\hat{\Theta}_k, \hat{\Theta}_t)$ as v_{kt}. Let $\hat{\Theta}_t = \sum_{s=1}^{n} d_{st}X_s$. Show that

$$\mathrm{Cov}\left(\sum_{i=1}^{n} a_{ij}X_i, \hat{\Theta}_t\right) = \sum_{i=1}^{n} a_{ij}d_{it}\sigma^2$$

$$= \delta_{jt}\sigma^2, \qquad \text{where } \delta_{jt} = 0, t \neq j, \delta_{jj} = 1$$

Hence or otherwise, deduce that

$$\sum_{k=1}^{m} b_{jk}v_{kt} = \delta_{jt}\sigma^2, \qquad j, t = 1, 2, \ldots, m \qquad (4.23)$$

The *m* equations for fixed $t(j = 1, 2, \ldots, m)$ have a unique solution for $v_{kt}(k = 1, 2, \ldots, m)$ since $\det(b_{jk}) = \det\left(\sum_{i=1}^{n} a_{ij}a_{ik}\right) \neq 0$ when the normal equations themselves have a unique solution.

4.14 Covariance matrix

For the random variables $X_1, X_2, \ldots, X_n$ let $\mathrm{Cov}(X_i, X_j) = \sigma_{ij}$ $(i, j, = 1, 2, \ldots, n)$. We shall define the covariance matrix, $\mathbf{V}(\mathbf{X})$, of the random vector $\mathbf{X} = (X_1, X_2, \ldots, X_n)'$ as the $n \times n$ matrix for which the (i, j)th element is σ_{ij}. Hence the (i, j)th element of the covariance matrix of $\mathbf{AX}$ is

$$\mathrm{Cov}\left[\sum_{t=1}^{n} a_{it}X_t, \sum_{s=1}^{n} a_{js}X_s\right] = \sum_t\sum_s a_{it}a_{js}\,\mathrm{Cov}(X_t, X_s)$$

$$= \sum_t\sum_s a_{it}\sigma_{ts}a_{js}$$

and it is straightforward to verify that this is the (i,j)th element of the matrix $\mathbf{A}\mathbf{V}(\mathbf{X})\mathbf{A}'$.

We can also verify that Equation (4.23) can be summarized as

$$\mathbf{A}'\mathbf{A}\mathbf{V}(\boldsymbol{\Theta}) = \mathbf{I}\sigma^2 \qquad (4.23')$$

In fact, the cumbersome manhandling which yielded up Equation (4.23) can more comfortably be obtained directly from Equation (4.8'):

$$\hat{\boldsymbol{\Theta}} = (\mathbf{A}'\mathbf{A})^{-1}\mathbf{A}'\mathbf{X}$$

hence
$$\begin{aligned}
\mathbf{V}(\hat{\boldsymbol{\Theta}}) &= (\mathbf{A}'\mathbf{A})^{-1}\mathbf{A}'\mathbf{V}(\mathbf{X})\mathbf{A}(\mathbf{A}'\mathbf{A})^{-1} \\
&= (\mathbf{A}'\mathbf{A})^{-1}\mathbf{A}'\mathbf{I}\mathbf{A}(\mathbf{A}'\mathbf{A})^{-1}\sigma^2 \\
&= (\mathbf{A}'\mathbf{A})^{-1}\sigma^2
\end{aligned}$$

For the same case, the b.l.u.e. of $\sum_{i=1}^{m} \mu_i\theta_i$ is $\sum_{i=1}^{m} \mu_i\hat{\Theta}_i = \boldsymbol{\mu}'\hat{\boldsymbol{\Theta}}$ which, from Equation (4.8'), is $\boldsymbol{\mu}'(\mathbf{A}'\mathbf{A})^{-1}\mathbf{A}'\mathbf{X}$. The variance of the estimator is $\mathbf{V}(\boldsymbol{\mu}'\hat{\boldsymbol{\Theta}}) = \boldsymbol{\mu}'\mathbf{V}(\hat{\boldsymbol{\Theta}})\boldsymbol{\mu} = [\boldsymbol{\mu}'(\mathbf{A}'\mathbf{A})^{-1}\boldsymbol{\mu}]\sigma^2$

Example 23.   When $(\mathbf{A}'\mathbf{A})^{-1}$ exists, $E[(\hat{\boldsymbol{\Theta}} - \boldsymbol{\theta})'\mathbf{A}'\mathbf{A}(\hat{\boldsymbol{\Theta}} - \boldsymbol{\theta})]$

$$\begin{aligned}
&= E\left[\sum_{i=1}^{n} \left\{ \sum_{k=1}^{m} a_{ik}(\hat{\Theta}_k - \theta_k) \right\}^2 \right] \\
&= \sum_{i=1}^{n} \left[\sum_{t=1}^{m} \sum_{s=1}^{m} a_{it}a_{is}E(\hat{\Theta}_t - \theta_t)(\hat{\Theta}_s - \theta_s) \right] \\
&= \sum_{t=1}^{m} \sum_{s=1}^{m} v_{st} \left[\sum_{i=1}^{n} a_{it}a_{is} \right] = \sum_{t=1}^{m} \sum_{s=1}^{m} b_{ts}v_{st}
\end{aligned}$$

where b_{ts} is the (t,s)th element of $\mathbf{A}'\mathbf{A}$.

Hence $\sum_{s=1}^{m} b_{ts}v_{st}$ is the (t,t)th element of $(\mathbf{A}'\mathbf{A})\mathbf{V}(\hat{\boldsymbol{\Theta}}) = (\mathbf{A}'\mathbf{A}) \times (\mathbf{A}'\mathbf{A})^{-1}\sigma^2 = \mathbf{I}\sigma^2$. The sum of the diagonal elements of $\mathbf{I}\sigma^2$ is finally $m\sigma^2$.

But $E[(\mathbf{X} - \mathbf{A}\boldsymbol{\theta})'(\mathbf{X} - \mathbf{A}\boldsymbol{\theta})] = n\sigma^2$, so, from Equation (4.3'),

$$E[(\mathbf{X} - \mathbf{A}\hat{\boldsymbol{\Theta}})'(\mathbf{X} - \mathbf{A}\hat{\boldsymbol{\Theta}})] = (n - m)\sigma^2$$

Hence $(\mathbf{X} - \mathbf{A}\hat{\boldsymbol{\Theta}})'(\mathbf{X} - \mathbf{A}\hat{\boldsymbol{\Theta}})/(n - m)$ is an unbiased estimator of σ^2.

Exercise 20.   Using a spring balance, a small container of unknown weight w_0 is weighed and recorded as x_1. An object of unknown weight w_1 is then put in the container and two separate weighings are recorded as y_1, y_2. The object is then replaced with another of unknown weight w_2 and three separate weighings are recorded as z_1, z_2, z_3. If all readings are regarded as independent and subject to errors with zero mean and the same variance σ^2, find the least-squares estimators of w_0, w_1, w_2 and their variances and covariances.

[Ans. $\hat{W}_0 = X_1, \hat{W}_1 = (Y_1 + Y_2 - 2X_1)/2$,
$\hat{W}_2 = (Z_1 + Z_2 + Z_3 - 3X_1)/3$]

Exercise 21. An experiment results in six independent observations $y_r (r = 1, 2, 3, 4, 5, 6)$ such that

$$E(Y_r) = \alpha \cos (2\pi r/6) + \beta \sin (2\pi r/6); V(Y_r) = \sigma^2$$

Find the least-squares estimators of α, β and verify that each of these estimates has variance $\sigma^2/3$.   (Univ. Leicester 1960)
[Ans. $\hat{\alpha} = (y_1 - y_2 - 2y_3 - y_4 + y_5 + 2y_6)/6$
$\hat{\beta} = (y_1 + y_2 - y_4 - y_5)/2\sqrt{3}$]

4.15 Relaxation of assumptions

What is to be done if the observations have different variances and are correlated? If their means are linear sums of unknown parameters, then we may still formally apply the method of least squares, though giving equal weight to observations may seem questionable. We obtain the same least-squares equations (4.7), and if these have a unique solution, then by the same argument subsequently employed the estimators are even unbiased. This mechanical application of the method inflicts a sacrifice – we have lost the minimum-variance property. This can be recovered at the cost of the further assumption that we *know* the variances and covariances of and between the observations. We use these to construct a new set of random variables which *do* have equal variances and *are* uncorrelated.

Example 24. $E(X_1) = E(X_2) = \theta$, but $V(X_1) = 5\sigma^2, \text{Cov}(X_1, X_2) = \sigma^2$, $V(X_2) = 2\sigma^2$. The (unmodified) least-squares estimate, found by minimizing $(x_1 - \theta)^2 + (x_2 - \theta)^2$, is $(x_1 + x_2)/2$ and $V[(X_1 + X_2)/2] = [V(X_1) + 2 \text{ Cov}(X_1, X_2) + V(X_2)]/4 = (5\sigma^2 + 2\sigma^2 + 2\sigma^2)/4 = 9\sigma^2/4$. Consider the random variables $Y_1 = g_1 X_1 + g_2 X_2, Y_2 = h_1 X_1 + h_2 X_2$, where we are to choose the coefficients g_1, g_2, h_1, h_2 so that $V(Y_1) = V(Y_2)$ and $\text{Cov}(Y_1, Y_2) = 0$.

That is,

$$5g_1^2 + 2g_1g_2 + 2g_2^2 = 5h_1^2 + 2h_1h_2 + 2h_2^2$$
$$5g_1h_1 + g_1h_2 + g_2h_1 + 2g_2h_2 = 0$$

One solution is $g_1 = g_2 = 1, h_1 = 1, h_2 = -2$.
Since $E(Y_1) = E(X_1 + X_2) = 2\theta, E(Y_2) = E(X_1 - 2X_2) = -\theta$, we
minimize $(x_1 + x_2 - 2\theta)^2 + (x_1 - 2x_2 + \theta)^2$, attained when

$$\hat{\theta} = (x_1 + 4x_2)/5$$

and $V[\hat{\Theta}] = 45\sigma^2/25$. Thus $(X_1 + 4X_2)/5$ is the b.l.u.e.

Exercise 22. In Example 24, show that if we choose $Y_1 = 2X_1 - X_2$,
$Y_2 = 3X_2$, then $V(Y_1) = V(Y_2) = 18\sigma^2$, Cov $(Y_1, Y_2) = 0$ and that
the value of θ which minimizes $(2x_1 - x_2 - \theta)^2 + (3x_2 - 3\theta)^2$ is
again $\hat{\theta} = (x_1 + 4x_2)/5$.

We shall not examine this topic more closely, since exact knowledge of the second moments is usually not available. The next exercise sets out the general position, and this is followed by the corresponding matrix formulation.

Exercise 23. Let $E(X_i) = \sum\limits_{k=1}^{m} a_{ik}\theta_k, i = 1, 2, \ldots, n$ and Cov $(X_i, X_j) = \sigma_{ij}, i, j = 1, 2, \ldots, n$. Consider a one-to-one transformation $Y_i = \sum\limits_{j=1}^{n} g_{ij}X_j$. Show that the restrictions $V(Y_i) = 1$, Cov $(Y_i, Y_j) = 0$, $i \neq j$, imply $\sum\limits_{s=1}^{n}\sum\limits_{t=1}^{n} g_{is}g_{jt}\sigma_{st} = \delta_{ij}$ where $\delta_{ij} = 0, s \neq t, \delta_{jj} = 1$. Derive the normal equations corresponding to minimizing $\sum\limits_{i=1}^{n} [y_i - E(Y_i)]^2$.

Matrix formulation for general linear model

Suppose $E(\mathbf{X}) = \mathbf{A}\theta$, $V(\mathbf{X}) = \mathbf{V}$ be positive definite and $\mathbf{G}$ be a non-singular matrix such that $\mathbf{Y} = \mathbf{GX}$ has $V(\mathbf{Y}) = \mathbf{I}$. That is, $V(\mathbf{Y}) = V(\mathbf{GX}) = \mathbf{GVG}' = \mathbf{I}$ and $E(\mathbf{Y}) = E(\mathbf{GX}) = \mathbf{GA}\theta$. Then the ordinary least-squares estimate $\hat{\theta}$, based on $\mathbf{y}$, is found by minimizing

$$(\mathbf{y} - \mathbf{GA}\theta)'(\mathbf{y} - \mathbf{GA}\theta)$$

and yields the normal equations

$$\mathbf{A'G'GA}\hat{\theta} = \mathbf{A'G'y}$$

But $\mathbf{GVG'} = \mathbf{I}$, or $\mathbf{G'G} = \mathbf{V}^{-1}$, since $\mathbf{G}$ is non-singular, so that

$$\mathbf{A'V^{-1}A}\hat{\theta} = \mathbf{A'V^{-1}x}$$

We have discussed, at some length, the properties of the two most commonly used types of estimator. It is time to review the situation. For the method of maximum likelihood, we need to know the type of distribution sampled apart, of course, from the parameters which are to be estimated. For small samples, no particular general optimum property is claimed. For large random samples, the estimators will generally be consistent. If, further, the distribution sampled has a sufficiently regular probability density function, then the maximum likelihood estimators are asymptotically normally distributed and efficient. If, however, the sample values are not independent or the number of parameters is not fixed, regardless of the sample size, then the classical asymptotic results may not hold. (See for instance, Cox and Hinkley, *Theoretical Statistics*, Chapter 9.)

The method of least squares can be used even when we do *not* know the probability density function of the distribution being sampled, and is particularly convenient when the sample values are independent. In many experimental situations it has been realistically supposed that the observations have been composed from a known number of fixed effects, together with an experimental error. We have devoted most of our attention to the case when the fixed effects can be represented as a linear combination of unknown parameters and the errors are independent with constant variances. For this case, the least-squares estimators are also the linear unbiased estimators with minimum variance. When it is known that the random variables are also normally distributed, then the least-squares estimators of the fixed effects coincide with the maximum likelihood estimators. (For some instructive comments on the historical interplay between these two methods of estimation see *Estimation Theory*, Deutsch.)

CHAPTER FIVE

Hypothesis testing I

5.1 Introduction

Someone holding shares in a company can adopt any of a wide variety of attitudes towards their disposal. These attitudes may vary from forgetting about them until retirement to considering afresh every day whether to sell them with a view to making a profit or minimizing a loss. He may have a cut-and-dried plan such as:

(a) sell when the profit reaches a certain minimum;

(b) sell when some relevant index reaches a certain level.

Such plans may become quite elaborate if they depend on several consecutive observations. Extra flexibility may be obtained by allowing the values of the 'readings' to affect only the probability of a sale. Thus some room might be left for the influence of mood, the political climate and those other forces which, because of our ignorance, tend to be regarded as chance effects. Any particular sale may entail a 'loss' in two different ways, either by being too soon or too late. The statistician can find himself in a similar situation. Consider the despatch of batches of items from a manufacturer to his customers. If a customer finds that the batch contains too many defectives, he may invoke penalty clauses or place future business elsewhere. However, the cost of checking every item in a batch may be prohibitive and the decision to despatch is then based on the quality of a limited sample of items. Suppose the item is a spare part for a machine which would be deemed to be defective if its working life were too short. A simple but tractable model is that the working life, T, for such a part is a random variable having an exponential distribution with unknown parameter λ. The mean of such a distribution is $1/\lambda$ and $\Pr(T \geqslant t_0) = \int_{t_0}^{\infty} \lambda e^{-\lambda t} dt = e^{-\lambda t_0}$. Good-quality parts will have a high probability of lasting at least until some reasonable time, t_0. Evidently, the smaller the value of λ, the greater is the chance of such a desirable feature. Thus, we can frame a requirement about quality in terms of the parameter λ, say $0 < \lambda \leqslant \lambda_0$, where λ_0 is stated. Some parts are then selected at random from the batch and allowed to work until they 'fail'. The observed failure time can neither prove nor disprove the claim that $0 < \lambda \leqslant \lambda_0$ but may be used as evidence in any decision to accept or reject such a claim.

The data obtained may lead us to a false conclusion in two different ways. If the claim is rejected when in fact it is true, a type I error has occurred. If the claim is accepted when it is false, a type II error has been made. For the present, we shall ignore the possible differing costs of these errors and concentrate on the bare probabilities involved. Suppose two parts are independently selected and tested for quality, then their 'working lives' are independent random variables, T_1, T_2, with a common exponential distribution. This is a situation where even this limited amount of information can be used in several ways. We may decide to reject the claim '$0 < \lambda \leqslant \lambda_0$' if both T_1, T_2 turn out to be too small.

Now
$$\Pr(T_1 \leqslant t_0 \text{ and } T_2 \leqslant t_0) = \Pr(T_1 \leqslant t_0)\Pr(T_2 \leqslant t_0)$$
$$= \left(\int_0^{t_0} \lambda e^{-\lambda t} dt \right)^2 = (1 - e^{-\lambda t_0})^2$$

This probability increases with λ, so the maximum probability of a type I error is $(1 - e^{-\lambda_0 t_0})^2$. If this same probability is to be equal to some pre-assigned level α, then $t_0 = -[\log(1 - \sqrt{\alpha})]/\lambda_0$. The probability of a type II error is $1 - \Pr(T_1 < t_0 \text{ and } T_2 < t_0)$ $= 1 - (1 - e^{-\lambda t_0})^2$. But $e^{-t_0} = (1 - \sqrt{\alpha})^{1/\lambda_0}$, so that $1 - (1 - e^{-\lambda t_0})^2$ $= 1 - [1 - (1 - \sqrt{\alpha})^{\lambda/\lambda_0}]^2$, $\lambda > \lambda_0$. A slight amendment produces another rule for testing the claim under consideration. We may reject the claim $0 < \lambda \leqslant \lambda_0$, if the first unit to fail does so before some time t'. Then $\Pr[\min(T_1, T_2) \leqslant t'] = 1 - \Pr[\min(T_1, T_2) > t'] = 1 - \Pr[T_1 > t' \text{ and } T_2 > t'] = 1 - [\int_{t'}^{\infty} \lambda e^{-\lambda t} dt]^2 = 1 - (e^{-\lambda t'})^2 = 1 - e^{-2\lambda t'}$. This again increases with λ and the maximum probability of a type I error is $1 - e^{-2\lambda_0 t'}$.

The question immediately arises as to which of these two 'rules' is to be preferred. To answer this, it is customary to match the maximum probabilities of type I error and then to compare the probabilities of a type II error. This matching requires $1 - e^{-2\lambda_0 t'} = \alpha$, or $t' = -[\log(1 - \alpha)]/2\lambda_0$ whence the probability of a type II error is

$$1 - (1 - e^{-2\lambda t'}) = e^{-2\lambda t'} = (e^{-2\lambda_0 t'})^{\lambda/\lambda_0}$$
$$= (1 - \alpha)^{\lambda/\lambda_0}, \qquad \lambda > \lambda_0$$

Consider the difference between the probabilities of type II error.

$$(1 - \alpha)^{\lambda/\lambda_0} - [1 - \{1 - (1 - \sqrt{\alpha})^{\lambda/\lambda_0}\}^2], \qquad \lambda > \lambda_0$$
$$= (1 - \alpha)^{\lambda/\lambda_0} - [1 - 1 + 2(1 - \sqrt{\alpha})^{\lambda/\lambda_0} - (1 - \sqrt{\alpha})^{2\lambda/\lambda_0}]$$
$$= [(1 - \sqrt{\alpha})(1 + \sqrt{\alpha})]^{\lambda/\lambda_0} - [2(1 - \sqrt{\alpha})^{\lambda/\lambda_0} - (1 - \sqrt{\alpha})^{2\lambda/\lambda_0}]$$
$$= (1 - \sqrt{\alpha})^{\lambda/\lambda_0}[(1 + \sqrt{\alpha})^{\lambda/\lambda_0} + (1 - \sqrt{\alpha})^{\lambda/\lambda_0} - 2] \geqslant 0,$$

since $0 \leqslant \alpha \leqslant 1$ and $\lambda/\lambda_0 > 1$.

Hence the probability of a type II error for the second rule is greater than for the first rule for each $\lambda > \lambda_0$. In the sense indicated, the first rule is better. For this problem there is yet another rule which is superior to both. This is based on the value of $T_1 + T_2$, which if too small leads to rejection of the claim that $0 < \lambda \leqslant \lambda_0$. If we match the maximum probability of a type I error, then the rule will have smaller probability of a type II error than either of the previous rules suggested. In fact, we shall show later that this rule is the best possible.

Exercise 1. Show that the sum of two independent random variables having common exponential distributions has probability density function $f(t) = \lambda^2 t e^{-\lambda t}, t > 0$. Hence show that $\Pr(T_1 + T_2 < t^* | \lambda) = 1 - (1 + \lambda t^*)e^{-\lambda t*}$ and deduce that, for fixed t^*, this probability is an increasing function of λ.

5.2 Statistical hypothesis

It is now time to outline a more formal language for describing the procedures adopted in problems of this kind. The observations, on the basis of which a decision is to be reached, are generally supposed to have been drawn from some family of distributions. The choice of family springs from some more or less plausible model for the process under inspection. A *statistical hypothesis* is any assumption made about the distribution of a random variable. If it completely specifies the distribution, the hypothesis is said to be *simple*, otherwise it is said to be *composite*. Thus, the hypothesis that a random variable is normally distributed with stated mean and unknown variance is composite. If the variance is also stated, the hypothesis becomes simple. The phenomena under study generally provoke reasoned conjectures as to the possible values of the parameters of the distributions postulated by the model. Such a conjecture which is generally of particular interest is often dignified with the title of the *null hypothesis* and is denoted H_0. Any other subset of the possible values of the parameters with which the null hypothesis is most particularly to be contrasted is termed the *alternative hypothesis* and denoted by H_1. Thus H_0 and H_1 are in a sense rivals and generally the data are used to decide in favour of one hypothesis or the other. There is usually no possibility of proving a hypothesis is true, though sometimes the data can show it is untrue. Where the family of distributions is understood from the context, the following compact notation describes our earlier examples:

$$H_0 : \lambda \leqslant \lambda_0 \, ; \, H_1 : \lambda > \lambda_0$$

Any rule or procedure for deciding whether or not to accept a hypothesis will be called a *test*. Any statistic which is employed to test a hypothesis is termed a *test statistic*. The most general approach is to define for each possible sample the probability of rejecting the null hypothesis. This conditional probability, as a function of the sample values $x_1, x_2, \ldots, x_n$, is called a *critical function* and is written $\phi(x_1, \ldots, x_n)$. The (unconditional) probability of rejecting H_0 is $E[\phi(X_1, \ldots, X_n)]$.

Example 1. X_1, X_2 is a random sample of two from the exponential distribution with parameter λ. $H_0 : 0 < \lambda \leqslant \lambda_0$; $H_1 : \lambda > \lambda_0$. Consider the critical function $\phi(x_1, x_2) = e^{-(x_1 + x_2)}$. This will serve as a probability since it is non-negative and lies between 0 and 1. How is such a function to be used? Suppose we observe $x_1 = 1$, $x_2 = 3$, then the value of ϕ is $e^{-4} = 0.018$. We perform the auxiliary experiment of drawing a random number between 0 and 1 and if it is less than 0.018, we reject H_0.

The probability of rejecting H_0 is

$$
\begin{aligned}
E[e^{-(X_1 + X_2)}] &= \int_0^\infty \int_0^\infty e^{-(x_1 + x_2)} f(x_1, x_2) dx_1 dx_2 \\
&= \int_0^\infty \int_0^\infty e^{-(x_1 + x_2)} \lambda^2 e^{-\lambda(x_1 + x_2)} dx_1 dx_2 \\
&= \left[\int_0^\infty \lambda e^{-x(\lambda + 1)} dx \right]^2 \\
&= \left(\frac{\lambda}{\lambda + 1} \right)^2
\end{aligned}
$$

For this test, the maximum probability of a type I error is $\left(\dfrac{\lambda_0}{\lambda_0 + 1}\right)^2$.

If the critical function takes only the values 0 and 1 then the test is said to be *non-randomized*, and the set of sample values $(x_1, \ldots, x_n)$ such that ϕ is 1 is called the *critical region* of the test. Other tests are said to be *randomized*.

Example 2. For the previous example, let $\phi(x_1, x_2) = 1$ if max $(x_1, x_2) \leqslant t_0$ and $\phi(x_1, x_2) = 0$ otherwise. The probability of rejecting H_0 is

$$E[\phi(X_1, X_2)] = 1 \times \Pr[\max(X_1, X_2) \leqslant t_0] = (1 - e^{-\lambda t_0})^2$$

The maximum value of the probability of a type I error is known as the *size* of the test and is denoted by α. If the test is non-randomized, the term 'size' is also applied to the critical region. The probability of rejecting the null hypothesis as a function of the underlying parameters is called the *power function* of the test. The value of the power function when the parameter values are included in the alternative hypothesis is called the *power*. Thus:

$$\text{Probability of a type II error} = 1 - \text{power}$$

We shall for the most part be concerned with non-randomized tests. For these tests the critical function need not be discussed at all, since such tests will always take the form: 'If a test statistic assumes a value in the critical region, reject the null hypothesis; otherwise accept the null hypothesis.'

5.3 Simple null hypothesis against simple alternative

It is possible to propose many tests of a particular hypothesis. We should prefer a good test which, roughly speaking, has acceptable probabilities of rejecting the rival hypotheses when they are false.

There is one situation where a 'best test' can be constructed. If the null and alternative hypothesis are both simple, a best test is one which for given size has maximum power. Neyman and Pearson proved the following:

Theorem. Let $X_1, X_2, \ldots, X_n$ have joint probability density function $f(x_1, x_2, \ldots, x_n \mid \theta_1, \theta_2 \ldots, \theta_p)$, $H_0 : \theta_i = \theta_i^0$, $H_1 : \theta_i = \theta_i^1$ where the θ_i^0, θ_i^1, $i = 1, 2, \ldots, K$, are known constants. Suppose further that U is the set of $(x_1, x_2, \ldots, x_n)$ such that

(a) $\dfrac{f(x_1, x_2, \ldots, x_n | H_1)}{f(x_1, x_2, \ldots, x_n | H_0)} > k, \qquad k > 0$

(b) $\Pr[(X_1, X_2, \ldots, X_n) \in U | H_0] = \alpha$

Then U is a best critical region of size α in the sense that no other critical region, of size α, has greater power when the alternative hypothesis is true. The theorem clearly refers to the class of non-randomized tests. It will later be shown that the test is optimal in the class of all tests of size α and hence may also be called *most powerful*.

Proof. We first remark that for any subset A of U, in virtue of (a),

$$\Pr[(X_1, X_2, \ldots, X_n) \in A | H_1] \geqslant k \Pr[(X_1, X_2, \ldots, X_n) \in A | H_0] \quad (5.1)$$

Correspondingly, if B includes no part of U,

$$\Pr[(X_1, X_2, \ldots, X_n) \in B | H_1] \leqslant k \Pr[(X_1, X_2, \ldots, X_n) \in B | H_0] \quad (5.2)$$

Any set V may have some points in common with U.

$$\Pr[(X_1, X_2, \ldots, X_n) \in U | H_1] - \Pr[(X_1, X_2, \ldots, X_n) \in V | H_1]$$

$= \Pr[(X_1, X_2, \ldots, X_n) \in (U \text{ and not } V) | H_1] - \Pr[(X_1, X_2, \ldots, X_n) \in (V \text{ and not } U) | H_1]$, since the points common to U and V may be omitted. Using Equations (5.1) and (5.2),

$$\Pr[(X_1, X_2, \ldots, X_n) \in U | H_1] - \Pr[(X_1, X_2, \ldots, X_n) \in V | H_1]$$

$\geqslant k \Pr[(X_1, X_2, \ldots, X_n) \in (U \text{ and not } V) | H_0] - k \Pr[(X_1, X_2 \ldots, X_n) \in (V \text{ and not } U) | H_0]$

$= k \{ \Pr[(X_1, X_2, \ldots, X_n) \in U | H_0] - \Pr[(X_1, X_2, \ldots, X_n) \in V | H_0] \}$

having restored the common part.

If the size of V does not exceed the size of U, this last quantity is non-negative. Hence the initial difference in powers is also non-negative. We remark that we would instinctively wish to reject H_0 if the sample values fall in a region less probable under H_0 than under H_1 and we shall show that the theorem tells us how to divide out the sample space most efficiently. There are several comments to make on the implication of this theorem, but we first consider some illustrative examples to catch the manner of its application.

Example 3. $X_1, X_2, \ldots, X_n$ is a random sample from the exponential distribution with parameter λ. $H_0 : \lambda = \lambda_0$; $H_1 : \lambda = \lambda_1 > \lambda_0$. Since the X_i are independent,

$$f(x_1, x_2, \ldots, x_n | \lambda) = \prod_1^n f_i(x_i | \lambda)$$

$$= \prod_1^n \lambda \exp(-\lambda x_i)$$

$$= \lambda^n \exp[-\lambda \sum x_i]$$

Hence, by the Neyman–Pearson theorem, the most powerful critical region of its size consists of those sample points which satisfy

$$\frac{\lambda_1^n \exp[-\lambda_1 \sum x_i]}{\lambda_0^n \exp[-\lambda_0 \sum x_i]} > k$$

$$\exp[(\lambda_0 - \lambda_1) \sum x_i] > k(\lambda_0/\lambda_1)^n$$

since $\lambda_1 > \lambda_0$, $\exp[(\lambda_0 - \lambda_1) \sum x_i]$ is a decreasing function of $\sum_1^n x_i$ and hence is greater than $k(\lambda_0/\lambda_1)^n$ when $\sum_1^n x_i$ is less than some constant. That is to say, a best critical region consists of those points with co-ordinates $x_1, x_2, \ldots, x_n$ such that $\sum_1^n x_i < c$. The size of such a test is $\Pr\left[\sum_1^n X_i < c | \lambda = \lambda_0\right]$. But the distribution of the sum of n such independent random variables, with a common parameter λ has a gamma distribution with parameters n, λ. The p.d.f. of such a distribution is

$$g(y | \lambda) = \lambda(\lambda y)^{n-1} \exp(-\lambda y)/(n-1)!, \qquad 0 \leqslant y < \infty$$

and the size of the test is

$$\int_0^c g(y | \lambda_0) \mathrm{d}y = \int_0^{\lambda_0 c} \{z^{n-1} \exp(-z)/(n-1)!\} \mathrm{d}z = \alpha, \text{ where } z = \lambda_0 y.$$

The power of this test is $\Pr\left[\sum_1^n X_i < c | \lambda = \lambda_1\right] = \int_0^c g(y | \lambda_1) \mathrm{d}y$

$$= \int_0^{\lambda_1 c} \{z^{n-1} \exp(-z)/(n-1)!\} \mathrm{d}z$$

It is to be seen that so long as $\lambda_1 > \lambda_0$, the form of the best test is unchanged and for each such λ, for fixed α, the value of c is determined by λ_0. Hence this is a *uniformly most powerful test* (u.m.p.) of $H_0 : \lambda = \lambda_0$ against the composite alternative $H_1 : \lambda > \lambda_0$.

Exercise *2*.   For Example 3 find the best test of $H_0 : \lambda = \lambda_0$ against
$H_1 : \lambda = \lambda_1 < \lambda_0$.

[Ans. $\sum_1^n x_i > d$]

Example 4. $X_1, X_2, \ldots, X_n$ is a random sample from the Poisson
distribution with parameter λ. $H_0 : \lambda = \lambda_0$; $H_1 : \lambda = \lambda_1 > \lambda_0$.

$$\frac{f(x_1, x_2, \ldots, x_n | \lambda = \lambda_1)}{f(x_1, x_2, \ldots, x_n | \lambda = \lambda_0)} = \frac{\prod_1^n f_i(x_i | \lambda = \lambda_1)}{\prod_1^n f_i(x_i | \lambda = \lambda_0)}$$

$$= \frac{\prod \lambda_1^{x_i} \exp(-\lambda_1)/x_i !}{\prod \lambda_0^{x_i} \exp(-\lambda_0)/x_i !}$$

$$= \frac{\lambda_1^{\Sigma x_i} \exp(-n\lambda_1)}{\lambda_0^{\Sigma x_i} \exp(-n\lambda_0)}$$

$$= (\lambda_1/\lambda_0)^{\Sigma x_i} \exp\left[n(\lambda_0 - \lambda_1)\right]$$

Since $\lambda_1 > \lambda_0$, this ratio is an increasing function of $\sum_1^n x_i$ and hence
exceeds some constant if $\sum_1^n x_i$ is sufficiently large. That is, the best
critical region consists of those $x_1, x_2, \ldots, x_n$ such that $\sum_1^n x_i > c$. The
distribution of the test statistic is Poisson with parameter $n\lambda$.
Hence the size of the test is $\Pr\left[\sum_1^n X_i > c \,|\, \lambda = \lambda_0\right] = \sum_{r=c+1}^{\infty} (n\lambda_0)^r \times$
$\exp(-n\lambda_0)/r!$, assuming c to be an integer, while the corresponding
power when $\lambda = \lambda_1$ is

$$\Pr\left[\sum_1^n X_i > c \,|\, \lambda = \lambda_1\right] = \sum_{r=c+1}^{\infty} (n\lambda_1)^r \exp(-n\lambda_1)/r!$$

Since the distribution of the test statistic is discrete, it is not always
possible to find a value of c which provides some particular pre-
assigned value of α. To arrange this, some randomization may be
required at the boundary value c. The following calculation illustrates the technique. Suppose $n = 10, \lambda_0 = 0.4$ and we require α to
be 0.05. From tables of the Poisson distribution we have

$$\Pr\left[\sum_1^{10} X_i > 8 \,|\, \lambda = 0.4\right] = 0.0214 \text{ and } \Pr\left[\sum_1^{10} X_i > 7 \,|\, \lambda = 0.4\right] = 0.0511$$

so that values $c = 7, 8$ bracket $\alpha = 0.05$. The probability that $\sum_1^{10} X_i = 8$ when $\lambda = 0.4$ is then 'split' to make up the required size. That is to say, γ is chosen so that

$$0.0214 + 0.0297\,\gamma = 0.05$$
$$\gamma = 0.963$$

The test then becomes 'If $\sum_1^{10} X_i > 8$, reject H_0; if $\sum_1^{10} X_i < 8$, accept H_0; while if $\sum_1^{10} X_i = 8$, reject H_0 with probability 0.963.' This is of course a randomized test, which, in terms of its critical function, may be restated as

$$\phi(x_1, x_2, \ldots, x_{10}) = 1, \qquad \sum_1^{10} x_i > 8$$

$$\phi(x_1, x_2, \ldots, x_{10}) = 0.963, \qquad \sum_1^{10} x_i = 8$$

$$\phi(x_1, x_2, \ldots, x_{10}) = 0, \qquad \sum_1^{10} x_i < 8$$

The power of this test is, when $\lambda = 0.5$,

$$\Pr\left[\sum_1^{10} X_i > 8 \,|\, \lambda = 0.5\right] + 0.963\left\{\Pr\left[\sum_1^{10} X_i = 8 \,|\, \lambda = 0.5\right]\right\} = 0.0843.$$

However, an experimentalist might well settle for the non-randomized test of size 0.0511, available by choosing $c = 7$, rather than incorporate any randomization which is not related to the experiment.

The question of bias

It would seem to be only sensible for a test to be less likely to reject the null hypothesis when it is true than when it is false. In fact, a test for which there exist values of the power less than the size is said to be biased. We should enquire how a most powerful non-randomized test for two simple hypotheses performs in this respect. Let α be the size of the critical region C, then

$\Pr[(X_1, X_2, \ldots, X_n) \in C \,|\, H_0] = \alpha$. So that

$$
\begin{aligned}
p &= \Pr[(X_1, X_2, \ldots, X_n) \in C \,|\, H_1] \\
&\geqslant k \Pr[(X_1, X_2, \ldots, X_n) \in C \,|\, H_0] = k\alpha
\end{aligned}
\tag{5.3}
$$

Similarly,

$$
\begin{aligned}
1 - p &= \Pr[(X_1, X_2, \ldots, X_n) \notin C \,|\, H_1] \\
&\leqslant k \Pr[(X_1, X_2, \ldots, X_n) \notin C \,|\, H_0] = k(1 - \alpha)
\end{aligned}
\tag{5.4}
$$

Now it is either the case that $k \geqslant 1$, when from the first inequality $p \geqslant \alpha$; or $k < 1$, when from the second inequality $p > \alpha$. In either case, the test is unbiased.

5.4 Applications of the Neyman-Pearson theorem

(*a*) Points of the sample space where both $f(x_1, x_2, \ldots, x_n \,|\, H_0)$ and $f(x_1, x_2, \ldots, x_n \,|\, H_1)$ are zero are not entertained since they cannot arise under either hypothesis.

If $f(x_1, x_2, \ldots, x_n \,|\, H_1) > k_1 f(x_1, x_2, \ldots, x_n \,|\, H_0)$, then for any $k_2 < k_1$, perforce

$$
f(x_1, x_2, \ldots, x_n \,|\, H_1) > k_2 f(x_1, x_2, \ldots, x_n \,|\, H_0)
$$

That is to say, best critical regions are nested. The two illustrative examples may have created the impression that best critical regions invariably lie in the tail of some statistic. The next exercise will dispel that impression.

Exercise 3. X is a single value from the distribution with probability density function

$$
f(x \,|\, \theta) = 1/[\pi\{1 + (x - \theta)^2\}], \qquad -\infty < x < +\infty
$$

$H_0 : \theta = -1$, $H_1 : \theta = 0$. Show that $f(x \,|\, 0)/f(x \,|\, -1) > 2$ for $0 \leqslant x \leqslant 2$.

(*b*) Any point such that $f(x_1, x_2, \ldots, x_n \,|\, H_1) \neq 0$ but $f(x_1, x_2, \ldots, x_n \,|\, H_0) = 0$ yields a ratio which exceeds every finite k and hence is included in every critical region. The set of all such points has zero probability under H_0 and is in fact the best critical region of size zero, for the omission of any subset of its points may decrease the power. This particular best test conforms to the Neyman-Pearson theorem if we allow $k = \infty$.

(c) There are some instances where the ratio of the probability density functions is constant for certain regions of the sample space.

Example 5. $X_1, X_2, \ldots, X_n$ is a random sample from the uniform distribution over $(0, \theta)$. $H_0 : \theta = \theta_0$; $H_1 : \theta = \theta_1 > \theta_0$.

$$f(x_1, x_2, \ldots, x_n | \theta) = \prod_1^n f_i(x_i | \theta) = 1/\theta^n, \max(x_i) < \theta.$$

$$\frac{f(x_1, x_2, \ldots, x_n | \theta_1)}{f(x_1, x_2, \ldots, x_n | \theta_0)} = \begin{cases} \infty, & \theta_0 < \max(x_i) < \theta_1 \\ \left(\dfrac{\theta_0}{\theta_1}\right)^n, & 0 < \max(x_i) \leqslant \theta_0. \end{cases}$$

Hence for $k < (\theta_0/\theta_1)^n$, every sample satisfies

$$\frac{f(x_1, x_2, \ldots, x_n | \theta_1)}{f(x_1, x_2, \ldots, x_n | \theta_0)} > k$$

However, the interval $\theta_0 < \max(x_i) \leqslant \theta_1$ has zero probability when H_0 is true and contributes nothing to the size, but as noted in remark (b), is included in any best critical region. To this interval we adjoin any other of size α. For example,

$$\Pr[0 < \max(X_i) \leqslant c | H_0] = \Pr[0 < X_i \leqslant c, i = 1, 2, \ldots, n | H_0]$$
$$= \{\Pr[0 < X \leqslant c | H_0]\}^n$$
$$= \left(\frac{c}{\theta_0}\right)^n$$

If this is required to be α, then $c = \theta_0 \alpha^{1/n}$.
Hence a best critical region of size α is the union of the intervals

$$(0 < \max(x_i) \leqslant \theta_0 \alpha^{1/n}), \qquad (\theta_0 < \max(x_i) \leqslant \theta_1)$$

The power, when H_1 is true, is

$$\Pr[0 < \max(X_i) \leqslant \theta_0 \alpha^{1/n} | H_1] + \Pr[\theta_0 < \max(X_i) \leqslant \theta_1 | H_1]$$

$$= \left(\frac{\theta_0 \alpha^{1/n}}{\theta_1}\right)^n + 1 - \left(\frac{\theta_0}{\theta_1}\right)^n$$

$$= 1 - \left(\frac{\theta_0}{\theta_1}\right)^n (1 - \alpha)$$

(d) The theorem does not require the sample values to be independent. The distributions specified need not even belong to the same family. We have focused on the case of one parameter, but the only restriction is that all the parameters be specified under either hypothesis,

Example 6. Let $X_1, X_2, \ldots, X_n$ be a random sample from the distribution $N(\mu, \sigma^2)$. $H_0 : \mu = \mu_0, \sigma = \sigma_0$; $H_1 : \mu = \mu_1, \sigma = \sigma_1$.

$$\frac{f(x_1, x_2, \ldots, x_n | \mu_1, \sigma_1)}{f(x_1, x_2, \ldots, x_n | \mu_0, \sigma_0)} = \frac{\prod \frac{1}{\sqrt{(2\pi)}\sigma_1} \exp\left[-\frac{1}{2}(x_i - \mu_1)^2/\sigma_1^2\right]}{\prod \frac{1}{\sqrt{(2\pi)}\sigma_0} \exp\left[-\frac{1}{2}(x_i - \mu_0)^2/\sigma_0^2\right]}$$

$$= \left(\frac{\sigma_0}{\sigma_1}\right)^n \exp\left[\frac{1}{2}\left\{\sum(x_i - \mu_0)^2/\sigma_0^2\right\}\right.$$
$$\left. - \frac{1}{2}\left\{\sum(x_i - \mu_1)^2/\sigma_1^2\right\}\right]$$

and this ratio depends on

$$\frac{\sum(x_i - \mu_0)^2}{\sigma_0^2} - \frac{\sum(x_i - \mu_1)^2}{\sigma_1^2}$$

or ignoring constants,

$$\left(\frac{1}{\sigma_0^2} - \frac{1}{\sigma_1^2}\right)\sum x_i^2 + 2\left(\frac{\mu_1}{\sigma_1^2} - \frac{\mu_0}{\sigma_0^2}\right)\sum x_i > k \qquad (5.5)$$

for best critical regions.

Case I : $\sigma_0 = \sigma_1$. In this case, Equation (5.5) reduces to $(\mu_1 - \mu_0)\sum_1^n x_i > l$, say. In the case $\mu_1 > \mu_0$, this implies $\sum_1^n x_i > d$.

Since $\sum_1^n X_i$ is the sum of independent normally distributed random variables, its distribution, when H_0 is true, is $N(n\mu_0, n\sigma_0^2)$.

$$\Pr\left[\sum_1^n X_i > d | H_0\right] = \Pr\left[\frac{\sum X_i - n\mu_0}{\sqrt{n}\sigma_0} > \frac{d - n\mu_0}{\sqrt{n}\sigma_0} \middle| H_0\right]$$

But $\sum_1^n (X_i - \mu_0)/(\sqrt{n}\sigma_0)$ has the $N(0,1)$ distribution, so that if c_α is the upper 100α per cent point of this distribution, the required best test is:

'If $\left(\sum_1^n x_i - n\mu_0\right)\middle/(\sqrt{n}\sigma_0) > c_\alpha$, reject H_0.'

Evidently, $d = \sqrt{n}\sigma_0 c_\alpha + n\mu_0$. For this case we can readily compute the power as

$$\Pr[\sum X_i > \sqrt{n}\sigma_0 c_\alpha + n\mu_0 | \mu_1, \sigma_0]$$

$$= \Pr\left[\frac{\sum X_i - n\mu_1}{\sqrt{n}\sigma_0} > \frac{n(\mu_0 - \mu_1)}{\sqrt{n}\sigma_0} + c_\alpha \Big| \mu_1, \sigma_0\right]$$

But when H_1 is true, $(\sum X_i - n\mu_1)/(\sqrt{n}\sigma_0)$ has the $N(0, 1)$ distribution and tables may now be used. In fact, the proposed test is a uniformly most powerful test of size α of $H_0 : \mu \leqslant \mu_0, \sigma = \sigma_0$ against $H_1 : \mu > \mu_0, \sigma = \sigma_0$.

Exercise 4.   For Example 6, construct the most powerful test of size α when

$$H_0 : \mu = \mu_0, \sigma = \sigma_0 ; H_1 : \mu = \mu_1 < \mu_0, \sigma = \sigma_0.$$

[Ans. $\sum x_i < d = n\mu_0 - \sqrt{n}\sigma_0 c_\alpha$]

Case II : $\mu_0 = \mu_1$.   The condition in Equation (5.5) depends on

$$\left(\frac{1}{\sigma_0^2} - \frac{1}{\sigma_1^2}\right)\sum_1^n (x_i - \mu_0)^2$$

If also $\sigma_0 < \sigma_1$, we need $\sum_1^n (x_i - \mu_0)^2$ to be sufficiently large. When H_0 is true, we employ the standard result that $\sum_1^n X_i - \mu_0)^2/\sigma_0^2$ has the χ_n^2 distribution. If the upper 100α per cent point of the χ_n^2 distribution is $c_\alpha(n)$, then the most powerful test of size α is:

'If $\sum_1^n (x_i - \mu_0)^2 > \sigma_0^2 c_\alpha(n)$, reject H_0.'

The power of this test is

$$\Pr\left[\sum_1^n (X_i - \mu_0)^2 > \sigma_0^2 c_\alpha(n) | \sigma = \sigma_1\right]$$

$$= \Pr\left[\sum_1^n (X_i - \mu_0)^2/\sigma_1^2 > c_\alpha(n)(\sigma_0/\sigma_1)^2 | \sigma = \sigma_1\right]$$

But now, when H_1 is true, $\sum_1^n (X_i - \mu_0)^2/\sigma_1^2$ has the χ_n^2 distribution and tables of the χ^2 distribution may be used. A glance back over the argument shows that the test is also uniformly most powerful against $H_1 : \sigma > \sigma_0, \mu = \mu_0$.

Exercise 5. In Example 6 if $H_0 : \mu = \mu_0, \sigma = \sigma_0$; $H_1 : \mu = \mu_1$, $\sigma = \sigma_1 > \sigma_0$, show that best critical regions consist of sufficiently large values of

$$\sum_1^n \left[x_i - \left(\frac{\mu_0 \sigma_1^2 - \mu_1 \sigma_0^2}{\sigma_1^2 - \sigma_0^2} \right) \right]^2$$

Exercise 6. $X_1, X_2, \ldots, X_n$ is a random sample from the distribution with probability density function $f(x|\theta) = \theta x^{\theta-1}, 0 < x < 1$. Construct a most powerful test of $H_0 : \theta = \theta_0$ against $H_1 : \theta = \theta_1 > \theta_0$. [Ans. $-\sum \log X_i < c$. Note $-\log X$ has exponential distribution with parameter θ]

Exercise 7. $X_1, X_2, \ldots, X_n$ is a random sample from the discrete distribution with probability density function $f(x|\theta) = \theta^x (1 - \theta)^{1-x}$, $x = 0, 1$. $H_0 : \theta = \theta_0; H_1 : \theta = \theta_1 < \theta_0$. Find the form of the most powerful non-randomized tests. Discuss uniformity against $H_1 : \theta < \theta_0$.
[Ans. Since $\theta_1(1 - \theta_0) < \theta_0(1 - \theta_1)$, sufficiently small values of $\sum x_i$ are uniformly most powerful.]

Exercise 8. $X_1, X_2, \ldots, X_n$ is a random sample from the distribution with probability density function

$$f(x|\theta) = \frac{1}{\sqrt{(2\pi)}\theta x} \exp\left[-\frac{1}{2}\left(\frac{\log x}{\theta}\right)^2 \right], \qquad 0 < x < \infty, \theta > 0$$

Show that there is a uniformly most powerful test of the null hypothesis $H_0 : \theta = \theta_0$ against the alternative $H_1 : \theta > \theta_0$.
[Ans. $\sum(\log x_i)^2 > c$. $Y = \log X$ is $N(0, \theta^2)$, Y^2/θ^2 is χ_1^2.]

Exercise 9. $X_1, X_2, \ldots, X_m$ is a random sample from the gamma distribution with known parameter n and unknown parameter θ. Show that there is a uniformly most powerful test of the null hypothesis $\theta = \theta_0$ against $\theta > \theta_0$ and explain how the critical region can be constructed to have a required size.
[Ans. $\sum x_i < c$, statistic has $\Gamma(nm, \theta_0)$ distribution when H_0 is true.]

5.5 Uniformly most powerful tests for a single parameter

We have noted several cases where a most powerful test of a simple hypothesis against a simple alternative was capable of generalization to a uniformly most powerful test of a composite null hypothesis against a composite alternative. These instances had certain features in common. Thus, the rival hypotheses claimed that the parameter was on one side, as against the other side of a boundary value θ_0 — sometimes described as a *one-sided* test. The power function was increasing, so that its value at θ_0 was in fact the size of the test. These features are reflected in the following more precise formulation. If the joint probability density function $f(x_1, x_2, \ldots, x_n | \theta)$ is such that, whenever $\theta_1 < \theta_2$,

$$\frac{f(x_1, x_2, \ldots, x_n | \theta_2)}{f(x_1, x_2, \ldots, x_n | \theta_1)}$$

is monotone in some function $t(x_1, x_2, \ldots, x_n)$ of the observations, then there exists a uniformly most powerful test of $H_0 : \theta \leqslant \theta_0$ against $H_1 : \theta > \theta_0$ based on the statistic $t(X_1, X_2, \ldots, X_n)$. We give a brief proof of the case when the ratio is a non-decreasing function of $t(x_1, x_2, \ldots, x_n)$.

When $t(x_1, x_2, \ldots, x_n) = t_0, f(x_1, x_2, \ldots, x_n | \theta_2) / f(x_1, x_2, \ldots, x_n | \theta_1)$ is some function of t_0, say $h(t_0)$. But since this is non-decreasing in t, we have

$$t(x_1, x_2, \ldots, x_n) < t_0 \text{ implies } \frac{f(x_1, x_2, \ldots, x_n | \theta_2)}{f(x_1, x_2, \ldots, x_n | \theta_1)} \leqslant h(t_0)$$

$$t(x_1, x_2, \ldots, x_n) > t_0 \text{ implies } \frac{f(x_1, x_2, \ldots, x_n | \theta_2)}{f(x_1, x_2, \ldots, x_n | \theta_1)} \geqslant h(t_0)$$

This is of the form required by the Neyman–Pearson theorem for a most powerful test of $\theta = \theta_1$ against $\theta = \theta_2$. In case the ratio is not strictly increasing in t, then for some test sizes we may have to randomize at some boundary point. If this is necessary, we shall continue to assume that a most powerful test is obtained. We can now find a uniformly most powerful test of $H_0 : \theta \leqslant \theta_0$ against $H_1 : \theta > \theta_0$. We first construct a most powerful test of $H'_0 : \theta = \theta_0$ against $H'_1 : \theta = \theta_2 > \theta_0$ of size α. Then for *any* $\theta_2 > \theta_0$ the test takes the same form, namely of rejecting H'_0 if $t(x_1, x_2, \ldots, x_n) > t_0$ or rejecting H'_0 with probability γ in case $t(x_1, x_2, \ldots, x_n) = t_0$. t_0 is to be determined by the distribution of $t(X_1, X_2, \ldots, X_n)$ when $\theta = \theta_0$. Suppose then such a test be constructed with size α.

It is uniformly most powerful against $\theta > \theta_0$. Now consider any

$$\theta = \theta_1 < \theta_0.$$

$$f(x_1, x_2, \ldots, x_n | \theta_0) / f(x_1, x_2, \ldots, x_n | \theta_1)$$

is an increasing function of $t(x_1, x_2, \ldots, x_n)$ and the test constructed must be a most powerful test of $H'' : \theta = \theta_1$ against $\theta = \theta_0$ (note the interchange of roles) of some size, say α'. But the power at θ_0, which is α, is therefore not smaller than α'. Hence the test constructed, of H'_0 against H'_1, can be taken to cover H_0 against H_1, since the probability of a type I error for any $\theta < \theta_0$ does not exceed the value at θ_0.

Exercise 10. State the obvious amendment if $f(x_1, x_2, \ldots, x_n | \theta_2) / f(x_1, x_2, \ldots, x_n | \theta_1)$ is a non-increasing function of $t(x_1, x_2, \ldots, x_n)$.

Example 7. $X_1, X_2, \ldots, X_n$ is a random sample from the Poisson distribution with parameter λ.

$$\frac{f(x_1, x_2, \ldots, x_n | \lambda_2)}{f(x_1, x_2, \ldots, x_n | \lambda_1)} = \left(\frac{\lambda_2}{\lambda_1}\right)^{\Sigma x_i} \exp\left[n(\lambda_1 - \lambda_2)\right]$$

For every $\lambda_1 < \lambda_2$, this is an increasing function of $\sum_1^n x_i$. Hence there is a uniformly most powerful test of $H_0 : \lambda \leqslant \lambda_0$ against $H_1 : \lambda > \lambda_0$ based on values of $\sum_1^n x_i$.

Exercise 11. Show that for a single value from the Cauchy distribution, $f(x | \theta_2) / f(x | \theta_1)$ is not monotone in x.

The obvious candidate for the statistic mentioned in the last theorem is a sufficient statistic for the parameter θ, when we have

$$\frac{f(x_1, x_2, \ldots, x_n | \theta_2)}{f(x_1, x_2, \ldots, x_n | \theta_1)} = \frac{h(t | \theta_2) g(x_1, x_2, \ldots, x_n)}{h(t | \theta_1) g(x_1, x_2, \ldots, x_n)}$$

$$= \frac{h(t | \theta_2)}{h(t | \theta_1)}$$

If now $h(t | \theta_2) / h(t | \theta_1)$ is monotone in t, the previous theorem may be applied.

The next exercise traces in detail what happens if $h(t | \theta_2) / h(t | \theta_1)$ is not monotone.

Exercise 12. X, Y have joint probability density function

$$f(x,y|\theta) = \frac{1}{2\pi\theta}\exp\left[-\frac{1}{2}\left\{\left(\frac{x+y-2\theta}{\theta}\right)^2 + y^2\right\}\right],$$

$$-\infty < x < +\infty, -\infty < y < +\infty.$$

Show that $T = X + Y$ is sufficient for θ.

If $H_0 : \theta = \frac{1}{2}$; $H_1 : \theta = 1$, show that best critical regions are based on the magnitude of $3t^2 - 4t$. Verify that the values of t for which $3t^2 - 4t \geqslant -1$ do not constitute a best critical region for testing $\theta = 1/2$ against $\theta = 2$.

Exercise 13.   If $X_1, X_2, \ldots, X_n$ is a random sample from the regular exponential family with probability density function

$$f(x|\theta) = \exp[\theta b(x) + c(\theta) + d(x)]$$

show that there is a uniformly most powerful test of $H_0 : \theta \leqslant \theta_0$ against $H_1 : \theta > \theta_0$.

5.6 Most powerful randomized tests

We now turn to the question of whether a most powerful test based on a best critical region can stand up to the competition.

   We shall lose nothing by restricting our remarks to the continuous case. Suppose, then, the joint probability density function is $f(x_1, x_2, \ldots, x_n|\theta)$, $H_0 : \theta = \theta_0$; $H_1 : \theta = \theta_1$ and $\phi(x_1, x_2, \ldots, x_n)$ is any critical function. That is, the probability of rejecting H_0 is

$$\int\int\cdots\int \phi(x_1, x_2, \ldots, x_n) f(x_1, x_2, \ldots, x_n|\theta)dx_1\,dx_2\ldots dx_n = P(\theta) \quad (5.6)$$

where P is the power function. Consider then, for any positive k, the difference

$$P(\theta_1) - kP(\theta_0) = \int\int\cdots\int \phi(x_1, x_2, \ldots, x_n)[f(x_1, x_2, \ldots, x_n|\theta_1)$$
$$- kf(x_1, x_2, \ldots, x_n|\theta_0)]dx_1\,dx_2\ldots dx_n \quad (5.7)$$

This integral will be maximized if for each $(x_1, x_2, \ldots, x_n)$ such that

$$f(x_1, x_2, \ldots, x_n|\theta_1) > kf(x_1, x_2, \ldots, x_n|\theta_0)$$

we assign $\phi(x_1, x_2, \ldots, x_n)$ the value 1 and for each $(x_1, x_2, \ldots, x_n)$

such that

$$f(x_1, x_2, \ldots, x_n | \theta_1) < kf(x_1, x_2, \ldots, x_n | \theta_0)$$

we assign $\phi(x_1, x_2, \ldots, x_n)$ the value 0. Samples for which

$$f(x_1, x_2, \ldots, x_n | \theta_1) = kf(x_1, x_2, \ldots, x_n | \theta_0)$$

contribute nothing to the integral in Equation (5.7) and the value of ϕ is immaterial; say it is γ. Denote then the critical function with such values as $\phi^*(x_1, x_2, \ldots, x_n)$ and let its corresponding power function be $P^*(\theta)$. By construction

$$P^*(\theta_1) - kP^*(\theta_0) \geqslant P(\theta_1) - kP(\theta_0), \tag{5.8}$$

or

$$P^*(\theta_1) - P(\theta_1) \geqslant k[P^*(\theta_0) - P(\theta_0)] \tag{5.9}$$

We deduce that $\qquad P(\theta_0) < P^*(\theta_0)$ implies $P^*(\theta_1) > P(\theta_1)$ (5.10)

So the most powerful test of its size of H_0 against H_1 takes the form:

If $f(x_1, x_2, \ldots, x_n | \theta_1) > kf(x_1, x_2, \ldots, x_n | \theta_0)$, reject H_0 (5.11)

If $f(x_1, x_2, \ldots, x_n | \theta_1) = kf(x_1, x_2, \ldots, x_n | \theta_0)$,
$\qquad$ reject H_0 with probability γ (5.12)

If $f(x_1, x_2, \ldots, x_n | \theta_1) < kf(x_1, x_2, \ldots, x_n | \theta_0)$, accept H_0 (5.13)

The most powerful test is thus essentially that provided by the Neyman–Pearson theorem. We have the additional information that any randomization required at the boundary, to obtain a particular size, still provides a best test. To obtain size α, for $0 < \alpha < 1$, if the test with $\gamma = 0$ has size $\alpha_1 < \alpha$ and with $\gamma = 1$ has size $\alpha_2 > \alpha$, then set $\gamma = (\alpha - \alpha_1)/(\alpha_2 - \alpha_1)$, thus splitting up the probability in the appropriate proportion. Two best tests of the same size are essentially identical except possibly at the boundary of their critical regions. The result does not apply when $k = 0$. There exist tests with power 1, for example 'If $f(x_1, x_2, \ldots, x_n | \theta_1) > 0$, reject H_0', corresponding to the Neyman–Pearson result with $k = 0$. By including extra points in the critical region corresponding to the last-mentioned test, we may increase the size of the test but cannot increase the power.

5.7 Hypothesis testing as a decision process

In our discussion of simple hypothesis testing there were only two 'states of nature' – the single parameter had the value θ_0 or θ_1. On the basis of a sample, together with an auxiliary randomization, we had to decide in favour of one value or the other. In the case of non-randomized tests there is an immediate correspondence with a non-randomized decision function $d(x_1, x_2, ..., x_n)$. We simply allow d to take the value θ_1 if the sample falls in the critical region, and θ_0 otherwise. If, however, the test is randomized, the relationship is not so obvious. Here the sample may provide only the probability of accepting θ_1. A randomized test is not immediately seen as a randomized decision function which would have to be constructed by randomizing over the non-randomized decision functions. In some instances, such a construction can be carried out. To avoid such difficulties, we find it convenient to take over the terminology of risk and loss functions and apply them directly to the use of tests.

For the problem of testing the simple null hypothesis $\theta = \theta_0$ against the simple alternative $\theta = \theta_1$, let l_{ij} be the loss for the decision $\theta = \theta_i$ when the value of the parameter is in fact θ_j, $i, j = 0, 1$. For a test with critical function ϕ, we take the decision $\theta = \theta_1$ with probability $\phi(x_1, x_2, ..., x_n)$ and the decision $\theta = \theta_0$ with probability $1 - \phi(x_1, x_2, ..., x_n)$. So that conditional expected loss for any particular sample, when θ_j is the true value of the parameter, is

$$l_{1j}\phi(x_1, x_2, ..., x_n) + l_{0j}[1 - \phi(x_1, x_2, ..., x_n)], \qquad j = 0, 1 \quad (5.14)$$

The risk is the expectation of this loss over the distribution of the sample values:

$$R(\phi, \theta_j) = l_{0j} + (l_{1j} - l_{0j})E[\phi(X_1, X_2, ..., X_n | \theta_j)], \qquad j = 0, 1 \quad (5.15)$$

We recognize that

$$E[\phi(X_1, X_2, ..., X_n | \theta_0)] = \alpha = \text{probability of a type I error} \quad (5.16)$$
$$E[\phi(X_1, X_2, ..., X_n | \theta_1)] = 1 - \beta$$
$$= 1 - \text{probability of a type II error} \quad (5.17)$$

So that we may also write the two risk values as

$$R(\phi, \theta_0) = l_{00} + (l_{10} - l_{00})\alpha \qquad (5.18)$$
$$R(\phi, \theta_1) = l_{11} + (l_{01} - l_{11})\beta \qquad (5.19)$$

where the notation suppresses the fact that the α, β in question depend on which ϕ we are talking about.

In principle, the risk set may now be plotted. For the special case $l_{00} = l_{11} = 0$ and $l_{10} = l_{01} = 1$ each point in the risk set has co-ordinates (α, β) such that $0 \leqslant \alpha \leqslant 1$, $0 \leqslant \beta \leqslant 1$, though for any

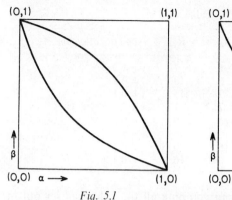

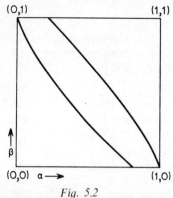

(0,1)   (1,1)

Fig. 5.1   Fig. 5.2

particular value α, only a limited range of values of β will be attainable. Indeed, the Neyman–Pearson theorem assures us that for each α there is a most powerful test for which β is a minimum.

Further, for each such best test, there is a complementary 'worst' test of size $1 - \alpha$ and power β. The line joining the points representing this pair of tests always contains the point $(\frac{1}{2}, \frac{1}{2})$. If the test with risks α_1, β_1 is chosen with probability p and the test with risks α_2, β_2 with probability $1 - p$, the result is a test with risks $p\alpha_1 + (1 - p)\alpha_2, p\beta_1 + (1 - p)\beta_2$. By the usual considerations, this test is represented by a point on the segment joining (α_1, β_1) to (α_2, β_2). Once again the risk sets are convex and Figs. 5.1 and 5.2 represent two possible risk sets.

For a most powerful test with risks $0 < \alpha^* < 1, 0 < \beta^* < 1$, we have, from Equation (5.9),

$$\beta - \beta^* \geqslant k(\alpha^* - \alpha) \qquad (5.20)$$

so that for $k > 0$, $\alpha < \alpha^*$ implies $\beta > \beta^*$, and $\beta < \beta^*$ implies $\alpha > \alpha^*$. All such tests are admissible. Also, $\beta^* + k\alpha^*$ is a minimum since from Equation (5.20) it is less than or equal to $\beta + k\alpha$.

Example 8. A single value y is drawn from the binomial distribution with parameters $n = 2, \theta$. $H_0 : \theta = \frac{3}{4}$; $H_1 : \theta = \frac{1}{4}$, $l_{00} = l_{11} = 0$, $l_{01} = l_{10} = 16$.

The sample value y can assume the values $0, 1, 2$ and we find the risks for the eight possible non-randomized tests. If the critical region consists only of the sample value $y = 0$,

$$R_0 = 16\alpha = 16 \Pr(Y = 0 | \theta = \tfrac{3}{4}) = 16(\tfrac{1}{4})^2 = 1$$
$$R_1 = 16\beta = 16 \Pr(Y = 1 \text{ or } 2 | \theta = \tfrac{1}{4}) = 16[2(\tfrac{1}{4})(\tfrac{3}{4}) + (\tfrac{1}{4})^2] = 7$$

Table 5.1

Critical region	R_0	R_1	Non-critical region
$y = 0$	1	7	$y = 1, 2$
$y = 1$	6	10	$y = 0, 2$
$y = 2$	9	15	$y = 0, 1$
$y = 0, 1$	7	1	$y = 2$
$y = 1, 2$	15	9	$y = 0$
$y = 0, 2$	10	6	$y = 1$
$y = 0, 1, 2$	16	0	
	0	16	$y = 0, 1, 2$

In the same manner we can compute all the values as set out in Table 5.1.

Figure 5.3 shows the convex risk set generated by the eight non-randomized tests listed. The usual routine is followed for detecting the most powerful tests among these.

$$\frac{f(y|p = \tfrac{1}{4})}{f(y|p = \tfrac{3}{4})} = \frac{\binom{2}{y}(\tfrac{1}{4})^y(\tfrac{3}{4})^{2-y}}{\binom{2}{y}(\tfrac{3}{4})^y(\tfrac{1}{4})^{2-y}}$$

$$= \frac{3^{2-y}}{3^y}$$

$$= \frac{1}{9^{y-1}}, \qquad \text{a decreasing function of } y.$$

The most powerful tests (of their size), based on critical regions determined by values of y such that $1/9^{y-1} > k$, are:

(a) $y \leqslant 2$, $1/9^{y-1} \geqslant 1/9$, size 1;
(b) $y \leqslant 1$, $1/9^{y-1} \geqslant 1$, size 7/16;
(c) $y \leqslant 0$, $1/9^{y-1} \geqslant 9$, size 1/16;
(d) reject $p = \tfrac{1}{4}$, whatever y, size 0.

As expected, these four tests correspond to admissible points (marked A, B, C, D in Fig 5.3) on the south-west boundary of the risk set. Suppose now we require the most powerful test of size 1/4. Since this size is intermediate between 1/16, 7/16 we must split the difference $7/16 - 1/16 = 6/16$ at $y = 1$ to make up $1/4 = 4/16$. Choose γ so that

$$\frac{1}{16} + \gamma \frac{6}{16} = \frac{4}{16}; \text{ i.e., } \gamma = \frac{1}{2}$$

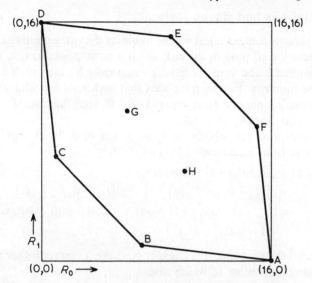

Fig. 5.3 A, B, C, D, E, F, G, H are the points in the risk set which correspond to the eight non-randomized tests.

Hence the required test is 'If $y = 0$, reject H_0; if $y = 1$, reject H_0 with probability $\frac{1}{2}$.' The probability of a type II error is

$$\binom{2}{2}\left(\frac{1}{16}\right) + \frac{1}{2}\binom{2}{1}\left(\frac{1}{4}\right)\left(\frac{3}{4}\right) = \frac{4}{16}$$

The risks for this test are $R_0 = 4$, $R_1 = 4$, which are the co-ordinates of the point midway between tests C, B, and is again admissible.

Evidently, the test proposed is equivalent to taking the critical region $y = 0, 1$ with probability $\frac{1}{2}$ or the critical region $y = 0$ with probability $\frac{1}{2}$.

This illustrates how a randomised test can be viewed as a randomized decision function. We draw on two other ideas met in connection with estimation. Since the line of equal risks first intersects the risk set at $(4, 4)$, the corresponding test is *minimax*. Finally, if the prior probability that $p = \frac{3}{4}$ is $\frac{1}{2}$, the Bayes risk is

$$\tfrac{1}{2} \times 16\alpha + \tfrac{1}{2} \times 16\beta = 8(\alpha + \beta)$$

This is minimized for all tests represented by points on the segment CB, the minimum Bayes risk being 4.

5.8 Minimax and Bayes tests

In the present context, a test will be minimax if its maximum risk is a minimum for all tests in the risk set. If a most powerful test, with size between 0 and 1, exists having equal risks R', then such a test must be minimax. For we have seen that such tests are admissible, so that there cannot be a test with risks R_0, R_1 such that $\max(R_0, R_1) \leqslant R'$ and $\min(R_0, R_1) < R'$.

Let the prior probability of θ_0 be g and of θ_1 be $(1-g)$. The Bayes risk from Equations (5.18) and (5.19) is

$$b(\phi, g) = gR(\phi, \theta_0) + (1-g)R(\phi, \theta_1)$$
$$= g[l_{00} + (l_{10} - l_{00})\alpha] + (1-g)[l_{11} + (l_{01} - l_{11})\beta]$$
$$= gl_{00} + (1-g)l_{11} + (1-g)(l_{01} - l_{11})[\beta + g(l_{10} - l_{00})\alpha/ \{(1-g)(l_{01} - l_{11})\}] \qquad (5.21)$$

In a 'sensible' problem, it is cheaper to make a correct rather than an incorrect decision. In which case, $l_{01} - l_{11} > 0$ and $l_{10} - l_{00} > 0$.

Suppose also $0 < g < 1$, then Equation (5.21) is minimized when

$$\beta + \frac{g(l_{10} - l_{00})\alpha}{(1-g)(l_{01} - l_{11})}$$

is a minimum. But this is of the form $\beta + k\alpha$ where $k > 0$, and, by Equation (5.20), is minimized by a critical region consisting of those samples such that $f(x_1, x_2, \ldots, x_n | \theta_1)/f(x_1, x_2, \ldots, x_n | \theta_0) > k$, where $k = g(l_{10} - l_{00})/[(1-g)(l_{01} - l_{11})]$. A test with minimum Bayes risk is said to be a *Bayes test*.

Example 9. In Example 8, if $g = \frac{1}{4}$, $k = \frac{1}{4}/\frac{3}{4} = \frac{1}{3}$, and the test corresponding to vertex C of the risk set minimizes the Bayes risk. On the other hand, if $g = \frac{1}{2}$, $k = \frac{1}{2}/\frac{1}{2} = 1$. Since

$$\frac{f(0 | p = \frac{1}{4})}{f(0 | p = \frac{3}{4})} = 9 > 1$$

the critical region $y = 0$ provides a test assuming minimum Bayes risk. But we also have

$$\frac{f(1 | p = \frac{1}{4})}{f(1 | p = \frac{3}{4})} = 1$$

and we may also reject $p = \frac{3}{4}$ with probability γ if $y = 1$ is observed. Since $0 \leqslant \gamma \leqslant 1$, any point on the segment CD minimizes the Bayes risk.

Exercise 14. Employ the method of minimizing the posterior expected loss to recover the result that a Bayes test is a most powerful test of $\theta = \theta_0$ against $\theta = \theta_1$.

Exercise 15. A single value is drawn from the distribution with probability density function $f(x|\theta) = \theta x^{\theta-1}, 0 < x < 1$. $H_0 : \theta = 2$; $H_1 : \theta = 4$. The loss function satisfies $l_{00} = l_{11} = 0, l_{10} = 1, l_{01} = 2$. Sketch the risk set, find the minimax test and the Bayes test when the prior probability that $\theta = 2$ is $\frac{3}{4}$.
[Ans. Minimax test rejects $\theta = 2$ if $x > 1/\sqrt{2}$. Bayes test rejects $\theta = 2$ if $x > \sqrt{3/2}$]

CHAPTER SIX

Hypothesis testing II

6.1 Two-sided tests for a single parameter

The most general situation so far has been testing $\theta \leqslant \theta_0$ against $\theta > \theta_0$. We next wish to consider testing $\theta_1 \leqslant \theta \leqslant \theta_2$ against the two-sided alternative $\theta < \theta_1$ or $\theta > \theta_2$. We can scarcely hope for a uniformly most powerful test for it would have to compete with the best available tests against the one-sided alternatives $\theta < \theta_1$ and $\theta > \theta_2$ taken separately. There are, however, distributions for which uniformly most powerful unbiased tests (u.m.p.u.) can be found. For any $\theta < \theta_1$ or $> \theta_2$, the power will not then be smaller than the size of the test. We review the situation with an illustrative example.

Example 1. A single value is drawn from the distribution with probability density function $f(x|\theta) = \theta x^{\theta-1}, 0 \leqslant x \leqslant 1$. $H_0 : \theta = 2$; $H_1 : \theta = 3$. The Neyman–Pearson theorem provides a most powerful test based on sufficiently large values of x. If the size is to be α, $\Pr(X \geqslant c | \theta = 2) = \alpha$ yields $c = (1 - \alpha)^{1/2}$. This test is unbiased and, since the same critical region is employed for each $\theta > 2$, it is uniformly most powerful against $\theta > 2$. Moreover, the power function, $\Pr(X \geqslant c | \theta) = 1 - c^\theta = 1 - (1 - \alpha)^{\theta/2}$, increases steadily with θ. So that the maximum probability of a type I error is attained at $\theta = 2$. Hence the test is uniformly most powerful for $\theta \leqslant 2$ against $\theta > 2$. If, however, the same critical region is used to test $1 \leqslant \theta \leqslant 2$ against $\theta < 1$ or $\theta > 2$, then its performance against $\theta > 2$ remains the best possible, but against $\theta < 1$ is as poor as can be. Evidently, the critical region should consist both of large and small values of x – it should be two-sided. A plausible test would make the probability of a type I error equal to α both when $\theta = 1$ and when $\theta = 2$. That is, we require constants c_1, c_2 such that

$$\Pr(X \leqslant c_1 | \theta = 1) + \Pr(X \geqslant c_2 | \theta = 1) = \alpha, \text{ and}$$
$$\Pr(X \leqslant c_1 | \theta = 2) + \Pr(X \geqslant c_2 | \theta = 2) = \alpha$$

The solutions are $c_1 = \alpha/2, c_2 = 1 - \alpha/2$ and thus the power function is

$$P(\theta) = \int_0^{c_1} \theta x^{\theta - 1} dx + \int_{c_2}^1 \theta x^{\theta - 1} dx$$
$$= c_1^\theta + 1 - c_2^\theta$$
$$= (\alpha/2)^\theta + 1 - (1 - \alpha/2)^\theta$$

For $1 < \theta < 2, P(\theta) < \alpha$ and for $\theta < 1$ or $\theta > 2, P(\theta) > \alpha$; hence the size of the critical region is α and the test is unbiased. We have no criterion for deciding whether the test is the best of this kind. For this we require an extension of the Neyman–Pearson theorem.

6.2 Neyman–Pearson theorem extension (non-randomized version)

Let $X_1, X_2, \ldots, X_n$ have joint probability density function $f(x_1, x_2, \ldots, x_n | \theta)$ and let U be the region of the sample space such that

$$f(x_1, x_2, \ldots, x_n | \theta^*) \geqslant k_1 f(x_1, x_2, \ldots, x_n | \theta_1)$$
$$+ k_2 f(x_1, x_2, \ldots, x_n | \theta_2) \qquad (6.1)$$

where $\theta_1, \theta_2, \theta^*$ are given values of θ. Then for any other region V, satisfying $\Pr(\mathbf{X} \in V | \theta_i) = \Pr(\mathbf{X} \in U | \theta_i), i = 1, 2$, we have

$$\Pr(\mathbf{X} \in U | \theta^*) \geqslant \Pr(\mathbf{X} \in V | \theta^*)$$

where $\mathbf{X}$ denotes the sample values

Proof

$$\Pr(\mathbf{X} \in U | \theta^*) - \Pr(\mathbf{X} \in V | \theta^*) \qquad (6.2)$$
$$= \Pr[\mathbf{X} \in \{(U \text{ and } V) \text{ or } (U \text{ and not } V)\} | \theta^*]$$
$$- \Pr[\mathbf{X} \in \{(V \text{ and } U) \text{ or } (V \text{ and not } U)\} | \theta^*]$$
$$= \Pr[\mathbf{X} \in (U \text{ and not } V) | \theta^*] - \Pr[\mathbf{X} \in (V \text{ and not } U) | \theta^*]$$

But in U, inequality (6.1) holds so that

$$\Pr[\mathbf{X} \in (U \text{ and not } V) | \theta^*] \geqslant k_1 \Pr[\mathbf{X} \in (U \text{ and not } V) | \theta_1]$$
$$+ k_2 \Pr[\mathbf{X} \in (U \text{ and not } V) | \theta_2] \qquad (6.3)$$

While outside U, inequality (6.1) does not hold and

$$\Pr[\mathbf{X} \in (V \text{ and not } U) | \theta^*] \leqslant k_1 \Pr[\mathbf{X} \in (V \text{ and not } U) | \theta_1]$$
$$+ k_2 \Pr[\mathbf{X} \in (V \text{ and not } U) | \theta_2] \qquad (6.4)$$

Using Equations (6.3) and (6.4), after restoring the common region U and V,

$$\Pr(\mathbf{X} \in U | \theta^*) - \Pr(\mathbf{X} \in V | \theta^*) \geqslant k_1 [\Pr(\mathbf{X} \in U | \theta_1) - \Pr(\mathbf{X} \in V | \theta_1)]$$
$$+ k_2 [\Pr(\mathbf{X} \in U | \theta_2) - \Pr(\mathbf{X} \in V | \theta_2)]$$
$$(6.5)$$

But by assumption, the coefficients of k_1, k_2 in Equation (6.5) are both zero.

Comment on the theorem

1. The X_i need not be independent.
2. $\theta_1, \theta_2, \theta^*$ may be vectors.
3. In terms of hypothesis testing, we obtain the best critical region for testing $\theta = \theta_1$ or θ_2 against $\theta = \theta^*$ for the specified probabilities of type I error at θ_1, θ_2. For k_1, k_2 both positive, no improvement is possible even by decreasing these last probabilities.
4. $k_1 \Pr(\mathbf{X} \in U | \theta_1) + k_2 \Pr(\mathbf{X} \in U | \theta_2) \leqslant \Pr(\mathbf{X} \in U | \theta^*)$.

Also

$$\Pr(\mathbf{X} \in U | \theta^*) = 1 - \Pr(\mathbf{X} \in \text{not } U | \theta^*)$$
$$> 1 - [k_1 \Pr(\mathbf{X} \in \text{not } U | \theta_1) + k_2 \Pr(\mathbf{X} \in \text{not } U | \theta_2)]$$
$$= 1 - [k_1 \{1 - \Pr(\mathbf{X} \in U | \theta_1)\} + k_2 \{1 - \Pr(\mathbf{X} \in U | \theta_2)\}]$$

For the case $\Pr(\mathbf{X} \in U | \theta_1) = \Pr(\mathbf{X} \in U | \theta_2)$, we have

$$\Pr(\mathbf{X} \in U | \theta^*) \geqslant (k_1 + k_2) \Pr(\mathbf{X} \in U | \theta_1) \text{ and}$$
$$\Pr(\mathbf{X} \in U | \theta^*) > 1 - (k_1 + k_2)[1 - \Pr(\mathbf{X} \in U | \theta_1)]$$

and whether $k_1 + k_2 \geqslant 1$ or $k_1 + k_2 < 1$, we have

$$\Pr(\mathbf{X} \in U | \theta^*) \geqslant \Pr(\mathbf{X} \in U | \theta_1).$$

That is to say, the test is then unbiased.

Example 2. A single value is drawn from the distribution with probability density function $f(x|\theta) = \theta x^{\theta-1}, 0 < x < 1$. It is required

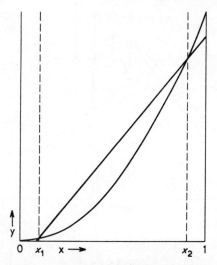

Fig. 6.1 Intersection of $y = 3x^2$ with $y = k_1 + 2k_2x$.

to find the most powerful test of the hypothesis that $\theta = 1$ or $\theta = 2$ (with probabilities of type I error α_1, α_2 respectively) against the alternative that $\theta = 3$.

Our object is to use the extension of the Neyman–Pearson theorem to discuss the best critical region. We seek those values of x such that

$$f(x|\theta = 3) \geqslant k_1 f(x|\theta = 1) + k_2 f(x|\theta = 2)$$

or $3x^2 \geqslant k_1 + 2x_2x$ $2k_2x$

The parabola $y = 3x^2$, meets the line $y = k_1 + 2k_2x$ in at most two points, (Fig. 6.1). The intervals where the inequality holds are of the form $0 \leqslant x \leqslant x_1$ or $x_2 \leqslant x \leqslant 1$ where we allow either $x_1 = 0$ or $x_2 = 1$. Now x_1, x_2 are determined by the requirements

$$\Pr(0 \leqslant X \leqslant x_1|\theta = 1) + \Pr(x_2 \leqslant X \leqslant 1|\theta = 1) = \alpha_1$$
$$\Pr(0 \leqslant X \leqslant x_1|\theta = 2) + \Pr(x_2 \leqslant X \leqslant 1|\theta = 2) = \alpha_2$$

We may further consider how the critical region performs for other values of θ (see Figs 6.2, 6.3, 6.4).

For each $\theta > 2$, $\theta x^{\theta-1}$ has positive and increasing slope and hence the line through $(x_1, \theta x_1^{\theta-1}), (x_2, \theta x_2^{\theta-1})$ is below $\theta x^{\theta-1}$ when and only when $0 \leqslant x < x_1$, or $x_2 < x \leqslant 1$. That is, there exist k_1, k_2 such

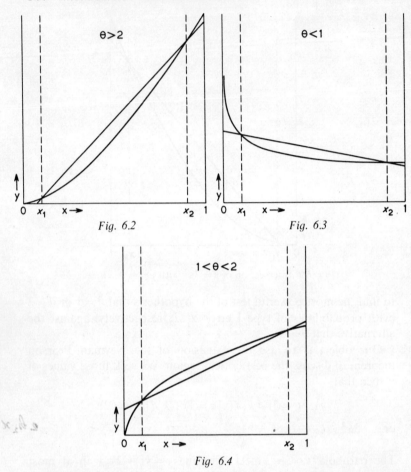

Fig. 6.2   Fig. 6.3

Fig. 6.4

that $\theta x^{\theta-1} \geqslant k_1 + 2k_2 x$ when $x \leqslant x_1$ or $x \geqslant x_2$ for any $\theta > 2$, (though not the same k_1, k_2 for each such θ). Similar conclusions are reached for each $\theta < 1$. When, however, $1 < \theta < 2$, precisely the opposite is the case: the line is higher than the curve when and only when $x < x_1$, or $x > x_2$.

Exercise 1. Show that for Example 2, $x_1 \leqslant x \leqslant x_2$ is the best critical region for testing $\theta = 1$ or $\theta = 2$ against $\theta = 3/2$, having probabilities of type I error $1 - \alpha_1, 1 - \alpha_2$ at $\theta = 1, \theta = 2$ respectively.

In Example 2, if $\alpha_1 = \alpha_2 = \alpha$, the critical region $0 \leqslant x \leqslant x_1$, $x_2 \leqslant x \leqslant 1$ provides a uniformly most powerful unbiased test of size α of the hypothesis that $1 \leqslant \theta \leqslant 2$ against $\theta < 1$ or $\theta > 2$.

6.3 Regular exponential family of distributions

It would of course be most convenient if instead of examining each case separately we could identify the position of the best critical region for testing two-sided hypotheses. This is possible for members of the regular exponential family, which we examine in the continuous case. Let X be drawn from the distribution with probability density function

$$f(x \mid \theta) = c(\theta)h(x)\exp(\theta x)$$

The null hypothesis is that $\theta = \theta_1$ or θ_2 ($\theta_1 < \theta_2$) and the alternative that $\theta = \theta^*$. The most powerful test with probability of type I error equal to α_1 when $\theta = \theta_1$, and α_2 when $\theta = \theta_2$, is the set of x such that

$$f(x \mid \theta^*) > k_1 f(x \mid \theta_1) + k_2 f(x \mid \theta_2) \text{ for some } k_1, k_2 \quad (6.6)$$

That is,

$$c(\theta^*)h(x)\exp(\theta^* x) > k_1 c(\theta_1)h(x)\exp(\theta_1 x)$$
$$+ k_2 c(\theta_2)h(x)\exp(\theta_2 x) \quad (6.7)$$

and where $h(x) \neq 0$,

$$1 > \frac{k_1 c(\theta_1)}{c(\theta^*)}\exp[(\theta_1 - \theta^*)x] + \frac{k_2 c(\theta_2)}{c(\theta^*)}\exp[(\theta_2 - \theta^*)x] \quad (6.8)$$

or, with evident identification,

$$1 > a_1 \exp(b_1 x) + a_2 \exp(b_2 x) \quad (6.9)$$

The function $a_1 \exp(b_1 x) + a_2 \exp(b_2 x)$ has slope $a_1 b_1 \exp(b_1 x) + a_2 b_2 \exp(b_2 x)$, hence there is a turning value at $x = x_0$ if

$$a_1 b_1 \exp(b_1 x_0) = -a_2 b_2 \exp(b_2 x_0) \quad (6.10)$$

The second derivative, evaluated at x_0, is

$$(b_2 - b_1)a_2 b_2 \exp(b_2 x_0) \quad (6.11)$$

There is at most one solution x_0 and the values of b_1, b_2, a_2 determine the nature of the turning value. Prompted by our previous example, we determine x_1, x_2 ($x_1 < x_2$) so that

$$\Pr(X \leqslant x_1 \mid \theta = \theta_1) + \Pr(X \geqslant x_2 \mid \theta = \theta_1) = \alpha_1$$
$$\Pr(X \leqslant x_1 \mid \theta = \theta_2) + \Pr(X \geqslant x_2 \mid \theta = \theta_2) = \alpha_2 \quad (6.12)$$

We leave as an exercise the determination of a_1, a_2 such that

$$a_1 \exp(b_1 x_1) + a_2 \exp(b_2 x_1) = 1$$
$$a_1 \exp(b_1 x_2) + a_2 \exp(b_2 x_2) = 1 \quad (6.13)$$

Looking at the solutions for a_1, a_2, there are three cases to consider.

1. If $0 < b_1 < b_2$, we have $a_1 > 0, a_2 < 0$. Hence there is a solution to Equation (6.10) and from Equation (6.11) it corresponds to a maximum. Hence if $x < x_1$ or $x > x_2, a_1 \exp(b_1 x) + a_2 \exp(b_2 x) < 1$ for any such b_1, b_2. That is, for any $\theta^* < \theta_1$ there exist k_1, k_2 such that Equation (6.6) is satisfied for $x < x_1$ or $x > x_2$.

2. If $b_1 < b_2 < 0$, we have $a_1 < 0, a_2 > 0$, and x_0 again corresponds to a maximum. Hence if $\theta^* > \theta_2$, there exist k_1, k_2 such that Equation (6.6) is satisfied for $x < x_1$ or $x > x_2$.

3. If $b_1 < 0 < b_2$, we have $a_1 > 0$ and $a_2 > 0$, and x_0 corresponds to a minimum between x_1 and x_2. That is, for $\theta_1 \leqslant \theta \leqslant \theta_2$, there exist k_1, k_2 such that Equation (6.6) is satisfied when and only when $x_1 \leqslant x \leqslant x_2$.

In summary, the critical region $x < x_1$ or $x > x_2$ is best for testing $\theta_1 \leqslant \theta \leqslant \theta_2$ against $\theta < \theta_1$ or $\theta > \theta_2$ among all those which have fixed power at $\theta = \theta_1$ and $\theta = \theta_2$. If we insist that those powers be equal (say to α), then the corresponding test is uniformly most powerful unbiased (of size α).

Exercise 2. A single value is drawn from the distribution with probability density function $f(x \mid \theta) = \theta e^{-\theta x}$. $H_0 : 1 \leqslant \theta \leqslant 2$; $H_1 : \theta < 1$ or $\theta > 2$. Construct the u.m.p.u. test of size α and show that the power function is $P(\theta) = 1 - (1 - \alpha/2)^\theta + (\alpha/2)^\theta$.

Exercise 3. A single value is drawn from the distribution $N(\mu, 1)$. Construct a u.m.p.u. test of size 5 per cent, of $1 \leqslant \mu \leqslant 2$ against $\mu < 1$ or $\mu > 2$.
[Ans. Critical region, $x < -0.67$ or $x > 3.67$]

It is to be observed that the case of a sample of n from the distribution $f(x \mid \theta) = c(\theta) h(x) \exp(\theta x)$ is not more general since the application of Equation (6.6) reduces the best test to a critical region based on the sum of the sample values. That is, we consider a single value of the sufficient statistic and this has a distribution which is again a member of the regular exponential family.

6.4 Uniformly most powerful unbiased test of $\theta = \theta_0$ against $\theta \neq \theta_0$

There remains outstanding the case of testing $\theta = \theta_0$ against $\theta \neq \theta_0$. If we select a particular $\theta = \theta^* \neq \theta_0$ as the alternative, then of course the ordinary Neyman–Pearson theorem provides us with a most powerful test of size α. We now seek the best test of given size for which the power function has given slope at $\theta = \theta_0$. Eventually we shall allow this slope to be zero, to obtain the property of unbiasedness.

Theorem. The random variables $X_1, X_2, \ldots, X_n$ have joint probability density function $f(x_1, x_2, \ldots, x_n | \theta)$ which is differentiable with respect to θ, and this operation can be interchanged with integration with respect to the x_i. The null hypothesis is that $\theta = \theta_0$ and the alternative that $\theta = \theta^* \neq \theta_0$. Then the most powerful test, of given size and for which the power function has given slope at θ_0, is provided by the critical region U consisting of those $x_1, x_2, \ldots, x_n$ such that

$$f(x_1, x_2, \ldots, x_n | \theta^*) > k_1 f(x_1, x_2, \ldots, x_n | \theta_0)$$
$$+ k_2 \left[\frac{\partial}{\partial \theta} f(x_1, x_2, \ldots, x_n | \theta) \right]_{\theta_0} \quad (6.14)$$

For let V be any other set such that

$$\Pr[\mathbf{X} \in V | \theta_0] = \Pr[\mathbf{X} \in U | \theta_0) \text{ and} \quad (6.15)$$

$$\left\{ \frac{\partial}{\partial \theta} \Pr[\mathbf{X} \in V | \theta] \right\}_{\theta_0} = \left\{ \frac{\partial}{\partial \theta} \Pr[\mathbf{X} \in U | \theta] \right\}_{\theta_0} \quad (6.16)$$

Now $\Pr[\mathbf{X} \in U | \theta^*] - \Pr[\mathbf{X} \in V | \theta^*]$

$= \Pr[\mathbf{X} \in (U \text{ and not } V) | \theta^*] - \Pr[\mathbf{X} \in (V \text{ and not } U) | \theta^*]$

$> k_1 \Pr[\mathbf{X} \in (U \text{ and not } V) | \theta_0]$

$\quad + k_2 \left\{ \frac{\partial}{\partial \theta} \Pr[\mathbf{X} \in (U \text{ and not } V)] | \theta \right\}_{\theta_0}$

$\quad - k_1 \Pr[\mathbf{X} \in (V \text{ and not } U) | \theta_0]$

$\quad - k_2 \left\{ \frac{\partial}{\partial \theta} \Pr[\mathbf{X} \in (V \text{ and not } U) | \theta] \right\}_{\theta_0}$

$= k_1 \{ \Pr[\mathbf{X} \in U | \theta_0] - \Pr[\mathbf{X} \in V | \theta_0] \}$

$\quad + k_2 \left(\frac{\partial}{\partial \theta} \{ \Pr[\mathbf{X} \in U | \theta] - \Pr[\mathbf{X} \in V | \theta] \} \right)_{\theta_0}$

When the conditions of Equations (6.15) and (6.16) hold, the coefficients of k_1, k_2 are both zero. For some distributions, the same U will serve as the best critical region for each $\theta \neq \theta_0$, thus providing a uniformly most powerful test (subject to the slope condition).

If, in addition, the power function has a minimum at θ_0, the test will be u.m.p.u. This situation will arise with the regular exponential family of distributions. For suppose the probability density function is $c(\theta)h(x)\exp(\theta x)$, then

$$\frac{\partial}{\partial\theta}[f(x|\theta)] = c'(\theta)h(x)\exp(\theta x) + c(\theta)h(x)\exp(\theta x)x$$

Hence, applying the theorem we require the set of x such that

$$c(\theta^*)h(x)\exp(\theta^* x) > k_1 c(\theta_0)h(x)\exp(\theta_0 x) + k_2[c'(\theta_0)h(x)\exp(\theta_0 x)$$
$$+ c(\theta_0)h(x)\exp(\theta_0 x)x]$$

or

$$\exp[x(\theta^* - \theta_0)] > [k_1 c(\theta_0) + k_2 c'(\theta_0) + k_2 c(\theta_0)x]/c(\theta^*)$$
$$= k_1^* + k_2^* x$$

Since $\exp[x(\theta^* - \theta_0)]$ is monotone with positive second derivative with respect to x, it is clear that if $x < x_1$ or $x > x_2$, then the inequality holds for some k_1^*, k_2^* for any $\theta^* \neq \theta_0$. [A rough sketch is helpful.] Thus, to construct a u.m.p.u. test of size α, for a continuous distribution, we must find x_1, x_2 such that

$$\Pr[X \leqslant x_1 \text{ or } X \geqslant x_2 | \theta = \theta_0] = \alpha$$

$$\left\{\frac{\partial}{\partial\theta}\Pr[X \leqslant x_1 \text{ or } X \geqslant x_2 | \theta]\right\}_{\theta_0} = 0$$

Exercise 4.   A single value is drawn from the exponential distribution, $f(x|\theta) = \theta\exp(-\theta x)$, $x > 0$. Construct a u.m.p.u. test of $\theta = 1$ against $\theta \neq 1$ of size 10 per cent.
[Ans. Critical region, $x < 0.084$ or $x > 3.945$].

Exercise 5. X_1, X_2 is a random sample of two from the distribution $N(0, \sigma^2)$. Construct the u.m.p.u. test of the null hypothesis $\sigma = 1$ against $\sigma \neq 1$ of size 2 per cent. Verify that a test which assigns 1 per cent to each tail when $\sigma = 1$ is biased for $1/\sqrt{2} < \sigma < 1$.

For discrete distributions, the size requirement is met by randomization at the boundary points.

Example 3.   A single value is drawn from a binomial distribution with $n = 4$ and parameter θ. To construct the u.m.p.u. test of the hypothesis $1/3 \leqslant \theta \leqslant 1/2$ against $\theta < 1/3$ or $\theta > 1/2$ of size 0.3, we compute $f(x|\theta = 1/3)$, $f(x|\theta = 1/2)$ for $x = 0, 1, 2, 3, 4$:

	0	1	2	3	4
$f(x|1/3)$	16/81	32/81	24/81	8/81	1/81

	0	1	2	3	4
$f(x|1/2)$	1/16	4/16	6/16	4/16	1/16

Suppose the null hypothesis is rejected with probability γ_1 when $x = 1$ and with probability γ_2 when $x = 3$. Then we must have

$$\frac{1}{16} + \frac{4}{16}\gamma_1 + \frac{4}{16}\gamma_2 + \frac{1}{16} = 0.3$$

$$\frac{16}{81} + \frac{32}{81}\gamma_1 + \frac{8}{81}\gamma_2 + \frac{1}{81} = 0.3$$

whence $\gamma_1 \approx 0.07$, $\gamma_2 \approx 0.63$

6.5 Nuisance parameters

It may happen that the hypotheses of interest do not specify some of the parameters, yet as the next example shows, they cannot just be ignored.

Example 4. X, Y have independent ordinary exponential distributions with parameters λ, $\theta\lambda$ respectively. The null hypothesis is that $\theta = 1$, the alternative that $\theta = \theta_1 > 1$. Both are composite, since nothing is said about λ, it is duly termed a *nuisance parameter*. To study the situation, we fix $\lambda = \lambda_0$ under the null hypothesis, and $\lambda = \lambda_1 > \lambda_0$ (say) under the alternative. We may now apply the Neyman–Pearson theorem:

$$\frac{f(x, y|\theta = \theta_1, \lambda = \lambda_1)}{f(x, y|\theta = 1, \lambda = \lambda_0)} = \frac{\lambda_1^2 \theta_1 \exp[-\lambda_1(x + \theta_1 y)]}{\lambda_0^2 \exp[-\lambda_0(x + y)]}$$

$$= \frac{\lambda_1^2 \theta_1}{\lambda_0^2} \exp[(\lambda_0 - \lambda_1)x + (\lambda_0 - \lambda_1\theta_1)y]$$

This ratio is governed by $(\lambda_0 - \lambda_1)x + (\lambda_0 - \lambda_1\theta_1)y$, and the distribution of the corresponding statistic depends on the value of λ. If we cannot ignore the nuisance parameter, then we can attempt to eliminate it. This may be accomplished by arguing conditionally on a statistic sufficient for the nuisance parameter when the null hypothesis is true. In this instance we have that $X + Y$ is sufficient for λ when $\theta = 1$. The position of the most powerful critical region for fixed $x + y$ is not immediately obvious. We rewrite the ratio obtained above so that terms involving $x + y$ are displayed. It is easily checked that

$$\frac{f(x, y \mid \theta = \theta_1, \lambda = \lambda_1)}{f(x, y \mid \theta = 1, \lambda = \lambda_0)} = \frac{\lambda_1^2 \theta_1}{\lambda_0^2} \exp\left[(\lambda_0 - \lambda_1)(x + y) + \lambda_1(1 - \theta_1)y\right]$$

For fixed $x + y = t$, this expression decreases with $y (\theta_1 > 1)$. Hence the most powerful such test of $\theta = 1$ against $\theta = \theta_1 > 1$ is based on small values of y given $x + y$. The remaining details concerning the construction of the conditional critical region are discussed in the next exercise.

Exercise 6.   When H_0 is true, the joint p.d.f. of X, Y is $f(x, y)$ $= \lambda_0^2 \exp\left[- \lambda_0(x + y)\right]$. Show that the joint distribution of $S = Y$, $T = X + Y$ has p.d.f. $h(s, t) = \lambda_0^2 \exp\left[- \lambda_0 t\right]$, $0 < s < t$. Hence show that $h(s \mid t) = 1/t$, $0 < s < t$. Evidently, the distribution of Y given $X + Y = t$ is uniform over $(0, t)$. Hence $\Pr(Y \leqslant c \mid X + Y = t) = c/t$, and for this to be α, we take $c = \alpha t$. The test is now straightforward – the sample values are observed to have sum t – if $y/t \leqslant \alpha$ then $\theta = 1$ is rejected with probability of type I error equal to α, *whatever the value of* λ, a property conferred by using the sufficient statistic. A sketch of the critical region in the x, y plane will be found instructive.

Exercise 7.   The conditional power of the test in Exercise 6 is now examined. Show that for general λ, θ

$$h(s, t \mid \lambda, \theta) = \lambda^2 \theta \exp\left[- s\lambda\theta + s\lambda - \lambda t\right], 0 < s < t, \text{ and } h(s \mid t, \lambda, \theta)$$
$$= \lambda(\theta - 1)\exp\left[- \lambda s(\theta - 1)\right]/(1 - \exp\left[- \lambda t(\theta - 1)\right], 0 \leqslant s \leqslant t.$$

Hence show that

$$\Pr(S \leqslant \alpha t \mid T = t, \lambda, \theta) = \{1 - \exp\left[- \lambda\alpha t(\theta - 1)\right]\}/$$
$$\{1 - \exp\left[- \lambda t(\theta - 1)\right]\}.$$

6.6 Similar tests

We take up the ideas generated by the above illustrative example. There the test had the property that the probability of rejecting the null hypothesis, when it was true, remained constant whatever the value of the nuisance parameter. Such a test is called a *similar test* (of size α) and the corresponding critical region is known as a *similar critical region* (of size α).

More generally, suppose that $\mathbf{X} = (X_1, X_2, \dots, X_n)$ has a probability density function which depends on $r + s$ parameters $(\theta_1, \theta_2, \dots, \theta_r, \theta_{r+1}, \dots, \theta_{r+s}) = (\boldsymbol{\theta}_r, \boldsymbol{\theta}_s)$. The null hypothesis asserts that the first r components assume the particular set of values $(\theta_{10}, \theta_{20}, \dots, \theta_{r0}) = \boldsymbol{\theta}_{r0}$ and nothing is asserted about $(\theta_{r+1}, \dots, \theta_{r+s}) = \boldsymbol{\theta}_s$. Then if a critical region, C, exists such that

$$\Pr(\mathbf{X} \in C \,|\, \boldsymbol{\theta}_{r0}, \boldsymbol{\theta}_s) = \alpha$$

for any $\boldsymbol{\theta}_s$, then C is said to be a *similar critical region* (of size α).

Example 5. $X_1, X_2, \dots, X_n$ is a random sample from the distribution $N(\mu, \sigma^2)$. The null hypothesis is $\sigma = \sigma_0$. The statistic $\sum_{i=1}^{n} (X_i - \bar{X})^2 / \sigma_0^2$ has the χ_{n-1}^2 distribution $(n \geq 2)$ whatever the value of μ, hence, in this case, there do exist similar critical regions of any size.

One way of constructing similar critical regions is via a statistic, $\mathbf{T}_s$, known to be sufficient for the nuisance parameter $\boldsymbol{\theta}_s$ when $\boldsymbol{\theta}_r = \boldsymbol{\theta}_{r0}$. For then $\Pr(\mathbf{X} \in C \,|\, \boldsymbol{\theta}_{r0}, \mathbf{T}_s = \mathbf{t}_s)$ does not depend on $\boldsymbol{\theta}_s$. These similar regions are generated by parts of curves on which the sufficient statistic is constant. This does not guarantee that there are not other similar critical region *not* based on the sufficient statistic. Such possibilities are ruled out if the statistic is also boundedly complete. For let D be any similar region of size α, then we have

$$\Pr[\mathbf{X} \in D \,|\, \boldsymbol{\theta}_r = \boldsymbol{\theta}_{r0}, \boldsymbol{\theta}_s] = \alpha$$

Conditioning on the sufficient statistic for $\boldsymbol{\theta}_s$,

$$E[\Pr(\mathbf{X} \in D \,|\, \boldsymbol{\theta}_{r0}, \boldsymbol{\theta}_s, \mathbf{T}_s)] = \alpha$$
$$E[\Pr(\mathbf{X} \in D \,|\, \boldsymbol{\theta}_{r0}, \mathbf{T}_s)] = \alpha$$
$$E[\Pr(\mathbf{X} \in D \,|\, \boldsymbol{\theta}_{r0}, \mathbf{T}_s) - \alpha] = 0$$

where the expectation is over the distribution of $\mathbf{T}_s$. But this distribution is boundedly complete, so that

$$\Pr(\mathbf{X} \in D \,|\, \boldsymbol{\theta}_{r0}, t_s) - \alpha = 0$$

Hence any contour in D for which $\mathbf{T}_s$ is fixed, has conditional size α.

These ideas are further explored in the next example, which eventually yields the 'usual solution' to a standard problem.

Example 6. $X_1, X_2, \ldots, X_n$ is a random sample from the distribution $N(\mu, \sigma^2)$. The null hypothesis is that $\mu = \mu_0$, the alternative that $\mu = \mu_1$, the nuisance parameter being unspecified. It is required to find a most powerful similar test. We have

$$\frac{f(x_1, \ldots, x_n | \mu = \mu_1, \sigma = \sigma_1)}{f(x_1, \ldots, x_n | \mu = \mu_0, \sigma = \sigma_0)} = \frac{(1/\sqrt{(2\pi)}\sigma_1)^n \exp\left[-\frac{1}{2}\sum(x_i - \mu_1)^2/\sigma_1^2\right]}{(1/\sqrt{(2\pi)}\sigma_0)^n \exp\left[-\frac{1}{2}\sum(x_i - \mu_0)^2/\sigma_0^2\right]} \tag{6.17}$$

We cannot proceed, without particular values σ_0, σ_1 in mind, to find an unrestricted best test. However, we can limit our choice to similar tests. We know that when $\mu = \mu_0, T = \sum_1^n (X_i - \mu_0)^2$ is a complete sufficient statistic for σ. We rewrite the ratio in Equation (6.17), to display the effect of keeping the statistic constant, as

$$\left(\frac{\sigma_0}{\sigma_1}\right)^n \exp\left\{\frac{1}{2}\left[\sum_1^n \frac{(x_i - \mu_0)^2}{\sigma_0^2} - \sum_1^n \frac{(x_i - \mu_0 + \mu_0 - \mu_1)^2}{\sigma_1^2}\right]\right\}$$

$$\propto \left(\frac{\sigma_0}{\sigma_1}\right)^n \exp\left\{\frac{1}{2}\left[\sum_1^n (x_i - \mu_0)^2\left(\frac{1}{\sigma_0^2} - \frac{1}{\sigma_1^2}\right) - \frac{2n(\bar{x} - \mu_0)(\mu_0 - \mu_1)}{\sigma_1^2}\right]\right\} \tag{6.18}$$

All that we need to deduce from this somewhat complicated expression is that, for fixed $\sum_1^n (x_i - \mu_0)^2$, it is increasing or decreasing with $\bar{x}$ according as $\mu_1 > \mu_0$ or $\mu_1 < \mu_0$. In principle, this settles the form of the most powerful conditional test—it is based on the distribution of $\bar{X}$ given $\sum_1^n (X_i - \mu_0)^2$. Moreover, so long as $\mu_1 > \mu_0$, the particular value of μ_1 plays no role. Thus, we have a uniformly most powerful similar test of $\mu = \mu_0$ against $\mu > \mu_0$. We say 'in principle', for the distribution of this statistic is by no means apparent! A further effort is required to cast the result in a standard form.

We require, then,

$$\Pr\left[\bar{X} > c(t) \middle| \sum_{i=1}^n (X_i - \mu_0)^2 = t, \mu = \mu_0\right] = \alpha$$

where $c(t)$ implies that the 'constant' depends possibly on the value of t which turns up.

$$\Pr\left[\frac{\bar{X}-\mu_0}{t^{1/2}}>\frac{c(t)-\mu_0}{t^{1/2}}\Big|\sum(X_i-\mu_0)^2=t, \mu=\mu_0\right]=\alpha$$

$$\Pr\left[\frac{\bar{X}-\mu_0}{\{\sum(X_i-\bar{X})^2+n(\bar{X}-\mu_0)^2\}^{1/2}}\right.$$
$$\left.>\frac{c(t)-\mu_0}{t^{1/2}}\Big|\sum(X_i-\mu_0)^2=t, \mu=\mu_0\right]=\alpha \qquad (6.19)$$

Now $\dfrac{\bar{X}-\mu_0}{\{\sum(X_i-\bar{X})^2+n(\bar{X}-\mu_0)^2\}^{1/2}}$ is a function of

$$S=(\bar{X}-\mu_0)\Big/\left[\frac{\sum(X_i-\bar{X})^2}{n(n-1)}\right]^{1/2}$$

and S has Student's t distribution (with parameter $n-1$). But, when $\mu=\mu_0$, the distribution of S does not depend on σ; hence S is then independent of the complete sufficient statistic $\sum_1^n (X_i-\mu_0)^2$. We may thus drop the condition $\sum_1^n (X_i-\mu_0)^2=t$ and write Equation (6.19) as

$$\Pr\left[\left\{\frac{n(n-1)}{S^2}+n\right\}^{-1/2}>\frac{c(t)-\mu_0}{t^{1/2}}\Big|\mu=\mu_0\right]=\alpha \qquad (6.20)$$

In fact, since the distribution of S does not depend on the value assumed by T, when $\mu=\mu_0$ the quantity $[c(t)-\mu_0]/t^{1/2}$ appearing in Equation (6.20) cannot depend on t either.

Exercise 8. $X_1, X_2, \ldots, X_n$ is a random sample from the normal distribution $N(\mu, \sigma^2)$. The null hypothesis is that $\sigma=\sigma_0$, the alternative that $\sigma=\sigma_1$ while μ is a nuisance parameter. Show that most powerful similar tests can be based on the statistic $\sum_1^n (X_i-\bar{X})^2 \; (n\geqslant 2)$ for both $\sigma_1>\sigma_0$ and $\sigma_1<\sigma_0$.

[Hint: $\bar{X}$ is a complete sufficient statistic for μ and $\sum_1^n (X_i-\mu)^2 = \sum_1^n (X_i-\bar{X})^2+n(\bar{X}-\mu)^2$].

Exercise 9. $X_1, X_2, \ldots, X_n$ is a random sample from $N(\mu_1, \sigma^2)$, $Y_1, Y_2, \ldots, Y_m$ is an independent random sample from $N(\mu_2, \theta^2\sigma^2)$.

The null hypothesis is that $\theta = 1$, the alternative that $\theta = \theta_1 > 1$, while the parameters μ_1, μ_2, σ are unspecified. Show that when $\theta = 1$, the statistics $\bar{X}, \bar{Y}, \sum_{1}^{n}(X_i - \bar{X})^2 + \sum_{1}^{m}(Y_i - \bar{Y})^2 = S_1^2 + S_2^2$ are jointly sufficient for μ_1, μ_2, σ. Show that most powerful tests of $\theta = 1$ can be based on the conditional distribution of S_2^2 given $\bar{x}, \bar{y}, s_1^2 + s_2^2$. Show further, that when $\theta = 1$, the distribution of S_1^2/S_2^2 does not depend on σ and is independent of $\bar{X}, \bar{Y}, S_1^2 + S_2^2$. Explain how most powerful similar tests can be based on a statistic having an 'F' distribution.

The topic of two-sided tests in the presence of nuisance parameters really requires a more advanced approach. [A full treatment is to be found in *Testing Hypotheses* by E.H. Lehman, John Wiley & Sons, 1959]. However certain tests for the normal distribution are so important that some discussion of the two parameter case is inevitable. We have already seen that although for certain two-sided tests a u.m.p. test does not exist, for one parameter members of the regular exponential family, we can construct a u.m.p.u. test. Now if **X** is a random sample from a distribution involving two parameters θ, ϕ then an unbiased, size α, test of $\theta = \theta_0$ against $\theta \neq \theta_0$ requires a critical region, C, such that

$$\Pr[\mathbf{X} \in C | \theta = \theta_0] = \alpha$$
$$\Pr[\mathbf{X} \in C | \theta \neq \theta_0] \geqslant \alpha$$

for all values of ϕ. By the first of these conditions, C is also a similar critical region. But if T is a boundedly complete sufficient statistic for ϕ when $\theta = \theta_0$, then the only tests of size α must also have conditional size α given $T = t$. In such a case, we look for the u.m.p.u. test based on the conditional distribution of the observations given $T = t$. For example, for the normal distribution $N(\mu, \sigma^2)$, suppose we wish to test $\mu = 0$ against $\mu \neq 0$ where σ is a nuisance parameter. We know that $T = \sum X_i^2$ is a complete sufficient statistic for σ when $\mu = 0$. Hence we should construct a test from the conditional distribution of the sample values given $\sum x_i^2$. The resulting critical region consists of large vales of $|\bar{X}|$ given $\sum x_i^2$ and this can be converted into an equivalent two-sided test based on

$$\sqrt{(n)}\bar{X}/[\sum(X_i - \bar{X})^2/(n-1)]^{1/2}$$

which has the t-distribution with parameter $(n-1)$ if $\mu = 0$ (when its distribution does not depend on σ). We offer only a plausible argument, based on Equation 6.14 (Section 6.4), which was limited to the case of one parameter.

If we test $\mu = 0$, $\sigma = \sigma_0$ against $\mu = \mu_1$, $\sigma = \sigma_1$, the best critical region for which the power function has zero slope with *respect to* μ at $\mu = 0, \sigma = \sigma_0$, consists of those $x_1, x_2, \ldots, x_n$ such that

$$\frac{1}{[\sqrt{(2\pi)}\sigma_1]^n} \exp\left[-\tfrac{1}{2}\sum (x_i - \mu_1)^2/\sigma_1^2\right]$$

$$> \frac{1}{[\sqrt{(2\pi)}\sigma_0]^n} \exp\left(-\tfrac{1}{2}\sum x_i^2/\sigma_0^2\right)(k_1 + k_2 \sum x_i/\sigma_0^2)$$

or

$$c(\sigma_0, \sigma_1, \mu_1) \exp\left[-\tfrac{1}{2}\sum x_i^2 \left(\frac{1}{\sigma_1^2} - \frac{1}{\sigma_0^2}\right) + \frac{n\bar{x}\mu_1}{\sigma_1^2}\right] > k_1 + \frac{nk_2\bar{x}}{\sigma_0^2}.$$

Such regions for which $\sum x_i^2$ is constant are satisfied by large values of $|\bar{x}|$, for some k_1, k_2. The reader should verify that if $X_1, X_2, \ldots, X_n$ is a random sample from the distribution $N(\mu, \sigma^2)$ then by the same kind of argument, a u.m.p.u. test of $\sigma = \sigma_0$ against $\sigma \neq \sigma_0$ can be based on $\sum (X_i - \bar{X})^2/\sigma_0^2$. The statistic has the χ_{n-1}^2 distribution when $\sigma = \sigma_0$.

6.7 Composite hypotheses several parameters

The reader may have noticed that the main emphasis has rested on testing a single parameter. Parameters, other than the one under scrutiny, were 'removed' by arguing conditionally on a sufficient statistic. Sometimes an hypothesis which appears to involve two parameters can be recast as a one-parameter problem.

Example 7. X_1, X_2 are independently distributed $N(\theta_1, 1), N(\theta_2, 1)$. It is required to test $H_0 : \theta_1 = \theta_2$ against $H_1 : \theta_1 > \theta_2$.

If we write $\phi_1 = \theta_1 - \theta_2$ and (say) $\phi_2 = \theta_1 + \theta_2$, then we are to test $H_0 : \phi_1 = 0$ against $\phi_1 > 0$ and ϕ_2 assumes the role of a nuisance parameter. The likelihood now becomes

$$\frac{1}{2\pi} \exp\left[-\tfrac{1}{2}\{[x_1 - (\phi_2 + \phi_1)/2]^2 + [x_2 - (\phi_2 - \phi_1)/2]^2\}\right]$$

$$= \frac{1}{2\pi} \exp\left[-\tfrac{1}{2}\{x_1^2 + x_2^2 - (x_1 + x_2)\phi_2 - (x_1 - x_2)\phi_1 + (\phi_2^2 + \phi_1^2)/2\}\right]$$

If ϕ_1 is known, then $X_1 + X_2$ is sufficient for ϕ_2, and we look for a good test of $\phi_1 = 0$ conditional on fixed $X_1 + X_2$. Alternatively, we could have changed the variables to $U = X_1 + X_2, V = X_1 - X_2$.

Exercise 10. Show for Example 7 that a u.m.p. similar test can be based on large values of $x_1 - x_2$ given $x_1 + x_2$. Check that $X_1 - X_2, X_1 + X_2$ are independent and hence construct a test with size 5 per cent.
[Ans. Critical region is $x_1 - x_2 \geqslant 1.64\sqrt{2}$]

The kind of adjustment just illustrated will not take us very far. Thus, if Example 7 is extended, so that the X_i are independently distributed $N(\theta_i, 1), (i = 1, 2, 3)$, then the null hypothesis $\theta_1 = \theta_2 = \theta_3$ cannot be expressed as a single constraint on some combination of the θ_i. We can, of course, manage to express it in terms of two such constraints. We may reparametrize so that

$$\phi_1 = (\theta_1 - \theta_2), \phi_2 = (\theta_1 + \theta_2 - 2\theta_3), \phi_3 = (\theta_1 + \theta_2 + \theta_3)$$

then $\theta_1 = \theta_2 = \theta_3$ implies $\phi_1 = 0$ and $\phi_2 = 0$.

Exercise 11. If $\phi_1 = (\theta_1 - \theta_2)/\sqrt{2}, \phi_2 = (\theta_1 + \theta_2 - 2\theta_3)/\sqrt{6}$, $\phi_3 = (\theta_1 + \theta_2 + \theta_3)/\sqrt{3}$, show that

$$\theta_1 = \frac{\phi_1}{\sqrt{2}} + \frac{\phi_2}{\sqrt{6}} + \frac{\phi_3}{\sqrt{3}}$$

$$\theta_2 = -\frac{\phi_1}{\sqrt{2}} + \frac{\phi_2}{\sqrt{6}} + \frac{\phi_3}{\sqrt{3}}$$

$$\theta_3 = -\sqrt{\left(\frac{2}{3}\right)}\phi_2 + \frac{\phi_3}{\sqrt{3}}$$

and that $\theta_1^2 + \theta_2^2 + \theta_3^2 = \phi_1^2 + \phi_2^2 + \phi_3^2$

Yet further complications may be involved if we wish to test a null hypothesis of the type $\theta_1 = 0$ and $\theta_2 = 0$. There is no difficulty if the alternative is also simple, for then we apply the ordinary Neyman–Pearson theorem.

Example 8. X_1, X_2 are independently distributed $N(\theta_1, 1), N(\theta_2, 1)$ respectively. $H_0 : \theta_1 = 0, \theta_2 = 0; H_1 : \theta_1 = \theta_1', \theta_2 = \theta_2', \theta_1'; \theta_2'$ known.

The ratio of likelihoods is

$$\exp\left[-\tfrac{1}{2}(x_1 - \theta_1')^2 - \tfrac{1}{2}(x_2 - \theta_2')^2\right]/\exp\left[-\tfrac{1}{2}(x_1^2 + x_2^2)\right]$$
$$\propto \exp\left[\theta_1' x_1 + \theta_2' x_2\right]$$

Most powerful tests are then based on the statistic $\theta_1' X_1 + \theta_2' X_2$.

Exercise 12. Show for Example 8 that if $\theta_1' = +1$, $\theta_2' = -1$, then the most powerful test is based on large values of $x_1 - x_2$.

We pause to remind ourselves that in Example 8, θ_1, θ_2 stand or fall together. This thought may cause us to back off and regret not being able to accept $\theta_1 = 0$ and reject $\theta_2 = 0$. After all, we can construct best tests of $\theta_1 = 0$, $\theta_2 = 0$ against particular alternatives. We then have two separate tests. How is the overall performance of such a procedure to be judged? Suppose the criterion is the rejection of at least one of the individual hypotheses.

Thus, if the individual tests are at levels α_1, α_2 respectively, then when in fact both $\theta_1 = 0$ *and* $\theta_2 = 0$, the probability that at least one of the separate hypotheses will be rejected is $1 - (1 - \alpha_1)(1 - \alpha_2)$.

Example 9. X_1 is distributed $N(\theta_1, 1)$. The u.m.p. test of $\theta_1 = 0$ against $\theta_1 > 0$ of size 5 per cent has critical region $x_1 > 1.64$. The power, when $\theta_1 = 1$, is

$$\Pr[X_1 > 1.64 | \theta_1 = 1] = \Pr[X_1 - 1 > 0.64 | \theta_1 = 1] = 0.2611$$

X_2 is distributed $N(\theta_2, 1)$ independently of X_1. The u.m.p. test of $\theta_2 = 0$ against $\theta_2 < 0$ of size 5 per cent has critical region $x_2 < -1.64$. The power when $\theta_2 = -1$ is again 0.2611. The probability of rejecting at least one of $\theta_1 = 0, \theta_2 = 0$ when both are true is $1 - (1 - 0.05)^2 = 0.0975$. The probability of rejecting at least one of $\theta_1 = 0, \theta_2 = 0$ when $\theta_1 = 1, \theta_2 = -1$ is $1 - (1 - 0.2611)^2 = 0.454$. On the other hand, the most powerful test of $\theta_1 = 0$ and $\theta_2 = 0$ against $\theta_1 = 1$ and $\theta_2 = -1$ is based on large values of $x_1 - x_2$ (exercise 12). The distribution of $X_1 - X_2$ is $N(\theta_1 - \theta_2, 2)$. Suppose the critical region is $x_1 - x_2 > d$, where $\Pr[X_1 - X_2 > d | \theta_1 = 0, \theta_2 = 0] = 0.0975$, then $d = (1.29)\sqrt{2}$ from tables. Finally,

$$\Pr[X_1 - X_2 > (1.29)\sqrt{2} | \theta_1 = 1, \theta_2 = -1] \approx 0.55$$

It might be thought that this most powerful test is none the less rather a shaky article compared to the separate tests which were individually *uniformly* most powerful against *their* alternatives. However, $\theta_1 = 0, \theta_2 = 0$ is included in $\theta_1 - \theta_2 = 0$ and the alternative $\theta_1 = 1$, $\theta_2 = -1$ belongs also to $\theta_1 - \theta_2 > 0$. The critical region $x_1 - x_2 > (1.29)\sqrt{2}$ is uniformly most powerful similar for testing $\theta_1 - \theta_2 = 0$ against $\theta_1 - \theta_2 > 0$ [see Exercise 10].

The saving clause which closes Example (9) is no help against two-sided alternatives. To see this, let the null hypothesis be $\theta_1 = 0$ and $\theta_2 = 0$, while the alternative is $\theta \neq 0$ and $\theta_2 \neq 0$. We have a starting-point for we know that we can construct uniformly most powerful *unbiased* tests for $\theta_i = 0$ against $\theta_i \neq 0$ separately. Unfortunately, although using the tests together will provide an unbiased test of $\theta_1 = 0$ and $\theta_2 = 0$ against $\theta_1 \neq 0$ and $\theta_2 \neq 0$, it will not be blessed with the property of uniformity. Thus if X_1 is distributed $N(\theta_1, 1)$, consider a two-sided critical region, of size α, which is u.m.p.u. for testing $\theta_1 = 0$ against $\theta_1 \neq 0$. Then its power against some particular θ_1 is $p_1(\theta_1) \geqslant \alpha$. If X_2 is independently distributed $N(\theta_2, 1)$ then another such test, of size α, has power against some particular θ_2 of $p_2(\theta_2) \geqslant \alpha$. The overall probability of rejecting at least one of $\theta_1 = 0, \theta_2 = 0$, when the same alternative pair is true, is $1 - [1 - p_1(\theta_1)][1 - p_2(\theta_2)] \geqslant 1 - (1 - \alpha)(1 - \alpha) = $ probability of rejecting least one of $\theta_1 = 0, \theta_2 = 0$ when both are true. Yet, by constructing separate tests at levels α_1, α_2 so that $1 - (1 - \alpha_1)(1 - \alpha_2) = 1 - (1 - \alpha)^2$, we have another unbiased test, at the same level, but with a different power function. Some numerical details are followed up in the next exercise.

Exercise 13. X_i is distributed $N(\theta_i, 1)(i = 1, 2)$. Consider the pair of u.m.p.u. tests of $\theta_i = 0$ of size 5 per cent which have critical regions $|x_i| \geqslant 1.96$ $(i = 1, 2)$. Calculate $\Pr[|X_1| \geqslant 1.96$ or $|X_2| \geqslant 1.96 | \theta_1 = 1, \theta_2 = -1]$.
[*Ans.* ≈ 0.31].

Alternatively, suppose whatever x_1 we accept $\theta_1 = 0$, i.e. $\alpha_1 = 0$, then the power against any $\theta_1 \neq 0$ is also zero. For testing $\theta_2 = 0$, find α_2 such that $1 - (1 - 0.05)^2 = 1 - (1 - \alpha_2)$
[Ans. $\alpha_2 = 0.0975$].
If $\Pr[|X_2| \geqslant d|\theta_2 = 0] = 0.0975$, calculate $\Pr[|X_2| \geqslant d|\theta_2 = -1]$.
[*Ans.* ≈ 0.26].

To put matters more bleakly, if X_1, X_2 are independently distributed and both members of one-parameter exponential families, then there does not exist a u.m.p.u. test of $\theta_1 = \theta_1'$ and $\theta_2 = \theta_2'$ against $\theta_1 \neq \theta_1'$ and $\theta_2 \neq \theta_2'$. Among the plain unbiased tests there is thus an embarrassment of choice. We can make a selection by picking out a symmetrical acceptance region. A square has already been considered in Exercise 13. Another such choice would be a circle. For example 9 we reject $\theta_1 = 0$ and $\theta_2 = 0$ if $x_1^2 + x_2^2 > c$ where $\Pr[X_1^2 + X_2^2 > c | \theta_1 = 0, \theta_2 = 0] = \alpha$, the size of the test. In fact, c is easily determined since when $\theta_1 = \theta_2 = 0$, $X_1^2 + X_2^2$ has a χ_2^2 distribution. The power is annoyingly difficult to calculate but it can be shown that $X_1^2 + X_2^2$ has a distribution which only depends on $\theta_1^2 + \theta_2^2$. That is, parameter points θ_1, θ_2 equidistant from $\theta_1 = 0, \theta_2 = 0$ give equal power, though this is probably obvious.

Exercise 14. If $X_1, X_2, \ldots, X_n$ are independently and normally distributed with means $\theta_1, \theta_2, \ldots, \theta_n$ and unit variance, show that the moment generating function of $S = \sum_{i=1}^{n} X_i^2$ is

$$E[\exp(St)] = (1 - 2t)^{-n/2} \exp\left[t \sum_1^n \theta_i^2 / (1 - 2t) \right]$$

The random variable S is said to have the non-central chi-squared distribution. Tables are available.

6.8 Likelihood ratio tests

As the rival hypotheses become increasingly complex, the greater will be the need for some general technique. We may be faced with several parameters, the null and alternative hypotheses concerning some of them being composite, the remainder being nuisance parameters. We shall shortly discuss the *likelihood ratio test* which can address itself to such problems. Unfortunately, it does not appear to be a best test in any general sense and the intuitive justification for its use is uncommonly difficult to express. Recall that the joint probability density function of the (fixed) sample values, regarded as a function of the parameters, is termed the likelihood. The likelihood has already played a key role in generating most powerful tests of simple hypotheses.

Indeed, one school of thought maintains that any inference from a sample is solely to be determined by the likelihood function. In particular, it has been suggested that the relative support provided by the sample for two different sets of values of the parameters should be provided by the corresponding ratio of the likelihood functions.

In hypothesis testing we want to know whether there is a sufficient measure of support for some set of values of the parameters. One way of assigning such a measure is to compare the likelihood function at a set of parameter values with the largest value achievable by varying the parameters (subject to any constraints). We can then divide the parameter values into acceptable and non-acceptable classes according as the corresponding ratio is high enough or small enough. But all of this has been put more vividly by Fisher and we cannot resist giving a brief quotation from his *Statistical Methods and Scientific Inference*. He has just discussed the observance of 3 successes in a series of 14 independent trials with an unknown probability of success, p, on each trial. He calculates, for instance, that the probability of 3 or fewer successes is less than 1 per cent if $p > 0.557$. [In the language of hypothesis testing, the best one-sided test of size 1 per cent would reject any $p > 0.557$]. We may call 0.557 an upper confidence limit for p. He then says:

Objection has sometimes been made that the method of calculating confidence limits by setting an assigned value such as 1 per cent on the frequency of observing 3 or less (or at the other end of observing 3 or more) is unrealistic in treating the values less than 3, in exactly the same manner as the value 3, which is the one that has been observed.

As an alternative, he suggests:

In the case under discussion, a simple graph of the values of the mathematical likelihood expressed as a percentage of its maximum, against the possible values of the parameter p, shows clearly enough what values of the parameter have likelihoods comparable with the maximum and outside what limits the likelihood falls to levels at which the corresponding values of the parameter become implausible.

It is usual to clothe the 'simple enough' with a probability structure. That is, to find a limit for the ratio below which it falls with a prescribed maximum probability.

Example 10. X_i is distributed $N(\theta_i, \sigma_0^2)$ $(i = 1, 2, \ldots, n)$ where $\sigma_0^2 > 0$ is known, $-\infty < \theta_i < +\infty$, and the X_i are independent. It is required to test $\theta_1 = \theta_2 = \ldots = \theta_n = 0$ against $\theta_i \neq 0$ $(i = 1, 2, \ldots, n)$. The likelihood is

$$L(x_1, x_2, \ldots, x_n, \theta_1, \ldots, \theta_n, \sigma_0)$$
$$= \frac{1}{(\sqrt{(2\pi)}\sigma_0)^n} \exp\left[-\frac{1}{2} \sum_{i=1}^{n} (x_i - \theta_i)^2 / \sigma_0^2 \right]$$

This has the value $[1/\{\sqrt{(2\pi)}\sigma_0\}^n \exp\left[-\frac{1}{2}\sum_{i=1}^{n} x_i^2/\sigma_0^2\right]$ when the null hypothesis is true. Since there are no restrictions on the θ_i, the likelihood is maximized when $\theta_i = x_i (i = 1, 2, \dots, n)$ and is then merely $1/\{\sqrt{(2\pi)}\sigma_0\}^n$. The ratio is $\exp\left[-\frac{1}{2}\sum_{i=1}^{n} x_i^2/\sigma_0^2\right]$. We now find c such that

$$\Pr\left[\exp\left(-\frac{1}{2}\sum_{i=1}^{n} X_i^2/\sigma_0^2\right) < c \,\middle|\, \theta_1 = \theta_2 = \dots = \theta_n = 0\right] = \alpha.$$

Since the ratio is a decreasing function of $\sum_{i=1}^{n} x_i^2$, we may equivalently find c^* such that

$$\Pr\left[\sum_{i=1}^{n} X_i^2 > c^* \,\middle|\, \theta_1 = \theta_2 = \dots = \theta_n = 0\right] = \alpha.$$

But when the θ_i are all zero, $\sum_{i=1}^{n} X_i^2/\sigma_0^2$ has the χ_n^2 distribution.

If the null hypothesis is composite, we transfer our attention to the maximum value that the likelihood can attain when the null hypothesis is true. This seems reasonable, for if the ratio of this maximum to that of the overall maximum appears to be unacceptable, then we should take the same view of any smaller likelihood *for the same sample*. Notationally, we write ω for the parameter space as constrained by the null hypothesis and Ω when it is not so constrained. We inspect $\sup_{\theta \in \omega} L(x_1, x_2, \dots, x_n, \boldsymbol{\theta})/\sup_{\theta \in \Omega} L(x_1, x_2, \dots, x_n, \boldsymbol{\theta})$, which is called the *likelihood ratio statistic*, written $\lambda(x_1, \dots, x_n)$ or λ. The ratio necessarily cannot be greater than 1 and a procedure for rejecting the null hypothesis based on its magnitude is called a *likelihood ratio test*. The size of such a test is

$$\max_{\theta \in \omega} \Pr[\lambda(X_1, X_2, \dots, X_n) \leqslant c \,|\, \boldsymbol{\theta} \in \omega],$$

where the critical region is $0 < \lambda \leqslant c < 1$.

Example 11. $X_1, X_2, \dots, X_n$ is a random sample from the distribution $N(\theta_1, \theta_2)$ where θ_1, θ_2 are both unknown. To construct the likelihood ratio test of the null hypothesis $\theta_1 = \theta_1'$ against $\theta_1 \neq \theta_1'$ where θ_2 is unspecified and θ_1' is known. Here Ω consists of all pairs $(\theta_1, \theta_2 > 0)$ and the likelihood must be maximized simultaneously with respect to θ_1, θ_2.

$$L(x_1, x_2, \ldots, x_n \boldsymbol{\Omega}) = (2\pi\theta_2)^{-n/2} \exp\left[-\frac{1}{2}\sum_{i=1}^{n}(x_i - \theta_1)^2/\theta_2\right]$$

$$\log L(\mathbf{x}, \boldsymbol{\Omega}) = -n\log\sqrt{(2\pi)} - \frac{n}{2}\log\theta_2 - \frac{1}{2}\sum(x_i - \theta_1)^2/\theta_2$$

$$\frac{\partial\log L}{\partial\theta_1} = \frac{\sum_{i=1}^{n}(x_i - \theta_1)}{\theta_2}, \qquad \frac{\partial\log L}{\partial\theta_2} = -\frac{n}{2\theta_2} + \frac{\sum_{i=1}^{n}(x_i - \theta_1)^2}{2\theta_2^2}$$

Whence readily, the maximum is at $\hat{\theta}_1 = \bar{x}, \hat{\theta}_2 = \sum(x_i - \bar{x})^2/n$.

$$\sup_{\theta_1, \theta_2} L(x_1, x_2, \ldots, x_n, \theta_1, \theta_2) = L(x_1, x_2, \ldots, x_n, \hat{\theta}_1, \hat{\theta}_2)$$

$$= \frac{1}{(2\pi)^{n/2}}\left(\frac{n}{\sum_{i=1}^{n}(x_i - \bar{x})^2}\right)^{n/2} \exp(-\tfrac{1}{2}n)$$

On the other hand, ω consists only of the pairs (θ_1', θ_2).

$$L(x_1, x_2, \ldots, x_n, \omega) = (2\pi\theta_2)^{-n/2} \exp\left[-\frac{1}{2}\sum_{i=1}^{n}(x_i - \theta_1')^2/\theta_2\right]$$

θ_1' is fixed and the maximum now occur at $\tilde{\theta}_2 = \sum_{i=1}^{n}(x_i - \theta_1')^2/n$.

$$\sup_{\theta_1', \theta_2} L(x_1, x_2, \ldots, x_n, \theta_1, \theta_2) = L(x_1, x_2, \ldots, x_n, \theta_1', \tilde{\theta}_2)$$

$$= \frac{1}{(2\pi)^{n/2}}\left(\frac{n}{\sum(x_i - \theta_1')^2}\right)^{n/2} \exp(-\tfrac{1}{2}n),$$

The likelihood ratio is

$$\lambda(x_1, x_2, \ldots, x_n) = \sup_{\theta_1', \theta_2} L \bigg/ \sup_{\theta_1, \theta_2} L = \left\{\frac{\sum_{i=1}^{n}(x_i - \bar{x})^2}{\sum_{i=1}^{n}(x_i - \theta_1')^2}\right\}^{n/2}$$

So the test is: reject $\theta_1 = \theta_1'$, when

$$\lambda = \left[\sum_{i=1}^{n}(x_i - \bar{x})^2 \bigg/ \sum_{i=1}^{n}(x_i - \theta_1')^2\right]^{n/2} \leqslant c.$$

There remains the little matter of fixing c. We do not recognize the distribution of $\lambda(X_1, X_2, \ldots, X_n)$, but it will serve if we can find a function of λ for which we can identify the distribution. Using the identity

$$\sum_{i=1}^{n} (x_i - \theta'_1)^2 = \sum_{i=1}^{n} (x_i - \bar{x})^2 + n(\bar{x} - \theta'_1)^2$$

$$\lambda^{2/n} = \cfrac{1}{1 + \cfrac{n(\bar{x} - \theta'_1)^2}{\sum (x_i - \bar{x})^2}} = \frac{1}{1 + t^2/(n-1)}$$

where $t = \sqrt{n}(\bar{x} - \theta'_1)/[\sum(x_i - \bar{x})^2/(n-1)]^{1/2}$. Thus, small values of λ correspond to large values of $|t|$. When $\theta_1 = \theta'_1$ the corresponding random variable T has Student's t-distribution with parameter $(n-1)$. In this instance, the likelihood ratio test is also the uniformly most powerful unbiased test of $\theta_1 = \theta'_1$ against $\theta_1 \neq \theta'_1$, where θ_2 is a nuisance parameter. A slight modification yields the likelihood ratio test of $\theta_1 = \theta'_1$ against $\theta_1 > \theta'_1$. Ω is now restricted to those pairs (θ_1, θ_2) where $\theta_1 \geq \theta'_1$. Consider again

$$\frac{\partial}{\partial \theta_1} \log L(x_1, x_2, \ldots, x_n, \Omega) = n(\bar{x} - \theta_1)/\theta_2$$

If $\bar{x} \geq \theta'_1$, then the turning value is at $\hat{\theta}_1 = \bar{x}$. If $\bar{x} < \theta'_1$ the partial derivative is negative and θ_1 is chosen as small as possible — that is, equal to θ'_1. But for this case, $\lambda = 1$ and the null hypothesis is not rejected. In the former case, we again have $[1 + t^2/(n-1)]^{-1}$ is to be small but with $t > 0$. Thus we have recovered the usual one-sided t-test, which is also uniformly most powerful similar.

Exercise 15. $X_1, X_2, \ldots, X_n$ is a random sample from the distribution $N(\theta_1, \theta_2)$. The null hypothesis is that $\theta_2 = \theta'_2$ a known constant, the alternative is that $\theta_2 \neq \theta'_2$ while θ_1 is unspecified. Show that the likelihood ratio statistic is

$$\lambda = \left(\frac{\hat{\theta}_2}{\theta'_2} \right)^{n/2} \exp\left[-\frac{n}{2} \left(\frac{\hat{\theta}_2}{\theta'_2} - 1 \right) \right]$$

where $\hat{\theta}_2 = \sum_{i=1}^{n} (x_i - \bar{x})^2/n$. Verify that λ is not a monotone function of $\hat{\theta}_2$ but has a single maximum. Hence show that an equivalent test may be based on $n\hat{\theta}_2/\theta'_2$, which when $\theta_2 = \theta'_2$ has a χ^2_{n-1} distribution, and explain how to construct a test of size α. [Tail areas sum to α from points with equal ordinates.]

Exercise 16. $X_1, X_2, \ldots, X_n$ is a random sample from $N(\theta_1, \theta_3)$, $Y_1, Y_2, \ldots, Y_m$ an independent random sample from $N(\theta_2, \theta_3)$, where $-\infty < \theta_1 < +\infty$, $-\infty < \theta_2 < +\infty$, $\theta_3 > 0$. The null hypothesis is that $\theta_1 = \theta_2$, the alternative that $\theta_1 \neq \theta_2$, θ_3 being unspecified. Show that the unrestricted likelihood is maximized when

$$\theta_1 = \hat{\theta}_1 = \bar{x},\, \theta_2 = \hat{\theta}_2 = \bar{y},\, \theta_3 = \hat{\theta}_3$$

$$= \left[\sum_{i=1}^{n} (x_i - \bar{x})^2 + \sum_{i=1}^{m} (y_i - \bar{y})^2 \right] \Big/ (m + n)$$

whereas when the null hypothesis is true, the likelihood is maximized when

$$\theta_1 = \theta_2 = \tilde{\theta}_1 = (n\bar{x} + m\bar{y})/(n + m),$$

$$\theta_3 = \tilde{\theta}_3 = \left[\sum_{i=1}^{n} (x_i - \tilde{\theta}_1)^2 + \sum_{i=1}^{m} (y_i - \tilde{\theta}_1)^2 \right] \Big/ (m + n).$$

Hence show that the likelihood ratio statistic can be written as

$$\left[\frac{n + m - 2}{(n + m - 2) + t^2} \right]^{(n+m)/2}$$

where $T = (\bar{X} - \bar{Y}) \Big/ \left[\left(\frac{1}{n} + \frac{1}{m} \right) \left\{ \frac{\sum (X_i - \bar{X})^2 + \sum (Y_i - \bar{Y})^2}{n + m - 2} \right\} \right]^{1/2}$

Explain briefly why T has Student's t-distribution with parameter $n + m - 2$ when $\theta_1 = \theta_2$.

Exercise 17. $X_1, X_2, \ldots, X_n$ is a random sample from the distribution $N(\theta_1, \theta_3)$, $Y_1, Y_2, \ldots, Y_m$ is an independent random sample from $N(\theta_2, \theta_4)$, where $-\infty < \theta_1 < +\infty$, $-\infty < \theta_2 < +\infty$, $\theta_3 > 0$, $\theta_4 > 0$. The null hypothesis is that $\theta_3 = \theta_4$, the alternative that $\theta_3 \neq \theta_4$; θ_1, θ_2 being unspecified under either hypothesis. Show that the likelihood ratio test can be based on the statistic

$$\frac{\displaystyle\sum_{i=1}^{n} (X_i - \bar{X})^2 / (n - 1)}{\displaystyle\sum_{i=1}^{m} (Y_i - \bar{Y})^2 / (m - 1)}$$

explain briefly why this statistic has the F distribution with parameters $n - 1$, $m - 1$ when $\theta_3 = \theta_4$.

6.9 Bayes methods

From some points of view, the use of a prior distribution appreciably simplifies the problem of testing hypotheses concerning a single parameter. For having computed the posterior distribution, we can, in principle, calculate the probability that a parameter lies in a certain interval as opposed to the probability of the complementary event that it does not. Even the presence of nuisance parameters will not hinder us, for these can be 'integrated out' and we may work with the marginal distribution of the parameter of interest. We shall look closely at what the reader may feel is an excessively trivial example. The truth is that more complex cases readily pose rather daunting computational problems.

Example 12. A single value, X, is drawn from the Bernoulli distribution with parameter θ. The prior distribution of Θ is uniform over $(0, 1)$. It is desired to compare the hypothesis $\theta \leqslant \theta_0$ with $\theta > \theta_0$.

Now even before we see x, we can calculate $\Pr[\Theta \leqslant \theta_0] = \theta_0$. So the *prior odds* are $\Pr[\Theta \leqslant \theta_0]/\Pr[\Theta > \theta_0] = \theta_0/(1 - \theta_0)$. Since $f(x|\theta) = \theta^x(1 - \theta)^{1-x}$, $x = 0, 1$ and $g(\theta) = 1$, $0 \leqslant \theta \leqslant 1$, we readily find that $g(\theta|x) = 2\theta^x(1 - \theta)^{1-x}$, $0 \leqslant \theta \leqslant 1$. For instance, if $x = 1$, $g(\theta|x = 1) = 2\theta$ and $\Pr[\Theta \leqslant \theta_0|x = 1] = \theta_0^2$ and the *posterior odds*, given $x = 1$, are $\theta_0^2/(1 - \theta_0^2)$. The allied question of a nuisance parameter is taken up in the next exercise.

Exercise 18. The discrete random variables X_1, X_2 have joint probability density function

$$f(x_1, x_2|\theta_1, \theta_2) = \theta_1^{x_1}\theta_2^{x_2}(1 - \theta_1 - \theta_2)^{1-x_1-x_2}, \qquad \begin{matrix} x_1 = 0, 1\, x_2 = 0, 1, \\ 0 \leqslant x_1 + x_2 \leqslant 1. \end{matrix}$$

The prior distribution of the continuous random variables Θ_1, Θ_2 is $g(\theta_1, \theta_2) = 2$, $0 \leqslant \theta_2 \leqslant 1$, $0 \leqslant \theta_1 \leqslant 1$, $0 \leqslant \theta_1 + \theta_2 \leqslant 1$. Calculate the prior probability that Θ_1 is less than θ_0.
[Ans. $1 - (1 - \theta_0)^2$]
Show that $g(\theta_1, \theta_2|x_1 = 1, x_2 = 0) = 6\theta_1$, $0 \leqslant \theta_1 + \theta_2 \leqslant 1$. Calculate $\Pr[\Theta_1 \leqslant \theta_0|x_1 = 1, x_2 = 0]$.
[Ans. $3\theta_0^2 - 2\theta_0^3$]

6.10 Loss function for one-sided hypotheses

If the null hypothesis is that $\theta \in \omega$, the alternative that $\theta \notin \omega$, then the simplest form of loss function assumes a zero loss when a correct decision is taken and a positive loss otherwise. Thus, presented with a sample, there are two actions available. If we decide, a_1, that θ does belong to ω, and this is incorrect, we lose a. If we decide, a_2, that θ does not belong to ω, and this is incorrect, we lose b. The Bayes solution selects that action for which the posterior expected loss is a minimum. For the one-sided hypothesis, ω is the interval $\theta \leqslant \theta_0$ and ω' is $\theta > \theta_0$. Before the sample is drawn, the expected losses are

$$E[l(a_1,\Theta)] = 0\Pr[\Theta \leqslant \theta_0] + a\Pr[\Theta > \theta_0] \qquad (6.21)$$

$$E[l(a_2,\Theta)] = b\Pr[\Theta \leqslant \theta_0] + 0\Pr[\Theta > \theta_0] \qquad (6.22)$$

Example 13. For Example 12, since the prior is uniform over $(0,1)$,

$$E[l(a_1,\Theta)] = a(1-\theta_0), E[l(a_2,\Theta)] = b\theta_0$$

Which decision is Bayes depends on the (known) value of θ_0

$$a(1-\theta_0) < b\theta_0 \text{ if, and only if, } \theta_0 > a/(a+b)$$

Having drawn the sample, we compare

$$E[l(a_1,\Theta)|\mathbf{x}] = a\Pr[\Theta > \theta_0|\mathbf{x}] \qquad (6.23)$$

$$E[l(a_2,\Theta)|\mathbf{x}] = b\Pr[\Theta \leqslant \theta_0|\mathbf{x}] \qquad (6.24)$$

Example 14. Again for Example 12, since $g(\theta|x=1) = 2\theta$, $g(\theta|x=0) = 2(1-\theta), 0 \leqslant \theta \leqslant 1$,

$$E[l(a_1,\Theta)|x=1] = a\int_{\theta_0}^{1} 2\theta\,\mathrm{d}\theta = a(1-\theta_0^2)$$

$$E[l(a_2,\Theta)|x=1] = b\int_{0}^{\theta_0} 2\theta\,\mathrm{d}\theta = b\theta_0^2$$

$$E[l(a_1,\Theta)|x=0] = a\int_{\theta_0}^{1} 2(1-\theta)\,\mathrm{d}\theta = a(1-\theta_0)^2$$

$$E[l(a_2,\Theta)|x=0] = b\int_{0}^{\theta_0} 2(1-\theta)\,\mathrm{d}\theta = b - b(1-\theta_0)^2$$

If $x = 1$, $a(1-\theta_0^2) < b\theta_0^2 \leftrightarrow \theta_0 > \sqrt{\{a/(a+b)\}}$.

If $x = 0$, $a(1-\theta_0)^2 < b - b(1-\theta_0)^2 \leftrightarrow \theta_0 > 1 - \sqrt{\{b/(a+b)\}}$.

In particular, if $1 - \sqrt{\{b/(a+b)\}} < \theta_0 < \sqrt{\{a/(a+b)\}}$, we take a_2 if $x = 1$ and a_1 if $x = 0$.

We can also obtain the Bayes risk for the possible Bayes solutions. Since $f(x|\theta) = \theta^x(1-\theta)^{1-x}(x = 0, 1)$, the marginal probability that

$X = 1$ is

$$\int_0^1 \theta g(\theta) d\theta = \int_0^1 \theta d\theta = \frac{1}{2}.$$

Hence the Bayers risk for a_2 if $x = 1$ and a_1 if $x = 0$ is

$$\tfrac{1}{2}b\theta_0^2 + \tfrac{1}{2}a(1 - \theta_0)^2$$

It is instructive to rework this example via the ordinary risk functions, and this is the aim of the next exercise.

Exercise 19. Any decision function of the data must be mapped onto one of the actions a_1, a_2. Since x takes the values $0, 1$, there are only four non-randomized decision functions

$$d_1(1) = a_1, d_1(0) = a_1$$
$$d_2(1) = a_2, d_2(0) = a_2$$
$$d_3(1) = a_1, d_3(0) = a_2$$
$$d_4(1) = a_2, d_4(0) = a_1.$$

Thus the risk for d_4 is

$$E\{l[d_4(X)]|\theta\} = l[d_4(0),\theta]\Pr(X = 0|\theta) + l[d_4(1),\theta]\Pr(X = 1|\theta)$$
$$= l(a_1,\theta)(1 - \theta) + l(a_2,\theta)\theta$$

When $\theta \leqslant \theta_0$, $l(a_1,\theta) = 0$, $l(a_2,\theta) = b$ and the risk is then $b\theta$. When $\theta > \theta_0$, the risk is $a(1 - \theta)$. The Bayes risk is the expected risk over the prior distribution of Θ and is

$$\int_0^{\theta_0} b\theta d\theta + \int_{\theta_0}^1 a(1 - \theta)d\theta = \tfrac{1}{2}[b\theta_0^2 + a(1 - \theta_0)^2]$$

Calculate the risks against $\theta \leqslant \theta_0, \theta > \theta_0$ and the Bayes risks for $d_i, i = 1, 2, 3$.
[Ans. $0, a, a(1 - \theta_0), b, 0, b\theta_0, b(1 - \theta_0), a\theta_0, \tfrac{1}{2}[b(1 - (1 - \theta_0)^2)$
$+ a(1 - \theta_0^2)]$]
Find the Bayes solutions and the intervals for θ_0 for which each is appropriate. Check agreement with Example 14.

Exercise 20. X has p.d.f. $f(x|\theta) = \theta e^{-\theta x}, x > 0$, and the prior distribution of Θ has p.d.f. $g(\theta) = \lambda e^{-\lambda\theta}, \theta > 0$, where λ is known. Confirm that the posterior distribution of Θ given x has p.d.f. $g(\theta|x) = (x + \lambda)^2 \theta \exp[-(x + \lambda)\theta]$.

Action a_1 is to accept $\theta \leqslant \theta_0$, a_2 to accept $\theta > \theta_0$. The loss function is

$$l(a_1, \theta) = 0, \theta \leqslant \theta_0, l(a_2, \theta) = b, \theta \leqslant \theta_0$$
$$l(a_1, \theta) = a, \theta > \theta_0, l(a_2, \theta) = 0, \theta > \theta_0$$

Calculate the expected losses for a_1, a_2 given x and show that a_1 is the Bayes action if

$$(a + b)[1 + (x + \lambda)\theta_0] \exp[-(x + \lambda)\theta_0] < b.$$

An obvious way to modify the loss function is to replace the constant penalty incurred by a wrong decision by one which is proportional to the distance from θ_0. That is,

$$l(a_1, \theta) = 0, \quad \theta \leqslant \theta_0, \quad l(a_2, \theta) = \theta_0 - \theta, \quad \theta \leqslant \theta_0 \qquad (6.25)$$
$$l(a_1, \theta) = \theta - \theta_0, \quad \theta > \theta_0, \quad l(a_2, \theta) = 0, \quad \theta > \theta_0$$

If $g(\theta | \mathbf{x})$ is the p.d.f. of the posterior distribution of Θ given the sample values, the expected posterior losses are

$$E[l(a_1, \Theta)|\mathbf{x}] = \int_{\theta_0}^{\infty} (\theta - \theta_0)g(\theta|\mathbf{x})d\theta \qquad (6.26)$$

$$E[l(a_2, \Theta)|\mathbf{x}] = \int_{-\infty}^{\theta_0} (\theta_0 - \theta)g(\theta|\mathbf{x})d\theta \qquad (6.27)$$

So that a_1 is Bayes if

$$\int_{\theta_0}^{\infty} (\theta - \theta_0)g(\theta|\mathbf{x})d\theta < \int_{-\infty}^{\theta_0} (\theta_0 - \theta)g(\theta|\mathbf{x})d\theta, \text{ that is,}$$

$$\int_{-\infty}^{+\infty} \theta g(\theta|\mathbf{x})d\theta < \theta_0 \int_{-\infty}^{+\infty} g(\theta|\mathbf{x})d\theta$$

or $\qquad E(\Theta|\mathbf{x}) < \theta_0 \qquad (6.28)$

Example 15. For Example 12,

$$g(\theta|x) = 2\theta^x(1 - \theta)^{1-x}, \qquad x = 0, 1$$

whence, easily, $E[\Theta|x] = (x + 1)/3$.

If $x = 1$, we accept $\theta \leqslant \theta_0$ when $\theta_0 > 2/3$ and the expected posterior loss is

$$\int_{\theta_0}^{1} (\theta - \theta_0)2\theta d\theta,$$

or we reject $\theta \leqslant \theta_0$ when $\theta_0 \leqslant 2/3$ and the expected posterior loss is

$$\int_{0}^{\theta_0} (\theta_0 - \theta)2\theta d\theta,$$

If $x = 0$, we accept $\theta \leqslant \theta_0$ when $\theta_0 > 1/3$ and the expected posterior loss is

$$\int_{\theta_0}^1 (\theta - \theta_0)2(1 - \theta)d\theta,$$

or we reject $\theta \leqslant \theta_0$ when $\theta_0 \leqslant 1/3$ and the expected posterior loss is

$$\int_0^{\theta_0} (\theta_0 - \theta)2(1 - \theta)d\theta$$

Exercise 21. For Exercise 20, suppose the loss function is as in Equation (6.25). Show that $a_1 = $ accept $\theta \leqslant \theta_0$ is Bayes if $2/(x + \lambda) < \theta_0$. In case $\theta_0 > 2/\lambda$, calculate the Bayes risk.
[Hint: in finding the Bayes risk, reverse the order of integration]
[Ans. $[\exp(-\lambda\theta_0)]/\lambda$]

For this (linear) loss function, there is little difficulty in deciding which of the two actions to take. The problem is to calculate the risk for the resulting Bayes solution in advance of the data.

6.11 Testing $\theta = \theta_0$ against $\theta \neq \theta_0$

When the prior distribution of Θ is continuous, we immediately face a difficulty. For $\Pr[\Theta = \theta_0] = 0$ for either the prior or posterior distribution. When all the random variables are discrete, the usual direct calculation of the posterior probabilities will serve. That is,

$$\Pr[\Theta = \theta_k | X = x] = \frac{\Pr[X = x | \Theta = \theta_k]\Pr[\Theta = \theta_k]}{\Pr[X = x]}$$

where $\Pr[X = x] = \sum_i \Pr[X = x | \theta_i]\Pr[\Theta = \theta_i]$

$$= \Pr[X = x | \theta_k]\Pr[\Theta = \theta_k] + \sum_{i \neq k} \Pr[X = x | \theta_i]\Pr[\Theta = \theta_i]$$

$$= \Pr[X = x | \theta_k]\Pr[\Theta = \theta_k]$$

$$+ \sum_{i \neq k} \Pr[X = x | \theta_i] \frac{\Pr[\Theta = \theta_i]}{\Pr[\Theta \neq \theta_k]} \Pr[\Theta \neq \theta_k] \qquad (6.29)$$

and the terms involved in the summation, $\sum_{i \neq k}$, can be written, $\Pr[\Theta \neq k] \sum_{i \neq k} \Pr[X = x | \theta_i]\Pr[\Theta = \theta_i | \Theta \neq \theta_k]$. We have changed temporarily to θ_k since, for the discrete case, we do not wish to imply that $i = 0$ is bound to be favoured as a candidate for testing.

From the very first line we can find $\Pr[\Theta = \theta_k | X = x]$ and $\Pr[\Theta \neq \theta_k | X = x] = 1 - \Pr[\Theta = \theta_k | X = x]$. We have developed the formula further to tackle the continuous case. For if θ_0 is so important, we can assign a prior probability, p, that $\Theta = \theta_0$ and the remaining amount, $1 - p$, can be spread out over a continuous distribution. That is, the prior distribution of Θ is mixed. We recover the posterior probability that $\Theta = \theta_0$, given x, by analogy with the above formulae as

$$\Pr[\Theta = \theta_0 | x] = \frac{pf(x|\theta_0)}{pf(x|\theta_0) + (1 - p)\int f(x|\theta)g(\theta)\mathrm{d}\theta} \tag{6.30}$$

Here $g(\theta)$ is the continuous part of the prior distribution and the integral may be taken over the whole range of θ since, for a continuous function, there is no contribution from an isolated point θ_0.

Example 16. $f(x|\theta) = \theta \mathrm{e}^{-\theta x}, x > 0$. The prior probability that $\Theta = \theta_0$ is p and the p.d.f. of Θ given $\Theta \neq \theta_0$ is $\mathrm{e}^{-\theta}, \theta > 0$.

$$\int_0^\infty \theta \mathrm{e}^{-\theta x} \mathrm{e}^{-\theta} \mathrm{d}\theta = \frac{1}{(x + 1)^2}$$

so that

$$\Pr[\Theta = \theta_0 | x] = \frac{p\theta_0 \exp(-\theta_0 x)}{p\theta_0 \exp(-\theta_0 x) + (1 - p)/(1 + x)^2},$$

and hence

$$\frac{\Pr[\Theta = \theta_0 | x]}{\Pr[\Theta \neq \theta_0 | x]} = \frac{p}{1 - p}(x + 1)^2 \theta_0 \exp(-\theta_0 x)$$

The answer has been displayed to show the effect on the prior odds.

Exercise 22. The distribution of X given θ is binomial with parameters n and θ. The prior probability that $\Theta = \frac{1}{2}$ is $p > 0$. The conditional p.d.f. of Θ, given $\Theta \neq \frac{1}{2}$, is uniform over $(0, 1)$. Show that the posterior probability that $\Theta = \frac{1}{2}$ is greater than p if and only if $\binom{n}{x}(1/2)^n > 1/(n + 1)$.

Exercise 23. X_1, X_2, X_n is a random sample from the distribution $N(\theta, 1)$. The prior probability that $\Theta = \theta_0$ is p. The condi-

tional p.d.f. of Θ, given $\Theta \neq \theta_0$, is $N(\mu,1)$.
Show that

$$\frac{\Pr[\Theta = \theta_0 | x_1, x_2, \ldots, x_n]}{\Pr[\Theta \neq \theta_0 | x_1, x_2, \ldots, x_n]}$$

$$= \frac{p}{1-p}(n+1)^{1/2} \exp\left\{\frac{n}{2}\left[\frac{1}{n+1}(\bar{x}-\mu)^2 - (\bar{x}-\theta_0)^2\right]\right\}.$$

We now briefly discuss the use of one possible loss function for this problem. Let a_1 be the action accept $\theta = \theta_0$, a_2 be the action accept $\theta \neq \theta_0$, and the loss function have the form:

$$l(a_1,\theta) = a(\theta - \theta_0)^2$$
$$l(a_2,\theta) = 0, \theta \neq \theta_0 \qquad (6.31)$$
$$l(a_2,\theta) = b, \theta = \theta_0$$

On the basis of assigning a discrete probability p to θ_0, we can now calculate the expected prior losses for the two possible actions.

$$E[l(a_1,\Theta)] = a(1-p)E[(\Theta - \theta_0)^2 | \Theta \neq \theta_0]$$
$$= a(1-p)\{V(\Theta) + [E(\Theta - \theta_0)]^2 | \Theta \neq \theta_0\} \quad (6.32)$$
$$E[l(a_2,\Theta)] = bp \qquad (6.33)$$

Example 17. If Θ is uniformly distributed over $(0,1)$ when $\Theta \neq \theta_0$, then for Equation (6.32),

$$E[\Theta | \Theta \neq \theta_0] = \tfrac{1}{2}, V[\Theta | \Theta \neq \theta_0] = 1/12, \text{ hence}$$

$$E[l(a_1,\Theta)] = a(1-p)\left[\frac{1}{12} + \left(\frac{1}{2} - \theta_0\right)^2\right].$$

Exercise 24. Show for Example 16, for the loss function of Equation (6.31),

$$E[l(a_1,\Theta)] = a(1-p)[1 + (1-\theta_0)^2].$$

Exercise 25. Show for Exercise 23 for the loss function of Equation (6.31),

$$E[l(a_1,\Theta)] = a(1-p)[1 + (\mu - \theta_0)^2].$$

Our real interest, however, is in computing the expected posterior loss for these two actions, conditional on the data. For this we require more than the posterior probability that $\Theta = \theta_0$ – we also need the posterior distribution of Θ when $\theta \neq \theta_0$. This is given by the usual formula,

$$\frac{f(x|\theta)g(\theta)}{\int f(x|\theta)g(\theta)d\theta} \tag{6.34}$$

where the integral is taken over all permitted values of θ.

Example 18. In Example 16 we have already recovered $\Pr[\Theta = \theta_0|x]$ as

$$\frac{p\theta_0 \exp(-\theta_0 x)}{p\theta_0 \exp(-\theta_0 x) + (1-p)/(1+x)^2}$$

From Equation (6.34),

$$g(\theta|x, \theta \neq \theta_0) = \frac{\theta \exp[-\theta(x+1)]}{\int_0^\infty \theta \exp[-\theta(x+1)]d\theta}$$

$$= (x+1)^2 \theta \exp[-\theta(x+1)].$$

This is the p.d.f. of $\Gamma(2, x+1)$ distribution, hence

$$E[\Theta|x, \theta \neq \theta_0] = \frac{2}{x+1}, V[\Theta|x, \theta \neq \theta_0] = \frac{2}{(x+1)^2}$$

So that

$$E[l(a_1, \Theta)|x] = a(1-p)\left[\frac{2}{(x+1)^2} + \left(\frac{2}{x+1} - \theta_0\right)^2\right]$$

and

$$E[l(a_2, \Theta)|x] = \frac{bp\theta_0 \exp(-\theta_0 x)}{p\theta_0 \exp(-\theta_0 x) + (1-p)/(x+1)^2}$$

where the loss function has the form of Equation (6.31).
The Bayes solution will be the smaller of these two expected posterior losses.

Exercise 26. For Exercise 22 and the loss function of Equation (6.31), calculate the expected posterior losses (given x).

[Ans. For a_1, $a(1-p)\left\{\dfrac{(x+1)(n-x+1)}{(n+2)^2(n+3)} + \left(\dfrac{x+1}{n+2} - \dfrac{1}{2}\right)^2\right\}$

For a_2, $bp(\tfrac{1}{2})^n / \left\{p(\tfrac{1}{2})^n + (1-p)/(n+1)\dbinom{n}{x}\right\}$

CHAPTER SEVEN

Interval estimation

7.1 One parameter, Bayesian confidence intervals

The use of a loss function focuses attention on one estimate of the parameter which appears to offer the 'best bargain'. If we are more interested in plausible values of the parameter, we replace our single point estimate by a collection of points which, in the light of the data, is thought to contain the parameter. Such a collection is broadly known as a *confidence region* and the probability that it contains the parameter is its *confidence coefficient*. For individual parameters, such regions will be most useful if they are undivided intervals.

When a prior distribution is believable, then such intervals may be constructed even in advance of the data. Thus, if Θ has a continuous probability density function $g(\theta)$ and $\int_{\theta_1}^{\theta_2} g(\theta) d\theta = p$, then it may fairly be claimed that (θ_1, θ_2) contains the unknown θ with probability p. Alternatively, and more usually, we can fix p and find suitable θ_1, θ_2. What is 'suitable' depends on the circumstances. Thus, if θ is known to be non-negative and we wish to be certain that $\theta_1 < \theta$, we choose $\theta_1 = 0$. If one end-point is not fixed by such considerations, then among optional choices with fairly obvious merits we have:

(a) The shortest interval, i.e. $\Pr[\theta_1 \leqslant \Theta \leqslant \theta_2] = p$ and $\theta_2 - \theta_1$ is a minimum.

(b) The interval of highest density, i.e. $g(\theta) \geqslant g(\theta')$ for every θ in (θ_1, θ_2) and every θ' not in (θ_1, θ_2). In an interval of highest density, $g(\theta) \geqslant k$ for some k.

It is intuitively clear that for many continuous distributions with a single maximum, the requirements are equivalent. Such intervals are of course only rephrasings of our beliefs concerning the prior distribution. Provided with data, we would compute the posterior distribution and find suitable θ_1, θ_2 such that

$$\int_{\theta_1}^{\theta_2} g(\theta|x_1, x_2, \ldots x_n) d\theta = p$$

Such intervals, constructed from the posterior distribution, are sometimes qualified as Bayesian confidence intervals or alternatively credible intervals.

Example 1. An observation on a random variable X which is uniformly distributed over $(0, \theta)$ is found to have the value $x_1 > 1$. If the prior density of Θ is $1/\theta^2$ for $\theta > 1$ and zero otherwise, find:
(a) The $100p$ per cent highest posterior density interval for θ in terms of p and x_1;
(b) The probability that a future observation on x will exceed x_1.
(Aberystwyth, 1975)

Since $1/\theta^2$ is decreasing, the $100p$ per cent highest *prior* density interval for θ is $(1, \theta_2)$ where

$$\int_1^{\theta_2} \frac{d\theta}{\theta^2} = p, \text{ or } \theta_2 = 1/(1-p)$$

Since $f(x|\theta) = 1/\theta, x \leqslant \theta, g(\theta) = 1/\theta^2, \theta > 1$, the joint probability density function of X, Θ is $1/\theta^3, 0 \leqslant x \leqslant \theta, \theta > 1$. Hence the marginal probability density function of X, *when* $x > 1$, is

$$\int_x^\infty \frac{1}{\theta^3} d\theta = \frac{1}{2x^2}$$

so that

$$g(\theta|x = x_1) = \frac{1}{\theta^3} \bigg/ \frac{1}{2x_1^2} = \frac{2x_1^2}{\theta^3}, \theta \geqslant x_1 > 1.$$

Since, again, $g(\theta|x)$ is decreasing in θ, the $100p$ per cent highest posterior density interval is (x_1, θ_2) where

$$\int_{x_1}^{\theta_2} \frac{2x_1^2}{\theta^3} d\theta = p \text{ or } \theta_2 = \frac{x_1}{\sqrt{(1-p)}}$$

The length of this Bayesian confidence interval is $\theta_2 - x_1 = x_1\left(\frac{1}{\sqrt{(1-p)}} - 1\right)$, which is actually greater than the $100p$ per cent highest *prior* density interval if

$$x_1\left(\frac{1}{\sqrt{(1-p)}} - 1\right) > \left(\frac{1}{1-p} - 1\right), \text{ or } x_1 > \frac{1}{\sqrt{(1-p)}} + 1$$

Exercise 1. Complete the second part of Example 1 by checking that a new value X will be greater than x_1 with probability $(\theta - x_1)/\theta$ for a particular θ and integrating this probability over the posterior distribution of Θ given $x_1 > 1$.
[Ans. 1/3]

Exercise 2. For Example 1, show that if $x_1 < 1, g(\theta | x_1) = 2/\theta^3, \theta > 1$, and that the $100p$ per cent highest posterior density interval is $(1, 1/\sqrt{(1 - p)})$.

Exercise 3. The prior distribution of a parameter Θ is $\lambda \exp(-\lambda\theta)$, $\theta > 0$. Show that the $100p$ per cent highest prior density interval is $(0, -[\log(1 - p)]/\lambda)$. Suppose for a single sample value x, the posterior distribution of Θ given x is $\Gamma(2, \lambda + x)$. Obtain two equations which determine the highest posterior density interval. Verify that this interval is the shortest Bayesian confidence interval with coefficient p.

Exercise 4. $X_1, X_2, \ldots, X_n$ is a random sample from $N(\theta, 1)$. If the prior distribution of Θ is $N(\mu, 1)$ then the posterior distribution of Θ is $N\left(\dfrac{\mu + n\bar{x}}{n + 1}, \dfrac{1}{n + 1}\right)$. Show that the $100p$ per cent Bayesian confidence interval of shortest length is

$$\left[\frac{\mu + n\bar{x}}{n + 1} - \frac{d}{\sqrt{(n + 1)}}, \frac{\mu + n\bar{x}}{n + 1} + \frac{d}{\sqrt{(n + 1)}}\right]$$

where d is the upper $\left[\left(\dfrac{1 - p}{2}\right)\right] 100$ per cent point of the $N(0, 1)$ distribution.

Exercise 5. Suppose Θ has probability density function $g(\theta)$ such that $g(\theta) = \theta/2, 0 < \theta < 1, g(\theta) = (4 - \theta)/6, 1 \leqslant \theta \leqslant 4$. Show that if $\Pr[\theta_1 \leqslant \Theta \leqslant \theta_2] = 1 - \alpha$, then the interval (θ_1, θ_2) of highest prior density is $(\sqrt{\alpha}, 4 - 3\sqrt{\alpha})$.

7.2 Two parameters, Bayesian confidence regions

If the parameters Θ, Φ have a joint prior distribution with density $g(\theta, \phi)$, then from the sample values $x_1, x_2, \ldots, x_n$ we can find the density of the posterior distribution of Θ, Φ given $x_1, x_2, \ldots, x_n$. Any region R such that $\Pr[\Theta, \Phi \in R | x_1, x_2, \ldots, x_n] = p$ is a $100p$ per cent Bayesian confidence region for θ, ϕ. For a reasonably behaved posterior distribution, with a single maximum, a region of highest posterior density, i.e. satisfying

$$g(\theta, \phi \mid x_1, x_2, \ldots, x_n) \geqslant k$$

will be connected.

Example 2. X given θ, ϕ has a uniform distribution over the interval (θ, ϕ). The prior distribution of the parameters has density $g(\theta, \phi) = 2/(\phi - \theta)^3, \theta < 0, \phi > 1$. A single value x is drawn and $0 < x < 1$. The joint probability density function of X, Θ, Φ is

$$\frac{1}{(\phi - \theta)} \frac{2}{(\phi - \theta)^3} = \frac{2}{(\phi - \theta)^4}, \theta < \min(0, x), \phi > \max(1, x)$$

For $0 < x < 1$, the marginal distribution of X has density

$$\int_{-\infty}^{0} \int_{1}^{\infty} \frac{2}{(\phi - \theta)^4} \, d\phi d\theta = \int_{-\infty}^{0} \frac{2}{3(1 - \theta)^3} \, d\theta = \frac{1}{3}$$

So that the posterior distribution has density

$$\frac{2}{(\phi - \theta)^4} \bigg/ \frac{1}{3} = \frac{6}{(\phi - \theta)^4} \text{ given } 0 < x < 1$$

Hence any region R such that

$$\iint_{R} \frac{6}{(\phi - \theta)^4} \, d\phi d\theta = p$$

is a $100 p$ per cent Bayesian confidence region for (θ, ϕ). Note that $g(\theta, \phi \mid x)$ is decreasing as $(\phi - \theta)$ increases, so that a region of highest posterior density consists of a triangle with sides $\phi = 1, \theta = 0, \phi - \theta = c$.

Exercise 6. Show for Example 2, that if $x > 1$,

$$g(\theta, \phi \mid x) = 6x^2/(\phi - \theta)^4, \phi > x, \theta < 0, \text{ but if } x < 0,$$
$$g(\theta, \phi \mid x) = 6(1 - x)^2/(\phi - \theta)^4, \theta < x, \phi > 1.$$

For the Bayesian, the construction of a confidence interval for one of several parameters is straightforward in principle. From the joint posterior distribution, the marginal posterior distribution of a parameter of interest is found by integrating out the remainder, and the problem is reduced to the one-parameter case.

Example 3. For Example 2, $g(\theta, \phi | x) = 6/(\phi - \theta)^4, 0 < x < 1$, $\theta < 0, \phi > 1$. Hence $g(\phi | x) = \int g(\theta, \phi | x) \mathrm{d}\theta = 2/\phi^3, \phi > 1$.

If $\int_1^{\phi_0} \dfrac{2}{\phi^3} \mathrm{d}\phi = p$, then $(1, \phi_0)$ is a 100 p per cent Bayesian confidence interval for ϕ.

7.3 Confidence intervals (classical)

Without a prior distribution, it is not possible to make direct probability statements about a parameter. We have a sample of values from a known type of distribution with fixed parameters, about which little may be known except, perhaps, broad features such as that they lie between certain bounds. We can proceed *indirectly* by constructing, from the sample values alone, a region which has a known probability of covering the parameter. To be of any real service, the 'known' probability should not involve the unknown parameters! In fact, it would be most desirable for the probability to be the same for all achievable values of the parameters. It may not be obvious that any such regions exist.

Example 4. X has probability density function $f(x | \theta) = \theta^{-1} \exp(-x/\theta), x > 0$. Even from a sample of one value, we can construct the interval $(k_1 x, k_2 x)$ where $0 < k_1 < k_2$. Now the interval contains θ unless the lower end is too large or the upper end is too small. That is to say, the probability of *failing* to cover θ is

$$
\begin{aligned}
\Pr[k_1 &X > \theta \text{ or } k_2 X < \theta] \\
&= \Pr[X > \theta/k_1] + \Pr[X < \theta/k_2] \\
&= \int_{\theta/k_1}^{\infty} \frac{1}{\theta} \exp\left(-\frac{x}{\theta}\right) \mathrm{d}x + \int_0^{\theta/k_2} \frac{1}{\theta} \exp\left(-\frac{x}{\theta}\right) \mathrm{d}x \\
&= \exp(-1/k_1) + 1 - \exp(1 - 1/k_2)
\end{aligned}
$$

Thus the probability that $(k_1 X, k_2 X)$ contains θ is $\exp(-1/k_2) - \exp(-1/k_1)$, *whatever the value of* θ.

In Example 4, we have displayed an interval which has a known probability of containing a parameter, and this probability is the same for any value of θ. More generally, if $X_1, X_2, \ldots, X_n$ is a sample from a distribution indexed by a single parameter θ and

$t_1(X_1, X_2, \ldots, X_n), t_2(X_1, X_2, \ldots, X_n)$ are two statistics such that

$$\Pr[t_1(X_1, X_2, \ldots, X_n) \leqslant \theta \leqslant t_2(X_1, X_2, \ldots, X_n) | \theta]$$

is constant for all θ, then $[t_1(X_1, X_2, \ldots, X_n), t_2(X_1, X_2, \ldots, X_n)]$ shall be called a *confidence interval* for θ. The same name is also commonly employed for the interval $[t_1(x_1, x_2, \ldots, x_n), t_2(x_1, x_2, \ldots, x_n)]$ computed from particular sample values. The fixed probability is called the *confidence coefficient* and this, for reasons which will appear, is denoted by $1 - \alpha$. The value of this coefficient may be controlled either by a different choice of statistic or by altering the sample size. The confidence interval fails to contain θ if either $T_1 > \theta$ or $T_2 < \theta$. Let the probabilities of these two mutually exclusive events be α_2, α_1. Then provided $\alpha_1 + \alpha_2 = \alpha$, the confidence coefficient will be $1 - \alpha$. If $\alpha_2 = 0$, then $\Pr[t_2(X_1, X_2, \ldots, X_n) > \theta | \theta] = 1 - \alpha$, and we may reasonably call T_2 an *upper confidence limit* for θ with coefficient $1 - \alpha$. Similarly, if $\alpha_1 = 0$, T_1 is a *lower confidence limit* for θ with coefficient $1 - \alpha$. If $\alpha_1 = \alpha_2 = \alpha/2$, then the confidence interval is said to be central.

Example 5. X has probability density function $f(x|\theta) = \theta^{-1} \exp(-x/\theta)$, $x > 0$. From Example 4, $(k_1 X, k_2 X)$ is a confidence interval with coefficient $\exp(-1/k_2) - \exp(-1/k_1)$.

(a) If $k_1 = 0$, since $\theta > 0$, the interval $(0, k_2 X)$ cannot fall entirely above θ. $k_2 X$ is an upper confidence limit for θ, with coefficient $\exp(-1/k_2)$.

(b) If $k_2 = \infty$, the interval $(k_1 X, \infty)$ cannot fall entirely below θ. $k_1 X$ is a lower confidence limit for θ, with coefficient $1 - \exp(-1/k_1)$.

(c) If k_1, k_2 are chosen so that $\exp(-1/k_1) = 1 - \exp(-1/k_2)$, the confidence interval $(k_1 X, k_2 X)$ is central, with coefficient $1 - 2\exp(-1/k_1)$.

It is all very well to say that we can 'freely choose k_1, k_2', but our ability to do so must be paid for in some other feature. Thus, in (a), if the confidence coefficient is to be large, then k_2 must be large, and hence possibly $k_2 x$ is a long way off!

In Example 4, there was an element of 'luck' in that the interval $(k_1 X, k_2 X)$ provided a confidence interval with fixed confidence coefficient regardless of the true value of θ. This desirable property stems from the fact that $\Pr[kX < \theta] = \Pr[(X/\theta < 1/k)]$ and for the random variable in question, the distribution of X/θ

does not depend on θ at all. This is an example of the *pivotal method*, which employs a function T of the observations and θ that has a distribution not involving θ. We have then

$$\Pr[t(X_1, X_2, \dots, X_n, \theta) \leqslant t]$$

is the same for each θ.

Of course, a little more is required—we should be able to solve the probability statement in terms of θ. If the solution does not lead to a connected interval, then there will be problems of interpretation.

Example 6. $X_1, X_2, \dots, X_n$ is a random sample from the distribution $N(\theta, \sigma_0^2)$ where σ_0^2 is a known constant. Since $\bar{X}$ has the distribution $N(\theta, \sigma_0^2/n)$, then $\sqrt{n}(\bar{X} - \theta)/\sigma_0$ has the distribution $N(0, 1)$, whatever θ. Hence from tables we can find c_1, c_2 such that

$$\Pr[c_1 \leqslant \sqrt{n}(\bar{X} - \theta)/\sigma_0 \leqslant c_2] = 1 - \alpha$$

This can be 'solved for θ' to read

$$\Pr\left[\bar{X} - \frac{c_2 \sigma_0}{\sqrt{n}} \leqslant \theta \leqslant \bar{X} - \frac{c_1 \sigma_0}{\sqrt{n}} \Big| \theta \right] = 1 - \alpha$$

so that $(\bar{X} - c_2 \sigma_0/\sqrt{n}, \bar{X} - c_1 \sigma_0/\sqrt{n})$ is a confidence interval for θ with coefficient $1 - \alpha$. From symmetry, the shortest such interval has $c_1 = -c_2$. [A common choice is $1 - \alpha = 0.95$, when $c_2 = +1.96$.]

That the property discussed is essential is readily seen. For suppose, in Example 4, that we proposed the interval $(kX, kX + c)$, $k > 0, c > 0$,

$$\Pr[kX \leqslant \theta \leqslant kX + c | \theta] = \exp[(c - \theta)/k\theta] - \exp(-1/k)$$

which contains the unknown parameter. This defect is here fatal, since the probability steadily decreases as θ increases. The question of a 'good' choice of statistic, from which confidence regions are to be constructed, emerges more forcibly for samples of more than one observations.

Example 7. X_1, X_2 are independent values from the distribution with probability density function $f(x|\theta) = \theta^{-1}\exp(-x/\theta), x > 0$. It is required to construct an upper confidence limit for θ with prescribed coefficient.

(a) Consider $U = X_1 + X_2$; this has density $\theta^{-2}u\exp(-u/\theta)$,

$u > 0$ and perforce, the distribution of U/θ does not depend on θ.

$$\text{Pt}[U/k > \theta|\theta] = \Pr[U > k\theta|\theta]$$

$$= \int_{k\theta}^{\infty} \frac{1}{\theta}\left(\frac{u}{\theta}\right)\exp\left(-\frac{u}{\theta}\right)du = e^{-k}(1 + k)$$

(b) Consider $V = \min(X_1, X_2)$. Since $\Pr[lV > \theta|\theta] = \Pr[lX_1 > \theta$ and $lX_2 > \theta|\theta] = [\Pr(X > \theta/l|\theta)]^2 = e^{-2/l}$, the distribution of V/θ does not depend on θ.

We conclude that $(X_1 + X_2)/k, l \min(X_1, X_2)$ are both upper confidence limits for θ which have the same coefficient when $e^{-k}(1 + k) = e^{-2/l}$.

To compare two proposed upper limits is not easy. There is no guarantee that one will be higher than the other, not even on the average.

Example 8.   (Example 7 continued.) If $k = 2$, then $l \approx 2.2$ If x_1 happens to be close to x_2, then $(x_1 + x_2)/2 < 2.2 \min(x_1, x_2)$; but, if, say, $x_1 > 4x_2$, then $(x_1 + x_2)/2 > 2.5x_2 > 2.2 \min(x_1, x_2)$. Moreover, $E[(X_1 + X_2)/k] = 2\theta/k$ while $E(l \min(X_1, X_2)] = l\theta/2$. From the equality of the confidence coefficients,

$$\exp\left(\frac{k}{2} - \frac{2}{l}\right) = (1 + k)\exp(-k/2)$$

The expression on the right-hand side at first increases with k and eventually decreases. Hence $2/k \not< l/2$ for all k, and the comparison between the expectations depends ultimately on the confidence coefficient.

7.4 Most selective limits

There is another criterion which turns out to be unambiguous for many standard distributions. For upper confidence limits we may put it this way. If θ' is any value of θ which exceeds the true value θ_0, then the best upper limit will be least likely to exceed θ'. Such a limit is said to be *most selective* (or most accurate).

Example 9.   (Example 8 continued.)

(a) $\Pr[(X_1 + X_2)/k > \theta'|\theta_0] = \Pr[(X_1 + X_2) > k\theta'|\theta_0]$

$$= \left(1 + \frac{k\theta'}{\theta_0}\right)\exp\left(-\frac{k\theta'}{\theta_0}\right)$$

(b) $\Pr[\min(lX_1, lX_2) > \theta'|\theta_0] = \exp\left(-\dfrac{2\theta'}{l\theta_0}\right)$

We require, of course, equality when $\theta' = \theta_0$. Thus

$$\exp\left(-\frac{2\theta'}{l\theta_0}\right) = \left[\exp\left(-\frac{2}{l}\right)\right]^{\theta'/\theta_0} = \left[(1+k)\exp(-k)\right]^{\theta'/\theta_0}$$

$$= (1+k)^{\theta'/\theta_0}\exp\left(-\frac{k\theta'}{\theta_0}\right)$$

It is readily verified, that since $k > 0$, when $\theta' > \theta_0$

$$(1+k)^{\theta'/\theta_0} > 1 + \frac{\theta'}{\theta_0}k$$

The upper limit $(X_1 + X_2)/k$ is superior, in the sense that it is less likely to trap an unwanted value of the parameter, and is indeed *uniformly* more selective than $l\min(X_1, X_2)$, since the result holds for all $\theta' > \theta_0$. We should wish to be assured that we have the best possible upper limit. It turns out that this is directly related to the best test of a particular one-sided hypothesis.

7.5 Relationship to best tests

We display a rather general way of generating confidence regions. For each $\theta = \theta_0$, construct any critical region $c(\theta_0)$ at level α. For each θ_0, the obtained sample $x_1, x_2, \ldots, x_n$ either belongs to $c(\theta_0)$ or it does not. If the sample does *not* belong to $c(\theta_0)$, then that particular θ_0 is included in the confidence region— otherwise it is excluded. By construction, the probability that the sample falls in $c(\theta_0)$, given $\theta = \theta_0$, is $\leq \alpha$, hence the probability that the sample does not fall in $c(\theta_0)$, given $\theta = \theta_0$, is $\geq 1 - \alpha$. Thus, the prescribed confidence region has a confidence coefficient of at least $1 - \alpha$. Without the imposition of some additional structure on the selection of the critical region in relation to the confidence coefficient, we could be landed with some peculiar confidence regions. Thus, if we wish to consider a sequence of confidence regions, for the same sample, but with increasing confidence coefficients, we should like each region to be contained in its successor. This has been called the *nesting principle*. There is one special circumstances which in general avoids pathological constructions and procures 'best' confidence regions. This is when there exists a uniformly most powerful (u.m.p.) test against one-sided alternatives.

We know that most powerful tests obey the nesting principle – that is, to decrease the size of the test, you shrink the critical region.

Thus if we require a lower confidence limit for θ, then we need a test such that, for any sample, there is a *least* θ^* which can be accepted at level α. Then θ^*, which is a function of the sample values, is a lower confidence limit for θ with coefficient $1 - \alpha$. If θ_0 is the true value of the parameter and $\theta_1 < \theta_0$ then, since the test of θ_1 against θ_0 is u.m.p., the probability of drawing a sample which accepts θ_1 is a minimum.

Example 10. $X_1, X_2, \ldots, X_n$ is a random sample from $N(\theta, \sigma_0^2)$ where σ_0^2 is a known constant. It is required to construct a lower confidence limit for θ with confidence coefficient $1 - \alpha$. We have seen that there exists a u.m.p. test of $\theta = \theta_0$ against $\theta > \theta_0$ based on large values of $\bar{x}$.

If $\Pr[\bar{X} > d \,|\, \theta_0] = \alpha$, then $d = \theta_0 + c_\alpha \sigma_0/\sqrt{n}$ where c_α is the upper 100α per cent point of the $N(0, 1)$ distribution. So if, for the obtained $\bar{x}$, we have $\bar{x} < \theta_0 + c_\alpha \sigma_0/\sqrt{n}$ or $\theta_0 > \bar{x} - c_\alpha \sigma_0/\sqrt{n}$, then that θ_0 is included in the confidence region and $\bar{X} - c_\alpha \sigma_0/\sqrt{n}$ is a lower confidence limit for θ with coefficient $1 - \alpha$. Moreover, if θ_0 is the true value of θ, then any $\theta_1 < \theta_0$ will be included in the confidence region with minimal probability. We say that $\bar{X} - c_\alpha \sigma_0/\sqrt{n}$ is a *uniformly most selective lower confidence limit* for θ with coefficient $1 - \alpha$.

Exercise 7. $X_1, X_2, \ldots, X_n$ is a random sample from the distribution $N(\mu_0, \sigma^2)$. If $c_\alpha(n)$ is the lower 100α per cent point of the χ_n^2 distribution, show that the uniformly most selective upper confidence limit for σ^2, with coefficient $1 - \alpha$, is

$$\sum_{i=1}^{n} (X_i - \mu_0)^2 / c_\alpha(n).$$

[μ_0 is a known constant.]

7.6 Unbiased confidence intervals

Suppose we require an interval (T_1, T_2) such that $\Pr[T_1 \leqslant \theta \leqslant T_2 \,|\, \theta] = 1 - \alpha$ for all θ. Any pair of lower and upper limits, T_1, T_2, with coefficients $1 - \alpha_1, 1 - \alpha_2$ such that $\alpha_1 + \alpha_2 = \alpha$, will suffice. We would not expect such an interval to be most selective against values either side of the true value of a parameter. One reasonable solution is to take $\alpha_1 = \alpha_2 = \alpha/2$ and ensure an equal chance that the entire interval falls above or below the true value. Such an interval is said to be central.

Example 11. $X_1, X_2, \ldots, X_n$ is a random sample from $N(\theta, \sigma_0^2)$ where σ_0^2 is known. The interval $(\bar{X} - c_{\alpha/2}\sigma_0/\sqrt{n}, \bar{X} + c_{\alpha/2}\sigma_0/\sqrt{n})$, where $c_{\alpha/2}$ is the upper $\alpha/2$ probability point of the distribution $N(0, 1)$, is a central confidence interval for θ with coefficient $1 - \alpha$. It is formed from a combination of most selective lower and upper limits.

Another solution is to construct intervals from the corresponding best unbiased tests. Suppose, then, for each $\theta = \theta_0$ we can construct a uniformly most powerful unbiased (u.m.p.u.) test against $\theta \neq \theta_0$, of size α, with $c(\theta_0)$ as critical region. Then for the data obtained, we include in the confidence region, any θ_0 for which the data do *not* belong to $c(\theta_0)$. Since: (*a*) from the size condition, $\Pr[(X_1, X_2, \ldots, X_n) \notin c(\theta_0)|\theta_0] = 1 - \alpha$; (*b*) from the unbiasedness, $\Pr[(X_1, X_2, \ldots, X_n) \notin c(\theta_0)|\theta] \leqslant (1 - \alpha)$; then the confidence region will have coefficient $1 - \alpha$ and be less likely to contain a false value than the true one. Indeed, among such confidence regions, it is least likely to contain a false value since it is constructed from a u.m.p.u. test. We may justifiably call such regions 'uniformly most selective unbiased'. For one-parameter members of the regular exponential family, such regions will be intervals. For these distributions we know in principle how to construct u.m.p.u. tests – the critical region lies in the tails and the corresponding power function has zero slope at θ_0.

Example 12. $X_1, X_2, \ldots, X_n$ is a random sample from $N(0, \sigma^2)$. It is required to construct a uniformly most selective unbiased confidence interval for σ^2 with coefficient $1 - \alpha$. We recall that $\sum X_i^2/\sigma^2$ has the χ_n^2 distribution. For a u.m.p.u. test of $\sigma = \sigma_0$ versus $\sigma \neq \sigma_0$, we require numbers c_1, c_2 such that if

$$P(\sigma) = \Pr\left[\sum_1^n X_i^2/\sigma_0^2 < c_1 \Big| \sigma\right] + \Pr\left[\sum_1^n X_i^2/\sigma_0^2 > c_2 \Big| \sigma\right]$$

then $P(\sigma_0) = \alpha$ and $\left(\dfrac{\mathrm{d}P}{\mathrm{d}\sigma}\right)_{\sigma_0} = 0$.

In such a case,

$$\Pr\left[c_1 \leqslant \sum_1^n X_i^2/\sigma^2 \leqslant c_2 \Big| \sigma\right] = 1 - \alpha$$

and $(\sum X_i^2/c_2, \sum X_i^2/c_1)$ is the required confidence interval.

Exercise 8. In Example 12, for $\alpha = 0.05, n = 2$, verify by direct integration that $c_1 = 0.084, c_2 = 9.54$ (approximately).

7.7 Nuisance parameters

The method of the last section may be extended to cover cases where there is a nuisance parameter. Suppose, then, there are two parameters θ, ϕ. For each $\theta = \theta_0$ it may be possible to find a critical region $c(\theta_0)$ such that:

(a) $\Pr[(X_1, X_2, \ldots, X_n) \notin c(\theta_0) | \theta_0, \phi] = 1 - \alpha$, for all ϕ;

(b) $\Pr[(X_1, X_2, \ldots, X_n) \notin c(\theta_0) | \theta, \phi] \leqslant 1 - \alpha$, for all ϕ.

For certain two-parameter distributions, best critical regions of this type can be derived via a sufficient statistic for the nuisance parameter.

Example 13. $X_1, X_2, \ldots, X_n$ is a random sample from $N(\phi, \sigma^2)$. It is required to construct a uniformly most selective unbiased confidence interval for σ^2 with coefficient $1 - \alpha$. Here the mean, ϕ, is the nuisance parameter. u.m.p.u. tests of $\sigma = \sigma_0$ versus $\sigma \neq \sigma_0$ are based on the statistic $\sum(X_i - \bar{X})^2/\sigma_0^2$ which is distributed, independently of ϕ, as χ_{n-1}^2 when $\sigma = \sigma_0$. We require two numbers d_1, d_2 such that if

$$P(\sigma) = \Pr\left[\sum_1^n (X_i - \bar{X})^2/\sigma_0^2 < d_1 | \sigma \right] + \Pr\left[\sum_1^n (X_i - \bar{X})^2/\sigma_0^2 > d_2 | \sigma \right]$$

then $P(\sigma_0) = \alpha$ and $\left(\dfrac{\mathrm{d}P}{\mathrm{d}\sigma}\right)_{\sigma_0} = 0$.

We have in general,

$$\Pr\left[d_1 \leqslant \sum_1^n (X_i - \bar{X})^2/\sigma^2 \leqslant d_2 | \sigma \right] = 1 - \alpha$$

and $\left[\sum_1^n (X_i - \bar{X})^2/d_2, \sum_1^n (X_i - \bar{X})^2/d_1 \right]$ is the required confidence interval. Since special tables are needed, many prefer to sacrifice the optimal property and rest content with central confidence intervals.

Example 14. $X_1, X_2, \ldots, X_n$ is a random sample from $N(\theta, \phi)$. It is required to construct a uniformly most selective unbiased confidence interval for the mean θ with coefficient $1 - \alpha$. Here the nuisance parameter is the variance. u.m.p.u. tests of $\theta = \theta_0$ versus $\theta \neq \theta_0$ are based on

$$T = \sqrt{n}(\bar{X} - \theta_0)/S, \text{ where } S^2 = \sum_1^n (X_i - \bar{X})^2/(n-1) \text{ and}$$

T has Student's distribution with parameter $n - 1$ when $\theta = \theta_0$. The *acceptance* region for a test of size α is

$$|T| \leqslant t_{n-1}(\alpha/2)$$

where $t_{n-1}(\alpha/2)$ is the upper $\alpha/2$ probability point of the t-distribution with parameter $n - 1$.

Hence $\Pr[-t_{n-1}(\alpha/2) \leqslant \sqrt{n}(\bar{X} - \theta)/S \leqslant t_{n-1}(\alpha/2)|\theta] = 1 - \alpha$ or 'solving' for θ,

$$\Pr\left[\bar{X} - \frac{St_{n-1}(\alpha/2)}{\sqrt{n}} \leqslant \theta \leqslant \bar{X} + \frac{St_{n-1}(\alpha/2)}{\sqrt{n}}\bigg|\theta\right] = 1 - \alpha$$

From symmetry, this confidence interval is also central.

Exercise 9. $X_1, X_2, \ldots, X_n$ is a random sample from $N(\theta_1, \phi)$; $Y_1, Y_2, \ldots, Y_m$ is an independent random sample from $N(\theta_2, \phi)$. Find a construction for a most selective unbiased confidence interval for $\theta_1 - \theta_2$, with coefficient $1 - \alpha$.

7.8 Discrete distributions

Similar methods can be employed for discrete distributions though, in general, prescribed confidence coefficients can only be attained conservatively. That is, for $\theta = \theta_0$, we can find a 'good' critical region $c(\theta_0)$ such that $\Pr[(X_1, X_2, \ldots, X_n) \in c(\theta_0)|\theta_0] \leqslant \alpha$, with equality only possible for some values θ_0. Hence the probability that the sample does *not* fall in the critical region is greater than or equal to $1 - \alpha$.

Example 15. X is a single value from a Poisson distribution with parameter λ. We wish to construct a (most selective) upper confidence limit for λ with confidence coefficient at least $1 - \alpha$.

There is a u.m.p. test of $\lambda = \lambda_0$ against $\lambda < \lambda_0$, and it is based on sufficiently small values of x. For each λ_0, there is a largest $x(\lambda_0)$ such that $\Pr[X \leqslant x(\lambda_0)|\lambda_0] \leqslant \alpha$. Suppose now x is observed and from tables of the Poisson distribution we can find λ_2 such that

$\Pr[X \leqslant x | \lambda_2] = \alpha$, then λ_2 is the required $1 - \alpha$ upper confidence limit for λ. For instance, if $x = 2$ and $1 - \alpha$ is to be 95 per cent, we have $\Pr[X \leqslant 2 | \lambda = 6.3] = 0 \cdot 0498$, so that the numerical value of the upper confidence limit is 6.3. For some values of $1 - \alpha$, the next exercise shows how ordinary tables of the chi-square distribution may be used.

Exercise 10. If X has the Poisson distribution with parameter λ,

show that
$$\Pr[X \leqslant k - 1 | \lambda] = \int_{\lambda}^{\infty} \frac{y^{k-1} \exp(-y)}{(k-1)!} \mathrm{d}y$$
$$= \int_{2\lambda}^{\infty} \frac{1}{2} \left(\frac{w}{2} \right)^{k-1} \frac{\exp(-w/2)}{\Gamma(k)} \mathrm{d}w$$

It is to be noticed that the integrand is the p.d.f. of a chi-square distribution with parameter $2k$. So, for example, if $\Pr[X \leqslant 2 | \lambda] = 5$ per cent, take $k = 3$. Then the upper 5 per cent point of the χ_6^2 distribution is 12.59; finally, $2\lambda_2 = 12.59$ or λ_2 is approximately 6.3.

Exercise 11. A single value is drawn from a Poisson distribution with parameter λ. Calculate an approximate 95 per cent central confidence interval for λ if the obtained value is 11.
[Ans. 5.5, 19.7]

Exercise 12. If X has the binomial distribution with parameters n, θ, show that
$$\Pr[X \leqslant k | \theta] = \frac{n!}{(n-k-1)! k!} \int_0^{1-\theta} (1-t)^k t^{n-k-1} \mathrm{d}t$$
$$= \frac{\Gamma(n+1)}{\Gamma(n-k) \Gamma(k+1)} \int_0^{(1-\theta)/\theta} \frac{y^{n-k-1}}{(1+y)^{n+1}} \mathrm{d}y, t = y/(1+y)$$

Hence, substituting $y(k+1)/(n-k) = u$, show that
$$\Pr[X \leqslant k | \theta] = \int_0^{(1-\theta)(k+1)/[\theta(n-k)]} \phi(u) \mathrm{d}u$$

where $\phi(u)$ is the probability density function of an F-distribution with parameters $2n - 2k, 2k + 2$. [Hint: integrate by parts.]

Exercise 13. In nine independent trials, with constant probability θ of success, four successes are observed. Show that the numerical value of an approximate 95 per cent central confidence interval is $[0.14, 0.79]$.

7.9 Relationship between classical and Bayesian intervals

Suppose $[\theta_1(X_1, X_2, \ldots, X_n), \theta_2(X_1, X_2, \ldots, X_n)]$ is a (classical) confidence interval for θ with coefficient $1 - \alpha$. We have $\Pr[\theta_1(X_1, X_2, \ldots, X_n) \leqslant \theta \leqslant \theta_2(X_1, X_2, \ldots, X_n) | \theta] = 1 - \alpha$ for all θ, where the probability has been computed with respect to the sample values given θ. Since the confidence coefficient is the same for all θ, it remains at $1 - \alpha$ even if it is assumed that Θ has a prior distribution.

Now we can also compute the Bayesian coefficient for the same interval as

$$\Pr[\theta_1(x_1, x_2, \ldots, x_n) \leqslant \Theta \leqslant \theta_2(x_1, x_2, \ldots, x_n) | x_1, x_2, \ldots, x_n]$$
$$= \gamma(x_1, x_2, \ldots, x_n)$$

based on the posterior distribution of Θ given $x_1, x_2, \ldots, x_n$. However, the unconditional distribution of the sample values is available in principle so that

$$E[\gamma(X_1, X_2, \ldots, X_n)] = 1 - \alpha.$$

Exercise 14. A single value X is drawn from the exponential distribution with parameter θ. Show that $(1/2X, 1/X)$ contains θ with probability $\exp(-\frac{1}{2}) - \exp(-1)$. If Θ has the prior distribution $\Gamma(1, 1)$, check that the posterior distribution of Θ given x is $\Gamma(2, 1 + x)$. Hence show that $\gamma(x) = \Pr\left[\dfrac{1}{2x} \leqslant \Theta \leqslant \dfrac{1}{x} \middle| x \right] = \dfrac{1 + 3x}{2x} \exp\left[-(1 + x)/2x\right] - \dfrac{1 + 2x}{x} \exp\left[-(1 + x)/x\right]$. Show that the distribution of X has p.d.f. $f(x) = 1/(1 + x)^2$ and verify that $\int_0^\infty \gamma(x) f(x) \, dx = \exp(-\frac{1}{2}) - \exp(-1)$.
[Hint: put $(1 + x)/x = u$ and integrate by parts.]

7.10 Large-sample confidence intervals

For a large random sample, from a distribution with a sufficiently regular probability density function, the maximum likelihood estimator has an asymptotically normal distribution (Section 4.8). More precisely, for the case of one parameter,

$$(\hat{\Theta} - \theta) / \left\{ -1 / E\left[\frac{\partial^2 \log L}{\partial \theta^2} \right] \right\}^{1/2} \tag{7.1}$$

where L is the likelihood, has a limiting distribution which is $N(0, 1)$.

This result may be exploited to construct confidence intervals with approximately the desired confidence coefficient.

Example 16. $X_1, X_2, \ldots, X_n$ is a random sample from the distribution $N(0, \theta)$. It is required to construct a central confidence interval with an approximate coefficient $1 - \alpha$.
Since

$$\frac{\partial \log L}{\partial \theta} = -\frac{n}{2\theta} + \frac{\sum X_i^2}{2\theta^2}$$

it is easy to check that,

$$\hat{\theta} = \sum x_i^2/n, \; E\left[\frac{\partial^2 \log L}{\partial \theta^2}\right] = -n/2\theta^2$$

Hence, if $c_{\alpha/2}$ is the upper 50α per cent probability point of the standardized normal distribution,

$$\Pr\left[-c_{\alpha/2} < \left(\frac{\sum X_i^2}{n} - \theta\right) \Big/ \left(\frac{2\theta^2}{n}\right)^{1/2} < +c_{\alpha/2}\right] = 1 - \alpha$$

That is to say,

$$\Pr[\theta(1 - \sqrt{(2/n)}c_{\alpha/2}) < \sum X_i^2/n < \theta(1 + \sqrt{(2/n)}c_{\alpha/2})] = 1 - \alpha$$

Hence the required confidence interval is

$$\left\{\frac{\sum X_i^2/n}{1 + \sqrt{(2/n)}c_{\alpha/2}}, \frac{\sum X_i^2/n}{1 - \sqrt{(2/n)}c_{\alpha/2}}\right\} \tag{7.2}$$

Exercise 15. $X_1, X_2, \ldots, X_n$ is a random sample from the exponential distribution with p.d.f. $f(x|\theta) = \theta \exp(-\theta x), x > 0$. Construct a central confidence interval for θ with an approximate coefficient $1 - \alpha$.

$$\left[\text{Ans.} \quad \left(\frac{\sqrt{n}}{\bar{X}(\sqrt{n} + c_{\alpha/2})}, \frac{\sqrt{n}}{\bar{X}(\sqrt{n} - c_{\alpha/2})}\right)\right]$$

There are some inconveniences attached to the method just discussed. To begin with, the interval is not invariant under transformations of the parameter.

Example 17. $X_1, X_2, \ldots, X_n$ is a random sample from $N(0, \theta^2)$. To construct a confidence interval for θ with an approximate coefficient $1 - \alpha$, we have

$$\frac{\partial \log L}{\partial \theta} = -\frac{n}{\theta} + \frac{\sum X_i^2}{\theta^3}$$

and hence

$$\hat{\theta} = (\sum x_i^2/n)^{1/2}, \quad E\left[\frac{\partial^2 \log L}{\partial \theta^2}\right] = -2n/\theta^2.$$

Thus,

$$\Pr\left[-c_{\alpha/2} < \left[(\sum X_i^2/n)^{1/2} - \theta\right]\left/\frac{\theta}{\sqrt{2n}} < c_{\alpha/2}\right.\right] = 1 - \alpha$$

or

$$\Pr\left[\theta\{1 - c_{\alpha/2}/\sqrt{(2n)}\} < (\sum X_i^2/n)^{1/2} < \theta\{1 + c_{\alpha/2}/\sqrt{(2n)}\}\right] = 1 - \alpha$$

In this case, the confidence interval for θ is

$$\left\{\frac{(\sum X_i^2/n)^{1/2}}{1 + c_{\alpha/2}/\sqrt{(2n)}}, \frac{(\sum X_i^2/n)^{1/2}}{1 - c_{\alpha/2}/\sqrt{(2n)}}\right\} \tag{7.3}$$

Since $\theta > 0$, we might take it into our heads to obtain a confidence interval for θ^2, again with coefficient $1 - \alpha$, merely by squaring the values obtained in Equation (7.3) and arrive at

$$\left\{\frac{\sum X_i^2/n}{\{1 + c_{\alpha/2}/\sqrt{(2n)}\}^2}, \frac{\sum X_i^2/n}{\{1 - c_{\alpha/2}/\sqrt{(2n)}\}^2}\right\}$$

This is not the same as the result in Equation (7.2). To be sure, $\{1 + c_{\alpha/2}/\sqrt{(2n)}\}^2 = 1 + \sqrt{(2/n)}c_{\alpha/2} + c_{\alpha/2}^2/2n$, so, for large n, the difference will scarcely be remarked.

There may also be some difficult in computing the end-points of the required confidence interval.

Example 18. $X_1, X_2, \ldots, X_n$ is a random sample from a Poisson distribution with parameter θ. We have

$$\frac{\partial \log L}{\partial \theta} = \frac{\sum X_i}{\theta} - n$$

hence $\hat{\theta} = \bar{x}$, $\quad E\left[\frac{\partial^2 \log L}{\partial \theta^2}\right] = -n/\theta$

If $\Pr\left[-c_{\alpha/2} < (\bar{X} - \theta)/\sqrt{(\theta/n)} < +c_{\alpha/2}\right] = 1 - \alpha$, then we cannot immediately 'solve for θ'. However, we have equivalently

$$\Pr\left[(\bar{X} - \theta)^2 < c_{\alpha/2}^2\theta/n\right] = 1 - \alpha$$

and the reader may, as an exercise, show that after rearranging as a quadratic form in θ, the required confidence interval is

$$\left\{ \bar{X} + c_{\alpha/2}^2/2n \pm \left(\frac{\bar{X}c_{\alpha/2}^2}{n} + \frac{c_{\alpha/2}^4}{4n^2} \right)^{1/2} \right\}$$

Exercise 16. $X_1, X_2, \ldots, X_n$ is a random sample from the Bernoulli distribution with parameter θ. Show that $\hat{\theta} = \bar{x}$ and $E\left[\dfrac{\partial^2 \log L}{\partial \theta^2} \right] = -n/[\theta(1 - \theta)]$. Hence calculate a central confidence interval for θ with an approximate coefficient $1 - \alpha$. If $n = 100$, $\hat{\theta} = 0.60$, $1 - \alpha = 0.95$, confirm that the interval is $(1/2, 9/13)$. [Take $c_{\alpha/2}$ as approximately 2.]

The difficulty highlighted in Example 3 can be evaded by replacing θ by the m.l.e. in the variance of the asymptotic distribution of $\hat{\Theta}$. That is, we treat

$$(\hat{\Theta} - \theta) \bigg/ \left\{ -1/E\left[\frac{\partial^2 \log L}{\partial \theta^2} \right] \right\}_{\hat{\theta}}^{1/2} \tag{7.4}$$

as having the distribution which tends towards $N(0, 1)$. This in practice gives the most convenient computational form.

Example 19.   For the Poisson distribution, Example 18, we have

$$\Pr\left[-c_{\alpha/2} < (\bar{X} - \theta)/(\bar{X}/n)^{1/2} < +c_{\alpha/2} \right] = 1 - \alpha$$

and the confidence interval is

$$\left[\bar{X} - c_{\alpha/2}(\bar{X}/n)^{1/2}, \bar{X} + c_{\alpha/2}(\bar{X}/n)^{1/2} \right]$$

Exercise 17. $X_1, X_2, \ldots, X_n$ is a random sample from $N(0, \theta)$. Use Equation (7.4) to construct a central confidence interval for θ, with an approximate coefficient $1 - \alpha$.
    [Ans. $(\{1 - c_{\alpha/2}\sqrt{(2/n)}\}\sum X_i^2/n, \{1 + c_{\alpha/2}\sqrt{(2/n)}\}\sum X_i^2/n)$]

We have not yet explored the possibility of constructing large-sample confidence intervals which are invariant under transformations of the parameter. Such a construction exists and shows how the asymptotic normality is ultimately grounded in the all-pervasive central-limit theorem. Suppose the probability density function, $f(x|\theta)$, is sufficiently regular for the random variable $(\partial/\partial\theta) \log f(X|\theta)$ to have zero expectation and finite variance, $-E[(\partial^2/\partial\theta^2) \log f(X|\theta)]$, for all θ.

If we have a random sample from such a distribution and $L = \prod_1^n f(X_i | \theta)$, then the random variable

$$\frac{\frac{\partial}{\partial \theta} \log L}{\sqrt{\left\{ - E\left(\frac{\partial^2 \log L}{\partial \theta^2}\right)\right\}}} \qquad (7.5)$$

has mean 0 and variance 1. Moreover, Equation (7.5) is easily written as the sample mean of the random variables $(\partial / \partial \theta) \log f(X_i | \theta)$, divided by its standard deviation. Hence, by the central-limit theorem, the limiting distribution of Equation (7.5) is $N(0, 1)$. Let ϕ be a strictly increasing function of θ. Then

$$\frac{\partial}{\partial \theta} \log L = \frac{\partial \log L}{\partial \phi} \frac{\partial \phi}{\partial \theta}$$

and $E[(\partial / \partial \theta) \log L] = 0 \Rightarrow E[(\partial / \partial \phi) \log L] = 0$.
Further,

$$\frac{\partial^2 \log L}{\partial \theta^2} = \frac{\partial^2 \log L}{\partial \phi^2}\left(\frac{\partial \phi}{\partial \phi}\right)^2 + \frac{\partial \log L}{\partial \phi}\left(\frac{\partial^2 \phi}{\partial \theta^2}\right)$$

hence

$$E\left[\frac{\partial^2 \log L}{\partial \theta^2}\right] = \left(\frac{\partial \phi}{\partial \theta}\right)^2 E\left[\frac{\partial^2 \log L}{\partial \phi^2}\right]$$

and evidently we have the desired invariance property in Equation (7.5).

Example 20. $X_1, X_2, \ldots, X_n$ is a random sample from $N(0, \theta^2)$. We have

$$\frac{\partial \log L}{\partial \theta} = -\frac{n}{\theta} + \frac{\sum X_i^2}{\theta^3}, \text{ and}$$

$$E\left[\frac{\partial^2 \log L}{\partial \theta^2}\right] = -2n/\theta^2$$

Hence,

$$\frac{\frac{\partial}{\partial \theta} \log L}{\sqrt{\left\{ - E\left[\frac{\partial^2 \log L}{\partial \theta^2}\right]\right\}}} = \frac{(\sum X_i^2 / \theta^2) - n}{\sqrt{(2n)}} \qquad (7.6)$$

For a central confidence interval, we use

$$\Pr\left[-c_{\alpha/2} < [(\sum X_i^2/\theta^2) - n]/\sqrt{(2n)} < +c_{\alpha/2}\right] = 1 - \alpha$$

and the interval is

$$\left\{\left(\frac{\sum X_i^2}{n + \sqrt{(2n)}c_{\alpha/2}}\right)^{1/2}, \left(\frac{\sum X_i^2}{n - \sqrt{(2n)}c_{\alpha/2}}\right)^{1/2}\right\} \tag{7.7}$$

Although this is not the same as Equation (7.3), we note that the difference is negligible since, for large n, $\{1 + \sqrt{(2/n)}c_{\alpha/2}\}^{1/2}$ is approximately $1 + \frac{1}{2}\sqrt{(2/n)}c_\alpha = 1 + c_{\alpha/2}/\sqrt{(2n)}$. Moreover, if we had regarded the variance of the normal distribution as the parameter θ, then this method would have yielded the confidence interval

$$\left\{\frac{\sum X_i^2/n}{1 + \sqrt{(2/n)}c_{\alpha/2}}, \frac{\sum X_i^2/n}{1 - \sqrt{(2/n)}c_{\alpha/2}}\right\}$$

and the end-points *are* the squares of those in Equation (7.7). In conclusion, confidence intervals based on Equation (7.5) have a certain optimum property, namely that (within a restricted class) they are, on average, the shortest. (Kendall and Stuart, *The Advanced Theory of Statistics*, Vol. 2, Chapter 9.)

Exercise 18.   Show that for a random sample from a distribution for which

$$\frac{\partial \log L}{\partial \theta} = a(\theta)[T - \theta]$$

then the random variable in Equation (7.1) is equivalent to Equation (7.5).

Appendix 1
Functions of random variables

A1.1 Introduction

The reader will likely have some experience of finding the distribution of sums of independent random variables. The following results are standard when $X_1, X_2, \ldots, X_n$ are independent random variables:

(a) X_i distributed $N(\theta_i, \phi_i)$, then $\sum\limits_{i=1}^{n} X_i$ is distributed

$$N\left(\sum_{i=1}^{n} \theta_i, \sum_{i=1}^{n} \phi_i \right).$$

(b) X_i distributed Poisson with parameter λ_i, then $\sum\limits_{i=1}^{n} X_i$ has a

Poisson distribution with parameter $\sum\limits_{i=1}^{n} \lambda_i$.

(c) X_i distributed $\Gamma(\alpha_i, \theta)$, then $\sum\limits_{i=1}^{n} X_i$ is distributed $\Gamma\left(\sum\limits_{i=1}^{n} \alpha_i, \theta \right)$.

These results are readily obtained using moment generating functions, or probability generating functions for discrete random variables whose only possible values are the non-negative integers. Our next example serves to revise these ideas.

Example 1. The discrete random variable X has p.d.f. $f(x|\theta) = (1-\theta)^x \theta$, $x = 0, 1, 2, \ldots$, $0 < \theta < 1$. Then the p.g.f. of X is

$$G_X(t) = E(t^X) = \sum_x t^x f(x|\theta) = \sum_{x=0}^{\infty} t^x (1-\theta)^x \theta$$

$$= \theta / [1 - (1-\theta)t]$$

If we require the p.g.f. of the sum of two such independent random

193

variables X_1, X_2, then

$$G_{X_1 + X_2}(t) = E(t^{X_1 + X_2}) = E(t^{X_1})E(t^{X_2})$$

$$= \frac{\theta}{[1 - (1 - \theta)t]}\frac{\theta}{[1 - (1 - \theta)t]}$$

$$= \frac{\theta^2}{[1 - (1 - \theta)t]^2}$$

$$= \theta^2 \sum_{u=0}^{\infty} (u + 1)(1 - \theta)^u t^u$$

So that $\Pr[X_1 + X_2 = u] = (u + 1)(1 - \theta)^u \theta^2$.

Exercise 1. Show that if the discrete random variable X has p.g.f. $G(t)$, then

$$E(X) = \frac{dG}{dt}\bigg]_{t=1}$$

If X_i has the binomial distribution with parameters n_i, θ find the p.g.f. of X_i and deduce the distribution of $X_1 + X_2$ when X_1, X_2 are independent.

A1.2 Transformations: discrete distributions

Eventually, considerable ingenuity is required to find the joint distribution of several functions of a set of random variables. Similar methods are available for continuous distribution, but based on moment generating functions, when these exist. Of course, the characteristic function, defined as $E[\exp(iXt)]$, always exists. The final problem is one of identification. That is, can we recognize, or recover by inversion, the distribution which has a particular generating function? An alternative technique is to work directly with the joint probability density function of the underlying random variables. Thus, suppose the discrete random variables $X_1, X_2, \ldots,$ X_n have joint probability density function $f(x_1, x_2, \ldots, x_n)$ and we require $\Pr[t(X_1, X_2, \ldots, X_n) = t]$ where T is a statistic. Then, equivalently, we must sum $f(x_1, x_2, \ldots, x_n)$ over all those $(x_1, x_2, \ldots, x_n)$ such that $t(x_1, x_2, \ldots, x_n) = t$.

Example 2. X_1, X_2 is a random sample of two from the distribution with p.d.f. $f(x|\theta) = (1 - \theta)^x \theta, x = 0, 1, 2, \ldots,$ Since X_1, X_2 are independent, $f(x_1, x_2) = f_1(x_1)f_2(x_2) = \theta^2(1 - \theta)^{x_1 + x_2}$.

If $t(X_1, X_2) = X_1 + X_2$,

$$
\begin{aligned}
\Pr[T = t] &= \sum_{x_1 + x_2 = t} \Pr[X_1 = x_1 \text{ and } X_2 = x_2] \\
&= \sum_{x_1 = 0}^{t} \Pr[X_1 = x_1 \text{ and } X_2 = t - x_1] \\
&= \sum_{x_1 = 0}^{t} \Pr[X_1 = x_1] \Pr[X_2 = t - x_1] \\
&= \sum_{x_1 = 0}^{t} (1 - \theta)^{x_1} \theta (1 - \theta)^{t - x_1} \theta \\
&= \sum_{x_1 = 0}^{t} \theta^2 (1 - \theta)^t = (t + 1) \theta^2 (1 - \theta)^t
\end{aligned}
$$

Exercise 2. For Example 2, if $t(X_1, X_2) = X_1 - X_2$, show that $\Pr[T = t] = (1 - \theta)^{|t|} \theta^2 / [1 - (1 - \theta)^2]$.

In order to keep track of all the sample values which satisfy a particular condition, it pays to make a formal change of variables. The new set should be in one-to-one correspondence with the old set and will include the statistics of particular interest as members. The remaining members will be a matter of convenience.

Example 3. For Example 2, if we change variables to $U_1 = X_1 + X_2, U_2 = X_1 \leqslant U_1$, then the joint probability density function of U_1, U_2 is

$$
\begin{aligned}
f(x_1, x_2) &]_{u_1, u_2} \\
&= [\theta^2 (1 - \theta)^{x_1 + x_2}]_{u_1, u_2} \\
&= \theta^2 (1 - \theta)^{u_1}, 0 \leqslant u_2 \leqslant u_1
\end{aligned}
$$

since $\Pr[U_1 = u_1 \text{ and } U_2 = u_2] = \Pr[X_1 = u_1 - u_2 \text{ and } X_2 = u_2]$

For discrete random variables, we merely express the joint probability density function of $X_1, X_2, \ldots, X_n$ in terms of the new variables.

Exercise 3. For Example 2, find the joint probability density function of $V_1 = X_1 + X_2$, $V_2 = X_1 - X_2$. By summing out v_1, show that the probability density function of V_2 is $\theta^2 (1 - \theta)^{|v_2|} / [1 - (1 - \theta)^2]$. [Hint: bear in mind that v_1, v_2 must be both even or both odd at points of positive probability. Since $v_1 \geqslant 0$, if $v_2 > 0$, $v_1 = v_2 + 2r$, while if $v_2 < 0$, $v_1 = -v_2 + 2r$, $r = 0, 1, \ldots$.]

Exercise 4.   The discrete random variables X_1, X_2 have joint probability density function

$$f(x_1, x_2) = \frac{n!}{x_1! x_2! (n - x_1 - x_2)!} \theta_1^{x_1} \theta_2^{x_2} (1 - \theta_1 - \theta_2)^{n - x_1 - x_2},$$

$$x_1 = 0, 1, \ldots, n, x_2 = 0, 1, \ldots, n, 0 \leqslant x_1 + x_2 \leqslant n.$$

Show that the distribution of $X_1 + X_2$ is binomial with parameters n and $\theta_1 + \theta_2$.

A1.3 Continuous distributions

To find the joint distribution of several functions of the sample random variables in the continuous case is not so immediately straightforward. We wish to keep the advantage of the method which changes the variables into a new set by mapping points onto points in a one-to-one correspondence. But, in the continuous case, points carry zero probability. We must compare regions of positive probability and then deduce the implication for the underlying probability density functions. Suppose then that the continuous random variables $X_1, X_2, \ldots, X_n$ have joint probability density function $f(x_1, x_2, \ldots, x_n)$, where reference to the parameters has been omitted. Let $Y_i = \phi_i(X_1, X_2, \ldots, X_n)$, $i = 1, 2, \ldots, n$, be a one-to-one correspondence between the X_i and the Y_i, and let the latter have probability density function $g(y_1, y_2, \ldots, y_n)$. Take any volume V such that $\Pr[(X_1, X_2, \ldots, X_n) \in V] > 0$ and suppose all the points of V are mapped onto U, then

$$\Pr[(X_1, X_2, \ldots, X_n) \in V] = \Pr[(Y_1, Y_2, \ldots, Y_n) \in U]$$

But both these probabilities are found by evaluating the appropriate multiple integral. That is

$$\int_V \ldots \int f(x_1, x_2, \ldots, x_n) dx_1 \ldots dx_n = \int_U \ldots \int g(y_1, y_2, \ldots, y_n) dy_1 \ldots dy_n$$

In each integral the limits are in the (usual) increasing order. In order to find a connection between the integrands, we make a formal change of variable from the x_i to the y_i in the left-hand side. Since the correspondence is one-to-one, we can solve uniquely for each x_i, so that $x_i = \psi_i(y_1, y_2, \ldots, y_n)$, $i = 1, 2, \ldots, n$. We now require a theorem from the calculus which states that if all the partial derivatives

$\dfrac{\partial x_i}{\partial y_j}(i, j = 1, 2, \ldots, n)$, are continuous, and the Jacobian,

$$J\left[\frac{\partial(x_1, x_2, \ldots, x_n)}{\partial(y_1, y_2, \ldots, y_n)}\right] = J_x \text{ is not zero over } V, \text{ then}$$

$$\int \cdots_V \int f(x_1, x_2, \ldots, x_n) dx_1 dx_2 \ldots dx_n$$

$$= \int \cdots_U \int [f(x_1, x_2, \ldots, x_n)|J_x|]_{y_1, y_2, \ldots, y_n} dy_1 dy_2 \ldots dy_n$$

Equating integrands, we have

$$g(y_1, y_2, \ldots, y_n) = [f(x_1, x_2, \ldots, x_n)|J_x|]_{y_1, y_2, \ldots, y_n}$$

That is to say, we multiply the joint probability density function of $X_1, X_2, \ldots, X_n$ by the modulus (positive value), of the Jacobian of the inverse transformation and express the product in terms of the new variables $y_1, y_2, \ldots, y_n$.

Note on Jacobians

The Jacobian J_x is defined as the determinant for which the element in the ith row and jth column is $\dfrac{\partial x_i}{\partial y_j}, i = 1, 2, \ldots, n, j = 1, 2, \ldots, n$. For example, if $n = 2$,

$$J_x = \begin{vmatrix} \dfrac{\partial x_1}{\partial y_1} & \dfrac{\partial x_1}{\partial y_2} \\ \dfrac{\partial x_2}{\partial y_1} & \dfrac{\partial x_2}{\partial y_2} \end{vmatrix} = \left(\frac{\partial x_1}{\partial y_1}\frac{\partial x_2}{\partial y_2} - \frac{\partial x_1}{\partial y_2}\frac{\partial x_2}{\partial y_1}\right)$$

The reason for taking the positive value is to retain the usual convention for evaluating integrals in terms of upper and lower limits. The reason for requiring the Jacobian to be non-zero is to preserve the uniqueness of the inverse transformation. However, if sets for which the Jacobian is zero have also zero probability then we may simply remove such sets. Furthermore, the Jacobian of the direct transformation J_y, defined as the determinant for which the element in the ith row and jth column is $\dfrac{\partial y_i}{\partial x_j}$, must satisfy

$$J_x J_y = 1$$

For if we first transform from $(x_1, x_2, \ldots, x_n)$ to $(y_1, y_2, \ldots, y_n)$ and then transform back to $(x_1, x_2, \ldots, x_n)$ then this double application is the identity transformation. It may be more convenient to calculate J_y.

Example 4. X_1, X_2 are independently distributed $N(0, 1)$ and it is required to find the joint distribution of $Y_1 = X_1 + X_2$, $Y_2 = X_1 - X_2$. Uniquely, $X_1 = (Y_1 + Y_2)/2$, $X_2 = (Y_1 - Y_2)/2$ and

$$
J_x = \begin{vmatrix} \dfrac{\partial x_1}{\partial y_1} & \dfrac{\partial x_1}{\partial y_2} \\[2mm] \dfrac{\partial x_2}{\partial y_1} & \dfrac{\partial x_2}{\partial y_2} \end{vmatrix} = \begin{vmatrix} \dfrac{1}{2} & \dfrac{1}{2} \\[2mm] \dfrac{1}{2} & -\dfrac{1}{2} \end{vmatrix} = -\dfrac{1}{2}
$$

$$
f(x_1, x_2) = f_1(x_1) f_2(x_2) = \frac{1}{2\pi} \exp\left[-\tfrac{1}{2}(x_1^2 + x_2^2) \right]
$$

$$
g(y_1, y_2) = \left\{ \frac{1}{2\pi} \exp\left[-\tfrac{1}{2}(x_1^2 + x_2^2) \right] | -\tfrac{1}{2}| \right\}_{y_1, y_2}
$$

$$
= \frac{1}{4\pi} \exp\left[-\frac{1}{2}\left(\frac{y_1 + y_2}{2} \right)^2 - \frac{1}{2}\left(\frac{y_1 - y_2}{2} \right)^2 \right]
$$

$$
= \frac{1}{4\pi} \exp\left[-\frac{1}{2}\left(\frac{y_1^2}{2} + \frac{y_2^2}{2} \right) \right], \ -\infty < y_1 < \infty,
$$

$$
-\infty < y_2 < \infty.
$$

Evidently, Y_1, Y_2 are independent $N(0, 2)$, a result reachable by several methods.

Exercise 5.   Solve Example 4 using the joint moment generating function $M_{Y_1, Y_2}(t_1, t_2) = E[\exp(Y_1 t_1 + Y_2 t_2)]$.

Exercise 6. X_1, X_2 are independently distributed $N(0, 1)$. Find the joint p.d.f. of $Y_1 = X_1 + X_2$, $Y_2 = X_1$.
[Ans. $\dfrac{1}{2\pi} \exp\{ -\tfrac{1}{2}(2y_2^2 - 2y_1 y_2 + y_1^2) \}$]
Recover the marginal distribution of Y_1.

Example 5. X_1, X_2 are independently distributed $N(0, 1)$. Find the distributions of R, Θ defined by $X_1 = R \cos \Theta$, $X_2 = R \sin \Theta$,

$0 < R, 0 \leqslant \Theta < 2\pi.$

$$J_x = \begin{vmatrix} \dfrac{\partial x_1}{\partial r} & \dfrac{\partial x_1}{\partial \theta} \\[2mm] \dfrac{\partial x_2}{\partial r} & \dfrac{\partial x_2}{\partial \theta} \end{vmatrix} = \begin{vmatrix} \cos\theta & -r\sin\theta \\ \sin\theta & r\cos\theta \end{vmatrix}$$

$$= r\cos^2\theta + r\sin^2\theta = r > 0.$$

All points $(r = 0, \theta)$ have the same inverse point $x_1 = 0$, $x_2 = 0$, but $X_1 = 0, X_2 = 0$ is an outcome with zero probability, hence $r = 0$ can be safely excluded.

$$g(r,\theta) = \frac{1}{2\pi}\exp\left[-\tfrac{1}{2}(r^2\cos^2\theta + r^2\sin^2\theta)\right]r$$

$$= \frac{r}{2\pi}\exp\left[-\tfrac{1}{2}r^2\right], r > 0, 0 \leqslant \theta < 2\pi$$

Whence

$$g_1(r) = \int_0^{2\pi} \frac{r}{2\pi}\exp\left[-\tfrac{1}{2}r^2\right]d\theta = r\exp\left[-\tfrac{1}{2}r^2\right], r > 0,$$

and

$$g_2(\theta) = \frac{1}{2\pi}\int_0^\infty r\exp\left[-\tfrac{1}{2}r^2\right]dr = \frac{1}{2\pi}, 0 \leqslant \theta < 2\pi,$$

R and Θ are independent.

Exercise 7. X_1, X_2, X_3 are independent $N(0,1)$. If $X_1 = R\cos\Theta\sin\Phi$, $X_2 = R\sin\Theta\sin\Phi$, $X_3 = R\cos\Phi$, $R > 0$, $0 \leqslant \Theta < 2\pi$, $0 \leqslant \Phi < \pi$, prove that the joint probability density function of R, Θ, Φ is $g(r,\theta,\phi) = \dfrac{r^2\sin\phi}{\{\sqrt{(2\pi)}\}^3}\exp\left[-\tfrac{1}{2}r^2\right]$ and deduce that they are independent.

Example 6. X_1, X_2 are independent, each having the exponential distribution with parameter θ. Show that $Y_1 = X_1 + X_2$, $Y_2 = X_1/(X_1 + X_2)$ are independent. We have $X_1 = Y_1Y_2, X_2 = Y_1(1 - Y_2)$ and the Jacobian of the inverse transformation is

$$J_x = \begin{vmatrix} y_2 & y_1 \\ 1-y_2 & -y_1 \end{vmatrix} = -y_1$$

$X_1 > 0, X_2 > 0$ implies $Y_1 > 0$ and $0 < Y_2 < 1$.

$$g(y_1,y_2) = [f(x_1,x_2)|J_x|]_{y_1,y_2}$$
$$= \{\theta^2 \exp[-\theta(x_1 + x_2)]y_1\}_{y_1,y_2}$$
$$= \theta^2 y_1 \exp(-\theta y_1), \qquad y_1 > 0, 0 < y_2 < 1$$

By factorization, Y_1, Y_2 are independent, having a $\Gamma(2,\theta)$, rectangular distribution respectively.

Exercise 8. X_1, X_2 are independently distributed $N(0,1)$. Find the joint distribution of $Y_1 = X_1/X_2, Y_2 = X_2$ and deduce that Y_1 has p.d.f. $1/[\pi(1 + y_1^2)]$, $-\infty < y_1 < \infty$.
{Note: all points $(y_1,0)$ must be excluded (why?), the Jacobian is y_2, hence $|y_2| = y_2$ if $y_2 > 0$ and $|y_2| = -y_2$ if $y_2 < 0$.}

Exercise 9. X_1 has p.d.f. $f_1(x_1|\alpha) = x_1^{\alpha-1}\exp(-x_1)/\Gamma(\alpha), X_2$ has p.d.f. $f_2(x_2|\beta) = x_2^{\beta-1}\exp(-x_2)/\Gamma(\beta)$ and X_1, X_2 are independent. Find the joint p.d.f. of $Y_1 = X_1/(X_1 + X_2), Y_2 = X_1 + X_2$, and deduce that the p.d.f. of Y_1 is

$$\frac{\Gamma(\alpha + \beta)}{\Gamma(\alpha)\Gamma(\beta)} y_1^{\alpha-1}(1 - y_1)^{\beta-1}, \qquad 0 < y_1 < 1.$$

Example 7.   (In which Student's t-distribution is derived.) Let X_1 have the distribution $N(0,1)$ and X_2, independently of X_1, have the χ_m^2 distribution: Let further, $T = X_1/\sqrt{(X_2/m)}, S = X_2 > 0$, hence $X_2 = S, X_1 = T\sqrt{(S/m)}$ and the Jacobian of the inverse transformation is

$$\left| \begin{matrix} \sqrt{\dfrac{s}{m}} & \dfrac{t}{2m}\left(\sqrt{\dfrac{s}{m}}\right)^{-1/2} \\ 0 & 1 \end{matrix} \right| = \sqrt{\dfrac{s}{m}}$$

whence the joint p.d.f. of S, T is

$$\left[\frac{1}{\sqrt{(2\pi)}}\exp[-x_1^2/2] \frac{(\frac{1}{2})^{m/2} x_2^{(m/2)-1}\exp[-x_2/2]}{\Gamma(m/2)} \sqrt{\frac{s}{m}} \right]_{s,t}$$

$$= \frac{1}{\sqrt{(2\pi)}}\exp[-st^2/2m] \frac{(\frac{1}{2})^{m/2} s^{(m/2)-1} e^{-s/2}}{\Gamma(m/2)} \sqrt{\frac{s}{m}}$$

$$= \frac{(\frac{1}{2})^{m/2}}{\sqrt{(2\pi m)}\Gamma(m/2)} s^{(m-1)/2}\exp[-\tfrac{1}{2}s(1 + t^2/m)],$$

$$-\infty < t < \infty, s > 0.$$

To find the marginal distribution of T we must integrate with respect to s. After substituting $u = \frac{1}{2}(1 + t^2/m)s$ and integrating with respect to u, we arrive at

$$g_1(t) = \frac{1}{\sqrt{(m\pi)}} \frac{\Gamma[(m+1)/2]}{\Gamma(m/2)} \frac{1}{[1 + t^2/m]^{(m+1)/2}}, \quad -\infty < t < \infty.$$

A continuous random variable T with this p.d.f. is said to have the t-distribution with parameter m (or m degrees of freedom).

Tables for this distribution are, of course, widely available, for example, *Cambridge Elementary Statistical Tables* by D.V. Lindley and J.C. Miller, or the rear-guard of most first-year textbooks.

Exercise 10. Write out the p.d.f. of the t-distribution for $m = 1$, $m = 3$ and note how $\Pr[T > c]$ can be obtained directly. Show that if $m > 1$, $E(T) = 0$.

Exercise 11. $Y_1, Y_2, \ldots, Y_n$ is a random sample from the distribution $N(\theta_1, \theta_2)$. Explain why

$$\frac{\sqrt{n}(\bar{Y} - \theta_1)/\sqrt{\theta_2}}{\sqrt{\left\{ \sum_{i=1}^{n} (Y_i - \bar{Y})^2 / [(n-1)\theta_2] \right\}}}$$

has the t-distribution with parameter $(n-1)$.

Exercise 12. If X_1 has the χ_n^2 distribution and X_2 has, independently of X_1, the χ_m^2 distribution, derive the joint distribution of $Y_2 = \dfrac{X_1}{n} \bigg/ \dfrac{X_2}{m}$, $Y_1 = X_2$, and hence show that the distribution of Y_2 has p.d.f.

$$\frac{\Gamma[(m+n)/2]}{\Gamma(m/2)\Gamma(n/2)} \left(\frac{n}{m}\right)^{n/2} \frac{y_2^{(n/2)-1}}{[1 + (ny_2/m)]^{(m+n)/2}}$$

A continuous random variable with this p.d.f. is said to have the $F_{n,m}$ distribution.

Exercise 13. If Y_2 has the $F_{n,m}$ distribution show:

(a) the p.d.f. of Y_2 has a mode at $y_2 = m(n-2)/[n(m+2)], n > 2$;
(b) $E(Y_2) = m/(m-2), m > 2$;
(c) $1/Y_2$ has the $F_{m,n}$ distribution.

Exercise 14. If $U_1, U_2, \ldots, U_n$ is a random sample from the distribution $N(\theta_1, \phi)$ and $V_1, V_2, \ldots, V_m$ is an independent random sample from the distribution $N(\theta_2, \phi)$, explain why

$$\frac{\sum_{i=1}^{n} (U_i - \bar{U})^2/(n-1)}{\sum_{i=1}^{m} (V_i - \bar{V})^2/(m-1)}$$ has the $F_{n-1, m-1}$ distribution.

A1.4 The order statistics

If a function of the sample values has no unique inverse, then the technique under discussion cannot be immediately applied. If the sample values $X_1, X_2, \ldots, X_n$ are arranged in order of increasing magnitude, then the kth in the sequence is called the kth order statistic and denoted $X_{(k)}$. Clearly,

$$X_{(1)} \leqslant X_{(2)} \leqslant \ldots \leqslant X_{(n)}$$

and in particular $X_{(1)} = \min(X_1, X_2, \ldots, X_n)$, and $X_{(n)} = \max(X_1, X_2, \ldots, X_n)$.

Now $X_{(n)}$ is a function of the sample values but the inverse can be any one of $X_1, X_2, \ldots, X_n$, hence is not unique. We shall restrict attention to continuous random variables when relatively straight-forward alternative derivations are available. These are based on the consideration of the type $X_{(k)} \leqslant x_{(k)}$ if and only if *at least k of the X_i are less than $x_{(k)}$*.

Example 8. $X_{(n)} \leqslant x_{(n)}$ if and only if all the X_i are less than $x_{(n)}$. Hence

$$\Pr[X_{(n)} \leqslant x_{(n)}] = \Pr[X_1 \leqslant x_{(n)} \text{ and } X_2 \leqslant x_{(n)} \ldots \leqslant X_n \leqslant x_{(n)}].$$

Since for a random sample, the X_i are independent with common p.d.f. f and distribution function F,

$$\Pr(X_{(n)} \leqslant x_{(n)}) = \{\Pr[X_1 \leqslant x_{(n)}]\}^n$$
$$= [F(x_{(n)})]^n$$

The p.d.f. of $X_{(n)}$ is found by differentiating with respect to $x_{(n)}$ and is $n[F(x_{(n)})]^{n-1} f(x_{(n)})$. For instance, if $f(x) = 2x, 0 < x < 1, n = 4$, then $F(x) = x^2$ and the p.d.f. of $X_{(4)}$ is $4(x^2)^3 2x = 8x^7, 0 < x < 1$. Similarly, $X_{(1)} \leqslant x_{(1)}$ if and only if at least one X_i is less than $x_{(1)}$. Hence $\Pr[X_{(1)} \leqslant x_{(1)}] = \Pr[\text{at least one } X_i \leqslant x_{(1)}] = 1 - \Pr[\text{all } X_i$

$> x_{(1)}] = 1 - [1 - F(x_{(1)})]^n$. Whence the p.d.f. of $X_{(1)}$ is $n[1 - F(x_{(1)})]^{n-1}f(x_{(1)})$.

Exercise 15. In a random sample of two from the distribution $N(0, \theta)$, show that $E[X_{(1)}] = -\sqrt{(\theta/\pi)}$.

Exercise 16. $X_1, X_2, \ldots, X_n$ is a random sample from a continuous distribution with distribution function F and density f. Show that the p.d.f. of the kth order statistic is

$$n\binom{n-1}{k-1}[F(x_{(k)})]^{k-1}[1 - F(x_{(k)})]^{n-k}f(x_{(k)}).$$

[Hint. The number of observations below $x_{(k)}$ has a binomial distribution with parameters n and $F(x_{(k)})$]

Exercise 17. A random sample of n is drawn from the uniform distribution over $(0, 1)$. Show that $E(X_{(k)}) = k/(n + 1)$.

Similarly, one way of finding the joint p.d.f. of two order statistics $X_{(i)}, X_{(j)}$ is to exploit the fact that $X_{(i)} < x_{(i)}$ and $X_{(j)} < x_{(j)}$ if and only if there are at least i sample values below $x_{(j)}$ *and* at least j below $x_{(j)}(i < j)$.

Example 9. $X_1, X_2, \ldots, X_n$ is a random sample from a continuous distribution with probability density function, f, and distribution function, F.

$$\Pr[X_{(1)} < x_{(1)} \text{ and } X_{(n)} < x_{(n)}]$$
$$= \Pr[\text{at least one } X_i < x_{(1)} \text{ and all } X_i < x_{(n)}]$$
$$= \Pr[\text{all } X_i < x_{(n)}] - \Pr[\text{no } X_i < x_{(1)} \text{ and all } X_i < x_{(n)}]$$
$$= [F(x_{(n)})]^n - [F(x_{(n)}) - F(x_{(1)})]^n$$

We have here the distribution function for $X_{(1)}, X_{(n)}$. On differentiating partially, first with respect to $x_{(1)}$ and then with respect to $x_{(n)}$, we arrive at

$$n(n - 1)[F(x_{(n)}) - F(x_{(1)})]^{n-2}f(x_{(1)})f(x_{(n)}), x_{(1)} < x_{(n)}.$$

Exercise 18. X_1, X_2, X_3 is a random sample of three from the exponential distribution with p.d.f. $f(x) = \exp(-x), x > 0$. Calculate the joint p.d.f. of $X_{(1)}, X_{(3)}$ and *hence* derive the marginal distributions of $X_{(1)}, X_{(3)}$.

[Ans. $6\{\exp(-2x_{(1)} - x_{(3)}) - \exp(-x_{(1)} - 2x_{(3)})\}, 0 < x_{(1)} <$
   $x_{(3)} < \infty; 3\exp(-3x_{(1)}), 0 < x_{(1)} < \infty; 3[1 - \exp(-x_{(3)})]^2$
   $\times \exp(-x_{(3)}), 0 < x_{(3)} < \infty]$

Once we have obtained the joint p.d.f. of $X_{(1)}, X_{(n)}$, we can study certain other statistics which are of practical interest – in particular, those for which the *range* $= X_{(n)} - X_{(1)}$ and the *centre* $= [X_{(n)} + X_{(1)}]/2$.

Example 10.   For Exercise 18, the joint p.d.f. of $X_{(1)}, X_{(3)}$ is
$6[\exp(-2x_{(1)} - x_{(3)}) - \exp(-x_{(1)} - 2x_{(3)})]$.
Consider $Z_1 = X_{(1)}, Z_2 = X_{(3)} - X_{(1)} > 0$. The Jacobian of the transformation is 1 and thence the joint p.d.f. of Z_1, Z_2 is

$$3\exp(-3z_1)[2\exp(-z_2) - 2\exp(-2z_2)], \qquad z_1 > 0, z_2 > 0$$

Z_1, Z_2 are in fact independent, the p.d.f. of Z_2 being $2\exp(-z_2) - 2\exp(-2z_2)$.

Exercise 19.   For a random sample of n from the uniform distribution over $(0,1)$ show that the p.d.f. of the range, $R = X_{(n)} - X_{(1)}$, is

$$n(n-1)r^{n-2}(1-r), \qquad 0 < r < 1$$

Exercise 20. $X_1, X_2, \ldots, X_n$ is a random sample from a continuous distribution with distribution function F and density f. Show that the joint p.d.f. of the order statistics $X_{(i)}, X_{(j)}$ is

$$\frac{n!}{(i-1)!(j-i-1)!(n-j)!}[F(x_{(i)})]^{i-1}[F(x_{(j)}) - F(x_{(i)})]^{j-i-1}$$
$$\times [1 - F(x_{(j)})]^{n-j}f(x_{(i)})f(x_{(j)})$$

Explain why $X_{(i)}, X_{(j)}$ are not independent.
{Note: This result may be found by an easier alternative route. Consider the simultaneous probability that one observation falls in $x_{(i)} + \delta x_{(i)}$ and another in $x_{(j)} + \delta x_{(j)}$. From the remaining $n-2$ values, $i-1$ are chosen to fall below $x_{(i)}$, with probability $\binom{n-2}{i-1}[F(x_{(i)})]^{i-1}$, and from the $n-i-1$ *then* remaining, $j-i-1$ to fall between $x_{(i)}$ and $x_{(j)}$, with probability $\binom{n-i-1}{j-i-1}[F(x_{(j)}) - F(x_{(i)})]^{j-i-1}$. The rest of the sample values must fall above $x_{(j)}$.}

Exercise 21. In a random sample of 5 from the continuous distribution with p.d.f. $f(x) = 3x^2$, $0 < x < 1$, show that $X_{(2)}/X_{(4)}$, $X_{(4)}$ are independent.

Exercise 22. The continuous random variable X has distribution function F. Show that the random variable $F(X)$ has the uniform distribution over $(0, 1)$. For a random sample $X_1, X_2, \ldots, X_n$, show that $F(X_{(k)})$ has a beta distribution.

Exercise 23. $X_1, X_2, \ldots, X_n$ is a random sample from a continuous distribution with distribution function F. Show that the expected number of observations falling below a fixed point, t, is $nF(t)$.

Finally, there is the matter of the joint distribution of all the order statistics for a random sample $X_1, X_2, \ldots, X_n$ from a continuous distribution with probability density function, f. Let $g(x_{(1)}, x_{(2)}, \ldots, x_{(n)})$ be the joint p.d.f. Then

$$\Pr[x_{(1)} < X_{(1)} < x_{(1)} + \delta x_{(1)} \text{ and } x_{(2)} < X_{(2)} < x_{(2)} + \delta x_{(2)}, \ldots$$
$$\text{and } x_{(n)} < X_{(n)} < x_{(n)} + \delta x_{(n)}]$$
$$= g(x_{(1)}, x_{(2)}, \ldots, x_{(n)})\delta x_{(1)} \delta x_{(2)} \ldots \delta x_{(n)} + o(\delta x_{(1)} \delta x_{(2)} \ldots \delta x_{(n)})$$

But this same outcome is realized if $x_{(i)} < X_i < x_{(i)} + \delta x_{(i)}$ ($i = 1, 2, \ldots, n$), which is but one of the $n!$ ways in which the sample values may be placed in the intervals $(x_{(i)}, x_{(i)} + \delta x_{(i)})$ ($i = 1, 2, \ldots, n$). Hence this probability is also

$$n! \Pr[x_{(1)} < X_1 < x_{(1)} + \delta x_{(1)} \text{ and } x_{(2)} < X_2 < x_{(2)} + \delta x_{(2)}, \ldots,$$
$$\text{and } x_{(n)} < X_n < x_{(n)} + \delta x_{(n)}]$$
$$= n! \prod_{i=1}^{n} [f(x_{(i)})\delta x_{(i)} + o(\delta x_{(i)})]$$
$$= n! \prod_{i=1}^{n} f(x_{(i)})\delta x_{(i)} + \text{terms all of which are } o(\delta x_{(1)} \delta x_{(2)} \ldots \delta x_{(n)})$$

Hence on division by $(\delta x_{(1)} \delta x_{(2)} \ldots \delta x_{(n)})$ and allowing all $\delta x_{(i)} \to 0$,

$$g(x_{(1)}, x_{(2)}, \ldots, x_{(n)}) = n! \prod_{i=1}^{n} f(x_{(i)}), \quad x_{(1)} < x_{(2)} < \ldots < x_{(n)}.$$

This formula may be used to find the distributions of individual order statistics but some care must be taken over the limits when carrying out integrations. An optional note on this follows.

Note. To find the p.d.f. of the distribution of $X_{(k)}$. By inspecting the inequalities

$$x_{(1)} < x_{(2)} \cdots < x_{(k-1)} < x_{(k)} < x_{(k+1)} \cdots x_{(n-1)} < x_{(n)}$$

we either:

(a) follow a sequence in which we integrate with respect to $x_{(k+1)}$ from $x_{(k)}$ to $x_{(k+2)}$, then $x_{(k+2)}$ from $x_{(k)}$ to $x_{(k+3)}, \ldots, x_{(n)}$ from $x_{(k)}$ to the upper limit of positive probability, followed by $x_{(k-1)}$ from $x_{(k-2)}$ to $x_{(k)}$, then $x_{(k-2)}$ from $x_{(k-3)}$ to $x_{(k)}, \ldots, x_{(1)}$ from the lower limit of positive probability to $x_{(k)}$;

(b) or we follow a sequence in which we start at the outside and work inwards, with respect to $x_{(n)}$ from $x_{(n-1)}$ to the upper limit of positive probability, then $x_{(n-1)}$ from $x_{(n-2)}$ to the upper limit of positive probability, $\ldots$, $x_{(k+1)}$ from $x_{(k)}$ to the upper limit of positive probability, followed by $x_{(1)}$ from the lower limit of positive probability to $x_{(2)}$ then $x_{(2)}, \ldots$

Example 11. X_1, X_2, X_3 is a random sample from the distribution for which $f(x) = \exp(-x), x > 0$. The joint p.d.f. of the order statistics is

$$g(x_{(1)}, x_{(2)}, x_{(3)}) = 3! \exp[-x_{(1)} - x_{(2)} - x_{(3)}], 0 < x_{(1)} < x_{(2)} < x_{(3)}.$$

To find the p.d.f. of the distribution of $X_{(1)}$ we evaluate either:

(a) $\displaystyle\int_{x_{(1)}}^{\infty} \left[\int_{x_{(1)}}^{x_3} g(x_{(1)}, x_{(2)}, x_{(3)}) dx_{(2)} \right] dx_{(3)}$

or

(b) $\displaystyle\int_{x_{(1)}}^{\infty} \left[\int_{x_{(2)}}^{\infty} g(x_{(1)}, x_{(2)}, x_{(3)}) dx_{(3)} \right] dx_{(2)}$

As an exercise, both integrals should be computed.
[Ans. $3 \exp(-3x_{(1)})$]

Appendix 2
The regular exponential family of distributions

A2.1 Single parameter

Suppose a random variable X has a p.d.f. of the form

$$f(x|\theta) = \exp[a(\theta)b(x) + c(\theta) + d(x)] \qquad (A2.1)$$

where the set of values of x in which $f(x|\theta)$ is positive does not depend on θ. Then, whether X is continuous or discrete, we say it belongs to the regular exponential family of distributions. The densities of many standard distributions can be written in this form.

Example 1. X is distributed $N(0, \theta)$.

$$f(x|\theta) = \frac{1}{\sqrt{(2\pi\theta)}} \exp\left[-\frac{1}{2}x^2/\theta\right] = \exp\left[\frac{-x^2}{2\theta} - \log\sqrt{(2\pi\theta)}\right],$$
$$-\infty < x < \infty.$$

This is of the form of Equation (A2.1) with:

$$a(\theta) = -1/2\theta, b(x) = x^2, c(\theta) = \log\sqrt{(2\pi\theta)}, d(x) = 0.$$

Example 2. X has the binomial distribution with parameters m and θ.

$$f(x|\theta) = \binom{m}{x}\theta^x(1-\theta)^{m-x}$$

$$= \exp\left[x\log\theta + (m-x)\log(1-\theta) + \log\binom{m}{x}\right]$$

$$= \exp\left[x\log[\theta/(1-\theta)] + m\log(1-\theta) + \log\binom{m}{x}\right]$$

$$x = 0, 1, 2, \ldots, m$$

This is of the form of Equation (A2.1) with
$a(\theta) = \log[\theta/(1-\theta)], b(x) = x, c(\theta) = m\log(1-\theta),$
$$d(x) = \log\binom{m}{x}.$$

Exercise 1. Show that the following are members of the regular exponential family:
(a) X is Poisson with parameter θ;
(b) X in $N(\theta, 1)$;
(c) X in $\Gamma(m, \theta)$ where m is a known integer.

On the other hand, the Cauchy distribution, for which

$$f(x|\theta) = \frac{1}{\pi[1 + (x-\theta)^2]},$$

cannot be written in the form of Equation (A2.1) and the truncated exponential, $f(x|\theta) = \exp(\theta - x), x > \theta$, seems to fit, but the domain of x for which the density is positive depends on θ.

General comments

(a) We exclude the trivial case $b(x)$ a constant.
(b) Since f is a p.d.f.,

$$\exp[-c(\theta)] = \int_{f(x|\theta)>0} \exp[a(\theta)b(x) + d(x)]\,dx$$

{summation for discrete case}
(c) Equation (A2.1) can be written

$$\exp[c(\theta)]\exp[d(x)]\exp[a(\theta)b(x)] = g(\theta)h(x)\exp[a(\theta)b(x)],$$

and $a(\theta)$ is said to be the natural parameter for the distribution. For the binomial distribution this is $\log[\theta/(1-\theta)]$ {see Example 2}. Indeed sometimes it is convenient to reparametrize by writing $\phi = a(\theta)$ and to change the variable to $y = b(x)$.

Suppose now we have a random sample $X_1, X_2, \ldots, X_n$ from a member of the regular exponential family. The joint p.d.f. of the sample values is, from Equation (A2.1),

$$\prod_{i=1}^{n} \{\exp[a(\theta)b(x_i) + c(\theta) + d(x_i)]\}$$
$$= \exp[a(\theta)\sum_{i=1}^{n} b(x_i)]\exp[nc(\theta)]\exp\left[\sum_{i=1}^{n} d(x_i)\right] \qquad (A2.2)$$

By the factorization displayed in Equation (A2.2), $\sum_{i=1}^{n} b(X_i)$ is sufficient for θ.

Example 3. Immediately we have, for Example 1, $\sum_{i=1}^{n} X_i^2$ is sufficient for θ.

Exercise 2. $X_1, X_2, \ldots, X_n$ are independent and the p.d.f. of X_i is

$$f_i(x_i \mid \theta) = \exp\left[a(\theta)b_i(x_i) + c_i(\theta) + d_i(x_i)\right]$$

Show that $\sum_{i=1}^{n} b_i(X_i)$ is sufficient for θ.

From Equation (A2.2) $T = \sum_{i=1}^{n} b(X_i)$ is sufficient for θ and moreover itself belongs to the regular exponential family of distributions. For instance, in the discrete case, to find the p.d.f. of T, we are to sum Equation (A2.2) over those $x_1, x_2, \ldots, x_n$ such that $\sum_{i=1}^{n} b(x_i) = t$. This is

$$\exp\left[a(\theta)t\right]\exp\left[nc(\theta)\right]\sum_{\Sigma b(x_i)=t} \exp\left[\sum d(x_i)\right] \qquad (A2.3)$$

Evidently, Equation A2.3) depends on the observations only through t and is of the same form as Equation (A2.1). {For the continuous case, see Exercise 4.}

Exercise 3. (Relating to Example 2. Show that

$$\sum_{x_1 + x_2 \ldots + x_n = t} \exp\left[\sum \log\binom{m}{x_i}\right] = \sum_{x_1 + x_2 \ldots + x_n = t} \prod_{i=1}^{n} \binom{m}{x_i} = \binom{mn}{t}$$

Exercise 4. For the continuous case, change the variables to the set $Y_i = X_i, i = 1, 2, \ldots, n-1, Y_n = \sum_{i=1}^{n} b(X_i)$. The Jacobian is $b'(x_n)$. Integrate out $y_1, \ldots, y_{n-1}$.

The reader may be thinking that there must be a more attractive way of deriving the distribution of T. Exercise 5 suggests such a way.

Exercise 5.   Without loss of generality, consider
$f(x|\phi) = \exp[\phi b(x) + c(\phi) + d(x)]$.
Show that the m.g.f. of $b(X)$, $E[\exp\{b(X)t\}]$, is $\exp[c(\phi) - c(\phi + t)]$.
State the m.g.f. of $\sum_{i=1}^{n} b(X_i)$ for a random sample of n. What do you deduce?

It is beyond the scope of this text to prove that for the regular exponential family of the form of Equation (A2.1), the sufficient statistic $T = \sum_{i=1}^{n} b(X_i)$ is also complete.

A2.2 Several parameters

Now suppose X has a distribution which depends on m parameters with p.d.f.

$$f(x|\theta_1, \theta_2, \ldots, \theta_m) = \exp\left[\sum_{j=1}^{k} a_j(\theta_1, \theta_2, \ldots, \theta_m)b_j(x)\right.$$
$$\left. + c(\theta_1, \theta_2, \ldots, \theta_m) + d(x)\right] \qquad (A2.4)$$

where the interval in which f is positive does not depend on any of the θ_i, then X belongs to the family of regular exponential distributions.

For a random sample of n from a distribution of the type in Equation (A2.4), the joint p.d.f. is

$$\prod_{i=1}^{n} \exp\left[\sum_{j=1}^{k} a_j(\theta_1, \theta_2, \ldots, \theta_m)b_j(x_i) + c(\theta_1, \theta_2, \ldots, \theta_m) + d(x_i)\right]$$
$$= \exp\left\{\sum_{j=1}^{k}\left[a_j(\theta_1, \ldots, \theta_m)\sum_{i=1}^{n} b_j(x_i)\right] + nc(\theta_1, \theta_2, \ldots, \theta_m)\right.$$
$$\left. + \sum_{i=1}^{n} d(x_i)\right\} \qquad (A2.5)$$

By factorization of Equation (A2.5), the statistics $T_j = \sum_{i=1}^{n} b_j(X_i)$, $j = 1, 2, \ldots, k$, are jointly sufficient for $\theta_1, \theta_2, \ldots, \theta_m$. The question of completeness is determined by the relationship between k and m. We state, unproved, the result that a necessary and sufficient condition for completeness is $k = m$. [It is intended that no T_j be a function of the remaining statistics and that the $a_j(\theta_1, \ldots, \theta_m)$ are not functionally related.]

Example 4. X has the distribution $N(\theta_1, \theta_2)$.

$$f(x|\theta_1, \theta_2) = \frac{1}{\sqrt{(2\pi\theta_2)}} \exp\left[-\tfrac{1}{2}(x - \theta_1)^2/\theta_2\right], \qquad -\infty < x < \infty$$

$$= \exp\left[-\frac{x^2}{2\theta_2} + \frac{\theta_1 x}{\theta_2} - \frac{\theta_1^2}{2\theta_2} - \log\sqrt{(2\pi\theta_2)}\right]$$

This is of the form of Equation (A2.4) with $m = 2$, $k = 2$.

$$a_1(\theta_1, \theta_2) = -\frac{1}{2\theta_2}; a_2(\theta_1, \theta_2) = \frac{\theta_1}{\theta_2}; c(\theta_1, \theta_2)$$

$$= -\frac{\theta_1^2}{2\theta_2} - \log\sqrt{(2\pi\theta_2)}; d(x) \equiv 0.$$

For a random sample, the statistics $T_1 = \sum\limits_{i=1}^{n} X_i, T_2 = \sum\limits_{i=1}^{n} X_i^2$ are jointly sufficient for θ_1, θ_2 and are complete.

Example 5. X has the distribution $N(\theta_1, \theta_1^2)$.

$$f(x|\theta_1) = \exp\left[-\frac{1}{2\theta_1^2}x^2 + \frac{x}{\theta_1} - \frac{1}{2} - \log\sqrt{(2\pi\theta_1^2)}\right],$$

$$-\infty < x < \infty.$$

This is a case of Equation (A2.4) with $m = 1, k = 2$. For a random sample of $n(\geqslant 2)$, the statistics $\sum\limits_{i=1}^{n} X_i, \sum\limits_{i=1}^{n} X_i^2$ are jointly sufficient for θ_1, but their distribution is not complete. Indeed, since $E(X_i^2) = 2\theta_1^2, E(\bar{X}^2) = \frac{\theta_1^2}{n} + \theta_1^2$, then

$$\frac{\sum\limits_{i=1}^{n} X_i^2}{2n} - \frac{n\bar{X}^2}{n+1}$$

has expectation zero but is not identically zero.

A2.3 The regular exponential family of bivariate distributions

The random variables X, Y belong to the regular exponential family of bivariate distributions if their joint p.d.f. is of the form

$$f(x,y|\theta_1,\ldots,\theta_m) = \exp\left[\sum_{j=i}^{k} a_j(\theta_1,\theta_2,\ldots,\theta_m)b_j(x,y)\right.$$

$$\left. + c(\theta_1,\ldots,\theta_m) + d(x,y)\right] \qquad \text{(A2.6)}$$

and is positive in a rectangle which does not depend on any of $\theta_1,\theta_2,\ldots,\theta_m$.

Exercise 6. Write the p.d.f. of the bivariate normal distribution in the form of Equation (A2.6) $[k = m = 5]$.

If $(X_1, Y_1),(X_2, Y_2),\ldots,(X_n, Y_n)$ is a random sample of n pairs from a member of the regular exponential family of bivariate distributions then their joint p.d.f. is, from Equation (A2.6),

$$\exp\left\{\sum_{j=1}^{k}\left[a_j(\theta_1,\ldots,\theta_m)\sum_{i=1}^{n}b_j(x_i,y_i)\right] + nc(\theta_1,\theta_2,\ldots,\theta_m)\right.$$

$$\left. + \sum_{i=1}^{n} d(x_i,y_i)\right\} \qquad \text{(A2.7)}$$

By the factorization theorem, the statistics $T_j = \sum_{i=1}^{n} b_j(X_i, Y_i)$, $j = 1,\ldots,k$, are jointly sufficient for the parameters $\theta_1,\theta_2,\ldots,\theta_m$.

Example 6.

$$f(x,y|\theta_1,\theta_2,\theta_3,\theta_4) = \frac{1}{2\pi\sqrt{(\theta_3\theta_4)}}\exp\left\{-\frac{(x-\theta_1)^2}{2\theta_3} - \frac{(y-\theta_2)^2}{2\theta_4}\right\}$$

$$= \exp\left[-\frac{x^2}{2\theta_3} - \frac{y^2}{2\theta_4} + \frac{\theta_1 x}{\theta_3} + \frac{\theta_2 y}{\theta_4} - \frac{\theta_1^2}{2\theta_3} - \frac{\theta_2^2}{2\theta_4}\right.$$

$$\left. - \log\{2\pi\sqrt{(\theta_3\theta_4)}\}\right]$$

For a random sample of n pairs, the statistics $T_1 = \sum_{i=1}^{n} X_i^2$, $T_2 = \sum_{i=1}^{n} Y_i^2, T_3 = \sum_{i=1}^{n} X_i, T_4 = \sum_{i=1}^{n} Y_i\,(k = 4)$ are jointly sufficient and complete statistics for $\theta_1,\theta_2,\theta_3,\theta_4\,(m = 4)$. {Check that even more is true – T_1, T_3 are jointly sufficient for θ_1,θ_3 when θ_2,θ_4 are known}. However in the subfamily for which $\theta_1 = \theta_2$, the statistics

T_1, T_2, T_3, T_4 remain sufficient for $\theta_1, \theta_3, \theta_4$ ($m = 3$) but their joint distribution is no longer complete! For instance, $E[T_3 - T_4] = n\theta_1 - n\theta_1 = 0$, although $T_3 - T_4 \not\equiv 0$.

Exercise 7. For Example 6, show that if $\theta_4 = \theta_3$, then $\sum X_i, \sum Y_i,$ $\sum X_i^2 + \sum Y_i^2$ are jointly sufficient for $\theta_1, \theta_2, \theta_3$ and if $\theta_4 = \theta_3, \theta_2 = \theta_1$ then $\sum X_i + \sum Y_i, \sum X_i^2 + \sum Y_i^2$ are jointly sufficient for θ_1, θ_3.

Further exercises

[The first number of a question indicates a relevant chapter]

2.1 $X_1, X_2, \ldots, X_n$ is a random sample from the continuous distribution with probability density function

$$f(x|\theta) = \frac{r\theta^r}{x^{r+1}}, \qquad \theta \leqslant x < \infty, \theta > 0, r > 1$$

Show that the statistic $T = \min[X_1, X_2, \ldots, X_n]$ is sufficient for θ and that the distribution of T is complete for θ. Hence or otherwise, derive the minimum-variance unbiased estimator of θ.

(Royal Holloway College BSc, 1975)

2.2 State and prove the Rao–Blackwell theorem for improving an unbiased estimator of a population parameter.

Independent observations $x_1, x_2, \ldots, x_n$ are drawn from the Poisson distribution with unknown parameter λ. An unbiased estimator is required of $\theta = \lambda e^{-\lambda}$, the probability that exactly one event occurs in a single realization. Show that the random variable y defined by

$$y = \begin{cases} 1 & (x_1 = 1) \\ 0 & (x_1 \neq 1) \end{cases}$$

provides an unbiased estimator of θ. Hence, or otherwise, show that an improved unbiased estimator of θ based on the sample mean $\bar{x}$ is given by

$$t = \bar{x}\left(1 - \frac{1}{n}\right)^{n\bar{x}-1}$$

{It may be assumed that if $x_i (i = 1, 2, \ldots, n)$ are independent Poisson random variables with parameters λ_i, then the con-

214

ditional distribution of x_1 given $\sum\limits_{i} x_i$ is binomial with index $\sum\limits_{i} x_i$ and parameter $\lambda_1 / \sum\limits_{i} \lambda_i$.}

(University of Leads MSc, 1977)

2.3 $X_1, X_2, \ldots, X_n$ is a random sample from the exponential distribution with p.d.f. $f(x|\theta) = \theta \exp(-\theta x)$. Show that $T = \sum\limits_{i=1}^{n} X_i$ is sufficient for θ and that the p.d.f. of X_1 given T is

$$g(x_1|t) = \frac{(n-1)(t-x_1)^{n-2}}{t^{n-1}}, \quad t > x_1$$

Confirm that the random variable $s(X_1)$ which is $X_1 - k$ when $X_1 > k$ and zero otherwise is, for positive k, an unbiased estimator of $\phi(\theta) = [\exp(-\theta k)]/\theta$, and hence derive the m.v.u.e. of $\phi(\theta)$.

3.1 (a) Define loss function.

(b) In a certain decision problem there are two decisions available, d_1, d_2, and two states of nature, ω_1, ω_2. The associated loss function is:

$$L(\omega_1, d_1) = L(\omega_2, d_2) = 0$$
$$L(\omega_1, d_2) = 5, L(\omega_2, d_1) = 10.$$

The prior probabilities on the states are:

$$P(\omega_1) = \tfrac{1}{4}, \ P(\omega_2) = \tfrac{3}{4}$$

A single, cost-free observation can be made of a random variable X which has the following conditional distributions:

$$P(X = 1|\omega_1) = \tfrac{3}{4}, \ P(X = 0|\omega_1) = \tfrac{1}{4}$$
$$P(X = 1|\omega_2) = \tfrac{1}{3}, \ P(X = 0|\omega_2) = \tfrac{2}{3}$$

Find the Bayes decision function and the Bayes risk.

(c) Suppose it is possible that we shall be faced with the above problem for different values of $P(\omega_1)$ (i.e. other than $\tfrac{1}{4}$). Give the solution for all values of $P(\omega_1)$ between 0 and 1.

(University College of Wales, Aberystwyth, 1972)

3.2 A decision problem has the following loss structure:

	θ_1	θ_2
d_1	0	l_{12}
d_2	l_{21}	0

and $p(\theta_1) = \alpha$. An experiment ε is available at cost f which will yield an observation which is either x_1 or x_2 with probabilities:

	θ_1	θ_2
x_1	p_1	$1 - p_2$
x_2	$1 - p_1$	p_2

(Without loss of generality, suppose $p_1/(1 - p_2) > 1$.) Write down the decision tree appropriate to the problem of deciding whether to perform ε or not, and whether to select d_1 or d_2. Let $K = (1 - \alpha)l_{12}/\alpha l_{21}$ and suppose

$$\frac{1 - p_1}{p_2} < K < \frac{p_1}{1 - p_2} \qquad (*)$$

Show that if ε is performed and x_i observed then the optimum decision is $d_i (i = 1, 2)$. Hence show that if ε is performed the expected loss is

$$(1 - p_2)(1 - \alpha)l_{12} + (1 - p_1)\alpha l_{21} + f$$

Hence or otherwise, determine the expected value of ε. (Hint: the cases $K < 1$ and $K > 1$ will have to be considered separately.) If the inequalities $(*)$ are not satisfied it is obvious that the expected value is negative: why?

(University College of Wales, Aberystwyth, Diploma 1972)

3.3 Discuss the relationship between Bayes and minimax estimators. A sequence of n independent identical Bernoulli trials with unknown probability of success $\theta (0 < \theta < 1)$ is observed with the purpose of estimating θ. *A priori* θ has a uniform distribution over $(0,1)$ and the loss in estimating θ by d is

$$l(d, \theta) = \frac{(d - \theta)^2}{\theta(1 - \theta)}$$

Determine the Bayes estimator of θ and show that it is also the minimax estimator of θ. Is it admissible?

(Imperial College London, BSc, 1977)

3.4 Let $Y_1, Y_2, \ldots$ be a sequence of independent, identically distributed random variables with probability density function

$$p(y|\lambda) = \begin{cases} \lambda e^{-\lambda y} & (y > 0) \\ 0 & \text{(otherwise)} \end{cases}$$

where λ is an unknown, positive parameter with prior density function

$$\pi(\lambda) = \begin{cases} \dfrac{a^r \lambda^{r-1} e^{-\alpha\lambda}}{\Gamma(r)} & (\lambda > 0) \\ 0 & \text{(otherwise)} \end{cases}$$

a and r being known, positive numbers. Find the posterior distribution of λ given

$$Y_1 = y_1, Y_2 = y_2, \ldots, Y_n = y_n$$

It is required to predict Y_{n+1} given the n observations

$$Y_1 = y_1, Y_2 = y_2, \ldots, Y_n = y_n$$

Show that, for any positive constant c,

$$\Pr\{Y_{n+1} > c \,|\, y_1, \ldots, y_n\} = \left(\frac{t+a}{t+a+c}\right)^{r+n}$$

where $t = \sum_{i=1}^{n} y_i$.

What is the probability that Y_{n+1} and Y_{n+2} will both be greater than c given

$$Y_1 = y_1, Y_2 = y_2, \ldots, Y_n = y_n?$$

(Imperial College London BSc, 1977)

3.5 The observations $x_1, x_2, \ldots, x_n$ are independent random variables having a common Poisson distribution of mean θ. The prior distribution of θ is:

$$e^{-\alpha\theta}\theta^{\beta-1}\alpha^{\beta}/(\beta-1)!$$

for some $\alpha, \beta > 0$. Write down the posterior distribution of θ given $x_1, x_2, \ldots, x_n$ and also the posterior expectation of $e^{-a\theta}, a > 0$.

It is required to select one of two decisions d_1, d_2 where the utilities are $A_i e^{-a_i\theta}$, with $A_1 > A_2 > 0, a_1 > a_2 > 0$. Show that, if θ is known, d_1 is selected if $\theta < c$ for a suitable c which should be found.

If θ is unknown, but has the posterior distribution described above with $\alpha = \beta = 0$, and n is large, show that d_1 is selected if $\bar{x} < c(1 + kn^{-1})$, and determine the value of k. Here $\bar{x} = \sum_{i=1}^{n} x_i/n$.

(University College London BSc, 1971)

{Note: utility is to be taken as negative loss, hence take decision with *greater* expected utility}.

3.6 Explain, briefly, what is meant by the Bayes solution of a decision-theory problem.

A boat manufacturer buys motors for assembly in a particular type of boat. The motors, independently, have probability θ of being faulty. If a faulty motor is incorporated in a boat a net loss of £25 arises for reassembly, etc. On the other hand, if a satisfactory motor is rejected by the manufacturer a net loss of £2 is incurred on administrative overheads. Faulty motors which are rejected involve negligible net loss. The manufacturer has two possible basic schemes of inspection; a quick check at negligible cost where there is a probability of 0.05 that a faulty motor will be accepted, and a probability of 0.10 that a satisfactory motor will be rejected, or a full technical examination with negligible error at a cost of £1. The manufacturer considers the following strategies:

(a) accept each motor without any inspection;

(b) subject each motor to the quick check;

(c) carry out a full technical examination of each motor;

(d) do the quick check on each motor, but carry out the full technical examination on any motor rejected on the quick check.

Are any of these strategies inadmissible? For what values of θ are the various strategies most profitable? If the prior distribution of θ has density function

$$f(\theta) = (20!/4!15!)\theta^4(1 - \theta)^{15}$$

what strategy should be adopted?

(University of Birmingham, BSc, 1968)

3.7 The distribution of X given θ has p.d.f. $f(x|\theta) = 1/\theta, 0 < x < \theta$, and the prior distribution of Θ has p.d.f. $g(\theta) = \theta \exp(-\theta)$, $\theta > 0$. Show that the posterior distribution of Θ given x has p.d.f. $\exp[-(\theta - x)], \theta > x$. If the loss function for the estimate $d(x)$ is $c[d(x) - \theta]^2, c > 0$, find the risk and Bayes risk for the

Bayes estimator. Calculate also the risk for the estimator $2X$.

3.8 Prove that if a parameter μ is, *a priori*, $N(\mu_0, \tau^2)$ and if x is $N(\mu, \sigma^2), \sigma^2$ known; then, *a posteriori*, μ is normal with mean $(x/\sigma^2 + \mu_0/\tau^2)/(1/\sigma^2 + 1/\tau^2)$ and variance $(1/\sigma^2 + 1/\tau^2)^{-1}$.

In order to measure the intensity, θ, of a source of radiation in a noisy environment, a measurement x_1 is taken without the source present and a second, independent measurement x_2 is taken with it present. It may be supposed that x_1 is $N(\mu, 1)$ and x_2 is $N(\mu + \theta, 1)$, where μ describe the noise. The amount of noise is fairly well known and, *a priori*, it may be supposed that μ is $N(\mu_0, 1)$. The prior distribution of θ is approximately uniform. Write down (apart from a constant of proportionality) the joint posterior distribution of μ and θ, and hence obtain that of θ. The usual estimate of θ is $x_2 - x_1$: explain why $\frac{1}{2}(2x_2 - x_1 - \mu_0)$ might be better.

(University College London BSc, 1974)

4.1 Components produced on a production line are monitored by a process which selects random batches of size k, and these batches are inspected for defectives. During a particular day a total of n such batches was inspected and the numbers of defectives were $r_1, r_2, \ldots, r_n$, respectively. It is required to estimate the probability that a batch of k components contains no defectives. If $\bar{r} = \sum_{i=1}^{n} r_i/n$, show that

(a) the maximum likelihood estimator of this probability is

$$(1 - \bar{r}/k)^k;$$

(b) the unbiased minimum variance estimator, using the Blackwell–Rao theorem, of this probability is

$$\prod_{s=1}^{k} \left(1 - \frac{n\bar{r}}{kn + 1 - s}\right); \text{ and that}$$

(c) both these estimators have, asymptotically for large n, variance $kp^{2 - 1/k}(1 - p^{1/k})/n$,

where p is the probability being estimated.

It may be assumed that each component produced has, independently, a constant probability of being defective.

(University of Birmingham, MSc, 1976)

4.2 State and prove the Cramer–Rao inequality. Find the conditions under which an unbiased estimator of a function of a single parameter attains its minimum-variance bound. Given a random sample of size n from the distribution

$$p(x;\theta) = c(\theta)x^\theta(1 - x), \qquad 0 \leqslant x \leqslant 1$$

show that

$$-\left(\sum_{i=1}^{n} \log x_i\right)\bigg/ n$$

is an unbiased estimator of $\dfrac{2\theta + 3}{(\theta + 1)(\theta + 2)}$ and that it attains its

minimum-variance bound.

(University College of Wales, Aberystwyth, Diploma 1972)

4.3 $X_1, X_2, \ldots, X_n$ are independent random variables. Each X_i is either, with probability $1 - p$, drawn from a distribution, which only yields zero values or, with probability p, drawn from a Poisson distribution with parameter θ. If f_r values are observed to take the value r, show that the maximum likelihood estimator of θ, satisfies

$$[1 - \exp(-\hat{\theta})]/\hat{\theta} = [n - f_0]/n\bar{x}$$

where $\bar{x} = \sum_{1}^{\infty} rf_r/n$. Show further that if all the zero values are discarded, then the maximum likelihood estimator, based on the truncated Poisson distribution, satisfies the same equation.

4.4 State and prove the Gauss–Markov theorem of least squares. Suppose $x_1, x_2, \ldots, x_n$ are random uncorrelated observations such that $E(x_i) = \mu, \mu$ unknown and var $(x_i) = \lambda^i\sigma^2$ for $i = 1, 2, \ldots, n$, where λ is a known constant. Show that the best linear unbiased estimate of μ is

$$t = \sum_{i=1}^{n} \lambda^{n-i} x_i \bigg/ \sum_{j=0}^{n-1} \lambda^j$$

Find the variance of t and prove that

(a) var$(t) < \lambda\sigma^2$ for $n > 1$;

(b) for large n, var$(t) \approx 0$ or $(\lambda - 1)\sigma^2$ according as $\lambda < 1$ or > 1 respectively.

Find the limit of var(t) as $\lambda \to 1$.

(University College of Wales, Aberystwyth, Diploma 1971)

4.5 State, without proof, the main properties of estimators derived by the method of least squares. State clearly the assumptions you have to make about the distribution of the observations.

An object is known to weigh exactly W grams. It is divided into n unequal pieces and the weights of these n pieces are estimated to be $w_1, w_2, w_3, \ldots, w_n$. If these estimates are independent and unbiased estimators of the true weights $W_1, W_2, W_3, \ldots, W_n$ with variance σ^2, show that the least-squares estimators of W_i are

$$\hat{W}_i = w_i - \frac{1}{n}\left[\sum_{i=1}^{n} w_i - W \right] \qquad (i = 1, 2, \ldots, n).$$

What is the variance of $\hat{W}_i$ and how might you estimate this variance?

(University of Reading, BSc, 1974)

4.6 A random sample $X_1, X_2, \ldots, X_n$ is drawn from a beta distribution with density function

$$f(x|\theta) = \theta(\theta + 1)x^{\theta - 1}(1 - x), \qquad 0 \leqslant x \leqslant 1$$

where $\theta > 0$ is an unknown parameter. Show that the mean and variance of this distribution are

$$\mu = \frac{\theta}{\theta + 2} \quad \text{and} \quad \sigma^2 = \frac{2\theta}{(\theta + 2)^2(\theta + 3)}$$

respectively.

Show that the maximum-likelihood estimator (m.l.e.) $\dot{\theta}$ of θ is given by

$$\dot{\theta} = \frac{(2 - T) + \sqrt{(T^2 + 4)}}{2T}$$

where $T = -\frac{1}{n}\sum \log X_i$. Hence or otherwise, show that $\dot{\theta}$ is sufficient for θ.

Write down the m.l.e. $\dot{\mu}$ of μ and compute its asymptotic variance.

The sample mean $\bar{X}$ is also an estimator of μ. Which would you use to estimate μ, $\bar{X}$ or $\dot{\mu}$, and why?

(University of Manchester, Diploma, 1978)

4.7 (i) A response variable y is dependent on two controllable variables x_1 and x_2. Observations on y are made at the following four points,

Observation	x_1	x_2
y_1	$\cos \theta$	$\sin \theta$
y_2	$- \sin \theta$	$- \cos \theta$
y_3	$\sin \theta$	$\cos \theta$
y_4	$- \cos \theta$	$- \sin \theta$

Obtain expressions for the least-squares estimators $\hat{\beta}_1$ and $\hat{\beta}_2$ of β_1 and β_2 in the assumed model

$$y = \beta_0 + \beta_1 x_1 + \beta_2 x_2 + e$$

where the values of e for the four observations are independently and normally distributed with mean zero and variance σ^2.

Show that $V(\hat{\beta}_1) = V(\hat{\beta}_2) = \dfrac{1}{\cos^2 2\theta}\dfrac{\sigma^2}{2}$.

(ii) If observations 1 and 2 were made at time $t = 0$ and observations 3 and 4 were made at time $t = 1$ and the true model is $y = \beta_0 + \beta_1 x_1 + \beta_2 x_2 + \gamma t + e$, show that the biases in $\hat{\beta}_1$ and $\hat{\beta}_0$ in (i) are

$$-\frac{(\cos\theta - \sin\theta)}{2(1 - \sin 2\theta)}\gamma \quad \text{and} \quad \frac{(\cos\theta - \sin\theta)}{2(1 - \sin 2\theta)}\gamma$$

respectively.

Discuss the implications of the results in (i) and (ii) for values of θ near $45°$.

(University of Reading, BSc, 1972)

4.8 A single trial must have one of four results, their probabilities being $p_1 = 1 - \theta$, $p_2 = \theta - \theta^2$, $p_3 = \theta^2 - \theta^3$ and $p_4 = \theta^3$ respectively, where $0 \leqslant \theta \leqslant 1$. Over n independent trials the total number of occurrences of each result are X_1, X_2, X_3 and X_4 respectively. Show that the maximum likelihood estimator of θ is

$$\hat{\theta} = (X_2 + 2X_3 + 3X_4)/(X_1 + 2X_2 + 3X_3 + 3X_4)$$

and determine the asymptotic variance of $\hat{\theta}$.

Determine values of constants a_i so that $T = \sum_{i=1}^{4} a_i X_i$ is an unbiased estimator of θ. Determine the variance of T and hence investigate how the efficiency of T relative to θ depends on the true value of θ.

(University of Edinburgh, Diploma, 1971)

5.1 A population has the truncated exponential distribution with density function

$$f(x;\theta,\phi) = \frac{1}{\phi}e^{-(x-\theta)/\phi}(x \geqslant \theta; -\infty < \theta < \infty; \phi > 0)$$

Prove that, for a sample of n independent values $x_1, x_2, \ldots, x_n$ from this population, the statistic $\left(x_{\min}, \sum_{i=1}^{n} x_i \right)$ is sufficient for (θ, ϕ).

It is desired to test the hypothesis $H_0 : \theta = \theta_0, \phi = \phi_0$ against $H_1 : \theta < \theta_0, \phi < \phi_0$. Show that there is a uniformly most powerful test of size α with critical region given by

$$C = \left\{ (x_1, x_2, \ldots, x_n) : x_{\min} < \theta_0 \text{ or } \sum_{i=1}^{n} x_i < nk_\alpha \right\}$$

where

$$k_\alpha = \theta_0 + \frac{\phi_0}{2n} \chi^2_{[2n]}(\alpha)$$

and $\chi^2_{[2n]}(\alpha)$ denotes the lower α per cent point of the χ^2 distribution with $2n$ degrees of freedom.

(Standard results relating to gamma distribution may be quoted without proof.)

(University of Leeds MSc, 1977)

5.2 $X_1, X_2, \ldots, X_n$ is a random sample from the distribution $N(\theta, \theta)$.

(a) Find the uniformly most powerful test of the null hypothesis $\theta = 1$ against alternatives $\theta > 1$.

(b) If $\hat{\theta}$ is the maximum likelihood estimator of θ, then show that $\hat{\theta}(1 + \hat{\theta})$ is an unbiased estimator of $\theta(1 + \theta)$ and has variance $2\theta^2(1 + 2\theta)/n$.

5.3 The random variable X has probability density function $f(x)$, the functional form of which is unknown. A random sample of size n is drawn to test the null hypothesis

$$H_0 : f(x) = f_0(x)$$

against the alternative $H_1 : f(x) = f_1(x)$. The functional forms of f_0 and f_1 are known. They have no unknown parameters, and the same domain.

By considering the probability density function

$$\lambda f_0(x) + (1 - \lambda) f_1(x)$$

show that H_0 and H_1 may be expressed parametrically. Hence show that if

$$f_0(x) = (2\pi)^{-1/2} \exp(-\tfrac{1}{2}x^2), \qquad -\infty < x < \infty$$
$$f_1(x) = \tfrac{1}{2} \exp(-|x|) \qquad -\infty < x < \infty$$

then the best critical region for the test of H_0 against H_1 is given by

$$\sum_{j=1}^{n} (|x_j| - 1)^2 \geqslant k$$

When $n = 1$ evaluate the best critical region for $(a) k = 1$, and $(b) k = \frac{1}{4}$. In case (a) is the test unbiased?

(University of Reading, BSc, 1974)

6.1 $X_1, \ldots, X_4, Y_1, \ldots, Y_4$ are two independent random samples of size 4 from $U[0, \theta]$, $U[0, \phi]$ respectively. Show that the likelihood-ratio test of $\theta = \phi$ against $\theta \neq \phi$ may be reduced to the form:

reject $\theta = \phi$ unless $k^{-1} X_{(4)} < Y_{(4)} < k X_{(4)}$.
Write down the joint density of $X_{(4)}$ and $Y_{(4)}$.
Determine the value of k that gives a test of size 5 per cent, and show that if $\theta = 3$, $\phi = 2$ this test has power approximately 1/8.

(University College of Wales, Aberystwyth, Statistics, 1977)
{Note, $U[0, \theta]$ is the p.d.f. of a random variable uniformly distributed over $[0, \theta]$.}

6.2 The continuous random variable X has probability density function $f(x | \theta)$. It is required to test the hypothesis $\theta = \theta_0$ against $\theta = \theta_1$. Show that the most powerful test of prescribed size *and* slope of power function at θ_0 has a critical region consisting of those x such that

$$f(x | \theta_1) > k_1 f(x | \theta_0) + k_2 \frac{\partial}{\partial \theta_0} [f(x | \theta)]$$

(It may be assumed that differentiation through the integral sign holds.)

Hence if $f(x | \theta) = \dfrac{1}{\pi[1 + (x - \theta)^2]}$, $\theta_0 = 0$, $\theta_1 = 1$, $k_1 = k_2 = 1$

find the corresponding critical region and show that the size of the test is

$$\frac{1}{\pi} \left[\frac{3\pi}{4} - \tan^{-1}\left(\frac{1}{3}\right) \right]$$

(Royal Holloway College, BSc, 1978)

6.3 A random sample of three observations is drawn from the distribution with probability density function

$$f(x|\theta_1, \theta_2) = \frac{1}{\theta_2} \exp\{-[x - \theta_1]/\theta_2\}, \qquad \theta_2 > 0, x > \theta_1$$

If Y_1, Y_2, Y_3 are the order statistics, show that the probability density function of $U_1 = Y_1$, $U_2 = Y_3 - Y_1$, $U_3 = -2Y_1 + Y_2 + Y_3$ is

$$h(u_1, u_2, u_3) = \frac{6}{\theta_2^3} \exp\{-[u_3 + 3u_1 - 3\theta_1]/\theta_2\}, \qquad \theta_1 < u_1,$$

$$\frac{u_3}{2} < u_2 < u_3.$$

Hence or otherwise, deduce that U_3, U_1 are independent and that U_1 is sufficient for θ_1. Find the most powerful similar test of $\theta_2 = \theta_2'$ against $\theta_2 = \theta_2'' > \theta_2'$ and discuss whether it is uniformly most powerful similar against $\theta_2 > \theta_2'$. Discuss *briefly* how the test is to be constructed.

(Royal Holloway College, BSc, 1978)

7.1 Let $X_{(1)}$ and $X_{(n)}$ be the minimum and maximum values, respectively, in a sample of size n from a distribution with probability density function

$$p(x|\theta) = \begin{cases} \dfrac{1}{\theta} & (0 \leqslant x \leqslant \theta) \\ 0 & \text{(otherwise)} \end{cases}$$

where θ is an unknown positive parameter. Find the joint distribution of $X_{(1)}$ and $X_{(n)}$. Show that $T = X_{(n)} - X_{(1)}$ has probability density function

$$\Pr(t|\theta) = \begin{cases} \dfrac{n(n-1)t^{n-2}(\theta - t)}{\theta^n} & (0 \leqslant t \leqslant \theta) \\ 0 & \text{(otherwise)} \end{cases}$$

Hence show that, for $0 < \alpha < 1$, if k is a function of α and n which satisfies

$$k^{n-1}\{n - (n-1)k\} = \alpha$$

then $[T, T/k]$ is a $100(1 - \alpha)$ per cent confidence interval for θ.

(Imperial College London, 1975)

7.2 A random sample $x_1, x_2, \ldots, x_n$ is taken from a population with probability density function $\lambda e^{-\lambda(x-\theta)}$, $x \geqslant \theta \geqslant 0$. When the observations are arranged in order of magnitude they become $y_1 < y_2 < \ldots < y_n$. Show that the joint probability density function of the y's is, when non-zero,

$$n!\,\lambda^n e^{-\lambda(y_1 + y_2 + \ldots y_n - n\theta)}$$

If $z_1 = ny_1$, $z_2 = (n-1)(y_2 - y_1)$, $z_3 = (n-2)(y_3 - y_2), \ldots$, $z_n = (y_n - y_{n-1})$, show that the z's are independent and that the probability density function of z_1 is $\lambda e^{-\lambda(z_1 - n\theta)}$, $z_1 \geqslant n\theta$, and of z_i is $\lambda e^{-\lambda z_i}$, $z_i \geqslant 0$, $i \neq 1$.

Hence, or otherwise, show how to obtain a confidence interval for θ with confidence coefficient $1 - \alpha$ using the ratio $(y_1 - \theta)(n-1)/(\bar{y} - y_1)$, where $\bar{y} = \sum_{i=1}^{n} y_i / n$. Show also that it is only possible for this interval to have a positive lower limit if

$$y_1 > k_\alpha \bar{y}/(n - 1 + k_\alpha)$$

where k_α is the upper 100α per cent point of the F-distribution with 2 and $2(n-1)$ degrees of freedom. Comment on this result.

(University of Birmingham MSc, 1976)

7.3 Let $x_1, x_2, \ldots, x_{n_1}$ be n_1 independent observations from $N(\rho\mu, 1)$ and $y_1, y_2, \ldots, y_{n_2}$ be n_2 independent observations from $N(\mu, 1)$. Write down the likelihood function $L(x, y | \rho, \mu)$ for the two unknown parameters. Show that $(\sum x_i, \sum y_i)$ is sufficient for (ρ, μ) and that if $\rho = \rho_0$ then $\rho_0 \sum x_i + \sum y_i$ is sufficient for μ.

Show that the distribution of $\bar{x} - \rho\bar{y}$ is independent of μ and use this to construct a 95 per cent confidence interval for ρ. Show that if $n_2 \bar{y}^2 > 3.84$ this interval is from ρ_1 to ρ_2, given by

$$\rho_1, \rho_2 = \frac{\bar{x}\bar{y} \pm \sqrt{\{3.84(n_1 \bar{x}^2 + n_2 \bar{y}^2 - 3.84)/n_1 n_2\}}}{\bar{y}^2 - 3.84/n_2}$$

but if $n_1 \bar{x}^2 + n_2 \bar{y}^2 < 3.84$ then the confidence interval includes all real values of ρ.

(University College London, BSc, 1976)

7.4 The time interval y between successive feeding of a certain type of insect has an exponential distribution whose mean is proportional to total body weight. Thus, for a sample of n insects with body weights $x_1, x_2, \ldots, x_n$ independently have probability densities

$$f(y|\beta) = \frac{1}{\beta x_i} \exp(-y/\beta x_i), \qquad i = 1, \ldots, n, \, y > 0$$

i.e. $\dfrac{2y_i}{\beta x_i}$ has a χ^2 distribution on 2 degrees of freedom. Show

that $z = \sum \dfrac{y_i}{x_i}$ is sufficient for β. Find point and interval estimates of the proportionally constant β from frequentist and Bayesian viewpoints, using a prior for β that is uniform over $(0, \infty)$. Show that the posterior distribution of β is such that

$$U = \frac{2z}{\beta}$$

has density

$$f(u) = \frac{1}{2^{n-1} \Gamma(n-1)} u^{n-2} e^{-u/2}$$

i.e. chi-square on $2(n-1)$ degrees of freedom.

(University College London, MSc, (1978) [slightly shortened])

7.5 Suppose a and b are unbiased estimates of two parameters α and β, respectively, such that

$$\text{Var}(a) = \lambda_1 \sigma^2; \quad \text{Var}(b) = \lambda_2 \sigma^2; \quad \text{and} \quad \text{Cov}(a, b) = \lambda_3 \sigma^2,$$

where λ_1, λ_2 and λ_3 are known constants, and s^2 is an independent estimate of σ^2.

Assuming that a and b are normally distributed and ns^2/σ^2 has a χ^2 distribution with n degrees of freedom, and by considering the statistic $a - \rho b$, or otherwise, obtain the appropriate 95 per cent confidence limits for the parametric ratio $\rho \equiv \alpha/\beta$, and hence verify that in the particular case when $\lambda_3 = 0$, the limits are

$$\frac{a}{b} \pm st_0 \left[\lambda_1 + \lambda_2 \left(\frac{a}{b}\right)^2 - \lambda_1 \lambda_2 \frac{s^2 t_0^2}{b^2} \right]^{1/2} \bigg/ \left[1 - \lambda_2 \frac{s^2 t_0^2}{b^2} \right]$$

t_0 being the 5 per cent point of Student's t-distribution with n degrees of freedom.

(University of Leicester, BSc, 1963)

A1.1 The random variable, X_1, follows a Weibull distribution with probability density function (p.d.f.)

$$p_1(x_1) = \frac{1}{6x_1^{1/2}} \exp - \left[\frac{x_1^{1/2}}{3} \right], \qquad \text{for } x_1 \geqslant 0$$
$$= 0 \text{ elsewhere}$$

A second random variable, X_2, follows a slightly different Weibull distribution with p.d.f.

$$p_2(x_2) = \frac{1}{4x_2^{1/2}} \exp - \left[\frac{x_2^{1/2}}{2} \right], \qquad \text{for } x_2 \geqslant 0$$

$$= 0 \text{ elsewhere}$$

Find the p.d.f. of the ratio $Y = X_1/X_2$ and hence deduce that $P(X_1 < X_2) = \frac{2}{5}$.

(University of Exeter, 1977)

A1.2 The two random variables, X_1 and X_2, follow a bivariate Dirichlet distribution with p.d.f.

$$f(x_1, x_2) = \frac{\Gamma(n_1 + n_2 + n_3)}{\Gamma(n_1)\Gamma(n_2)\Gamma(n_3)} x_1^{n_1 - 1} x_2^{n_2 - 1} (1 - x_1 - x_2)^{n_3 - 1}$$

$$\text{for } x_1, x_2 \geqslant 0 \text{ and } x_1 + x_2 \leqslant 1$$

$$= 0 \text{ elsewhere}$$

where n_1, n_2 and n_3 are known constants.

Use the standard transformation-of-variable technique to find the joint distribution of the two new random variables, Y_1 and Y_2, defined by $Y_1 = X_1$ and $X_2 = Y_2(1 - X_1)$. Hence show that *marginally* both Y_1 and Y_2 have beta distributions.

Z_1, Z_2 and Z_3 are three independent random variables with gamma distributions and parameters n_1, n_2 and n_3 respectively. Show that

$$U_1 = \frac{Z_1}{Z_1 + Z_2 + Z_3} \text{ and } U_2 = \frac{Z_2}{Z_1 + Z_2 + Z_3}$$

follow a bivariate Dirichlet distribution.

Note: A gamma variate with parameter $n(>0)$ has p.d.f.

$$f(x) = \frac{1}{\Gamma(n)} e^{-x} x^{n-1} \text{ for } x \geqslant 0$$

$$= \text{otherwise}$$

(University of Exeter, 1976)

Brief solutions to further exercises

No examining body is responsible for any suggested solution.
Note: in some cases the notation used in the original question has been used.

2.1 If $T = \min[X_1, X_2, \ldots, X_n]$, since $\Pr[X \leqslant x] = 1 - \theta^r/x^r$, the p.d.f. of T is $rn\theta^{rn}/t^{rn+1}$, $t > \theta$.

Conditional distribution of $X_1, X_2, \ldots, X_n$ given t does not depend on θ.

If $E[u(T)] = \displaystyle\int_\theta^\infty \{u(t)\, rn\theta^{rn}/t^{r_1+1}\}\, \mathrm{d}t = 0$ then

$\displaystyle\int_\theta^\infty \{u(t)/t^{rn+1}\}\, \mathrm{d}t = 0$. Differentiate with respect to θ for $u(\theta) = 0$, $E[T] = nr\theta/(nr-1)$. Hence $(nr-1)T/nr$ is m.v.u.e.

2.2 $\lambda\exp(-\lambda) = \Pr[X_1 = 1]$, since X_1 has Poisson distribution. $E[Y] = 1 \cdot \Pr[X_1 = 1] + 0 \cdot \Pr[X_1 \neq 1] = \lambda\exp(-\lambda) = \theta$.

$T = \displaystyle\sum_{i=1}^n X_i$ is a complete sufficient statistic for λ. By Rao–Blackwell theorem, $E[Y|T]$ is unbiased and best. But $X_1|t$ is binomial, with parameters t and $1/n$.

$$E[Y|t] = 1\Pr[X_1 = 1|t] = \binom{t}{1}\left(\frac{1}{n}\right)^1\left(1 - \frac{1}{n}\right)^{t-1}$$

2.3 T distributed $\Gamma(n, \theta)$. T given $X_1 = x_1$ has the unconditional distribution of $\displaystyle\sum_{i=2}^n X_i + x_1$ with p.d.f.

$$\frac{\theta^{n-1}(t-x_1)^{n-2}\exp[-\theta(t-x_1)]}{(n-2)!}, \qquad t > x_1$$

(since $\displaystyle\sum_{i=2}^n X_i$ has $\Gamma(n-1, \theta)$ distribution). Multiply by p.d.f. of

229

X_1 and divide by p.d.f. of T for first result.

$$E[s(X_1)] = \int_k^\infty (x_1 - k)\theta \exp(-\theta x_1)dx_1 = \exp(-\theta k)/\theta$$

$$E[s(X_1)|t] = \int_k^t (x_1 - k)g(x_1|t)dx_1$$
$$= (t - k)^n/nt^{n-1}$$

Exercise: Check directly that this estimator is unbiased for $\phi(\theta)$.

3.1 One way is to work with posterior losses. If the prior probability of ω_1 is g, then posterior

$$\Pr[\omega_1|X = 1] = \frac{3g/4}{3g/4 + (1-g)/3},$$

$$\Pr[\omega_1|X = 0] = \frac{g/4}{g/4 + 2(1-g)/3}$$

The expected posterior loss if $d(1) = \omega_1$ is

$$10[\tfrac{1}{3}(1-g)]/[\tfrac{3}{4}g + \tfrac{1}{3}(1-g)]$$

and if $d(1) = \omega_2$ is

$$5[\tfrac{3}{4}g]/[\tfrac{3}{4}g + \tfrac{1}{3}(1-g)]$$

$d(1) = \omega_1$ is cheaper on average if $g > 8/17$.

Similarly, if $d(0) = \omega_1$, expected posterior loss is

$$10[\tfrac{2}{3}(1-g)]/[\tfrac{1}{4}g + \tfrac{2}{3}(1-g)]$$

If $d(0) = \omega_2$

$$5[\tfrac{1}{4}g]/[\tfrac{1}{4}g + \tfrac{2}{3}(1-g)]$$

$d(0) = \omega_1$ is preferred if $g > 16/19$.

Shorter, but requiring to remember equivalent Neyman–Pearson test: best critical region for testing $\omega = \omega_1$ versus $\omega = \omega_2$ consists of those x such that

$$\frac{\Pr[X|\omega_1]}{\Pr[X|\omega_2]} \leqslant \frac{(1-g)l(\omega_2,d_1)}{gl(\omega_1,d_2)} = \frac{10(1-g)}{5g}$$

so if $x = 1$, for those g such that

$$\frac{\tfrac{3}{4}}{\tfrac{1}{3}} \leqslant \frac{2(1-g)}{g}, \text{ prefer } \omega_2.$$

If $x = 0$, for those g such that

$$\frac{\frac{1}{4}}{\frac{2}{3}} < \frac{2(1-g)}{g}, \text{ prefer } \omega_2.$$

3.2 Two states of nature, θ_1, θ_2, two possible sample values, x_1, x_2, hence four (non-randomized) decision functions

	Risk $|\theta_1$	*Risk* $|\theta_1$
(a) $d_1(x_1) = \theta_1, d_1(x_2) = \theta_1$	0	l_{12}
(b) $d_2(x_1) = \theta_2, d_2(x_2) = \theta_2$	l_{21}	0
(c) $d_3(x_1) = \theta_1, d_3(x_2) = \theta_2$	$(1-p_1)l_{21}$	$(1-p_2)l_{12}$
(d) $d_4(x_1) = \theta_2, d_4(x_2) = \theta_1$	$p_1 l_{21}$	$p_2 l_{12}$

Since the data are ignored, there is no extra cost for d_1, d_2. If ε is performed, the Bayes losses for d_3, d_4 are

$$(1-p_1)l_{21}\alpha + (1-p_2)l_{12}(1-\alpha) + f$$
$$p_1 l_{21}\alpha + p_2 l_{12}(1-\alpha) + f$$

If $(1-p_1)/p_2 < K < p_1/(1-p_2)$, then d_3 is better.

3.3 The Bayes estimator minimizes the expected loss over the posterior distribution of Θ. Let $\sum_{i=1}^{n} x_i = r$ be the number of successes. The posterior distribution of Θ given r is beta $(1+r, n+1-r)$.

$$E\left[\frac{(d-\Theta)^2}{\Theta(1-\Theta)}\bigg| r\right]$$

after a little cancelling and using $\Gamma(x+1) = x\Gamma(x)$, is

$$\frac{n(n+1)}{r(n-r)} \int_0^1 (d-\theta)^2 \phi(\theta)\mathrm{d}\theta, \qquad r \neq 0, r \neq n$$

where ϕ is the p.d.f. of a beta $(r, n-r)$ distribution. This is minimized when d is the mean of the distribution with p.d.f. ϕ – to wit, $r/(r+n-r) = r/n$. But the ordinary risk of $d = R/n$ is

$$E\left[\frac{\{(R/n)-\theta\}^2}{\theta(1-\theta)}\bigg|\theta\right] = \frac{V[R/n|\theta]}{\theta(1-\theta)} = \frac{\theta(1-\theta)}{n\theta(1-\theta)} = \frac{1}{n}$$

Hence R/n has constant risk – but it is also **Bayes** and therefore minimax. The values $r = 0, r = n$ are easily checked. Interesting to see the 'usual' maximum likelihood estimator turning up for *this* loss function.

3.4 The posterior density of λ is $\Gamma(n + r, a + t)$. The conditional density of Y_{n+1} given $y_1, y_2, \ldots, y_n$ is found by integrating out λ.

$$
\begin{aligned}
h(y_{n+1} | y_1, y_2, \ldots, y_n) &= \int p(y_{n+1} | \lambda) \pi(\lambda | y_1, \ldots, y_n) \mathrm{d}\lambda \\
&= \int_0^\infty \lambda e^{-\lambda y_{n+1}} \frac{(a+t)^{n+r} \lambda^{n+r-1} e^{-\lambda(a+t)}}{\Gamma(n+r)} \mathrm{d}\lambda \\
&= \frac{(n+r)(a+t)^{n+r}}{(y_{n+1} + a + t)^{n+r+1}}
\end{aligned}
$$

Now integrate the density from c to ∞.

The corresponding joint p.d.f. of Y_{n+2}, Y_{n+1} given $y_1, y_2, \ldots, y_n$ is

$$
\frac{(n+r)(n+r+1)(a+t)^{n+r}}{(y_{n+2} + y_{n+1} + a + t)^{n+r+2}}
$$

{Note: Y_{n+2}, Y_{n+1} are only conditionally independent given λ.}

3.5 If we denote the prior distribution as a $\Gamma(\beta, \alpha)$ distribution, by a standard result, the posterior is $\Gamma(\beta + \sum x_i, \alpha + n)$.

By considering the m.g.f. of a gamma distribution,

$$
E[\exp(-a\Theta) | \sum x_i] = \left[\frac{\alpha + n}{\alpha + n + a} \right]^{\beta + \Sigma x_i}
$$

we have $A_1 \exp(-a_1 \theta) > A_2 \exp(-a_2 \theta)$

$$
\text{if } \frac{A_1}{A_2} > \exp[\theta(a_1 - a_2)]
$$

$$
\text{or } \theta < \frac{1}{a_1 - a_2} \log\left(\frac{A_1}{A_2} \right) = c
$$

If θ is unknown, compare the expected posterior utilities. $\alpha = \beta = 0 \Rightarrow d_1$ is preferred if

$$
A_1 \left(\frac{n}{n + a_1} \right)^{n\bar{x}} > A_2 \left(\frac{n}{n + a_2} \right)^{n\bar{x}}
$$

$$
n\bar{x} \log\left[1 - \frac{a_1 - a_2}{n + a_1} \right] > \log \frac{A_2}{A_1}
$$

Taking $\log(1 - t)$ as approximately $-t$ leads to $\bar{x} < c(1 + a_1/n)$.

3.6 There are two states of nature, faulty (F), satisfactory (S). There are two actions, accept (a_1) and reject (a_2).

(a) $R(a_1|F) = 25, R(a_1|S) = 0$
(b) d_b: accept if motor passes check: if it fails, reject.
     $R(d_b|F) = (0.05)25 = 1.25$
     $R(d_b|S) = (0.1)(2) = 0.2$
(c) $R(d_c|F) = (0)(25) + 1 = 1$
     $R(d_c|S) = +1 = 1.$
(d) $R(d_d|F) = (0.05)(25) + (0.95)1 = 2.20$
     $R(d_d|S) = (0.90)(0) + (0.1)(1) = 0.1$

All admissible. Since probability of F is θ, of S is $1 - \theta$, average risks $25\theta, 0.2 + 1.05\theta, 1, 0.1 + 2.1\theta$.

Θ has beta $(5, 16)$ distribution with expectation $5/21$ when d_b is best.

3.7 Joint p.d.f. of X, Θ is $(1/\theta)\,\theta\exp(-\theta) = \exp(-\theta), 0 < x < \theta$. Marginal p.d.f. of X is $\int_x^\infty \exp(-\theta)\mathrm{d}\theta = \exp(-x)$. Posterior p.d.f. of $\Theta|x$ is $\exp[-(\theta - x)], \theta > x$. Bayes estimator, for the quadratic loss function, is the mean of the posterior distribution and is $X + 1$. The Bayes risk is

$$c\int_0^\infty \left[\int_x^\infty (\theta - x - 1)^2 \exp(-\theta + x)\mathrm{d}\theta\right]\exp(-x)\mathrm{d}x, \text{ or}$$

$$c\int_0^\infty V[\Theta|x]\exp(-x)\mathrm{d}x = c$$

The ordinary risk is

$$c\int_0^\theta (\theta - x - 1)^2 \frac{1}{\theta}\mathrm{d}x = c\left(\frac{\theta^2}{3} - \theta + 1\right).$$

The ordinary risk for $2X$ is

$$c\int_0^\theta (\theta - 2x)^2 \frac{1}{\theta}\mathrm{d}x = c\theta^2/3.$$

3.8 The distributions of $X_1|\mu$ and $X_2|\mu, \theta$ are independent. The prior distributions of μ, θ are independent. The posterior density of $\mu, \theta|x_1, x_2$ is proportional to

$$\exp\left[-\tfrac{1}{2}(x_1 - \mu)^2\right]\exp\left[-\tfrac{1}{2}(x_2 - \mu - \theta)^2\right]\exp\left[-\tfrac{1}{2}(\mu - \mu_0)^2\right]$$
$$\propto \exp\left\{-\tfrac{1}{2}[3\mu^2 - 2\mu(x_1 + x_2 - \theta + \mu_0) + \theta^2 - 2\theta x_2]\right\}$$
$$= \exp\left\{-\frac{1}{2}\left[3\left(\mu - \frac{x_1 + x_2 - \theta + \mu_0}{3}\right)^2\right.\right.$$
$$\left.\left. - \left(\frac{x_1 + x_2 - \theta + \mu_0}{3}\right)^2 + \theta^2 - 2\theta x_2\right]\right\}$$

After integrating out μ, the posterior distribution of $\theta | x_1, x_2$ has p.d.f.

$$\propto \exp\left\{ -\frac{1}{2}\left[\frac{2\theta^2}{3} - \frac{2\theta(2x_2 - x_1 - \mu_0)}{3} \right] \right\}$$

$$\propto \exp\left\{ -\frac{1}{2}\left[\frac{2}{3}(\theta - \frac{1}{2}(2x_2 - x_1 - \mu_0))^2\right] \right\}$$

corresponding to a normal distribution with mean $(2x_2 - x_1 - \mu_0)/2$. The 'usual' estimate of θ is the maximum likelihood estimator, derived from the likelihood,

$$\frac{1}{\sqrt{(2\pi)}} \exp\left[-\frac{1}{2}(x_1 - \mu)^2 \right] \frac{1}{\sqrt{(2\pi)}} \exp\left[-\frac{1}{2}(x_2 - \mu - \theta)^2 \right]$$

4.1   Let θ be the probability that an item is defective. The distribution of R_i is binomial (k, θ) and of $\sum R_i$ is binomial (nk, θ). Hence $\sum R_i / nk = \bar{R}/k$ is m.l.e. of θ. Probability of no defective in batch of k is $(1 - \theta)^k$, hence result. $T = \sum R_i$ is complete sufficient statistic for θ. To invoke the Blackwell theorem we need an unbiased estimator of $(1 - \theta)^k$. Consider the random variable

$$s(R_1) = 0, \text{ if } R_1 \geqslant 1, \; s(R_1) = 1, \; R_1 = 0, \; E[s(R_1)] = (1 - \theta)^k.$$

The discrete distribution of $R_1 | T = t$ has p.d.f.

$$\Pr[R_1 = r_1 | T = t] = \frac{\Pr[R_1 = r_1 \text{ and } R_2 + R_3 \ldots + R_n = t - r_1]}{\Pr[R_1 + R_2 + \ldots + R_n = t]}$$

$$= \frac{\Pr[R_1 = r_1] \Pr\left[\sum_{2}^{n} R_i = t - r_1\right]}{\Pr[\sum R_i = r]}$$

Using the properties of the various binomial distributions [being binomial (k, θ), $[(n - 1)k, \theta]$, (nk, θ) in that order], we have

$$\Pr[R_1 = r_1 | t] = \binom{k}{r_1}\binom{nk - k}{t - r_1} \bigg/ \binom{nk}{t}.$$

From one point of view, the answer is obvious. There are t defectives in all; the places for these can be chosen in $\binom{nk}{t}$ ways and there are $\binom{k}{r_1}$ ways of assigning r_1 to the first batch. $E[s(R_1)|t]$ is merely $\Pr[R_1 = 0 | T = t]$. After unravelling the factorials we have the answer. The last part follows from the Cramér lower-bound theorem.

4.2 The likelihood is $[c(\theta)]^n \prod (x_i)^\theta \prod (1 - x_i)$.

$$\frac{\partial}{\partial \theta} \log L = \frac{nc'(\theta)}{c(\theta)} + \sum \log x_i = -n\left[-\frac{\sum \log x_i}{n} - \frac{c'(\theta)}{c(\theta)} \right].$$

Since $p(x; \theta)$ is a p.d.f., $c(\theta) = (\theta + 1)(\theta + 2)$, and $\frac{\partial}{\partial \theta} \log L$ is in the from for attaining the m.v.b.

4.3 Some care needed with zero values. Suppose A is the population of zeros and B is the Poisson distribution.

$$\Pr[X = 0] = \Pr[X = 0 | A]\Pr(A) + \Pr[X = 0 | B]\Pr(B)$$
$$= 1(1 - p) + \exp(-\theta)p.$$

$$\Pr[X = r] = \Pr[X = r | B]\Pr(B) = \frac{\theta^r \exp(-\theta)}{r!}p.$$

Hence $L \propto [(1 - p) + p\exp(-\theta)]^{f_0} \theta^{n\bar{x}} p^{n-f_0} \exp[-\theta(n - f_0)]$. Take logs, and minimize with respect to θ, p. Interestingly, $\hat{p} = \bar{x}/\hat{\theta}$. (Note that $\sum_0^\infty f_r = n$.) If zero values discarded,

$$L = \prod_{r=1}^\infty \left[\frac{\theta^r \exp(-\theta)/r!}{1 - \exp(-\theta)} \right]^{f_r}$$

4.4 To equalize the variance, minimize $\sum[(x_i - \mu)^2/\lambda^i \sigma^2]$,

$$t = \sum_{i=1}^n \frac{x_i}{\lambda^i} \bigg/ \sum_{i=1}^n \frac{1}{\lambda^i}. \qquad V(T) = \sigma^2 \bigg/ \sum_{i=1}^n \frac{1}{\lambda^i} < \lambda\sigma^2.$$

If $\lambda > 1, \sum_1^n \frac{1}{\lambda^i} \to \lambda - 1$; if $\lambda < 1, \sum_1^n \frac{1}{\lambda^i} \to \infty$.

σ^2/n for all n.

4.5 Minimize $\sum(w_i - W_i)^2 + \lambda(\sum W_i - W)$, where λ is a Lagrange multiplier.

$$-2(w_i - \hat{W}_i) + \lambda = 0$$

Sum over i, $-2(n\bar{w} - W) + n\lambda = 0$. Hence λ and result.

$$V(\hat{W}_i) = V[w_i - \bar{w}] = \sigma^2 + \frac{\sigma^2}{n} - \frac{2\sigma^2}{n} = \sigma^2\left(1 - \frac{1}{n}\right).$$

4.6 $E(X) = \displaystyle\int_0^1 \theta(\theta + 1)x^\theta(1 - x)\mathrm{d}x$

$\quad\quad = \dfrac{\theta}{\theta + 2}\displaystyle\int_0^1 (\theta + 1)(\theta + 2)x^\theta(1 - x)\mathrm{d}x = \dfrac{\theta}{\theta + 2}.$

$L = \theta^n(\theta + 1)^n\left(\displaystyle\prod_1^n x_i\right)^{\theta - 1}\prod(1 - x_i)$ and $\displaystyle\prod_1^n x_i = \exp(-nT)$

is sufficient for θ. $\dfrac{\partial \log L}{\partial \theta} = 0$ yields $T\theta^2 + (T - 2)\theta - 1 = 0$

and acceptable root is $\dot\theta$.

$$\dot\mu = \dot\theta/(\dot\theta + 2) = 1 - 2/(\dot\theta + 2).$$

Asymptotic variance $= \left(\dfrac{\mathrm{d}\mu}{\mathrm{d}\theta}\right)^2 \Big/ - E\left[\dfrac{\partial^2 \log L}{\partial \theta^2}\right]$

$\quad\quad\quad\quad\quad\quad\quad\quad\quad = 4\theta^2(1 + \theta)^2/[n(1 + 2\theta + 2\theta^2)(\theta + 2)^4].$

$V(\bar X) = \sigma^2/n = 2\theta/[n(\theta + 2)^2(\theta + 3)].$

$\dot\mu$ is asymptotically efficient.

4.7   Least-square equations,

$$\hat\beta_0 = \bar y$$
$$\sum y_i x_{1i} - 2\hat\beta_1 - 2\sin(2\theta)\hat\beta_2 = 0$$
$$\sum y_i x_{2i} - 2\hat\beta_2 - 2\sin(2\theta)\hat\beta_1 = 0$$

For instance,

$$\hat\beta_2 = (\sum y_i x_{2i} - \sin(2\theta)\sum y_i x_{1i})/2\cos^2 2\theta.$$

4.8 $L(x_1, x_2, x_3, x_4) \propto (1 - \theta)^{x_1}(\theta - \theta^2)^{x_2}(\theta^2 - \theta^3)^{x_3}\theta^{3x_4}$

$\quad\quad\quad\quad\quad\quad\quad = [(1 - \theta)^{x_1 + x_2 + x_3}]\theta^{x_2 + 2x_3 + 3x_4}$

$\dfrac{\partial \log L}{\partial \theta} = -\dfrac{x_1 + x_2 + x_3}{1 - \theta} + \dfrac{x_2 + 2x_3 + 3x_4}{\theta}$, whence $\hat\theta$.

$$-E\left[\dfrac{\partial^2 \log L}{\partial \theta^2}\right] = \dfrac{n(1 + \theta + \theta^2)}{\theta(1 - \theta)}$$

$V(\hat\theta)$ asymptotically $\dfrac{\theta(1 - \theta)}{n(1 + \theta + \theta^2)}.$

$$E[T] = a_1 n(1 - \theta) + a_2 n\theta(1 - \theta) + a_3 n\theta^2(1 - \theta) + na_4\theta^3.$$

If $E(T) \equiv \theta$, equate coefficients $T = (X_2 + X_3 + X_4)/n = (n - X_1)/n$, $V(T) = V(X_1/n) = \theta(1 - \theta)/n$.

5.1 The p.d.f. of $X_{(1)}$ is $(n/\phi)\exp[-n(x_{(1)} - \theta)/\phi], x_{(1)} > \theta$. The likelihood can be written

$$\frac{n}{\phi}\exp[-n(x_{(1)} - \theta)/\phi]\frac{\exp[-(\sum x_i - nx_{(1)})/\phi]}{n\phi^{n-1}}$$

Try $\theta = \theta_0, \phi = \phi_0$ against $\theta = \theta_1 < \theta_0, \phi = \phi_1 < \phi_0$ in the ordinary Neyman–Pearson test. For $x_{(1)} < \theta_0$ the likelihood is zero under H_0 so is included in the best critical region. Otherwise the ratio of the likelihoods is a function of $\sum x_i$. The distribution of $\sum X_i - n\theta_0$ is $\Gamma(n, 1/\phi_0)$ when H_0 is true.

5.2 (a) Apply Neyman–Pearson to $\theta = 1$ against $\theta = \theta_1 > 1$. Most powerful test consists of large values of

$$\exp[\tfrac{1}{2}(1 - \theta_1^{-1})\sum x_i^2]$$

or, since $\theta_1 > 1$, large values of $\sum x_i^2$.

(b) At the turning value of the log likelihood,

$$\hat\theta + \hat\theta^2 = \frac{1}{n}\sum_{i=1}^{n} x_i^2$$

$$E(X_i) = \theta, \quad E(X_i^2) = \theta + \theta^2$$

$$V[\hat\Theta + \hat\Theta^2] = \frac{1}{n}V(X^2)$$

5.3
$$\prod_{1}^{n}\tfrac{1}{2}\exp(-|x_i|)\Big/\prod_{1}^{n}\frac{1}{\sqrt{(2\pi)}}\exp(-\tfrac{1}{2}x_i^2)$$
$$\propto \exp[\tfrac{1}{2}(\sum|x_i^2| - 2\sum|x_i|)]$$
$$\propto \exp[\tfrac{1}{2}\sum(|x_i| - 1)^2].$$

Sufficiently large when $\sum_{1}^{n}(|x_i| - 1)^2$ sufficiently large. $|x| > 2$, $|x| > 3/2$ or $|x| < 1/2$.

6.1 Unrestricted m.l.e. of θ is $\max[X_1, X_2, X_3, X_4] = X_{(4)}$; of ϕ is $Y_{(4)}$, if $\theta = \phi$, $\max[X_{(4)}, Y_{(4)}]$. Hence likelihood-ratio test is based on small values of $x_{(4)}^4 y_{(4)}^4 / [\max(x_{(4)}, y_{(4)})]^8$. Consider $x_{(4)} < y_{(4)}$ and $y_{(4)} < x_{(4)}$, leading to two-tailed critical region. Since $X_{(4)}, Y_{(4)}$ independent, joint p.d.f. is

$$4\left(\frac{x_{(4)}}{\theta}\right)^3\frac{1}{\theta}4\left(\frac{y_{(4)}}{\phi}\right)^3\frac{1}{\phi}, 0 < x_{(4)} < \theta, 0 < y_{(4)} < \phi.$$

The likelihood ratio test is equivalent to values of $Y_{(4)}/X_{(4)} <$

k^{-1} or $Y_{(4)}/X_{(4)} > k$. So change variables to

$$S_1 = Y_{(4)}/X_{(4)}, S_2 = X_{(4)}.$$

Careful with the limits – since $Y_{(4)} = S_1 S_2 < \phi$ also $S_2 = X_{(4)} < \theta$ hence $S_2 < \min[\theta, \phi/S_1]$ for points of positive probability (and $\theta < \phi/S_1$ if $S_1 < \phi/\theta$).

$$g(s_1, s_2) = \frac{16(s_2^3)(s_1 s_2)^3 s_2}{\theta^4 \quad \phi^4}, \qquad \begin{matrix} s_1 < \phi/\theta, & 0 < s_2 < \theta \\ s_1 > \phi/\theta, & 0 < s_2 < \phi/s_1 \end{matrix}$$

and is zero otherwise. To find the p.d.f. of S_1, integrate s_2 from 0 to θ when $s_1 < \phi/\theta$ and from 0 to ϕ/s_1 when $s_1 > \phi/\theta$. When $\theta = \phi$, the p.d.f. of S_1 does not depend on common value. Use size condition to fix $k(>1)$ which satisfies $1/k^4 = 5$ per cent. $[\Pr(S_1 < 1/k \text{ or } S_1 > k | \theta = \phi) = 5\%]$.

6.2 Direct application of the theorem provides the set of x such that

$$\frac{1}{\pi[1 + (x-1)^2]} > \frac{1}{\pi(1+x^2)} + \frac{2x}{\pi(1+x^2)^2}.$$

After simplification

$$1 + 2x - 3x^2 = (1-x)(1+3x) < 0$$
$$x > 1 \text{ or } x < -\tfrac{1}{3}.$$

The size of the test is

$$\int_{-\infty}^{-1/3} \frac{dx}{\pi(1+x^2)} + \int_1^\infty \frac{dx}{\pi(1+x^2)}$$

6.3 The p.d.f. of the order statistics is

$$\frac{6}{\theta_2^3} \exp\{-[y_1 + y_2 + y_3 - 3\theta_1]/\theta_2\}, \quad \theta_1 < y_1 < y_2 < y_3 < \infty.$$

The Jacobian of the transformation is -1. Integrating the variable u_2 between the limits $u_3/2, u_3$, the joint p.d.f. of U_1, U_3 is

$$\frac{3}{\theta_2^3} \exp\{-[u_3 + 3u_1 - 3\theta_1]/\theta_2\} u_3$$

$$H_0: \theta_1 = \theta_1', \theta_2 = \theta_2', H_1: \theta_1 = \theta_1'', \theta_2'' > \theta_2'$$

Best critical region consists of those u_1, u_2, u_3 such that

$$\frac{\dfrac{6}{(\theta_2'')^3} \exp[(-u_3 - 3u_1 + 3\theta_1'')/\theta_2'']}{\dfrac{6}{(\theta_2')^3} \exp[(-u_3 - 3u_1 + 3\theta_1')/\theta_2']} \geqslant k$$

$$\exp\left[u_3\left(\frac{1}{\theta_2'}-\frac{1}{\theta_2''}\right)\right]\exp\left[3u_1\left(\frac{1}{\theta_2'}-\frac{1}{\theta_2''}\right)\right]\geqslant c(\theta_1',\theta_1'',\theta_2',\theta_2'')$$

Among those tests for which u_1 is fixed, since $\theta_2'' > \theta_2'$, we require large values of u_3. Uniformly most powerful similar test based on distribution of U_3 given u_1. But U_3 is independent of U_1; hence on unconditional distribution of U_3, which has p.d.f.

$$\frac{u_3}{(\theta_2')^2}\exp(-u_3/\theta_2'),$$

when H_0 is true.

7.1 The joint distribution of $X_{(1)}, X_{(n)}$ has p.d.f.

$$n(n-1)[x_{(n)}-x_{(1)}]^{n-2}/\theta^n, 0\leqslant x_{(1)}\leqslant x_{(n)}\leqslant\theta.$$

The joint distribution of the new variables, $T = X_{(n)} - X_{(1)}$, $S = X_{(1)}$, has p.d.f. $n(n-1)t^{n-2}/\theta^n, 0\leqslant s\leqslant\theta-t$.
Thence integrate s from 0 to $\theta - t$ to obtain p.d.f. of T.

$$\Pr[T>\theta]=0, \Pr[T/k<\theta]=\Pr[T<k\theta]=\alpha$$

leads to condition on k.

7.2 Jacobian of the transformation from $(z_1,\ldots,z_n)$ to $(y_1,\ldots,y_n)$ is $n!$ hence first result.

$$\frac{(y_1-\theta)(n-1)}{\bar{y}-y_1}=\frac{\left(\dfrac{z_1}{n}-\theta\right)(n-1)}{\dfrac{\sum z_i}{n}-\dfrac{z_1}{n}}=\frac{(z_1-n\theta)(n-1)}{\displaystyle\sum_2^n z_i}$$

$$=2\lambda(z_1-n\theta)\left/\dfrac{2\lambda\displaystyle\sum_2^n z_i}{n-1}\right.$$

$2\lambda(Z_1 - n\theta)$ has a χ_2^2 distribution and is independent of $2\lambda\displaystyle\sum_2^n Z_i$, which has a χ_{2n-2}^2 distribution. Hence ratio has $F(2, 2n-2)$ distribution.

7.3 $L = \dfrac{1}{\{\sqrt{(2\pi)}\}^{n_1}}\exp\left[-\dfrac{1}{2}\sum_1^{n_1}(x_i-\rho\mu)^2\right]$

$\times\dfrac{1}{\{\sqrt{(2\pi)}\}^{n_2}}\exp\left[-\dfrac{1}{2}\sum_1^{n_2}(y_i-\mu)^2\right]$

$\propto\exp\left[\dfrac{1}{2}\left(2\rho\mu\sum_1^{n_1}x_i+2\mu\sum_1^{n_2}y_i-n_1\rho^2\mu^2-n_2\mu^2\right)\right]$

By factorization, $\sum_{i=1}^{n_1} X_i$, $\sum_{i=1}^{n_2} Y_i$ jointly sufficient for ρ, μ. Similarly, if $\rho = \rho_0, \rho_0 \sum_{i=1}^{n_1} X_i + \sum_{i=1}^{n_2} Y_i$ sufficient for μ. $\bar{X} - \rho\bar{Y}$ distributed $N\left(0, \frac{1}{n_1} + \frac{\rho^2}{n_2}\right)$,

$$\Pr\left[-1.96 < \frac{\bar{X} - \rho\bar{Y}}{\sqrt{\left(\frac{1}{n_1} + \frac{\rho^2}{n_2}\right)}} < +1.96\right] = 0.95 \text{ for all } \mu.$$

Square out and rearrange as a quadratic form in ρ for confidence interval. If $n_1\bar{x}^2 + n_2\bar{y}^2 < 3.84$, no real roots.

7.4 $$L = \frac{1}{\prod x_i}\left[\frac{1}{\beta^n}\exp\left(-\frac{1}{\beta}\sum_{i=1}^{n}\frac{y_i}{x_i}\right)\right]$$

By factorization, $Z = \sum_{i=1}^{n}\frac{Y_i}{X_i}$ is sufficient for β.

Maximum likelihood estimator is $\frac{1}{n}\sum_{i=1}^{n}\frac{Y_i}{X_i}$. Also $\frac{2}{\beta}\sum_{i=1}^{n}\frac{Y_i}{X_i}$ has χ^2_{2n} distribution for frequentist (classical) confidence intervals. If β has uniform (improper) prior then posterior distribution of β, given z, has density $\propto \frac{1}{\beta^n}\exp\left(-\frac{z}{\beta}\right)$, with mode at z/n.

Change variable to $u = 2z/\beta$.

7.5 $$V(a - \rho b) = V(a) - 2\rho C(a,b) + \rho^2 V(b)$$
$$= \sigma^2(\lambda_1 - 2\rho\lambda_3 + \rho^2\lambda_2)$$

If $\rho \equiv \alpha/\beta, a - \rho b$ is distributed $N[0, \sigma^2(\lambda_1 - 2\rho\lambda_3 + \rho^2\lambda_2)]$ and $(a - \rho b)/\sqrt{\{(\lambda_1 - 2\rho\lambda_3 + \rho^2\lambda_2)s^2\}}$ has t-distribution.

A1.1 The joint p.d.f. of X_1, X_2 (since independent) is

$$\frac{1}{24\sqrt{(x_1 x_2)}}\exp\left[-\frac{\sqrt{x_1}}{3} - \frac{\sqrt{x_2}}{2}\right], x_1 \geq 0, x_2 \geq 0.$$

Change variables to $Y_1 = X_1/X_2, Y_2 = X_2$. The Jacobian of the inverse transformation is y_2. The joint p.d.f. of Y_1, Y_2 is

$$\frac{1}{24\sqrt{y_1}}\exp\left[-\sqrt{y_2}\left(\frac{\sqrt{y_1}}{3} + \frac{1}{2}\right)\right]$$

Find the p.d.f. of Y_1, note $\Pr(X_1 < X_2) = \Pr[(X_1/X_2) < 1] = \Pr[Y_1 < 1]$. It helps to substitute $\sqrt{y_1} = 3(t - \frac{1}{2})$.

A1.2 $X_1 = Y_1, X_2 = Y_2(1 - Y_1)$. The Jacobian of *this* transformation is $1 - y_1$. Conditions $x_1 \geqslant 0, x_2 \geqslant 0, x_1 + x_2 \leqslant 1 \Rightarrow (1 - y_1)(1 - y_2) \geqslant 0$.

The joint p.d.f. of Y_1, Y_2 can be written

$$\frac{\Gamma(n_1 + n_2 + n_3)}{\Gamma(n_1)\Gamma(n_2 + n_3)} y_1^{n_1 - 1}(1 - y_1)^{n_2 + n_3 - 1}$$
$$\times \frac{\Gamma(n_2 + n_3)}{\Gamma(n_2)\Gamma(n_3)} y_2^{n_2 - 1}(1 - y_2)^{n_3 - 1}$$

Hence result. In the last part, a convenient solution depends on a suitable choice of a third 'topping up' random variable for the transformation. For instance $U_3 = Z_1 + Z_2 + Z_3$. The Jacobian of the inverse transformation is

$$\begin{vmatrix} u_3 & 0 & u_1 \\ 0 & u_3 & u_2 \\ -u_3 & -u_3 & 1 - u_1 - u_2 \end{vmatrix} = u_3^2$$

The joint p.d.f. of Z_1, Z_2, Z_3 is

$$\frac{1}{\Gamma(n_1)\Gamma(n_2)\Gamma(n_3)} z_1^{n_1 - 1} z_2^{n_2 - 1} z_3^{n_3 - 1} \exp(-z_1 - z_2 - z_3)$$

Change the variables and integrate out u_3.

Further reading

Reference has been made to the following texts:

(1) Cox, D. R. and Hinkley, D. V. (1974), *Theoretical Statistics*, Chapman and Hall, London.
(2) Kendall, M. G. and Stuart, A. (1961), *The Advanced Theory of Statistics*, Griffin, London.

They are both advanced in standard and wide in scope. They also discuss the general principles of statistical inference, matters scarcely touched on in the present text. For a detailed discussion of classical estimation techniques and some historical background, there is:

(3) Deutsch, R. (1965), *Estimation Theory*, Prentice-Hall, Englewood Cliffs, New Jersey.

For a presentation mainly from the point of view of decision theory.
(4) Ferguson, T. S. (1969), *Mathematical Statistics: a decision theoretic approach*, Academic Press, New York.

Author and subject indexes

Author index

Subject index